Penguin Handbooks
The Best of Bee Nilson

Bee Nilson was born in New Zealand where she received her professional training. After graduating as Bachelor of Home Science of the University of Otago, she came to England and settled in London where she has been teaching and writing about cookery and nutrition ever since. She is a State Registered Dietitian, a member of the British Dietetic Association, the New Zealand Dietetic Association, and the Nutrition Society. She also holds the Diploma in Education of London University.

During the war she was at the Ministry of Food and compiled the *A.B.C. of Cookery* and other Stationery Office publications. Her other books include the Penguin Handbooks *The Penguin Cookery Book* and *Cooking for Special Diets*, *The Book of Meat Cookery*, *Pears Family Cookbook* and *Deep Freeze Cooking*. She edited *The W.I. Diamond Jubilee Cookbook*.

Bee Nilson

The Best of
Bee Nilson

Penguin Books

Penguin Books Ltd, Harmondsworth
Middlesex, England
Penguin Books, 625 Madison Avenue,
New York, New York 10022, U.S.A.
Penguin Books Australia Ltd, Ringwood,
Victoria, Australia
Penguin Books Canada Ltd, 2801 John Street,
Markham, Ontario, Canada L3R 1B4
Penguin Books (N.Z.) Ltd, 182–190 Wairau Road,
Auckland 10, New Zealand

First published by Michael Joseph Ltd 1975
Published in Penguin Books 1978
Copyright © Bee Nilson, 1975
All rights reserved

Made and printed in Great Britain by
Richard Clay (The Chaucer Press) Ltd, Bungay, Suffolk
Set in Monotype Bembo

Except in the United States of America, this book is
sold subject to the condition that it shall not, by
way of trade or otherwise, be lent, re-sold, hired out,
or otherwise circulated without the publisher's prior
consent in any form of binding or cover other than
that in which it is published and without a similar
condition including this condition being imposed on
the subsequent purchaser

Contents

Introduction 7
Weights and Measures 9

1 Basics 13
2 Sauces 45
3 Starters 71
4 Soups 80
5 Cheese 94
6 Eggs 103
7 Fish 122
8 Meat 154
9 Poultry and Game 219
10 Vegetables 250
11 Salads 304
12 Pasta and Rice 325
13 Sandwiches and Snacks on Toast 338
14 Fruits and Fruit Desserts 351
15 Puddings and Sweets 377
16 Cakes, Biscuits, Scones and Bread 427
17 Drinks 461
18 Planning and Preparing Meals 471

Index 485

Introduction

This book is a collection of my favourite recipes and cooking methods, those I use for everyday meals as well as those reserved for special occasions. But it is not just a recipe book.

You will also find it contains a lot of useful reference material covering important things like what to look for when buying food, how to store it to prevent waste and keep it fresh and safe to eat; how to plan and prepare meals; doing advance cooking; and coping with emergency meals. In addition, each chapter has information on the foods suitable for home freezing, how to freeze them and how to use the frozen food.

Owners of electric blenders will find I have given alternative methods in many recipes, one using the blender and one without. I have not made any special mention of things like electric beaters, power-driven mincers, sieves and shredders. Their use is obvious as an alternative to hand-operated tools; but they are not a necessity for making any of the recipes.

The sort of cooking I do is a mixture of basic British and adaptations from other countries around the world. While I enjoy cooking there are also lots of other things I like to do with my time, so my choice of recipes and methods tends towards the simple rather than the complicated and I make considerable use of good quality convenience foods.

While it is true that some modern foods are not of as good quality as those known to older generations of cooks, many more are infinitely better and safer to eat and the variety available is much greater. To me it seems a futile exercise to bemoan inevitable changes, but a rewarding one to take the best of that which is available and make something good with it, not just for the special occasion but to give pleasure and health to the family every day of the year.

Weights and Measures

All measures used in this book are level measures

For those who like to measure ingredients rather than use scales, I have given many of the dry ingredients in cup equivalents of ounces and pounds. Many more have been given in spoons, which I think is particularly useful for quantities less than one ounce or twenty-five grams because many domestic scales do not weigh accurately below this. The spoon measures apply both to cooking imperial and cooking metric.

The spoons I have used are those defined in the British Standards Institution, *British Standard* 1348:1970, *Specification for Kitchen Measuring Spoons and Jugs*.

The level capacities of these spoons are 20 ml, 15 ml, 10 ml, 5 ml, 2·5 ml and 1·25 ml.

The one I have used as a tablespoon is 15 ml and the teaspoon 5 ml. These are the same size as medicinal tablespoons and teaspoons and are the sizes used by other countries with the metric system. When buying a set of kitchen measuring spoons check to see that you have got the full range of sizes, or at least have a 15 ml and 5 ml spoon. Not all manufacturers include the whole range in their sets.

If you use ordinary tablespoons and teaspoons for measuring, the majority of these are approximately 15 ml for a tablespoon and 5 ml for a teaspoon, though there are considerable variations and it is worth checking yours against a medicinal measuring glass or spoon.

The cup I have used is a ½ pt or 10 fl oz (284 ml).

IMPERIAL WEIGHTS AND MEASURES

16 ounces (oz)	1 pound (lb)
20 fluid ounces (fl oz)	1 pint (pt)
2 pints	1 quart (qt)
8 pints	1 gallon

The Best of Bee Nilson

METRIC WEIGHTS AND MEASURES

1,000 grams (g)	1 kilogram (kg)
100 millilitres (ml)	1 decilitre (dl)
1,000 millilitres	1 litre (l)
1 centimetre (cm)	100 millimetres (mm)

The metric weights and measures in the recipes are not exact translations, which would give amounts impossible to weigh or measure with domestic equipment. They have been adjusted to make them practical quantities for use with domestic scales and measures. For example, ¼ pt could be translated as 125 ml, 142 ml (exact) or 150 ml. The first and last of these are easy to measure, the exact one impossible without laboratory equipment. I have chosen the one most appropriate to the particular recipe so sometimes you may find ¼ pt as 125 ml and sometimes as 150 ml to fit in with the conversion of the other ingredients.

In some cases the metric version will be a trifle smaller than the original, in others a little larger; but the difference is not enough to matter.

METRIC EQUIVALENTS

1 ounce (oz)	28·35 grams (g)
1 pound (lb)	453·6 grams
1 pint (pt)	568·2 millilitres (ml)
1 inch (in)	2·54 centimetres (cm)
1 fluid ounce (fl oz)	28·4 millilitres

AMERICAN EQUIVALENTS

1 American cup	8 fl oz or approx 230 ml
1 American tablespoon	½ fl oz or approx 14 ml
1 American teaspoon	⅙ fl oz or approx 5 ml
1 American pint	16 fl oz or approx 454 ml

If standard American measures are used with this book, the spoons can be taken as the same size as those used in the recipes, but count 1 cup as equivalent to 1¼ American cups.

Abbreviations

°F degrees Fahrenheit
°C degrees Celsius

G	gas
Tbs	level tablespoon(s)
tsp	level teaspoon(s)
c	level cup(s)
oz	ounce(s)
pt	pint(s)
qt	quart(s)
lb	pound(s)
min(s)	minute(s)
hr(s)	hour(s)
in	inch(es)
g	gram(s)
kg	kilogram(s)
mm	millimetre(s)
cm	centimetre(s)
m	metre(s)
ml	millilitre(s)
l	litre(s)

American terminology

American names	English names
American cheese	Cheddar
biscuit	scone
broil	grill
confectioner's sugar	icing sugar
cornstarch	cornflour
cracker	water biscuit
farina	semolina
French fried potatoes	chips
Graham flour	wholewheat flour
ground	minced
mince	chop finely
molasses	black treacle
pan frying	shallow frying
pie	open tart
double pie	two-crust pie or plate pie
deep dish pie	pie
skillet	shallow pan with a lid
Swiss cheese	Emmental

Using the recipes

It pays to do as much preparation as possible before actually starting to cook. This makes cooking simpler and more trouble-free, which is particularly important when you are trying a recipe for the first time.

The method I have used for writing the recipes makes them very simple to follow. You can see clearly which ingredients are used together and can put them together as you do the necessary advance preparation. Some hints on advance preparation will be found under Advance Preparation, page 475.

1. Basics

Here I have included methods and recipes which are mentioned in more than one chapter, for example, stock, pastry, flavourings, basic cooking methods and so on.

Some of the basic recipes will no doubt already be familiar to you, depending on how experienced you are. I am not suggesting you must make them my way. Mine are here for your convenience.

Many basic preparations used in cooking are available in the form of packaged and canned foods. Whether or not you decide to use these or to start with the raw materials is up to you. Personally, I do a bit of both, as convenient, and according to whether I consider one is much better than the other, taking into account cost, quality and the time factor.

PREPARING INGREDIENTS

Blanching

This is a preliminary stage in many cooking operations. It is used to help remove skins from tomatoes, nuts and stone fruits. Put the fruit or nuts in a bowl, pour boiling water over it, leave for a few minutes, pour off the hot water, replace with cold and then the skins should come off easily.

It is also used for removing salt from preserved foods, to remove a strong or bitter taste or to help keep the food a good colour. The recipe indicates when this is necessary. In this case the food is put in cold water, brought to the boil and boiled for a few minutes or even half-cooked, the water poured off and the cooking continued with fresh water or by some other method.

Boning

Most butchers and fishmongers will do boning for you if you ask them. If you want to do it for yourself the most important thing is to find the position and shape of the bones, then to cut close to them with a scraping action which does not tear the flesh. To watch an expert do it is the best way of learning.

Special thin, pointed knives are the best to use; otherwise boning is difficult to do without waste and damage to the flesh.

Breadcrumbs

Buttered breadcrumbs. These are made from fresh breadcrumbs coated with melted butter or margarine. They are used for gratin dishes and as a topping for many sweet and savoury dishes, and are much better than using dry crumbs dotted with bits of butter or margarine. For every pint (½ l) of breadcrumbs melt 1 oz (25 g) of butter or margarine and stir the crumbs round in it until they are coated. They can be prepared in advance and stored in the refrigerator for a week or so, or longer in the freezer.

Dried breadcrumbs. These are made from bread dried in a very slow oven until it is crisp. If the drying is very slow the crumbs will remain white, otherwise they will be pale brown.

The simplest way of turning the dried bread into crumbs is to break the bread into small bits and feed them into the electric blender with the motor running, but keep your hand over the top, or the crumbs will fly out. They can also be made by mincing the bread with a bag tied over the end of the mincer to catch the crumbs, or by crushing them with a rolling pin and sieving to remove coarse pieces. Keep them in a covered container in a dry place.

Dried crumbs are used for coating food before frying. White crumbs are the best for deep-fat frying, as others tend to turn very dark in the hot fat.

Fresh breadcrumbs. These are made from the crumbs of stale but not dried bread. They can be made in the electric blender; or use a grater; or rub the bread through a sieve. See also Stuffings, page 26.

Fried breadcrumbs. These are used to garnish roast game and other dishes. Use fresh breadcrumbs and fry them brown and crisp in the minimum amount of butter or oil, stirring frequently, as they burn easily.

Chopping food

A meat chopper or cleaver, which is like a curved axe-head with a short handle, is used for chopping bones and cutting up large joints of meat. It is not an essential tool in the small kitchen as the butcher will usually do such chopping for you.

A good chopping knife, on the other hand, is an essential tool in a well-equipped kitchen. This is a knife with a sharp point to the blade which broadens to a wide base near the handle. They are usually called cook's knives and come in many sizes. It is useful to have a small and a large one, the small one doubling as a paring knife. For chopping, the food is first sliced roughly, then the point of the knife is held on the chopping board with one hand and the knife pivoted up and down about this point as chopping proceeds.

There are many gadgets designed to make chopping easier but they are seldom an improvement on a good sharp cook's knife. A good mincer or an electric blender are time-saving when large amounts of food have to be chopped.

Clarified butter

Butter which has been salted or which contains much butter-milk will turn brown when used for frying. This does not matter for most operations but if you want to avoid the browning, clarify the butter first. Heat the butter in a saucepan and remove any scum which rises to the top. Don't heat enough to colour the butter. Then pour off the clear butter, leaving the salty sediment in the bottom of the pan. Use this and the scum for other cooking purposes, for example, dressing vegetables.

Fruit

See Chapter 14.

Gelatine

Powdered gelatine sold in packets is the best. It is often packed in sachets, each containing sufficient gelatine to set 1 pt (600 ml) of liquid. This is usually $\frac{1}{2}$ oz ($1\frac{1}{2}$ Tbs). In some recipes less than this is recommended, for example, when the liquid is already partially thickened such as with whipped cream or a custard. Occasionally more is needed, for example, if a lot of lemon juice is added or when no refrigerator is available for setting the jelly. Gelatine may be soaked in cold water and then dissolved in hot liquid, sprinkled into hot liquid, or heated with other ingredients. In each recipe you will find I have recommended the best method for that particular one.

Grating

For small amounts of food a conventional metal grater is the most useful. It usually has a minimum of four different sizes of grating surface. The finest is used for foods like nutmeg and the zest of oranges or lemons; the next for fine grating of cheese, vegetables and also orange or lemon rind; the next for coarse grating of cheese, vegetables and butcher's suet; while the coarsest is for slicing vegetables.

For grating large quantities of any food an electrically driven grater or shredder is a time-saver, and most grating jobs can be done even faster in an electric blender.

Nuts

Chestnuts, to shell and skin. There are several ways of doing this. First the shell must be cut in some way, either by slicing off the pointed top or by cutting a slit in the rounded side, or a cross on the flat side. To remove the shells and skins the nuts must be heated, and the easiest way of doing this is either to grill them or bake in a hot oven for about 20 minutes. Remove the shells, and the skins should come away too. They are more easily shelled while still fairly hot, so do not heat them all at once if there are a lot to be prepared. Some people prefer to boil the nuts for about 10 minutes before shelling them.

To make a chestnut purée, boil the shelled nuts (there is no need to remove all the skins beforehand). Use only a little water and boil until the nuts are quite soft. Drain and rub through a sieve.

Praline is made by heating together in a small pan:

3 oz caster sugar (6 Tbs or 75 g)　　　　3 oz unblanched almonds (75 g)

Heat slowly until the sugar melts and begins to colour. Stir and continue cooking until the sugar is nut-brown in colour. Turn into an oiled sandwich tin about 6 in (15 cm) and leave to become cold. Break it up into small pieces and either blend it to a powder (small bits at a time), or crush with a rolling pin, or mince finely. Put the praline in an airtight container and store in a dry place.

Toasted nuts. These are nuts which are browned by baking in a hot oven or by frying in a little oil or butter. Turn them frequently and watch carefully as they burn easily and then are very bitter. Unblanched hazel nuts are toasted until the skins rub off easily; use the oven.

Shredding

This is cutting in thin slices or strips. For small quantities use either a sharp cook's knife or a coarse grater. For larger quantities a shredding attachment on an electric mixer is a great time-saver and there are various hand-operated mechanical shredders on the market. Both these have a selection of cutting blades for fine or coarse shredding.

Sieving and sifting

For sieving a small quantity of food use a small round plastic sieve and a wooden spoon to rub the food through. These can be used for making a purée or for sifting such things as flour or icing sugar, or for straining lumps out of liquids.

For sieving larger quantities there are attachments for electric mixers, or hand-operated mechanical sieves. For making a purée the electric blender is the fastest tool to use.

Vegetables

See Chapter 10.

STOCK

Stock is important for adding flavour to soups, sauces, stews and casseroles. I was brought up in the stock era when everyone who aspired to be a good cook had a stockpot simmering on the hob of their solid fuel cooker. The only time I make stock today is when I have a chicken or other carcass of a bird, or some beef or veal bones that it seems a pity to waste. Even then I make the stock in a pressure cooker in a mere half-hour of cooking time. I also make vegetable stock when there are pieces too old for other use and fish stock when there are skins or bones going to waste. These are the recipes I have included here.

If there is no stock available I use chicken or beef cubes or meat or vegetable extracts, and for better quality dishes a canned consommé or canned beef stock. Any of these may have additions made such as mushroom ketchup or a little wine or cider. Canned vegetable juices and tomato juice or the liquid from canned or boiled vegetables are also suitable.

There is no need to throw away good materials just because you don't happen to want stock immediately. It will keep for a week in the refrigerator and many weeks in the freezer. Unless you have plenty of room in the freezer, it is a help to boil the stock to concentrate it, then cool it, chill it in the refrigerator, remove any fat from the top and freeze it. Alternatively, freeze it in ice-cube trays and store the cubes in bags. To use, cubes can be dropped into hot liquid or the frozen stock can be melted over a gentle direct heat.

For refrigerator storage, cool the stock, put in containers with a lid and store.

Bone stock

Cooking time $\frac{1}{2}$ hr in a pressure cooker or 2–3 hrs ordinary boiling.

bones, cooked or raw, or the carcass of a bird	a bouquet garni carrots and onions

If necessary, chop or saw the bones into convenient sizes to fit the pan. For pressure cooking, use just enough water to cover and do not have the cooker more than half full of bones and water. Use more water for ordinary boiling or top up during cooking. Add a scraped carrot and a peeled or unpeeled onion for each pint of water used ($\frac{1}{2}$ l), and the bouquet garni.

When the stock is cooked, strain it into a bowl, and when it is cold remove any fat from the top.

Fish stock

Cooking time 5 mins pressure cooking or 20 mins ordinary boiling.

8 oz fish trimmings (250 g)	1 clove
1 small peeled onion	$\frac{1}{4}$ bay leaf
1 small sprig parsley	

For the fish trimmings use bones, skin, head and other trimmings. Put all in the pan with cold water to cover and boil gently for 20 mins or pressure cook for 5 mins. Strain.

Giblet stock

Use the neck, gizzard, heart, liver and any trimmings from the bird. Make it in the same way as bone stock, see above.

Mushroom stock

Cooking time 10–15 mins.

Use the stalks, washed and sliced, and if the mushrooms have been peeled use the skins as well. Cover with cold water and boil for 10–15 mins. Strain before using.

Vegetable stock

Cooking time 5–10 mins pressure cooking or 20–30 mins ordinary boiling.

Use any mixture of vegetables such as ones too old for other use, outside leaves of cabbage, cauliflower stalks and leaves, the green tops of leeks, watercress stalks, mushroom trimmings, celery trimmings and outside stalks, and any other vegetables available.

Wash well, chop or shred them finely, add boiling water to come three quarters of the way up.

a few bacon rinds (optional)
a few peppercorns 1–2 cloves
a bouquet garni or a few sprigs of other herbs

Cover and cook, then strain.

Aspic jelly

For one made with meat stock, use a clear home-made stock set with gelatine or use a can of consommé. If it is concentrated it may not need any gelatine, otherwise use about a quarter of the amount of gelatine you would use for setting other jellies.

Fish and vegetable aspics are made with clear stock and gelatine. For one without stock use the following recipe.

$\frac{1}{2}$ oz gelatine ($1\frac{1}{2}$ Tbs)
$\frac{1}{2}$ pt hot water (300 ml)
2 tsp sugar
$\frac{1}{2}$ tsp salt
2 Tbs tarragon vinegar
2 Tbs lemon juice

Sprinkle the gelatine into the hot water and stir until it is dissolved. This quantity of gelatine makes a firm aspic; less may be used if you prefer a softer one. Add the other ingredients. Cool and then use as required.

FLAVOURINGS

These are the main ingredients and preparations used in flavouring foods.

Alcoholic flavourings

Beer, stout, cider, wine, use in place of some of the stock or other liquid in a recipe.

Brandy, liqueurs, madeira, marsala, rum, sherry, vermouth, whisky, use in smaller amounts; spirits and liqueurs are used for a flambé.

All of these, except the sweet liqueurs, are suitable for either savoury or sweet dishes.

Condiments

Cayenne pepper, the hottest of all peppers.
Chillies, whole or ground, also very hot.
Mustard, English or French (see recipe below).
Salt, free-running table or cooking, iodized, sea salt, spiced (see recipe below).
Paprika pepper, mild in flavour, good colour for garnishing.
White and black peppercorns, best if freshly ground in a pepper mill.
Vinegar, malt – the strongest flavour, wine vinegar (white or red) – best for general purposes, cider vinegar, herb vinegars of many flavours (see recipe on page 24).

French mustard

6 Tbs dry mustard (90 mg)

Put in a small basin and mix to a stiff paste with cold water.

1 tsp sugar	1 tsp salt
1 Tbs olive oil	2 tsp tarragon vinegar
1 tsp anchovy essence	1 tsp mushroom ketchup
a good pinch of powdered marjoram	

Add all the ingredients to the mustard and mix thoroughly. If the mustard seems a little stiff, add more vinegar. Store in a covered jar or mustard pot.

Seasoned flour

4 oz flour (¾ c or 100 g)   1 Tbs salt
¼ tsp freshly ground pepper

Mix these together and keep in a dredger for coating meat and fish before frying.

Spiced salt

To use at table as a condiment, or for cooking, for flavouring soups, casseroles, sauces, meat and fish for grilling, for sprinkling on roasts, and indeed, whenever salt is used and the flavour of herbs would improve the dish.

Quantities for 5 oz (150 g) of spiced salt.

2 oz free-running cooking salt (50 g)   1 oz celery salt (25 g)
½ oz ground black pepper (15 g)

Mix these in a small bowl.

½ oz each (15 g) of dried thyme,   1 Tbs dried sage
marjoram and savory

Pound these finely in a mortar or put them in the electric blender with the cayenne pepper and spices and blend to a powder. Add to the salt mixture:

½ tsp cayenne pepper   ¼ tsp ground cloves
¼ tsp ground mace   ¼ tsp ground allspice

Mix thoroughly with the other ingredients. Put in a bottle with a cork or lid. For table use, put the salt in a salt shaker.

Essences used for sweet recipes

Almond.

Lemon.

Peppermint.

Ratafia, similar to almond.

Rosewater, old-fashioned delicate flavour; chemists sell it.

Vanilla essence or pods, which are stored with sugar to give vanilla-flavoured sugar, or infused with hot liquids.

Various synthetic fruit flavourings, never as good as using fruit juices, fruit purées or grated rind of citrus fruits.

Herbs, spices and vegetables used for flavouring

Allspice, whole, mostly for savoury cooking (mixed ground spice is different).

Anise, leaves used in soups, salads and as a garnishing herb, seeds as a spice with fish, bread, cakes, biscuits, desserts.

Balm, fresh leaves for sweet or savoury dishes, use a fair amount.

Basil, fresh or dried, fairly strong.

Bay leaf, alone in sweet or savoury recipes, as part of a bouquet garni for savoury dishes.

Capers, pickled.

Cardamon, seeds used as a spice in Eastern cookery (curries, pilau), also in pickled herrings, mulled wine.

Celery, fresh, as celery salt, seeds or dried leaves.
Celeriac, in place of celery as a flavouring vegetable.
Chervil, fresh leaves, strong flavour, for savoury dishes and garnishing.
Chives, fresh, the mildest of the onion family.
Cinnamon, as small sticks or ground, for sweet or savoury recipes.
Cloves, whole or ground, for sweet or savoury.
Coriander, fresh leaves and dried seeds, in sweet or savoury dishes.
Cumin, seeds as a spice in far Eastern cookery, also used in pickles.
Curry, various blends of powder, also curry pastes; strengths of both vary.
Dill, ripe seeds and fresh or dried leaves, especially for fish or lamb.
Fennel, ripe seeds or fresh leaves, like dill but stronger.
Fenugreek, leaves used as a vegetable or salad, seeds in Indian cooking, especially curries.
Garlic, as fresh cloves, dried, or garlic salt; the strongest of the onion family.
Ginger, fresh or dried root, ground, preserved in syrup, crystallized, for sweet or savoury cooking.
Horseradish, fresh grated root or grated bottled, strong and hot.
Mace, blades or ground, similar to nutmeg but milder, for sweet or savoury recipes.
Marjoram, fresh leaves or dried, many kinds; oregano is the strongest.
Mint, fresh leaves or dried, for sweet or savoury cooking.
Mushrooms, fresh or dried.
Nasturtium, fresh leaves and flowers for salads, seeds pickled to use as capers.
Nutmeg, whole or ground – whole needs grating but flavour better than ready-grated; for sweet or savoury cooking.
Onion, large, Spanish the mildest flavour, small pickling the strongest.
Parsley, fresh leaves in season all the year, stalks used alone for flavouring.
Poppy seeds, as a spice for sprinkling on bread, cakes and biscuits; also used in curries.
Rosemary, fresh or dried crushed, for sweet or savoury cooking, strong flavour.
Sage, fresh or dried leaves, a strong flavour, good with fatty meats and poultry.
Savory, fresh or dried leaves, fairly strong distinctive flavour.
Sesame seeds, oily and with a nutty flavour, used as a spice for sprinkling on bread, cakes, biscuits and pastry; also used in curries.
Shallots, small, mild onions.
Sweet peppers, fresh or canned; dried as paprika pepper.
Tarragon, fresh leaves, strong flavour.
Thyme, fresh or dried leaves, strong flavour; lemon thyme best.
Turmeric, as a spice in pickles and curries.

Bouquet garni
(also called a faggot)

This is the traditional bouquet of herbs used in French cookery. It consists of a bay leaf, a sprig of parsley or some parsley stalks, and a sprig of thyme. These are tied together with a piece of white cotton or tied in a muslin bag. Remove the bouquet before serving the food.

Dried herbs can be used and dried bouquets garnis are sold ready made up in muslin bags. The snag with these is that you never know how old they are and stale herbs can be tasteless. It can be better to make your own, especially if you grow the herbs and dry your own or store them in the freezer.

Other herbs are often included in flavouring bouquets, the herbs varying according to the food being cooked. A small piece of celery stick is often included.

It helps, when the time comes to remove the bouquet, if the thread used for tying it is made long enough to reach out of the pan and be tied to the handle. Mixtures which are strained before using can obviously have the herbs put in loose.

Fines herbes

A mixture of equal quantities of finely chopped fresh parsley, chervil, tarragon and chives.

Herb seasoning

Use this for flavouring any savoury dish. For variety of flavour, add spices such as nutmeg, mace, cloves, ginger or allspice, adding them to the recipe rather than to the herb flavouring.

Finely grated rind of 1 lemon

Spread this out on a saucer or piece of paper and put it in a warm place to dry. Do this if possible the day before you want to make up the mixture.

1 Tbs crushed dried marjoram	$\frac{1}{2}$ Tbs dried thyme
$\frac{1}{2}$ Tbs crushed dried basil	1 Tbs dried savory
$\frac{1}{4}$ tsp powdered dried bay leaf	

If the crushed leaves are already fairly fine the mixture can simply be bottled as it is, but a better blend of flavours results if the ingredients are pounded together in a mortar or in an electric blender. The mixture can then be sieved to remove any remaining large pieces. Add the dried lemon rind, mix and put in a covered jar.

Use the mixture in approximately the proportion of ½ tsp to a pint (½ l) of sauce, soup, stew and so on.

Mixed herb vinegar

Use thyme, marjoram, basil, savory, tarragon, chives, mint, selecting at least four different herbs. Fill a 1 pt (½ l) jar with small sprigs or leaves of the chosen herbs. Do not pack down.

a few slices of shallot or onion or   1 strip lemon rind
   some coarsely sliced chives

Add to the herbs and fill the jar with wine vinegar. Leave for 14 days or until the vinegar is well flavoured. Strain and bottle.

Various flavourings

Most of these can be used in small amounts in savoury cooking, but are chiefly for sweet things.

Black treacle and golden syrup for sweetness plus colour and flavour; treacle slightly bitter-sweet.

Cocoa and chocolate, cocoa better as it gives a stronger chocolate flavour.

Honey as sweetness plus flavour.

Lemon, orange, grapefruit; finely grated rinds and juice.

Sugar, white for sweetness; brown for sweetness plus colour and flavour.

MARINADES AND BASTING SAUCES

Marinades are for steeping foods (meat, game, fish and poultry) before cooking; basting sauces are for brushing on grills or roasts during cooking. Any excess marinade is often used as a basting sauce during the subsequent cooking, and the same recipe can usually serve either as a basting sauce or marinade.

Because salt tends to draw out the juices, it is not usually added to meat marinades, but it is often included in fish marinades as drawing out some moisture makes the flesh firmer, which is particularly useful for items like kebabs.

Marinated food needs to be steeped for 1-2 hours for small thin pieces, 24 hours or more for large pieces such as a joint of meat. This is to allow flavours from the marinade to penetrate the meat. Lengthy marinating is best done in a covered dish in the refrigerator.

Marinades and basting sauces can be prepared well in advance, covered, and stored in the refrigerator. This allows time for dried herbs to release their flavour and blend with the other flavourings.

When marinades are used for brushing food during grilling, they need to be strained first to remove any larger pieces of flavourings which might burn and spoil the food being grilled.

Barbecue basting sauce

Quantities for 4.

1 tsp dry mustard
2 Tbs vinegar (wine or herb)
1 clove garlic (optional)
2 tsp Worcester sauce
3 Tbs oil

If garlic is used, crush it and then strain out before use.

Ginger and lemon marinade or basting sauce

Quantities for 4.

½ clove crushed garlic
¼ tsp ground ginger
2 Tbs oil
¼ tsp freshly ground pepper
1 Tbs finely chopped onion
4 Tbs lemon juice (60 ml)

Mix together and leave to infuse for several hours or overnight. Strain before using.

Sherry and herb basting sauce or marinade

Quantities for 4–6.

1 tsp dry mustard
pinch of dried garlic
½ tsp dried marjoram
1 tsp brown sugar
pinch of dried thyme
pinch of black pepper

Put in a small basin.

4 Tbs sherry (60 ml)
2 Tbs oil (30 ml)

Mix these gradually into the dry ingredients.

Wine marinade and basting sauce

Quantities for 4.

5 Tbs red or white wine (75 ml)
1 small bay leaf
½ clove crushed garlic

5 Tbs oil (75 ml)
¼ tsp chopped fresh herbs

After marinating the food, strain any liquid left before using it as a basting sauce.

STUFFINGS

Stuffings are used chiefly to add flavour to meat, poultry and fish and to make an interesting accompaniment. When used for stuffing vegetables they add bulk and calories, making them suitable for a main dish.

Packet stuffings are the choice of many people and they can be improved with additional flavourings of your own choice. Those who prefer to start with the basic materials can keep a store of breadcrumbs in a bag in the refrigerator for a week or so or many weeks in the freezer. This is a good way of dealing with stale bread, particularly if you have an electric blender or a grating attachment for a mixer. You then have a store of crumbs not only for stuffings but for puddings and cooking in general. Frozen crumbs thaw very quickly at room temperature, and you can just use what you want from a bag, re-seal and put back in the freezer.

Herbs are another important ingredient for stuffings. Chopped fresh or dried herbs can be used, but be sure the latter are not stale and tasteless. In a blender, fresh herbs can be chopped with pieces of bread for the crumbs.

Stuffings should be mixed so that they are dry enough to keep their shape, but not stodgy. Sometimes the mixture is moulded into small balls which are cooked separately to use as a garnish. Tiny ones are used as a garnish for soups and other savoury dishes. The best way of cooking them is in a moderate oven, with very little fat or oil.

Stuffed meat or poultry should always be thoroughly cooked because it has been handled during boning, cleaning and stuffing and any contamination introduced can grow to dangerous proportions if the meat is not well cooked. If the stuffing is prepared in advance of cooking time, store it separately from the meat or poultry, in a refrigerator or cold larder. If the meat or poultry is being cooked to serve cold, the stuffing should be removed after cooking, cooled and stored separately. This also applies to freezing stuffed meat.

Bacon and nut stuffing for fish

This can be used to stuff a whole large fish or small ones. It is very good used as a stuffing for rolled fillets. Pack the rolls in a flat baking dish, pour a little white wine in to moisten and bake.

Quantities for 4.

1 rasher fat bacon finely chopped | 1 slice of onion, finely chopped

Heat the bacon in a small pan until the fat runs, then fry the onion with the bacon until it begins to colour.

1 oz fresh breadcrumbs (25 g)
1 Tbs chopped parsley
¼ tsp celery salt
1 egg, beaten

1 oz finely chopped hazel nuts (25 g)
½ Tbs lemon juice
pinch of pepper
a little chopped tarragon or savory

Put in a basin with the bacon and onion and mix thoroughly.

Cheese and rosemary stuffing for lamb or veal

Quantities for a 3–4 lb shoulder (1½–2 kg).

2 oz fresh breadcrumbs (50 g)
2 oz onion, finely chopped (50 g)
1 tsp concentrated tomato purée
½ tsp dried crushed rosemary or 1 tsp chopped fresh
pinch of pepper

1 oz grated cheese (25 g)
1 egg, beaten
½ oz melted butter (15 g)
2 Tbs white wine
½ tsp salt

Mix all the ingredients together, adding more wine if needed to bind the ingredients.

Chestnut stuffing for turkey

Quantities for a 12–14 lb turkey (5–6 kg).

2 lb chestnuts (1 kg)

Shell the chestnuts, see page 16.

stock

Barely cover the shelled nuts with stock and bring to the boil. Cover, and cook slowly until they are tender and almost dry. Rub through a sieve or purée in several lots in the electric blender. While fresh chestnuts have the better flavour either unsweetened canned purée or cooked dried chestnuts may be used instead (1 lb or ½ kg). The latter should be cooked like the fresh, but use more stock or add some water.

6 oz fresh breadcrumbs (175 g)	1 Tbs chopped parsley
1 lb pork sausage meat (500 g)	1 Tbs salt
stock to moisten	¼ tsp pepper
4 oz melted butter or dripping (125 g)	

Mix these ingredients into the chestnut purée, adding just enough stock to moisten well.

Lemon stuffing for chicken, duck, veal, lamb or fish

Quantities for 1 small chicken.

2 oz melted butter (50 g)	½ Tbs lemon juice
grated rind of ½ lemon	2 Tbs chopped parsley
pinch of salt and pepper	1 small egg or ½ large one, beaten
pinch each of dried thyme and rosemary	2 oz fresh breadcrumbs (⅔ c or 50 g)

Mix all the ingredients together thoroughly.

Prune and apple stuffing for pork, duck or goose

Quantities for 1 medium-sized goose.

1 lb prunes (500 g)

Soak overnight in cold water to cover. Next day remove the stones, discarding the soaking water.

2 lb apples (1 kg)

Peel, core and dice.

1 oz butter or margarine (25 g)	3 oz sugar (6 Tbs or 75 g)
1 Tbs water	

Put in a pan with the apples and prunes and cook over a low heat or in a slow oven for 2–3 hrs until the mixture is the consistency of jam. Stir frequently. Allow to become cold before using.

Sage and onion stuffing for duck, goose or pork

Quantities for 1 small goose or 2 ducks.

4 large onions

Skin and boil in a little salted water for 5 mins. Drain and cool.

10 fresh sage leaves or 1 tsp dried sage

Dip fresh sage in boiling water for a minute. Dry and chop or mince with the onion. Add dried sage to the chopped or minced onion.

1 oz melted butter or margarine (25 g)
2 tsp salt

4 oz breadcrumbs (1⅓ c or 100 g)
½ tsp freshly ground pepper

Mix carefully with the onion and sage.

Walnut stuffing for pheasant

Quantities for 1–2 birds.

8 oz chopped lean pork (250 g)   1½ oz butter (40 g)

Melt the butter in a frying pan and cook the pork in it until it is cooked through.

1 oz breadcrumbs (⅓ c or 25 g)
2 oz chopped walnuts (¼ c or 50 g)
pinch of pepper
1 tsp salt

1 tsp chopped thyme
2 Tbs chopped parsley
2 Tbs red wine
½ egg, beaten

Mix thoroughly with the pork and allow to become cold before using.

COOKING PROCESSES

Boiling

At normal atmospheric pressure, water boils at 100° C (212° F) and the surface bubbles owing to pockets of water vapour escaping as the water evaporates.

If the pressure above the liquid is more than atmospheric, as in a pressure cooker, the water boils at a higher temperature which varies with the pressure. The result is that pressure-cooked food needs only about a quarter of the normal boiling time.

Keeping a high heat under a pan produces violent and rapid boiling but it does not raise the temperature or hasten the cooking; it simply increases the rate of evaporation and the pan may boil dry. The violent agitation of the water tends to make food break up, for example, when boiling potatoes. Fast boiling should not, therefore, be used in ordinary cooking but only when rapid evaporation of the liquid is wanted to make it more concentrated, as might be required for making a thick syrup or concentrating a gravy.

Many foods which are spoken of as 'boiled' are in fact best cooked at a temperature below boiling – that is, simmering or poaching. In this case the surface of the liquid wobbles rather than bubbles.

Casserole cooking

Any ovenproof dish can be used as a casserole, either with its own lid or one of foil. The most useful casseroles are those which can be used on hotplate or burner as well as in the oven and which are sufficiently attractive to send to table. Any food which is suitable for cooking in a saucepan (with the exception of green vegetables), can equally well be cooked in the oven in a casserole. The cooking time will usually be longer than with hotplate boiling and will vary with the temperature of the oven. The most commonly used casserole temperature is about 180° C (350° F; G4). but it may be higher or lower.

It should be remembered that a casserole takes time to heat through and the thicker it is, the longer it takes before the contents actually start to cook. To bring the contents to simmering point on the hotplate reduces this preliminary heating up time, otherwise you need to add anything up to $\frac{1}{2}$ hr to the specified cooking time to allow the contents to heat up. Alternatively, the casserole can be put into a hot oven to start it off quickly and then cooked at a reduced heat.

Double boiler – use of

This is a double saucepan with one saucepan fitting into the top of another. The lower one contains boiling or hot water depending on whether the food in the top saucepan is to be cooked or just kept hot. It is useful for keeping sauces hot and for mixtures which tend to stick and burn when cooked over a direct heat, for example milk puddings and milk sauces. An improvised double boiler can be made by putting a basin in the top of a saucepan but this is not as convenient as a proper double boiler because the food cannot be brought to the boil in a basin as it can in a top saucepan used on its own. This process speeds up the cooking. Otherwise cooking can take half as long again in a basin.

Frying

IN A FRYING PAN

Use a good quality pan with a really thick base. Thin pans can become buckled, making the frying difficult. A pan with a lid is useful when the cooking process continues after the preliminary browning. If such a pan has two short handles instead of one long one, it can double up for oven cooking.

Use just enough fat or oil to prevent the food from sticking and make it really hot before adding the food. This is particularly important with foods which are absorbent like cooked potatoes, rissoles, mushrooms and onions. They can soak up a lot of fat and become unpleasantly greasy. Meat needs very little fat, fish rather more depending on whether it has been coated, eggs need enough to have a little to spoon over the tops and help them to set.

DEEP-FAT FRYING

Food properly fried in deep fat (preferably oil), is not greasy, and is very delicious, but it is rarely to be found in restaurants and probably not often in the home either. The chief reason for this is that few people bother to use a thermometer to test the temperature of the fat or oil, and many try to fry too much food at once in too little fat. The result is that the food cooks at too low a temperature, soaks up fat, and becomes greasy and flabby instead of crisp and succulent. Another common fault in frying is using stale or dirty fat which imparts a disagreeable flavour to the food. Fat should be strained after each use and discarded when it shows any signs of developing a strong flavour. The modern thermostatically controlled deep-fat fryer is the answer to the problem of getting the correct temperature and is a good investment for those who do a lot of this sort of frying. Most frying is done at about 190° C (375° F), so any thermometer designed for use at this sort of temperature can be used when you are frying without automatic temperature control.

It is better to use oil than fat as it can be heated to a higher temperature without burning. Only half fill the pan, which can be a saucepan or a special deep-fat frying pan. The latter will probably have its own frying basket; if not, you can use any perforated spoon or ladle for putting food in and out. Avoid putting in too much food at a time, or any wet food, as this causes violent frothing and the oil may spill over and catch fire. How much food you can put in at a time depends on the amount of oil you are using and on whether you have enough heat under the pan to prevent a rapid drop in temperature. It is best to err on the cautious side until you are experienced.

Drain the cooked food on absorbent kitchen paper and, if it is not to be served immediately, put it in a moderate oven to keep it crisp; but don't try to keep it long. Keeping the food in a single layer helps to retain its crispness.

Food which has been coated with batter should be dropped gently into the hot fat, not put in the frying basket as this makes it liable to stick to the wires. Have the basket in the pan by all means, and use it for lifting the food out when it is cooked.

Grilling

Grilled foods are only good if freshly cooked, and should not be kept hot for longer than it takes to eat the first course of soup or starter.

As far as the actual cooking process is concerned, grilling is the same whatever type of grill is used. The only thing likely to vary is the cooking time because some grills are hotter than others. With some it may not be possible to vary the heat, nor the distance you can place the food from the heat source, in order to slow up the cooking when this is desirable; in these cases there are a few grilled foods requiring gentle heat which it may be difficult to do to perfection. So, if you are buying a new cooker or separate grill, bear these points in mind.

In the recipes, I have given guide-times, but if your instruction booklet says to use different times, follow these to begin with. Then, if necessary, experiment to get exactly the results you like.

A very important point to remember is to heat the grill in good time so that it is at maximum heat when you start operations.

Many foods are improved in flavour and succulence if they are either marinaded or brushed with a basting sauce. You will find recipes for these on page 24.

For details of how to grill different foods, see the chapters on meat, fish, etc.

Kebabs and brochettes

It is important to have the right size and kind of skewer for these. Skewers are supplied with some portable grills and rôtisseries. They should be square skewers, not round. This is to hold the meat in position and prevent it from slipping round and cooking unevenly. Special square kebab or brochette skewers are usually about 10 in (25 cm) long, which is satisfactory for most grills. One skewer of that size holds enough for one portion.

The only difference between cooking kebabs with an ordinary grill and cooking them on a rôtisserie is that the skewers have to be turned over by hand when grilling (once is usually sufficient), while in the case of the revolving spit they turn automatically.

If the meat used is not fatty, kebabs need to be basted with oil or a basting

Basics 33

sauce. Alternatively, pieces of fat bacon may be threaded on the skewers next to the meat to supply basting fat.

Ingredients for a kebab can be prepared in advance and stored for an hour or so in the refrigerator, either on or off the skewers, and can be marinaded in the basting sauce to give them extra flavour (see page 24).

For kebab recipes, see the index.

Poaching

See boiling, page 29.

Pressure cooking

This reduces the cooking time to about a quarter of the normal boiling time.

Pressure cookers are sold in a variety of sizes, but a fairly large one is more useful than the smaller sizes.

Because steam cannot escape freely from a pressure cooker once it has reached the pressure point, less water is required than for ordinary boiling. The amount of liquid required depends on the cooking time rather than on the amount of food being cooked, for example, $\frac{1}{2}$ pt water (300 ml) is needed for the first 15 mins of cooking and another $\frac{1}{4}$ pt (150 ml) for every additional $\frac{1}{2}$ hr. Never use less than $\frac{1}{2}$ pt (300 ml) of water.

The maker's instructions for using the cooker should always be followed carefully. The most important instructions to observe are those relating to the amount that the cooker will safely hold, cooling instructions after cooking has finished, and the use of the pressure gauge.

A pressure cooker is of greatest benefit when used for speeding up long cooking processes such as making stocks and soups, softening tough meat, or cooking vegetables like beetroot or dried beans (be careful with lentils because they froth), the Christmas pudding and dried fruits.

Sauté

This is food fried in shallow fat in a sauté pan, a deep frying pan with sloping sides and a lid. The food is browned at a high heat and then the lid put on and the heat reduced to continue cooking at a lower temperature. It is specially useful for chicken joints and large pork or veal chops. A sauce is often added towards the end of the cooking time. Recipes for sautés will be found in Chapters 8 and 9.

COOKING TECHNIQUES

Beating and whisking

Beating usually means vigorous stirring with a wooden spoon to make a mixture smooth. Whisking is usually done to beat air into the food and for this an egg beater or whisk is used.

The best hand whisks are either the balloon-shaped ones made of many strands of thick wire, or the flatter whisks which are basically a coil of wire. It is useful to have a small one of these even if you have an electric beater for large amounts of food.

When you are using the rotary or electric type of beater, choose a bowl small enough to allow the mixture to come well up the sides of the blades of the beater, otherwise it takes a long time to beat the mixture satisfactorily.

To use the electric blender is a very quick way of beating eggs and batters.

Blending and liquidizing

The use of an electric blender or liquidizer takes a lot of hard work out of many cooking operations. Blenders may be attachments for a mixing machine or free-standing with their own motor. Large blenders are more useful than small ones, not only because they hold more food but because they are more powerful and efficient.

They are specially useful for the following cooking jobs:

Beating eggs for cakes, omelets and scrambled eggs; or for beating a batter, one minute only required with all ingredients in together.

Blending solids and liquids smoothly together for drinks, sauces and soups.

Chopping herbs for sauces and soups with a little water or other liquid, such as some of the sauce or soup. Fine chopping in the blender can take the place of grating for making breadcrumbs, grating cheese or chocolate and fine chopping of nuts. For these jobs the food is usually cut in small pieces and fed in through the top while the motor is running; keep one hand over the top to prevent food from being thrown out. In some cases the makers recommend using the on/off technique, putting the food in and then switching on and off until it is chopped. It is always best to follow the recommendations of the maker of your particular machine.

MAKING PURÉES

When sieving is required for making a purée you can get the same result much faster by putting the food in the blender, and there is less waste too. Sometimes small seeds of berries do not blend smooth but it is much easier to sieve a blended pulp than the whole fruit. Blending is particularly useful for fruit and vegetables but cooked meat or raw liver and fish can be made into a purée provided some liquid is added. It is also useful for making smooth sandwich spreads and dips.

You will find I have given blending as an alternative method of preparation for a great number of the recipes in this book.

Consistencies in mixing

Wherever possible I have given quantities of liquids to use when making batters, cakes and doughs but frequently these need to be adjusted because the other ingredients vary in their moisture content. Thus it is important to know what is meant by the various terms used to describe consistency. The thinnest is a thin batter, which is like a pouring cream or single cream and will flow readily from a jug; a thick batter will flow but is thick and sluggish; a dropping or soft cake consistency is too thick to pour but drops easily from the mixing spoon; a stiff cake consistency is thick enough to stand up in rocky lumps; a soft dough is thicker still, being stiff enough to handle and roll out, but is still soft to the touch; a stiff dough has the minimum amount of liquid needed to hold the ingredients together and is firmer and drier than a soft dough.

Creaming fat and sugar

Creaming can be quite hard work if you do it by hand. It is easy if you have an electric mixing machine. Some fats are much easier to cream than others, for example, soft margarines, but if the fat is firm or cold from the refrigerator, warm the mixing bowl before adding the fat. It should be soft but not melted.

The finer the sugar the easier it is to make a good creamed mixture, which is why so many cake recipes specify caster sugar; but you can substitute a coarser sugar if you wish. Creaming is continued until the sugar has more or less melted to give a light smooth mixture like very thick whipped cream.

Do not add ice-cold eggs to a creamed mixture as this will make it curdle. If the eggs are cold, break them into a warm bowl and whisk lightly before beating them into the creamed mixture. If several eggs are being added it is a good plan to beat a spoonful of the flour into the mixture between each addition of an egg.

Flamber or flaming

Flaming of food may be done during the cooking process, or at the time of serving, as with the lighted rum or brandy on the Christmas pudding. For good results you must use a spirit or liqueur because only these contain enough alcohol to burn satisfactorily. Unless the alcohol is being added to a very hot dish, as when frying, it is better to warm it first and set it alight before adding it to the food, otherwise it will not burn well. Neither will it burn well if there is a lot of juice or gravy with the food, as this will quickly douse the flames. The alcohol can be warmed and set alight in a large metal spoon or ladle, or use a small metal chauffe sauce. Be careful not to heat the alcohol far in advance or make it too hot as it evaporates very quickly.

Folding in

This method of mixing is used to combine ingredients gently in order to retain air which has been beaten in, for example, folding flour into beaten eggs, sugar into beaten egg whites or whipped cream into a purée. A metal spoon is used and one mixture is folded over the other gently, with the spoon being used to cut through the mixture to the bottom to lift up the lower layers and fold them over the top until all is smoothly combined.

Some electric mixers have a 'fold' setting but this is really gentle stirring, which is not quite the same thing. However, it can be satisfactory if carried out for the minimum time needed to blend the ingredients.

Rubbing in

This is the traditional method of combining fat with flour when making pastry and plain cake mixtures. The fat is cut into small pieces and dropped into the flour, then fingers and thumbs of both hands are used to work the flour and fat together until the mixture looks like fine breadcrumbs. As the rubbing is done the hands are continually lifted up so that the rubbed mixture falls back into the basin. This process helps to mix in air and keep the mixture cool. Don't ever rub between the palms of the hands as this makes the fat too hot and prevents it from combining as it should.

Today we have two other methods of doing this job, either using an electric mixer or using a very soft fat and simply stirring it into the flour with a little water or other liquid.

In the recipes I have advised rubbing in but you can use either of the other methods if you find them easier.

BASIC DUMPLING, PANCAKE AND PASTRY RECIPES

Dumplings

To serve with stews of meat, game or poultry or with boiled salt beef and other boiled meats. Tiny dumplings are also used for garnishing soups.

Cooking time $\frac{1}{2}$–$\frac{3}{4}$ hr for large dumplings; 15–20 mins for small ones.
Quantities for 4 large dumplings.

2 oz self-raising flour (6 Tbs or 50 g)	$\frac{1}{4}$ tsp salt
1 oz fresh grated or packet suet (4 Tbs or 25 g)	1 Tbs fresh chopped herbs or $\frac{1}{4}$–$\frac{1}{2}$ tsp dried (optional)

Good herbs to use are thyme, marjoram, savory, tarragon, parsley or chervil, or use a mixture. Pulverize dried herbs before using them.

Mix all the ingredients together thoroughly. Then, using a knife for mixing, quickly add enough cold water to make a soft dough, softer than for pastry, but not sticky. Flour your hands and roll the mixture into smooth balls.

Steaming is the best method of cooking dumplings for serving with boiled meats or stews cooked on the hob. Put the dumplings in a steamer top over rapidly boiling water. Cover the steamer and cook until they are risen and light. Do not lift the lid for the first 15 mins of cooking or the dumplings may become heavy.

Baking is a good method for a casserole. Put the dumplings in the bubbling casserole about $\frac{3}{4}$ hr before the end of cooking. Cover with the lid. If a crisp crust is wanted the dumpling mixture can be shaped in one piece. When it is risen and set, remove the casserole lid and allow the top to brown, increasing the oven temperature if necessary.

For soup either boil tiny dumplings in the soup or steam them separately as described above.

Pancakes

Cooking time 1–2 mins per pancake. *Quantities* for 8 pancakes.

4 oz plain flour ($\frac{3}{4}$ c or 125 g) $\frac{1}{2}$ tsp salt

Put in a basin and make a well in the centre.

2 eggs $\frac{1}{2}$ pt milk (300 ml)

Break the eggs into the well in the flour and begin mixing with a wooden spoon, working from the centre and gradually bringing in the flour. Add milk as it becomes thick, until half the milk has been added. Then beat the batter very thoroughly before adding the rest of the milk. Pour the batter into a jug.

ALTERNATIVE METHOD

Put all the ingredients in the blender goblet and process at high speed for 1 min.

COOKING

Use a 6–6½ in (15–16 cm) frying pan and add a knob of lard. When this is very hot tip out any surplus and pour in a thin layer of the batter. The pan must be really hot before you do this, or the batter may stick. Cook until brown underneath, turn or toss and cook the other side. Tip the pancakes on to a hot flat plate or a piece of greaseproof paper. Either fill and roll up or put the pancakes in a pile as they are made and fill them all at the end. To serve them plain, sprinkle with lemon juice and a little sugar before rolling them up.

Herb pancakes

Add to the batter 1–2 Tbs chopped fresh herbs, either of one kind or a mixture.

STORING PANCAKES

Pancakes can be made in advance and kept in the refrigerator. When they are cold, cover and store. To use them put the pancakes on trays and heat them through in a moderate oven. If you are serving them stuffed, add the filling to the cold pancakes, put in a baking dish and heat for not less than 20 mins in a moderate oven to make sure the filling is really hot. If a sauce is included in the recipe this can be added before heating the pancakes.

Pancakes can also be frozen successfully; frozen stuffed pancakes with a sauce are especially useful. Pack the stuffed pancakes in a single layer in a foil dish and cover them with the sauce, then cover the dish and freeze. To use, heat them at 200° C (400° F; G6) for ½–¾ hr or until they are hot right through and the sauce is bubbling.

Pastry

When one of my recipes specifies short-crust pastry it has been tested with the old-fashioned kind made with plain flour and a mixture of lard and butter or margarine. If you prefer a different kind of pastry, such as the quick-mix using soft margarine or oil, or a pastry made with self-raising flour, these can be used instead.

Below, I give my short-crust recipe and another one using egg, which makes it richer and more suitable for flans and quiches. Some people find this kind easier to make successfully.

The quick flaky pastry recipe is one I learnt to make when a teenager, and I find it perfectly adequate when this type of pastry is required.

I gave up making puff pastry several years ago when a really good ready-made version came on the market. Any of my recipes which use puff pastry have been tested with the commercial kind.

PASTRY FOR THE FREEZER

Freeze the pastry in quantities of not more than 1 lb ($\frac{1}{2}$ kg) per pack, shaping the dough to a flat oblong. This will freeze and thaw faster than a ball or a lump of pastry. Wrap it closely in foil or polythene. To use, thaw it at room temperature until it is soft enough to roll.

FREEZING FLANS, PIES AND TARTS

Flan or quiche cases. Freeze unfilled cases, raw or cooked, unwrapped and then stack in a box with cellophane or polythene between layers. Thaw cooked cases at room temperature for about 1 hr. Bake raw cases at 200° C (400° F; G6) for 20–25 mins.

Cooked savoury flans and quiches. Cool, chill and freeze, either before or after wrapping. To serve cold, thaw in the refrigerator for at least 6–8 hrs. To serve hot, cook at 180° C (350° F; G4) for 20 mins or until heated through.

Fruit pies. Use foil pie dishes. Freeze raw, then wrap. Avoid putting heavy packages on top. Cook at 200° C (400° F; G6) for 1 hr. Cut a vent in the top of the crust after the pie has been in the oven for about 15 mins.

Meat pies. Either freeze the raw or cooked meat filling and the pastry separately or make up the pie and freeze it raw. Do not cut a vent in the crust before freezing.

To cook a pie with flaky or puff pastry bake at 250° C (475° F; G9) for 25 mins, then cut a slit in the crust and continue cooking at 190° C (375° F; G5) for 2 hrs or whatever the normal cooking time would be.

To cook a pie with short pastry crust bake at 220° C (425° F; G7) for 15 mins, then cut a vent in the crust and continue cooking at 190° C (375° F; G5) for 2 hrs or whatever the normal cooking time would be.

In both cases the crust can be brushed with egg or milk before baking, and if it tends to become too brown it can be covered loosely with foil.

Pasties and turnovers. Freeze raw or cooked on a tray and then wrap. To cook raw ones, brush with egg or milk and bake at 200° C (400° F; G6) for 50–55 mins. For serving cold, thaw cooked ones for 12 hrs in the refrigerator; to serve hot, reheat for 20 mins in a hot oven.

Plate pies or double crust tarts. Either make in foil plates or in other dishes removing the tart when it is frozen and returning for cooking. Freeze raw and unwrapped, then protect the top with a foil plate and wrap. Cook at 200° C (400° F; G6) for 20 mins then at 180° C (350° F; G4) for 35 mins or until the filling is cooked.

Quick flaky pastry

8 oz plain flour (1½ c or 200 g)
½ tsp salt
3–4 Tbs water

3 oz butter (75 g) and 3 oz lard (75 g), or use 6 oz of a firm margarine (150 g)

Put the flour and salt in a basin. Cut the fat in pieces and add to the flour. The fat should be as firm as possible. Use two knives, one in each hand, and cut the fat into the flour, using a scissor-like action, until it is the size of large peas. Use a knife for mixing and add cold water to combine the ingredients into a very stiff dough.

Roll this to a rectangle about ¼ in (6 mm) thick, keeping the sides and ends as straight as possible. Fold the pastry by bringing the longest sides to the middle, then top and bottom edges to the middle, fold in half and press the edges together with the rolling pin. Put the pastry in a cold place to rest for ½ hr or longer.

To roll out, turn the pastry so that the unbroken fold is on your left-hand side. Roll out thinly and shape as required. Rest it again in a cold place before baking.

Short-crust pastry

8 oz plain flour (1½ c or 200 g)
2 oz butter or margarine (50 g)
2–3 Tbs cold water

½ tsp salt
2 oz lard (50 g)

Put the flour and salt in a basin, cut the fat in small pieces, add it to the flour and use the tips of your fingers to rub the fat into the flour. Use both hands and lift fat and flour up, letting the rubbed mixture fall back into the basin. Continue until the mixture looks like fine breadcrumbs. Sprinkle in 2 Tbs cold water and use a knife to mix it in, adding the extra water only if necessary. The less water you use the shorter the pastry will be. You only want enough to make the ingredients hold together and roll out without cracking.

Put a little flour on your bench or table top, roll the pastry to the thickness specified in the recipe and use as required.

All pastry benefits from a rest in a cold place after rolling and before baking. If it is a flan you are making, line the flan ring and put it in a cold place for about

20 minutes to rest. If it is for covering a pie, fold the pastry in four, put it on a plate and put it in a cold place to rest.

The secrets of success are using the right kind of fat, adding the minimum amount of water and letting the pastry rest before baking.

MACHINE-MIXED PASTRY

Allow the fat to soften at room temperature and cut it in small pieces before adding it to the flour. Use the attachment recommended by the maker of the mixer and mix until it looks like fine breadcrumbs. Then proceed by hand as above, which usually gives better results than doing the whole thing by machine.

DRY PASTRY MIX

This will keep for several weeks in the refrigerator. Make as above but do not add the water. Put the dry mixture in polythene bags or boxes and store in the refrigerator. It is a good idea to make double or treble the recipe.

6 oz (175 g) of the mix will be enough for a 7 in (18 cm) flan and 8–12 oz (250–350 g) will make a plate tart. Weigh out the required amount and add water to mix, in the proportions of 1–2 Tbs per 6 oz (175 g) of mix.

Short-crust pastry with egg

This pastry is richer and lighter than the previous recipe. Sometimes it cracks during shaping, but cracks can easily be pressed together without spoiling it.

8 oz plain flour (1½ c or 200 g)	¼ tsp salt
2 oz butter or margarine (50 g)	2 oz lard (50 g)

Rub the fat into the flour by hand or machine as described for short-crust pastry, above.

1 egg, beaten

Add to the flour and use your hands to work it in, only adding water if absolutely necessary; a standard sized egg probably won't need any at all. Roll and use as in the recipe. This pastry also benefits from a rest in a cold place, as with the previous recipe.

Flan or quiche cases

These can be made in a flan ring on a baking tray, in a flan tin with fluted sides or in a pie plate. Use short-crust pastry made with or without egg.

For a 7–8 in (18–20 cm) flan use 4 oz (100 g) of flour. This will make a thin pastry case; if you like it thicker use 6 oz (150 g) of flour, or use 8 oz (250 g) of ready-made pastry.

Roll the pastry into a circle a little larger than the flan case. Lift it carefully into the case, easing and not stretching it. Press the bottom down firmly and then the sides. Trim off surplus pastry either by using a knife or by passing the rolling pin over the top to cut off the surplus. Prick the bottom of the pastry and refrigerate it for 20 minutes or so before baking.

TO BAKE BLIND

Line the pastry case with foil and bake until the pastry is set, then remove the foil and finish cooking until the pastry is well dried inside. Bake at 200–220° C (400–425° F; G6–7) for about 20 mins.

Refrigerated flan

Quantities for an 8 in (20 cm) flan.

6 oz digestive biscuits (175 g)	1 Tbs honey or syrup
3 oz butter (75 g), or use half butter and half margarine	¼ tsp ground cinnamon

Crumb the biscuits by mincing or rolling, or use the electric blender. Put in a mixing bowl. Just melt the fat, honey or syrup and the cinnamon. Add to the crumbs, stir well. Put the flan ring on a serving dish, tip the mixture into the centre and use the back of a spoon to mould it to fit the ring. Mould the sides first and then spread the rest of the mixture evenly over the bottom. Chill in the refrigerator to set the flan, and remove the ring before adding the filling.

An alternative to the flan ring is to use a glass pie plate, or a sandwich tin lined with foil. Peel off the foil when the flan has been refrigerated to make it firm.

ALTERNATIVE VERSION

Use ginger biscuits instead of the digestives; this is especially good with a lemon filling. Omit the cinnamon and honey or syrup.

Sponge flan

Cooking time 20 mins.
Temperature 190° C (375° F; G5).
Quantities for an 8 in (20 cm) flan. Use a special sponge flan tin and grease it well, then dust with flour.

2 eggs　　　　　　　　　　　　　　　3 oz granulated sugar (6 Tbs or 75 g)

Make sure the eggs are at room temperature, or heat the mixing bowl with hot water. Beat until the eggs are light, add the sugar and beat until the mixture is very thick like whipped cream.

3 oz plain flour (⅔ c or 75 g)   pinch of salt
1 tsp baking powder

Sift into the egg mixture and fold together. Put in the prepared tin and bake until it feels springy when pressed lightly in the centre. Turn out on to a wire rack to cool. Put on a serving dish and add the filling.

Pies, to cover

QUICK METHOD FOR SHORT-CRUST PASTRY

Fill the pie up above the level of the rim to give support to the pastry. If the filling is not sufficient for this, use a pie funnel or inverted egg-cup placed in the middle of the filling. Roll the pastry about ¼ in (6 mm) thick and 2 in (5 cm) wider than the size of the top of the pie dish. Wind the pastry gently round the rolling pin and lift it on to the pie, unrolling it without stretching. Trim off surplus pastry leaving ½ in (1 cm) overhanging. Turn that piece under to make it level with the edge of the dish. Damp the flat rim of the pie dish and press the folded pastry down all round. Decorate the edge by slashing the pastry horizontally with a small knife and then scallop by pressing each piece with the thumb of one hand and cutting round it with a knife held in the other hand. Cut a slit in the centre of the crust to let out steam. Brush with beaten egg and water or with milk and bake.

STANDARD METHOD FOR ANY PASTRY

Fill the pie dish as above and roll out the pastry. Cut a strip or strips of pastry the length and width of the rim of the dish. Damp the edges of the dish and press the pastry strip right round. Brush the top of the rim with water. Lift the large piece of pastry on top, as above, and trim off surplus pastry level with the edge of the dish. Press down the rim, trim off surplus and decorate as above.

Vol-au-vents

Cooking time 15–20 mins.
Temperature 230° C (450° F; G8).
Quantities for 4 good-sized vol-au-vents.

1 lb puff pastry (500 g)

This amount of pastry will allow you to cut all four vol-au-vents from the first rolling. The trimmings can be refrigerated or frozen and used later for a pie covering or for sweet pastries or savoury pasties.

Roll the pastry about ⅛ in (3 mm) thick. Then lift it up from the board to let air get under and relax any stretching. Use a plain 3½ in (9 cm) circular cutter and stamp out 8 rounds. Put four of these on a baking tray. With a 2½ in (5 cm) cutter remove the centres from the remaining rounds. This size of cutter gives plenty of room for the filling. Put the small rounds on a separate baking tray. Brush the large rounds with beaten egg and water or with milk and carefully stick the circles on top, being sure to have them on straight or they will topple over during cooking. Put them in the refrigerator to chill for ½ hr or so. Before baking them brush with egg or milk round the top rim and brush the small pieces. These will be cooked in about 10 mins so remove them first.

Vol-au-vents are nicest if served freshly baked and hot but you can cook them in advance and re-heat before filling and serving them.

2. Sauces

Most sauces can be made in advance and kept hot for $\frac{1}{2}$ hr or so in a bain-marie or double boiler with the water hot, but not boiling; or they can be kept in a warming cupboard. Some sauces kept hot in this way are liable to form a skin on top and should be given an occasional whisk to keep them smooth. Should a sauce become lumpy with keeping, it can either be strained before use, or put in an electric blender for a second or two to make it smooth again. Sweet sauces can have some of the sugar in the recipe reserved to sprinkle over the top, which will prevent a skin from forming.

Sauces made with milk or stock will keep for 1–2 days in a refrigerator. As soon as the sauce is made, put it in a container and stand this in cold water to cool the sauce as quickly as possible. Cover when cold and store in the refrigerator. When the sauce is to be warmed, either whisk well to make it smooth or put it in the electric blender for a second or two. If the recipe contains egg or cream, add these after the sauce has been re-heated and just before serving.

Mayonnaise and similar cold sauces will keep for up to two weeks in the refrigerator.

For still longer storage the freezer can be used for any sauce except mayonnaise and its derivatives. These tend to separate when frozen, although very small amounts mixed with other food are not affected. Put the sauce to be frozen in tubs and cool it quickly by standing the tubs in cold water, then cover and chill in the refrigerator before finally transferring to the freezer. It is advisable to season the sauce lightly and add more seasoning during the re-heating. To use, re-heat the sauce in a double boiler or over a very gentle direct heat. Stir and break up the sauce as soon as it starts to melt. Stir vigorously or whisk frequently to make it smooth. It may be necessary to thin the sauce before serving it.

NOTE

If oil is preferred, use 2 Tbs oil to replace 1 oz (25 g) of butter, margarine or other solid fat.

HOT SAVOURY SAUCES

Anchovy sauce

(for fish or eggs)

Cooking time about 10 mins. *Quantities* for 4.

½ oz butter or margarine (15 g)   ½ oz flour (1½ Tbs or 15 g)

Melt the fat in a saucepan and stir in the flour. Cook until it looks crumbly.

½ pt liquid (300 ml)

The liquid can be milk or a mixture of milk and fish or chicken stock according to the way it will be used and the liquid available. Add to the pan and stir until the sauce is smooth and boiling. Boil gently for 5 mins.

2–3 tsp anchovy essence   chopped capers (optional)
pepper to taste

Add to the sauce, taste for seasoning and serve hot.

Apple sauce

Cooking time ½ hr. *Quantities* for 4–6.

1 lb cooking apples (500 g)   2 oz sugar (4 Tbs or 50 g)

Peel, core and slice the apples and cook them in a saucepan with just enough water to prevent burning. Cook to a pulp. If a smooth sauce is wanted, rub the pulp through a sieve or put it in the electric blender. Add the sugar and reheat. Serve hot.

Béchamel or white sauce

Cooking time about ½ hr. *Quantities* for 4.

½ pt milk (300 ml)   small piece of celery stick
1 slice of onion   ½ bay leaf
1 small piece of carrot   4 peppercorns

Put all the ingredients in a pan and bring to the boil. Remove from the heat and leave to infuse for 5 mins. Then strain and cool for a while. It is easier to make a smooth sauce with lukewarm or cold liquid. Rinse the pan.

½ oz butter or margarine (15 g)   salt
1½ Tbs flour   2 Tbs cream

Melt the butter or margarine in the saucepan and stir in the flour. Cook gently for 2–3 mins. Remove from the heat and beat in the strained milk in three or four lots, each time beating smooth. Return to the heat, stir until boiling. Boil gently for about three minutes or cook in a double boiler for 10 mins. Add cream and salt and serve.

Blender sauces

Two basic methods for sauces with a flour or starch thickening:

METHOD 1

Melt the fat in a small pan. Put the cold liquid, flour or other thickening and the seasonings in the blender and mix well. Add to the fat, stir until the sauce boils and boil gently for 5 mins, or cook longer over boiling water.

METHOD 2

Use hot liquid and blend all the ingredients together. Return to the pan, stir until it boils and cook for 3 mins, or cook longer over boiling water.

Bread sauce

Cooking time 25 mins. *Quantities* for 4.

1 onion	4 cloves
½ pt milk (250 ml)	

Skin and slice the onion and cook with the other ingredients for about 10 mins or until the milk is well flavoured. Strain.

2 oz fresh breadcrumbs (⅔ c or 50 g)

Add to the milk and heat slowly, without boiling, until the crumbs have thickened the milk.

1 oz butter or margarine (25 g)   Salt and pepper

Add to the sauce, seasoning well, and serve hot.

Brown butter sauce

(for fish, vegetables or eggs)

Cooking time a few mins. *Quantities* for 4.

2–4 oz butter (50–100 g)

Heat in a small saucepan until the butter turns nut-brown.

1–2 tsp chopped parsley   1–2 tsp vinegar

Add parsley to the butter and cook for a few minutes, then add the vinegar and pour the sauce quickly over the food.

Caper sauce

Although this sauce is most often served with boiled mutton it is also very good with other boiled meats such as tongue or bacon, and with boiled or steamed fish, in fact, with any food where a sharp flavour would be an improvement. Pickled nasturtium seeds can replace the capers.

Cooking time 10–15 mins. *Quantities* for 4–6.

2 oz butter or margarine (50 g)   2 oz flour (6 Tbs or 50 g)

Melt the fat in a saucepan and add the flour. Stir and cook for a few minutes. Remove from the heat.

1 pt fish or meat stock (600 ml)

Gradually add to the pan, stirring or whisking until the sauce is smooth. Return to the heat and stir until it boils, boil for 5 mins.

2 Tbs chopped capers   1½ Tbs vinegar from the capers, or
salt and pepper   use lemon juice

Add to the sauce and serve hot.

ALTERNATIVE

Use lemon juice instead of vinegar and add 1 Tbs anchovy essence.

Cheese sauce (Mornay)

Cooking time about 10 mins. *Quantities* for 4.

½ oz butter or margarine (15 g)   pinch of dry mustard
½ oz flour (1½ Tbs or 15 g)

Melt the fat in a saucepan and add flour and mustard. Stir and cook until it looks crumbly. Remove the pan from the heat.

½ pt milk (300 ml)

Stir in the milk, mixing or whisking until the sauce is smooth. Return to the heat and stir until it boils. Boil gently for 5 mins.

2 oz grated cheese (50 g)   salt and pepper
pinch of ground mace or nutmeg

Processed and other soft cheeses need not be grated, simply chop them in small pieces. A strongly flavoured cheese makes the best sauce. Heat the sauce until the cheese melts. Season and serve hot.

BLENDER METHOD

Cut the cheese in pieces and heat the milk. Put all ingredients in the goblet and process until smooth. Tip into a saucepan and stir until the sauce boils. Boil gently for 3 mins.

Cranberry sauce

Cooking time 10 mins. *Quantities* for 4.

8 oz cranberries (250 g)   ¼ pt water (150 ml)

Boil the cranberries in the water, crushing them with a spoon as they soften. When all are tender, rub them through a sieve or pulp them in the electric blender.

4 oz sugar (½ c or 125 g)

Add to the cranberry pulp and re-heat, stirring to dissolve the sugar. If required cold, pour into a small mould and leave for at least 12 hrs before using. If to be served hot, thin it with hot water to give it the consistency of a thick sauce.

Cucumber sauce

(for grilled lamb cutlets, veal escalopes or chops, grilled fish, or chicken)

Cooking time about 20 mins. *Quantities* for 4.

8 oz cucumber (250 g)

Peel, cut in strips and then in small dice.

½ oz butter (15 g)

Melt in a small saucepan, add the cucumber and stew it slowly until it is almost soft.

1 Tbs flour

Mix into the cucumber.

¼ pt white stock (150 ml)

Stir in and bring to the boil, cook for 5 mins.

2 heaped Tbs chopped dill   salt and pepper

Add to the sauce. There should be enough dill to make it look green.

5 Tbs soured or cultured cream (75 ml), or use fresh double cream with a squeeze of lemon

Add and heat just to boiling before serving.

Curry sauce

Cooking time ½ hr. *Quantities* for 4.

1 oz fat (25 g)   1 onion, chopped

Heat the fat in a small saucepan and fry the onion until brown.

1 oz flour (3 Tbs or 25 g)   1 Tbs curry powder, more or less

Add to the pan, mix and cook for a few minutes.

½ pt stock or milk (300 ml)

Remove the pan from the heat, add the liquid and stir or whisk. Return to the heat and stir until it boils.

1 apple, chopped	1 small tomato, chopped
Grated rind and juice of ½ small lemon	1 bay leaf
1 Tbs chutney	1 tsp brown sugar
	½ tsp salt

Add to the pan, cover and boil gently for 20 mins or more. Strain and re-heat before serving.

Espagnole sauce

(a brown sauce for meat, poultry or game)

Cooking time about 1 hr. *Quantities* for 6 or more.

2 oz butter (50 g)   2 oz chopped ham or bacon (50 g)

Heat the butter in a saucepan and fry the meat in it for a few minutes.

1 medium-sized onion, chopped   2 oz mushrooms or stalks, chopped
1 small carrot, chopped   (50 g)

Add to the pan and continue frying until the vegetables begin to brown.

1 oz flour (3 Tbs or 25 g)

Sprinkle into the pan, stir and cook until the flour begins to brown.

1 pt stock (600 ml)   2 Tbs concentrated tomato purée

Add to the pan and stir until the sauce boils. Boil gently for ¾ hr, adding more stock if it seems necessary. Strain the sauce through a fine sieve.

5 Tbs sherry or madeira (75 ml)   salt and pepper

Add to the sauce, re-heat to boiling and season to taste. Serve hot.

Fennel sauce

(for lamb or mutton, poultry, rabbit, fish or vegetables)

Cooking time about 10 mins. *Quantities* for 4–8.

1½ oz butter or margarine (40 g)   1½ oz flour (4½ Tbs or 40 g)

Melt the fat in a saucepan, add the flour, mix and cook until it looks crumbly. Remove from the heat.

1 pt white, fish or vegetable stock (600 ml)

Stir or whisk into the pan until the sauce is smooth. Return to the heat and stir until it boils, boil gently for 5 mins.

1 egg yolk   1 tsp sugar
1½ Tbs vinegar or lemon juice   salt and pepper
4 Tbs finely chopped fresh fennel

Mix the egg, sugar and vinegar or lemon juice and add to the sauce. Stir and heat to thicken without boiling. Add the fennel and seasoning and serve.

Gravy

THIN GRAVY

Remove the roast meat to a hot dish. Tilt the roasting pan to make the drippings flow down to one corner. Wait a few moments for the sediment to settle and then gently pour off most of the fat, leaving sediment and meat juices behind. Add stock and/or wine and stir to incorporate all the brown bits stuck to the pan. Bring this to the boil either in the roasting pan or in a small saucepan. Season and strain.

THICK GRAVY

Make it either in the roasting pan or in a small saucepan. As before, pour off the fat, except for about 2 tablespoons. Add 2 tablespoons of flour or one of cornflour, stir well and cook until it begins to brown. Add half a pint (300 ml) of stock, stir until it boils, cook for a few minutes. Season and strain.

Hollandaise sauce

Quantities for 4 or more.

4 oz butter (100 g)　　　　　　　　　2 egg yolks
1 Tbs lemon juice

Put the egg yolks, lemon juice and a third of the butter in the top of a double boiler or in a basin over boiling water. Just melt the rest of the butter in a small pan.

Cook the egg mixture over simmering water, beating with a wire whisk, until the butter is melted. Gradually whisk in the rest of the butter and continue whisking until the sauce begins to thicken slightly.

2–3 Tbs boiling water　　　　　　　　¼ tsp salt
a few grains cayenne pepper

Add boiling water to make a thin sauce and beat for a minute longer. Add the seasoning and remove from the heat. This sauce is served warm and it is advisable to make it at the last minute before serving the meal, though it can be kept warm for a short while. Should the sauce separate, add 2 Tbs double cream or boiling water, drop by drop, beating hard all the time.

Lemon and sage sauce

(for duck, goose, pork, boiled ham or bacon)

Cooking time 35 mins. *Quantities* for 4.

½ oz butter or margarine (15 g)　　　1 Tbs flour

Melt the fat in a small pan, stir in the flour and cook for a minute or two.

1 oz finely chopped onion (25 g)　　　1 tsp grated lemon rind
½ oz finely chopped sage (15 g)　　　(¾ pt [400 ml] of loosely packed sage
1 tsp vinegar　　　　　　　　　　　　leaves makes about ½ oz [15 g] when
¼ pt stock (150 ml)　　　　　　　　　chopped.)
salt and pepper

Add to the pan and stir until the sauce boils, cover and boil gently for ½ hr, adding more stock as needed to prevent burning. It should be a thick sauce. Serve hot.

Mushroom sauce

Cooking time 10–15 mins. *Quantities* for 4.

½ oz butter (15 g)   1 Tbs finely chopped onion

Melt the butter in a small pan and cook the onion gently until it is soft but not brown.

4 oz button mushrooms, whole or   4 Tbs good beef stock or canned
  chopped (125 g)   consommé (60 ml)
4 Tbs white wine (60 ml)

Add to the pan and bring to the boil, cook gently until the mushrooms are tender.

¼ pt double cream (150 ml)   chopped parsley
salt and pepper

Add to the sauce and heat, seasoning to taste. Serve hot. If a smooth sauce is preferred, rub through a sieve or put in the electric blender, then re-heat.

Mustard sauce

Cooking time 10 mins. *Quantities* for 4 or more.

2 oz butter or margarine (50 g)   2 Tbs. flour

Melt the fat in a small saucepan and stir in the flour. Cook for a minute without allowing the flour to colour.

½ pt stock (250 ml)

Add to the pan and stir or whisk until the sauce is smooth. Bring to the boil and cook for 5 mins.

2 Tbs dry mustard   2 Tbs tarragon or other herb vinegar

Mix to a smooth paste and add to the sauce just before serving. If necessary add salt to taste.

Onion sauce

Cooking time 30 mins. *Quantities* for 4.

8 oz onions (250 g)   1 oz butter or margarine (25 g)

Skin and slice the onions finely, or chop them. Melt the fat in a saucepan and stew the onions in it slowly until they are soft but not browned.

1 Tbs flour
salt and pepper
½ pt milk (250 ml)
grated nutmeg or mace

Stir the flour into the onions and then add the milk. Stir until it boils and then cook gently for 15 mins or until the onions are cooked. Serve as it is, or to make it smooth rub through a sieve or put it in the electric blender. Re-heat if necessary and season to taste.

cream (optional)

Add single cream just before serving.

Parsley sauce

Cooking time 8–10 mins. *Quantities* for 4.

½ oz butter or margarine (15 g)
½ oz flour (1½ Tbs or 15 g)
½ pt milk or half milk and half stock (300 ml)

Melt the fat in a small pan, add the flour and mix and cook for a minute or so. Add the liquid and stir until the sauce is smooth and boiling, boil gently for 5 mins.

2 Tbs or more of chopped parsley
lemon juice to taste
salt and pepper

Add to the sauce, which should be really green with parsley and taste distinctly of it.

Tomato sauce

(to serve with pasta)

Cooking time 30 mins. *Quantities* for 1 lb (½ kg) pasta.

2 medium-sized onions, chopped
2 Tbs oil

Heat the oil and fry the onion in it for 5 mins.

1 small tin of concentrated tomato purée (2½ oz or 75 g)

Add to the onion, stir and cook for a minute or two.

salt and pepper
pinch of dried thyme
1 pt water (500 ml)

Add to the pan, stirring until the sauce boils. Boil gently, uncovered, for about 25 mins, or until it is a creamy consistency. Season and serve hot.

Tomato sauce, quick

Quantities for 4.

½ pt can condensed tomato soup (284 ml)
1 Tbs Worcester sauce
1 Tbs tarragon vinegar
1 tsp brown sugar
salt and pepper

Mix all together, bring to the boil and serve.

Velouté sauce

(for poultry or vegetables)

Cooking time 10 mins. *Quantities* for 4.

½ oz butter or margarine (15 g)
½ pt chicken stock (300 ml)
ground nutmeg or mace
½ oz cornflour (1½ Tbs or 15 g)
salt and pepper

Melt the fat in a small pan and stir in the cornflour. Stir and cook over a gentle heat until the mixture becomes runny. Cook for a minute longer. Add the cold stock, stir and heat until the sauce boils, boil gently for 5 mins. Season to taste.

White sauce

See béchamel sauce.

COLD SAVOURY SAUCES

Apple and horseradish sauce

(for cold meat, poultry or fish)

Quantities for 4.

½ tsp dry mustard
1 tsp water

Combine to make a smooth paste.

2 medium-sized apples, or 1 apple and 1 medium-sized carrot
3 Tbs lemon juice

Peel the apple and carrot and grate fairly finely, mixing at once with the lemon juice. Mix in the mustard.

| 1 tsp sugar | 2 Tbs grated horseradish |

Add and mix well.

Béarnaise sauce

Cooking time a few mins. *Quantities* for 4–6.

| 1 tsp finely chopped shallot or onion | a sprig each of tarragon and chervil |
| pinch of salt | 5 Tbs white wine vinegar (75 ml) |

Cut the tarragon and chervil up roughly, put all the ingredients in the top of a double boiler and boil over direct heat until the liquid is reduced to about a dessert spoonful. Remove from the heat and cool a little.

| 2 egg yolks | 3 oz melted butter (75 g) |

Add the yolks to the vinegar and herbs and put the pan over boiling water. Whisk to mix in the egg yolks and then add the butter. Continue whisking until the sauce thickens. Rub it through a small nylon sieve.

1 tsp each of chopped chervil and cayenne pepper
 tarragon

Add to the strained sauce and serve cold.

Breton sauce

Quantities for 4.

1 Tbs French mustard	2 egg yolks
1 Tbs wine vinegar	¼ tsp salt
pinch of pepper	

Mix together in a small basin until well blended. Stand the basin in a bowl of warm water.

2 oz butter (50 g)

Soften until almost melted and then whisk into the egg mixture until the sauce is the consistency of mayonnaise.

2 Tbs chopped fresh herbs

Mix into the sauce and serve cold.

Butters, savoury or compound

(to serve with grilled meat and fish, to dress vegetables, for baked potatoes, for canapés)

To make these, the butter should be softened but not melted and the ingredients beaten together until creamy and smooth. For use with grills and vegetables, shape the mixture into small pats and chill them in the refrigerator. Put on the hot food just before serving it.

The butters can be prepared in advance and stored for several days in a refrigerator, wrapped in foil; or for weeks in a freezer. For the freezer, the mixture can be formed into a thin roll and frozen, then thawed enough to slice for serving.

ANCHOVY BUTTER

4 oz softened butter (100 g)	2 tsp anchovy essence

BASIL BUTTER

4 oz softened butter (100 g)	1 Tbs finely chopped fresh basil or 1 tsp powdered dried

CURRY BUTTER

4 oz softened butter (100 g)	1 tsp curry powder
salt	onion juice or onion salt

GARLIC BUTTER

4 oz softened butter (100 g)	1 small clove minced garlic

Leave to stand for an hour or more before using.

MAÎTRE D'HÔTEL OR PARSLEY BUTTER

4 oz softened butter (100 g)	2 Tbs chopped parsley
lemon juice to taste	

MINT BUTTER

4 oz softened butter (100 g)	½ pt mint leaves (250 ml)
½ pt parsley sprigs (250 ml)	

Wash the mint and parsley leaves and boil them in the smallest possible amount of water until they are pulpy. Rub through a sieve and work into the butter.

MUSTARD BUTTER

4 oz softened butter (100 g)	2 Tbs French mustard

PAPRIKA BUTTER

4 oz softened butter (100 g)   1 Tbs chopped onion
a good pinch of paprika pepper

Fry the onion in ½ oz (15 g) of the butter, adding the paprika during fying. Cool. Work into the butter and then rub through a sieve. Add more paprika if liked, but avoid over-seasoning.

ROSEMARY BUTTER

4 oz softened butter (100 g)   1 tsp powdered dried rosemary or 1 Tbs finely chopped fresh young rosemary leaves

TARRAGON BUTTER

4 oz softened butter (100 g)   ¼ pt tarragon leaves (150 ml)

Pour boiling water over the tarragon leaves, then plunge them in cold water, drain and dry in paper towels. Chop the leaves and work them into the butter, finally rub through a sieve. This makes a well-flavoured green butter.

Cream cheese and horseradish sauce

(for cold meats, grilled meat or fish or meat fondue)

Quantities for 4.

4 oz cream cheese (125 g)   1–2 Tbs bottled horseradish sauce
1–2 Tbs mayonnaise

Mash the cheese with a fork, gradually working in first some horseradish, then some mayonnaise until you have the consistency and flavour you like. Refrigerate until required. Serve cold.

Cumberland sauce

(for cold meats or a meat fondue)

Quantities for 8 or more.

8 Tbs port wine or red wine (4 fl oz   4 Tbs redcurrant jelly
or 120 ml)

Put in a small pan and heat gently, stirring to dissolve the jelly.

1 tsp grated orange rind
2 Tbs orange juice
1 tsp dry mustard
cayenne pepper

1 tsp grated lemon rind
1 Tbs lemon juice
pinch of ground ginger

Mix together and add to the melted jelly. Allow to become cold before using. It will keep well in a covered container in the refrigerator.

Horseradish sauce

Quantities for 4 or more.

4 Tbs grated horseradish
1 tsp wine vinegar
½ tsp salt
pinch of paprika pepper

2 tsp dry mustard
¼ pt yogurt, soured cream or double fresh cream (150 ml)

Mix all together, cover and store in the refrigerator.

Mint sauce

Quantities for 4.

½ pt mint leaves (250 ml)
5 Tbs malt or wine vinegar (75 ml)

1–2 oz caster sugar (2–4 Tbs or 25–50 g)

Chop the mint finely and mix it with the sugar and vinegar, stirring to dissolve the sugar. Leave to infuse for about 2 hrs before using.

USING THE ELECTRIC BLENDER

Put the ingredients in the goblet and process at slow speed until the mint is finely chopped. Leave to infuse.

FOR THE FREEZER

Mix mint and sugar and pour in boiling water barely to cover. Allow to cool and then put in a small container, seal and freeze. When required, add vinegar to the frozen mint and leave the sauce to thaw at room temperature.

Mint sauce with lemon

Quantities for 4.

4 Tbs chopped fresh mint (60 ml)
2 Tbs warm water

2 Tbs caster sugar
8 Tbs lemon juice (120 ml)

Mix together until the sugar dissolves. Leave to infuse for at least ½ hr before using.

Mustard sauce

(for grilled meat or fish, poached fresh or smoked fish, and meat fondue)

Quantities for 4.

¼ pt soured cream (150 ml)
1 Tbs very finely chopped onion
a little lemon juice
1½ Tbs French mustard
salt and pepper

Combine the ingredients and serve cold.

Rémoulade sauce

(for grilled meat or fish and cold meat or fish)

Quantities for 4 or more.

¼ pt mayonnaise (150 ml)
½ Tbs chopped gherkins
½ Tbs chopped fresh herbs (parsley, chervil, tarragon, mixed)
½ Tbs chopped capers
¼ tsp anchovy essence
½ Tbs French mustard

Mix all together.

Salsa verde or green sauce

(for boiled meats or fish, or cold meat)

Quantities for 8 or more.

4 Tbs olive oil (60 ml)
2 oz roughly cut parsley and stalks (50 g)
1 oz pickled gherkins or cucumber (25 g)
pepper, salt and a pinch of sugar
¼ pt wine vinegar (150 ml)
1 oz drained and rinsed capers (25 g)
pinch of dried garlic or ½ clove fresh garlic
1 oz bread (1 slice) or 1 small cooked potato

Put all ingredients in the goblet of an electric blender and mix until smooth.

Soured cream sauce

(for hot or cold meat, poultry or fish)

Quantities for 4 or more.

½ pt soured cream (250 ml)
2 Tbs lemon juice
¼ tsp freshly ground white pepper
¼ tsp salt
1 Tbs chopped chives
1 tsp Worcester sauce

½ tsp dry mustard
2–4 Tbs finely chopped onion

2 Tbs finely chopped parsley or other fresh herbs

Combine ingredients thoroughly, cover and store in the refrigerator.

Tartare sauce

Quantities for 4 or more.

½ pt mayonnaise (250 ml)
2 Tbs finely chopped gherkins or capers

1 tsp finely chopped onion
a little wine or wine vinegar

Mix the ingredients together, adding wine or wine vinegar to make it the right consistency; this should only be necessary if the mayonnaise is very thick.

SALAD DRESSINGS

Cream dressing

Quantities for 4.

1 Tbs oil
salt and sugar
flavouring, see below

1 Tbs wine vinegar
2 Tbs soured cream

Whisk together thoroughly.

ALTERNATIVE FLAVOURINGS

a little finely chopped onion and some chopped herbs
a little horseradish sauce
tomato purée or paprika pepper for a pink dressing

plenty of chopped chives
French mustard
finely grated lemon rind
1 tsp finely chopped onion and plenty of chopped fresh dill or fennel

French dressing

Quantities for a salad for 4.

1½ Tbs olive oil
¼ tsp sugar (optional)
½ Tbs vinegar (wine, cider, tarragon or other flavour) or 1 Tbs lemon juice

¼ tsp dry mustard
pinch of pepper
¼–½ tsp salt

Mix the seasonings with the oil, add the vinegar or lemon juice and stir before using. The simplest way of mixing is to use the salad bowl, then add the salad ingredients and mix or toss.

If preferred, make a larger amount to store in a bottle and use as required. For this use:

2 tsp sugar
¼ tsp pepper
4 Tbs vinegar (60 ml) or 6 Tbs lemon juice (90 ml)

2–3 tsp salt
2 tsp dry mustard
¼ pt oil (150 ml)

Lemon curry dressing

Quantities for 4 or more.

½ tsp salt
1 tsp sugar
¼ pt yogurt or soured cream (150 ml)

1–2 tsp curry powder
Finely grated rind of ½ lemon

Mix the flavourings with the yogurt or cream, cover and store the dressing in the refrigerator for at least ½ hr before using it.

Mayonnaise

2 egg yolks
½–1 tsp salt
½ tsp dry mustard

pinch of cayenne pepper
1 Tbs vinegar or lemon juice

Mix these to a smooth paste in a small basin.

½ pt salad or olive oil (250 ml)

Using a wooden spoon or a small wire egg whisk, stir the mixture vigorously and continuously, adding the oil drop by drop from a spoon. Have the oil and eggs at room temperature, neither hot nor very cold. Wait until each addition of oil has been blended in before adding the next. When half the oil has been used, begin adding it a spoonful at a time but always mixing it in thoroughly before adding more.

1 Tbs vinegar or lemon juice or more to taste

Add when all the oil is mixed in, to give the flavour and consistency you want.

Mayonnaise sometimes curdles, usually because the oil has been added too quickly at the beginning. If this happens put another egg yolk into a clean basin and beat the curdled mayonnaise into it gradually.

Electric blender mayonnaise

I find this recipe, which uses a whole egg, very successful. The mayonnaise is light in colour and texture. If you want a more yellow mayonnaise, add an extra yolk to the egg.

1 egg	pinch of sugar
2 Tbs lemon juice or 1 Tbs vinegar	pinch of salt
1 tsp French mustard	$\frac{1}{4}-\frac{1}{2}$ pt oil (150–250 ml)

Put all except the oil in the goblet of the blender. Turn the speed to maximum and remove the cap from the lid or add the oil through the hole provided in the lid. Continue mixing until the mayonnaise is the desired consistency. The amount of oil 1 egg will emulsify is more than $\frac{1}{4}$ pt and may be as much as $\frac{1}{2}$ pt.

Mayonnaise variations

To $\frac{1}{4}$ pt (150 ml) of mayonnaise made by either of the above recipes add any of the following flavours.

AURORE

1 Tbs double cream $\frac{1}{2}-1$ Tbs concentrated tomato purée
A dash of Worcester sauce

CURRY

Beat in

1 Tbs curry powder, more or less

FENNEL

1–2 Tbs chopped fresh fennel leaves

PAPRIKA

1 tsp or more paprika pepper

For other sauces made with mayonnaise, see rémoulade sauce and tartare sauce.

Mustard dressing

Quantities for 4.

2 Tbs dry mustard	1 Tbs sugar
pinch of pepper	

Put in a small basin or in the salad bowl and add enough cold water to mix to a smooth paste.

½ Tbs oil
1 Tbs single cream

1 Tbs vinegar

Add to the mustard mixture and combine thoroughly. Mix with the salad ingredients. This is very good with a potato salad or one containing beef, tongue, ham or smoked fish.

Turkish dressing

Quantities for 4 or more.

¼ pt yogurt (150 ml)
1 Tbs bottled horseradish sauce
¼ tsp garlic salt
½ tsp salt

1 Tbs lemon juice
½ tsp paprika pepper
1–2 Tbs chopped chives and other fresh herbs

Beat together until frothy.

Yogurt dressings

The simplest of all, and very good, is just to add seasoning to plain yogurt and use this for any kind of salad. The variations given below are for quantities for 4 or more.

1. STANDARD

¼ pt yogurt (150 ml)
pinch of pepper

¼ tsp mustard
¼ tsp salt

2. CURRY DRESSING

1 tsp caster sugar
pinch of pepper
¼ pt yogurt (150 ml)
1 Tbs chopped sweet pickle or chutney

¼ tsp salt
1 Tbs lemon juice
2 Tbs single cream
2 or more tsp curry powder

3. HERB DRESSING

To dressing No. 1 add chopped fresh herbs to make it really green; use just one herb or a mixture.

4. PIQUANT DRESSING

To dressing No. 1 add

1 tsp Worcester sauce
1 tsp paprika pepper

a few grains cayenne pepper
garlic salt or a little crushed fresh garlic

SWEET SAUCES

Caramel sauce

(for ice-cream, fruit and other cold sweets)

Cooking time 5 mins. *Quantities* for 4.

4 oz sugar (½ c or 125 g)   4 Tbs water (60 ml)

Heat these together in a small pan, stirring until the sugar dissolves, then boil hard, without stirring, until the mixture turns amber coloured. Remove the pan from the heat and allow it to cool a little.

4 Tbs water (60 ml)

Add to the caramel and heat and stir until it dissolves. Serve hot or cold.

Chantilly cream

Quantities for 4 or more.

½ pt whipping cream (250 ml)   vanilla to taste
1 oz sifted icing sugar (4 Tbs or 25 g)

Whip the cream until light and thick, then whip in the sugar and flavouring. This can be prepared in advance, covered and stored in the refrigerator for an hour or so.

VARIATION

For a liqueur-flavoured cream, towards the end of whipping add 1 Tbs brandy, rum or liqueur instead of the vanilla. The sugar may be omitted if preferred.

Cherry sauce

(for ice-cream, baked or steamed puddings)

Quantities for 4.

8 oz can morello cherries or 8 oz   4 oz red currant jelly (125 g)
stewed (250 g)   kirsch to taste

Strain the cherries and put the juice in a small pan with the jelly. Heat and stir until the jelly dissolves. Rub the cherries through a sieve, combine with the jelly. Serve hot or cold with kirsch to taste.

ALTERNATIVE METHOD

Remove the stones from the cherries, put the hot liquid, jelly and stoned cherries in the electric blender and process until smooth.

Chocolate sauce

(to serve hot or cold)

Prepare in advance for serving cold.

Quantities for 4.

2 oz butter (50 g)
½ tsp vanilla essence
2 oz sugar (4 Tbs or 50 g)
4 Tbs cocoa powder
3 Tbs water

Put all ingredients in a small pan and heat gently until the butter melts, stirring all the time. When the ingredients are smoothly blended, just bring to the boil. If too thick, thin with cream or milk.

Chocolate mocha sauce

Use the above recipe but reduce the cocoa to 3 Tbs and add 1-2 tsp soluble coffee, or to taste.

Custard sauce

This is a better sauce than one made just with custard powder, but is less difficult than using egg alone for thickening.

Cooking time 3-4 mins. *Quantities* for 4.

1 egg
1 oz sugar (2 Tbs or 25 g)
vanilla or other flavouring
1 Tbs custard powder
½ pt milk (250 ml)
½ oz butter (15 g)

Put the custard powder, sugar and egg in a small basin and whisk together until smooth. Add a little of the cold milk and heat the remainder. Pour the hot milk into the egg mixture, stirring well, return to the pan and stir until the sauce just comes to the boil. Remove from the heat, add the butter and stir to melt it, then add the flavouring. Serve hot or cold, diluting cold sauce with milk or cream if necessary. If you give the sauce an occasional stir while it is beginning to cool, no skin should form on top.

Fruit sauce 1

(hot or cold)

Use canned or stewed fruit: the best ones are apricot, black currant, greengage, raspberry, loganberry or strawberry. Drain the fruit and remove any stones. Either rub the fruit through a sieve, or put fruit and some of the liquid in the electric blender and process to a smooth pulp.

Put pulp and liquid in a pan and boil rapidly until the sauce thickens enough to coat the back of a wooden spoon. Flavour to taste with essence or a liqueur.

When the sauce is served hot, add a knob of butter.

Fruit sauce 2

(cold)

Quantities for 4.

8 oz raw ripe fruit (250 g)   caster or icing sugar

Juicy fruits such as cherries, black and red currants, raspberries, strawberries and other berries are the best to use. Partially thawed frozen fruit is also suitable.

Wash fresh fruit and remove stones and stalks. Either rub the fruit through a sieve or put it in the electric blender to make a pulp, adding sugar to taste. Strain the blended fruit if necessary to remove pips. If the sauce becomes frothy during blending leave it to stand a while before serving.

The addition of a little kirsch or other liqueur is an improvement.

Ginger sauce

(for ice-cream)

Quantities for 4.

1 Tbs potato flour or arrowroot   ½ pint water (250 ml)

Mix the flour smooth with the water and heat, stirring all the time until it just comes to the boil. Remove from the heat.

3 Tbs finely chopped ginger in syrup   4 Tbs of the ginger syrup (60 ml)
3 Tbs orange juice (45 ml)

Mix into the sauce and leave it to become cold. If necessary, thin down with a little more orange juice or ginger syrup.

Hard sauce for steamed puddings or cake fillings

2 oz butter (50 g)
4 oz icing sugar (¾ c) or 4 oz caster sugar (½ c or 100 g)
½ tsp vanilla essence or 1 Tbs rum, sherry or brandy

Warm the butter enough to soften it without melting. Cream the ingredients together thoroughly and flavour to taste. Serve it in a small bowl for portions to be put on the hot pudding as it is served.

VARIATION

To make Cumberland rum butter substitute fine light brown or soft sugar, add ground nutmeg and cinnamon to taste and flavour with rum.

Honey sauce

(for hot or cold puddings)

Quantities for 4.

4 oz honey (4 Tbs or 125 g)
rind and juice of ½ lemon
¼ pt water (150 ml)

Heat together until the honey has dissolved. Use hot or cold.

Honey fudge sauce

(for ice-cream)

Quantities for 4.

3 oz soft brown sugar (6 Tbs or 75 g)
1 oz butter (25 g)
2 Tbs honey
4 Tbs evaporated milk (60 ml)

Put in the top of a double boiler or in a basin over boiling water. Heat until the ingredients are melted into a smooth sauce. Stir gently during heating and serve warm.

Jam sauce

(hot or cold)

Quantities for 4.

6 Tbs jam of good flavour (6 oz or 150 g)
6 Tbs water, more or less (90 ml)
lemon juice or liqueur to taste

The simplest way of making this is to process the jam and hot water in the electric blender until smooth. Flavour to taste and serve cold or heat gently.

Alternatively, heat jam and water and boil and whisk until smooth; sieve if necessary. Flavour to taste and serve hot or cold.

Lemon sauce

(for steamed or baked puddings)

Quantities for 4.

½ oz cornflour, arrowroot or potato flour (1½ Tbs or 15 g)	½ pt water (300 ml) grated rind of 1 lemon

Mix the thickening to a smooth cream with a little of the cold water, heat the remainder with the lemon rind and when it is boiling add the blended mixture. Mix well, return to the pan, and stir until the sauce boils. Cornflour should be cooked for a further 5 mins.

sugar	juice of 1 lemon

Add the lemon juice and then sweeten the sauce to taste. Serve hot or cold; sprinkle the top with a little sugar to prevent a skin from forming during cooling.

Melba sauce

(for ice-cream and as a sauce for fresh or frozen strawberries or raspberries)

Cooking time 10–15 mins. *Quantities* for 4.

12 oz fresh or frozen raspberries (350 g)

Cook without any water until the fruit is reduced to a pulp. Sieve.

½ Tbs cornflour or potato flour

Blend with a little cold water and stir into the purée. Stir and heat until it thickens. Cook cornflour for a further 5 mins.

sugar	lemon juice

Add these to taste and serve cold.

Orange sauce

(for ice-cream and steamed or baked puddings)

Use a blender for this.

Quantities for 4.

¼ pt evaporated milk (150 ml)
1 oz sugar (2 Tbs or 25 g)
flesh and juice of 1 orange
2 Tbs lemon juice
outside peel of ½ orange

Use only the very thin orange-coloured peel. Put it in the blender goblet with the flesh and juice of the orange and the other ingredients. Blend at high speed for 1 min.

Serve cold, or heat gently, without boiling, and serve warm.

Raisin sauce

(for ice-cream and steamed or baked puddings)

Quantities for 4–6.

4 oz seedless raisins (⅔ c or 125 g)
4 fl oz water (8 Tbs or 120 ml)
1 tsp grated orange rind

Chop the raisins coarsely and simmer with the other ingredients for 5 mins.

2 Tbs sherry

Stir in and leave the sauce to become cold.

¼ pt cream, whipped (150 ml)

Fold the sauce into the cream and serve very cold.

Spiced blackberry sauce

(for ice-cream and other cold sweets or steamed puddings)

Quantities for 4.

8 oz fresh or frozen blackberries (250 g)
¼ tsp ground cinnamon
2 oz sugar (4 Tbs or 50 g)
¼ tsp grated nutmeg

Put in a small pan, bring to the boil and cook until the berries are soft and the sugar melted. Serve hot or cold.

3. Starters

The most practical starters for family meals or for the cook-hostess are not the mixed hors d'œuvre of the restaurant menu but those which are suitable for serving on their own, perhaps with a salad garnish. Most of these are cold starters for which the ingredients can be prepared in advance and stored in the refrigerator or freezer. The recipes in this chapter are for that type of starter.

The alternative is a hot or cold soup, recipes for which are given in the next chapter.

Artichokes vinaigrette

Serve cold boiled globe artichokes, page 252, with French dressing.

Avocado pear

Allow 1 pear for 2 portions.

Buy the pears a few days in advance and keep them in a warm place such as the airing cupboard. They should be really ripe when served.

Cut in half lengthwise and remove the stone. Serve the pear in small dishes or on small plates with the centres filled with French dressing, or serve plain and hand lemon separately.

Alternatively, fill the centres with shelled shrimps dressed with lemon juice, salt and pepper.

Cheese creams

Quantities for 4.

¼ pt whipping cream (150 ml)   ½ tsp salt
pinch each of pepper and dry mustard

Whip the cream and add the seasoning.

¼ pt melted aspic jelly (150 ml), see page 19.   2 oz finely grated Parmesan cheese (½ c or 50 g)

The aspic jelly should be cold, but not set. Add it to the cream and add the cheese. Combine gently. Pour the mixture into 4 small moulds or dishes or use one border mould. Cover and store in the refrigerator. Unmould and garnish with

salad vegetables.

Chicken liver pâté

Cooking time 8–10 mins. *Quantities* for 4 or more.

8 oz chicken livers (250 g)

Wash the livers, drain and dry on paper towels. Remove any stringy bits or skin.

½ small onion

Skin and chop finely.

1 oz butter (25 g)

Heat some of the butter and fry the liver quickly in it for 3–4 mins. Remove. Heat more butter and fry the onion until tender. Add any remaining butter and allow to melt. Put the liver and onion through a sieve or put it in the electric blender to make a pulp.

¼ tsp salt
pinch of powdered marjoram
2 Tbs sherry, marsala or brandy
pinch of cayenne pepper
pinch of ground mace

Add to the liver purée and mix well. Put in a small dish and allow to become quite cold. Cover and store in the refrigerator. Serve with

thin crisp toast.

Chicken mousse

Quantities for 6.

8 oz cold chicken (250 g), or use some chicken and some ham

Remove all skin and gristle. Mince the chicken and ham finely, or put it in the electric blender with the stock and gelatine mixture and the milk, and process until smooth.

½ oz gelatine (1½ Tbs or 15 g)   ¼ pt hot chicken stock (150 ml)

Sprinkle the gelatine into the stock and stir to dissolve it.

¼ pt evaporated milk (150 ml)   pinch of cayenne pepper
¼ pt mayonnaise (150 ml)   ½ tsp salt
1 tsp bottled horseradish sauce

Mix with the stock and gelatine and then stir in the chicken.

1 egg white, beaten stiff

Fold into the chicken mixture and pour into one large mould or six small ones. Cover and refrigerate until set. Unmould and garnish to taste.

Crab scallops

Cooking time 5 mins. Quantities for 4.

8 oz crab meat (250 g), fresh, canned or frozen   4 Tbs mayonnaise
½ tsp made mustard   1 Tbs Worcester sauce

Thaw frozen crab meat. Mix all the ingredients together and put it into buttered scallop shells or small flat fireproof dishes.

buttered breadcrumbs   grated Parmesan cheese

Melt a little butter and mix fresh breadcrumbs in to coat them. Allow about two tablespoons of crumbs for the four portions, the amount depending on the size of the dishes. Mix with some cheese and sprinkle on top of the crab to make a thin layer. Heat under a moderate grill to warm the mixture through and brown the top. Serve hot.

Cucumber and green pepper cocktail

Quantities for 4–6.

1 lb cucumber (500 g)   salt and pepper

Peel the cucumber and cut it in small dice. Put it in a shallow dish and sprinkle with salt. Leave for 20–30 mins. Drain well, return to the dish and sprinkle with pepper.

4 Tbs finely chopped green pepper   ¼ clove crushed garlic, or to taste
½ pt thick yogurt (300 ml)

Combine these and then mix with the cucumber. Cover and refrigerate until well chilled.

chopped fresh mint or other herbs

Serve the chilled mixture in small glasses, garnished with the herbs.

Eggs en cocotte

See page 104.

Fish cocktail

Quantities for 4–6.

¼ pt tomato ketchup (150 ml)	1 tsp Worcester sauce
¼ tsp dry mustard	1 Tbs bottled horseradish sauce
½ Tbs lemon juice	¼ pt double cream (150 ml)

Mix these together in a small basin.

½ pt flaked, cooked white fish or shellfish (250 ml), or a mixture

Add to the sauce and mix gently.

4–6 lettuce leaves

Wash, dry, shred finely and put some in the bottom of each glass or bowl. Put the fish mixture on top.

chopped parsley or other herbs such as dill or fennel

Use to decorate the top.

Fish mousse

Quantities for 4–6.

8 oz cooked or canned fish (250 g)   1 Tbs tarragon vinegar
pinch of paprika pepper

Mash or sieve the fish, or put fish, vinegar and dissolved gelatine in the blender and process until smooth.

½ oz gelatine (1½ Tbs or 15 g)   4 Tbs hot water (60 ml)

Sprinkle the gelatine into the water and stir to dissolve it. Mix it with the fish and leave to cool.

5 Tbs whipping cream (75 ml)

Whip the cream lightly and fold it into the cold fish mixture. Pour into one mould or individual moulds, cover and refrigerate. Unmould and serve garnished with

salad vegetables.

Herring with cheese and cream

Quantities for 4 or more.

4 fillets of salt herring

Put in a shallow dish, cover with water or milk and soak overnight. Drain and return to the dish. Discard the liquid.

1 Tbs finely chopped onion	2 Tbs sugar
pepper	¼ pt wine vinegar (150 ml)

Mix together and pour over the herring. Leave to marinate in a cold place for 5–6 hrs, or longer in the refrigerator. Drain from the marinade, which is discarded.

3 oz curd or cream cheese (75 g)	about ¼ pt soured cream (150 ml), or
1 Tbs lemon juice	use fresh double cream

Beat together until a smooth coating sauce is formed, using the necessary amount of cream to achieve this.

2 medium-sized apples

Wash well and grate coarsely. Put a bed of apple on the serving dish or individual dishes, the herrings on top and mask with the sauce.

chopped parsley or chives   brown bread or hot toast

Garnish with the herbs and serve bread or toast separately.

Herring with dill and tomato

Quantities for 4–8.

4 fillets of salt herring

Put in a shallow dish and cover with milk or water. Soak overnight. Drain, rinse and make sure there are no bones left in the fillets. Discard the soaking liquid. Slice each fillet diagonally in ½ in (1 cm) strips and arrange these in a flat dish, each in the shape of the original fillet.

3 Tbs oil	1 Tbs herb or wine vinegar
1 Tbs concentrated tomato purée	1 Tbs water
¼ tsp freshly ground pepper	¼ tsp ground or crushed allspice
1–2 tsp chopped fresh dill or fennel, or ½ tsp dried	½–1 Tbs sugar

Mix all together and pour over the fish.

chopped parsley

Sprinkle a little over the fish and serve.

Kipper pâté

Cooking time 5–10 mins. *Quantities* for 8 or more.

1½ lb kippers (700 g) or 12 oz kipper fillets (350 g)

Put the kippers in a jug deep enough to take them with a little room to spare. Pour in boiling water to cover them. Put a saucer or a piece of foil on top of the jug and stand it in a warm place for 5–10 mins. Drain the kippers and leave them to become cool enough to handle. Remove bones and skin. Rub the fish through a sieve.

8 oz butter or margarine (250 g)	1 tsp anchovy essence
pepper	lemon juice, about 2 Tbs

Warm the fat to soften but not melt it. Add to the kipper, with the flavourings, and work all into a smooth paste. Put in a container and when it is quite cold, cover and store in the refrigerator. Serve with

thin crisp toast.

ALTERNATIVE METHOD

Instead of sieving the kippers, use an electric blender. Put in the flaked kipper and melted butter or margarine and process until smooth. Tip into a bowl and work in the flavourings to taste.

Liver terrine

Cooking time 1½ hrs.
Temperature 180° C (350° F; G4).
Quantities for 8 or more.

8 thin rashers streaky bacon (8 oz or 250 g)

Remove the rinds and use the bacon to line a 2 lb (1 kg) loaf tin or a baking dish such as a pie dish.

4 oz chicken livers (125 g)	4 oz pig's liver (125 g)
1 lb calf's or lamb's liver (500 g)	

Remove any skin and tubes from the liver, cut in strips, rinse in cold water and drain. Then mince finely.

4 Tbs double cream	1 egg, beaten
1 clove garlic, finely chopped, or ¼ tsp dried garlic	1 Tbs lemon juice
	2 Tbs brandy or sherry
salt and pepper	

Mix these with the liver and pour into the bacon-lined tin. Stand this in a baking tin of hot water, cover the terrine with foil and bake. Remove from the water and allow to cool for a while, then put a weight on top and leave until quite cold before storing in the refrigerator or freezer.

To serve, cut in slices and serve with fresh rolls or French bread, or with thin crisp toast.

Mackerel pâté

Quantities for 4 or more.

about 8 oz smoked mackerel (250 g)

Remove all skin and bone. If there are roes, use them as well. Flake the fish and put fish and roes in a basin.

4 Tbs single cream (60 ml)	4 oz cream cheese (100 g)
2 Tbs white wine	1 Tbs lemon juice
a few chopped chives	$\frac{1}{4}$ tsp paprika pepper
2 oz softened butter or margarine (50 g), or 4 Tbs oil	salt and pepper

Add to the fish and mix and mash into a smooth paste. Press into a small mould or into a serving dish, smooth the top, cover and refrigerate until required. Remove in time for it to reach room temperature for serving. Serve with

thin crisp toast.

Melon

Wash the melon and dry the skin. Cut the melon in half or in thick slices, remove the seeds and serve it in any of the following ways:

with caster sugar and ground ginger handed separately
with wedges of lemon
a slice served with cold ham
a slice served with raw Italian ham (prosciutto)
a small melon cut in half with the centre filled with port wine and left to marinate before serving.

Ratatouille with yogurt

Cooking time $\frac{1}{2}-\frac{3}{4}$ hr. *Quantities* for 4–6.

1 green pepper	1 aubergine
2 courgettes	1 onion
3 medium-sized tomatoes	

Cut the pepper in half, remove the seeds, pith and stem and slice the flesh. Wash and slice the aubergine and courgettes. Skin and slice the onion and tomatoes.

3 fl oz olive oil (6 Tbs or 90 ml)   pinch of thyme

Heat the oil in a fairly large frying or sauté pan and cook the onion and thyme fairly slowly until the onion is tender and yellow. Add the pepper, courgettes and aubergine and fry for about 10 mins, turning frequently. Add the tomatoes, reduce the heat and simmer until the vegetables are quite tender.

Season well with salt and pepper and turn the mixture into a flat dish. Leave to cool.

¼ pt yogurt (150 ml)   garlic salt or crushed garlic
pepper

Beat the yogurt until smooth and season to taste. Pour it over the vegetables and serve.

Sausage

Many continental-type sausages are sold ready for serving. They make very good starters, the most popular being salami, garlic sausage and mortadella. Serve just one kind or a mixture.

Suitable accompaniments are French bread or fresh rolls, and radishes when in season, or a garnish of gherkins.

Smoked fish

There are a number of these sold ready for serving. They include:

Buckling. Allow 1 fish per portion. Remove the skin and serve the fish on the bone or filleted. Serve with lemon and brown bread and butter.

Cod's roe. Allow 2 oz (50 g) per portion. Remove any hard skin and cut the roe in slices or, if it is very soft, put a spoonful on a small lettuce leaf. Serve with lemon and hot crisp toast.

Eel. Allow 2 oz (50 g) fillet per portion. This may be sold in small fillets or in a piece with the skin on. For the latter, skin and cut in slices or separate lengthwise into fillets. Serve with lemon and brown bread and butter.

Mackerel. Allow 4 oz (100 g) on the bone or 2 oz (50 g) fillet per portion. If the mackerel are small, allow one per portion, but they are usually rather large for this. Skin and fillet them and serve a portion on a small lettuce leaf with lemon and brown bread and butter. For serving a whole mackerel, remove the skin and serve the fish on the bone. Horseradish sauce is often served with this.

Salmon. Allow 2 oz (50 g) per portion. Salmon is usually sold ready sliced and is served plain with lemon and brown bread and butter.

Sprats. Allow 4 oz (100 g) per portion. Sprats are sold as whole fish and served as such with lemon and brown bread and butter. Horseradish sauce is a good alternative to the lemon.

Trout. Allow 1 small fish per portion. These are sold on the bone. To serve, remove the skin but leave the head and tail on. Serve with lemon or horseradish sauce and brown bread and butter.

Sweet peppers with yogurt

See page 291.

Tomato juice cocktail

Quantities for 6 or more.

- 1 pt (600 ml) tomato juice
- 2 Tbs lemon juice
- ½–1 tsp salt
- Worcester sauce
- 2 tsp finely chopped fresh basil, or 1 tsp dried
- 2 tsp scissor-snipped fresh savory
- 1 Tbs orange juice
- 2 tsp sugar
- paprika pepper
- 2 tsp chopped fresh tarragon
- 2 tsp chopped chives or a little chopped onion

Combine the ingredients, cover and leave in the refrigerator to steep for an hour or so or until the tomato juice is flavoured to taste. Strain before serving.

4. Soups

Be it hot or cold, for those who like soup there is no finer starter to a meal. The range is enormous, from the light consommé or broth to the really substantial soup which can be both starter and main course in one. For those who lack the time and energy to make their own soups, canned and packet versions are important, the more adventurous using these as a basis to which is added an individual touch in the way of flavourings and additional ingredients. Others prefer to start from the basic ingredients, including making their own stock, for which recipes may be found in Chapter 1.

In terms of time and energy saving, apart from a pressure cooker for making stock, an electric blender is the best piece of equipment soup-makers can possibly have. Use it for making purées from canned, raw or cooked vegetables or to purée a completed soup.

Soups can be made in advance and stored in the refrigerator, when they should be used within 1–2 days, or in the freezer, where they will keep for many weeks. To save freezer space they can be made with less than the normal amount of liquid and the remainder put in the pan with the block of frozen soup for re-heating. Ingredients to keep in the freezer for making soups are vegetable purées, frozen sliced vegetables, especially mushrooms, sweet pepper, and herbs for flavouring.

When a recipe contains pasta, potatoes, rice, eggs or cream, it is usually more satisfactory to add these after thawing and re-heating. Season soups rather lightly before freezing them and add more seasoning later. They may be thawed and heated either over a direct gentle heat or in a double boiler.

Canned soups with yogurt

TO SERVE HOT

Use any canned soup, but yogurt is particularly good with thick cream soups as it reduces their tendency to be stodgy, without harming the flavour.

QUANTITIES

To each 10–15 oz can (284–425 g) of soup (not concentrated), add ¼ pt (150 ml) of yogurt. Heat and serve. For additional flavour add chopped fresh or powdered dried herbs, or spices.

TO SERVE COLD

Use the same proportions as for hot soup. Mix soup and yogurt, whisking to combine well, add any additional flavourings you like and refrigerate the soup until you are ready to serve it.

GOOD MIXTURES

Cream of tomato with chopped fresh tarragon
Cream of chicken with chopped fresh tarragon
Cream of asparagus with chopped parsley and a pinch of ground mace
Cream of celery with a pinch of ground nutmeg and chopped chives.

HOT SOUPS

Blender cream soup

This may be made using a can of vegetables and gives a completely different soup from a canned or packet vegetable soup. It is different in both flavour and texture, for this soup has no flour thickening. Instead of the canned vegetables you might use left-over cooked vegetables and some additional stock, or mix canned and left-over vegetables.

Vegetables to use: asparagus, carrots, garden peas, artichoke bottoms, celery, broad beans, sweet corn, spinach.

Cooking time 3–4 mins. *Quantities* for 4–6.

12–15 oz can vegetables (340–425 g)

Empty the contents of the can into the blender goblet, including the liquid in the can. Blend until smooth and then pour into a saucepan.

½ pt milk (300 ml)
½ pt stock (300 ml), or use a cube
salt and pepper

pinch of ground mace or other spice or herbs to taste

Add to the pan and bring to the boil, stirring frequently.

4 Tbs evaporated milk or cream (60 ml)

Add just before serving.

Bortsch

Cooking time 45 mins. *Quantities* for 4–6.

6 oz onion (175 g)	8 oz raw beetroot (250 g)

Skin the onion, scrub the beetroot and trim top and root end. Shred onion and beetroot.

1 Tbs sugar	1 Tbs vinegar
2 pt beef stock (1¼ l)	

Put in a pan with the beetroot and onion and boil gently for about 20 mins.

6 oz cabbage (175 g)

Wash and shred, add to the soup and boil for a further 20 mins.

2 Tbs concentrated tomato purée   salt and pepper

Add to the soup, together with some more stock if needed. Cook until the cabbage is tender.

soured cream or yogurt

Put a spoonful in each plate as the soup is served.

Cauliflower soup

(for the blender)

This can be made with either left-over or freshly cooked cauliflower. It makes a smooth, thin creamy soup, but if a thick soup is preferred, a tablespoon of cornflour or potato flour can be blended with the other ingredients.

Cooking time a few mins. *Quantities* for 4.

8 oz cooked cauliflower (250 g)	½ pt milk (250 ml)
1 chicken cube in water, or ½ pt chicken stock (250 ml)	1 oz diced strong cheese (25 g)
	salt and pepper
pinch of ground mace or nutmeg	cream, optional

Put half the cauliflower in the goblet with the milk, cheese, chicken stock and seasonings. Blend for 30 seconds. Add the rest of the cauliflower and blend for a further 30 seconds, or until the soup is quite smooth. Tip into a saucepan. Use ½ pt water or another ½ pt chicken stock to rinse out the goblet. Add to the soup, heat to boiling and taste for seasoning. Add a little cream, if liked. Serve garnished with

paprika pepper or chopped herbs.

Celery soup

(for the blender)

Cooking time 30–45 mins. *Quantities* for 4–6.

8 large sticks celery	2 rashers streaky bacon
1½ pt white stock (850 ml)	1 oz butter or margarine (25 g)
salt	pinch of ground mace or nutmeg
1 tsp sugar	

Wash the celery and slice it. Remove bacon rinds and cut the rashers in pieces. Put all the ingredients in a pan and boil gently until the celery is tender. Cool a little and then blend until smooth in two or more lots depending on the capacity of the blender. Rinse the pan and strain the soup back into it. Straining is not essential, but it does remove any tough fibres which may have failed to blend completely. Re-heat the soup.

¼ pt cream or evaporated milk (150 ml)

Taste for seasoning and use the cream or milk to dilute to taste. Serve hot.

Celery and tomato soup

Cooking time about 1 hr. *Quantities* for 4.

1 small onion, sliced	8 oz outside stalks celery (250 g)
1 oz fat (25 g) or 2 Tbs oil	

Scrub the celery and slice it. Heat the fat in a saucepan and stew the onion and celery in it with about 1 Tbs water. Cover the pan and cook slowly for about 15 mins without allowing the vegetables to brown. Stir or shake the pan occasionally.

1½ pt stock (850 ml)

Add to the vegetables, bring to the boil, cover and boil gently until the celery is tender. Either rub the soup through a sieve or purée it in the electric blender.

2 Tbs concentrated tomato purée	pinch of ground mace or nutmeg, or a
salt and pepper	pinch of dried marjoram or basil

Return the soup to the pan with the remaining ingredients. Re-heat and serve hot, thinning if necessary, with a little stock.

Chicken and rice soup with yogurt

Cooking time 20 mins. *Quantities* for 3-4.

1½ pt chicken stock (850 ml)   1 oz rice (2 Tbs or 25 g)

Bring the stock to the boil, add the rice, cover and boil gently for 15 mins.

2 tsp potato flour   1 egg yolk
¼ pt yogurt (150 ml)

Mix the potato flour and egg yolk and gradually beat in the yogurt. Remove the soup from the heat and stir in the yogurt mixture. Return the pan to the heat and stir until the soup just comes to the boil. Remove from the heat and taste for seasoning.

chopped fresh mint, tarragon or fines   salt and pepper
  herbes

Season to taste and serve the soup sprinkled with chopped herbs.

Consommé with mushrooms and herbs

Cooking time 5-10 mins. *Quantities* for 4.

2 oz mushrooms, sliced (50 g)   2 Tbs lemon juice

Put the mushrooms in a small dish and sprinkle the lemon juice over them. Leave for 5 mins. Frozen mushrooms can be used for this, sprinkling the lemon over them and leaving them to thaw.

1½ pt consommé or clear stock   salt and pepper
  (850 ml)

Use canned consommé (two 15 oz cans), canned meat broth or a well-flavoured home-made bone stock. Season to taste. Heat just to boiling and add the mushrooms.

1 tsp chopped fennel, chives or dill

Sprinkle into the soup just before serving it.

Crème de volaille princesse

(Cream of chicken)

Quantities for 4.

1½ pt thin velouté sauce (850 ml)   ½ pt thick chicken purée (250 ml)

Make the velouté sauce with chicken stock. Make the purée either by rubbing cooked chicken through a sieve or by putting it in the blender with enough chicken stock to moisten. Allow about 8 oz chicken (250 g).

chicken stock or milk   salt and pepper
cream

Heat the sauce and add the purée together with enough stock or milk to give the desired consistency. Season to taste and add 3–4 Tbs cream, or to taste. Serve garnished with

chopped fresh chives, parsley or tarragon.

VARIATIONS

Crème d'artichauts. Substitute cooked or canned globe artichoke bottoms for the chicken.
Crème d'asperges vertes. Substitute canned green asparagus for the chicken.
Crème de celeri. Substitute fresh cooked or canned celery for the chicken.

Lamb or mutton soup

This is a good way of using up the bones and last bits of meat on a cooked leg or shoulder, or you could make it with fresh scrag or neck of lamb or mutton.

Cooking time after the stock has been made, 20 mins. *Quantities* for 3–4.

About 1 lb bones and meat (500 g)   1 onion
1 bay leaf

If you are using cooked meat, remove this before making stock with the bones, but with fresh meat, leave the meat on the bones. Add the onion and bay leaf and either make the stock in a pressure cooker ($\frac{1}{2}$ hr) or boil for 2 hrs. Use water to cover in each case. Strain and remove freshly cooked meat from the bones. Cut either meat in small pieces.

1 small chopped onion   2 Tbs oil

Heat the oil in a saucepan and fry the onion until it is beginning to brown.

1 oz rice (2 Tbs or 25 g)   salt and pepper
$1\frac{1}{2}$ pt stock (850 ml)   the pieces of meat
plenty of chopped fresh mint

Add to the pan and simmer until the rice is cooked, 10–15 mins. Taste for seasoning.

yogurt

As each portion is served, put a good tablespoon of yogurt in the middle, more if liked.

Lentil soup

Cooking time 1–2 hrs. *Quantities* for 4–5.

1 carrot, sliced	1 onion, sliced
1 stick celery, sliced	1 small turnip, sliced
1 oz fat (25 g)	

Melt the fat in a saucepan and cook the vegetables in it over a low heat for 10–15 mins.

8 oz lentils (1 c or 200 g)	4 rashers streaky bacon, or a ham bone
fresh or dried thyme or savory	
pepper	2 pt stock or water (1¼ l)

Cut bacon in small pieces and put all the ingredients in the pan with the vegetables. Bring to the boil and cook slowly until the lentils are soft. The exact time is not important. If not required for service at once put the soup in a bowl, cool and store in the refrigerator.

milk or cream and milk   salt and pepper

Thin the soup with this as it is heated. Taste for seasoning.

chopped parsley

Sprinkle on and serve.

ALTERNATIVE

Add small pieces of cooked chopped ham and some mushroom ketchup or Worcester sauce.

Mushroom soup

Cooking time about 20 mins. *Quantities* for 4.

4 oz mushrooms (125 g)

Wash, drain and slice.

2 oz butter (50 g)   1 tsp finely chopped onion
1 tsp finely chopped parsley

Melt the butter in a large saucepan and stew the mushrooms, onion and parsley in it for about 5 mins without allowing the mixture to brown.

1 oz flour (3 Tbs or 25 g)   1½ pt stock (850 ml)

Stir in the flour and cook for a minute longer. Then stir in the stock and stir until the soup boils. Boil gently for 10–15 mins or until the onion and mushrooms are cooked.

¼ pt soured cream (150 ml)　　　　　　lemon juice
salt and pepper

Stir the cream into the soup and re-heat without boiling. Season and add lemon juice to taste.

Paprika soup

Cooking time about 1 hr. *Quantities* for 4.

1 oz butter (25 g)　　　　　　　　　　1 small onion, chopped
1 small stalk celery, chopped　　　　　1 green pepper, chopped

Melt the butter in a saucepan and stew the vegetables, without browning, for 10–15 mins.

¾ pt milk (400 ml)　　　　　　　　　　¾ pt stock (400 ml)
½ tsp salt　　　　　　　　　　　　　　pinch of pepper
¼ tsp paprika pepper

Add to the pan, bring to the boil, cover and cook gently until the vegetables are quite tender.

4 oz cottage cheese (125 g)　　　　　　4 Tbs single cream (60 ml)

Add to the soup and heat without boiling. Taste for seasoning and serve.

Parsley soup

Cooking time about 15 mins. *Quantities* for 4–6.

2 oz butter (50 g)　　　　　　　　　　4 Tbs finely chopped onion (60 ml)

Melt the butter in a large saucepan and stew the onion in it gently until it is softened but not brown.

2 Tbs flour

Add to the pan and stir and cook for a minute.

2 pt milk or milk and white stock　　　salt and pepper
　mixed (1¼ l)

Stir the liquid into the pan and stir until the soup boils. Boil gently for 5 mins. Season to taste.

about ¼ pt chopped parsley (150 ml)

Add enough parsley to make the soup really green. Make sure it is hot and serve.

Potato and onion soup

Cooking time ¾–1 hr. *Quantities* for 6 or more.

2 medium-sized onions, chopped
1 oz butter or margarine (25 g)

1 lb old potatoes (500 g), peeled and sliced thinly

Melt the fat in a saucepan and stew the vegetables in it gently for about 10 mins, without allowing them to brown. Keep the pan covered and stir occasionally.

1½ pt white stock (850 ml)

Add to the pan, bring to the boil and cook gently until the vegetables are tender, about 30–40 mins. Rub through a sieve or process in the electric blender. Return to the pan.

½ pt milk (250 ml)
salt and pepper

a knob of butter
a little Worcester sauce

Add to the soup and re-heat, seasoning to taste. Serve with

plenty of chopped parsley, marjoram, sage or thyme.

Soupe Flamande

Cooking time ½ hr. *Quantities* for 4–6.

1 lb brussels sprouts (500 g)

Wash and trim the sprouts. Cook them in a very little lightly salted water until they are half-done. Drain.

3 oz butter (75 g)

Melt in a saucepan and stew the sprouts in it until the butter is almost absorbed.

1 pt white stock (600 ml)   2 medium-sized old potatoes

Peel and quarter the potatoes and add them to the pan with the stock. Boil gently for 20 mins or until the vegetables are tender. Either sieve the soup or put it in the electric blender and process until smooth. Return to the pan.

½ pt milk (250 ml)   salt and pepper

Add to the soup, re-heat and season to taste. Add more milk or cream if the soup requires thinning. Serve hot.

Straciatella

Cooking time a few mins. *Quantities* for 4.

2 eggs
chopped parsley
salt and pepper

1 oz grated Parmesan cheese (25 g)
pinch of grated nutmeg

Whisk together in a small bowl.

2 pt consommé or stock (1¼ l)

Beat about ¼ pt (150 ml) of the stock into the egg mixture. Heat the remaining stock and, when it boils, gradually whisk in the egg mixture. Bring back to the boil and serve at once.

Watercress and cheese soup

Cooking time 10-15 mins. *Quantities* for 3-4.

1 oz butter or margarine (25 g)
½ tsp dry mustard

1 tsp cornflour

Melt the fat in a saucepan and stir in the cornflour and mustard. Cook gently for a minute.

1 pt milk (600 ml)
salt and pepper

2 oz grated cheese (50 g)

Add the milk to the pan and stir until the soup is smooth and boiling. Boil for 2-3 mins, then add the cheese and allow it to melt. Season to taste.

1 oz watercress (25 g)

Wash the watercress and remove any discoloured leaves. Chop it finely and add to the soup. Serve hot.

ALTERNATIVE METHOD

Cut the cheese in cubes and blend smooth with the soup, using the electric blender. Add the whole sprigs of watercress and blend a second or so to chop it. Re-heat and serve.

COLD SOUPS

Beetroot soup or bortsch

Quantities for 4.

10½ oz can of concentrated consommé (300 ml)
salt and pepper
a slice of onion, finely chopped

8 oz cooked beetroot (200 g)
2 Tbs evaporated milk
3 Tbs lemon juice or to taste

Skin the beetroot, and either rub it through a sieve or put it in the blender goblet with all the other ingredients and process until smooth. As there is no wastage with blending you may need to thin the soup with some stock, or use a little less beetroot.

Mix sieved beetroot with the other ingredients.

Cover the soup and chill it in the refrigerator.

chopped fennel or chives, and/or evaporated milk or cream

Serve the soup in bowls or large cups, the tops garnished with herbs and a swirl of milk or cream.

ALTERNATIVE METHOD

If freshly cooked beetroot is not available, use the small pickled baby beets, first rinsing them before blending or sieving. Taste the soup before deciding to add lemon juice. Pre-packed cooked beetroot is usually treated with vinegar and it is best to rinse this kind before using it.

Cold consommé with mushrooms

Cooking time 15–20 mins. *Quantities* for 4.

4 oz small mushrooms (125 g)

Wash and remove the stalks.

½ pt water (250 ml)   1 tsp wine vinegar

Heat in a small pan and poach the mushrooms in it until they are tender. Lift out and distribute between four individual soup bowls or small dishes. Keep the cooking liquid and add it to the consommé.

1 Tbs gelatine   ½ pt canned consommé (250 ml)

Heat the consommé, sprinkle in the gelatine and stir to dissolve it.

soy sauce
salt and pepper

Worcester sauce

Season the consommé and pour it over the mushrooms. Leave to become cold and then refrigerate until set and chilled.

Curried chicken soup

Quantities for 4.

2 cans condensed cream of chicken soup (21 oz or 595 g)
1 tsp curry powder

1 pt milk (600 ml), or the equivalent of the two cans of soup

Chill the soup in the refrigerator for several hours. Open the cans and turn the soup into a bowl. Add chilled milk equal to the soup in volume. Add it gradually, stirring and beating to blend well; or mix it in the electric blender. Beat in the curry powder. If necessary, return to the refrigerator to keep it cold. Serve in soup cups or cereal bowls.

chopped spring onions, chives or parsley

Sprinkle a little in the centre of each portion.

Gaspacho

Quantities for 8.

1½ pt canned tomato juice (850 ml)

1 lb cucumber (500 g or 1 large)

Peel the cucumber and either rub it through a sieve or pulp it in the electric blender, using a little tomato juice to supply enough liquid for this. Add the rest of the tomato juice.

2 Tbs olive oil
2 Tbs red wine
fresh or dried garlic

4 Tbs wine vinegar (60 ml)
sugar, salt and pepper

Add to the tomato mixture, flavouring to taste. Cover and refrigerate until the soup is well chilled. Serve cold, garnished with

chopped parsley.

Onion soup

(to serve hot or cold)

Cooking time about ¾ hr. *Quantities* for 3–4.

½ oz butter or other fat (15 g)   1 large onion

Skin the onion and chop it finely. Heat the fat in a saucepan and stew the onion in it for 10 mins without browning.

1½ pt white stock (850 ml)   celery salt

Add to the onion, bring to the boil, cover and simmer for ½ hr or until the onion is quite tender. If a completely smooth soup is preferred it may be sieved or blended at this stage.

1 tsp potato flour   3 Tbs soured cream
½ tsp wine vinegar   ½ tsp sugar

Mix the potato flour to a smooth paste with the cream, add the other ingredients and stir into the soup. Just bring to the boil.

salt and pepper   1–2 Tbs chopped parsley

Season to taste, stir in the parsley and serve hot, or cool and then chill in the refrigerator to serve cold.

Pea soup

(to serve hot or cold)

Cooking time 5–10 mins. *Quantities* for 4.

8 oz fresh or frozen peas (200 g)

Cook until tender in a little lightly salted water. Drain, keeping the cooking liquid. Either rub the peas through a sieve or put them in the electric blender with ¼ pt (150 ml) of the cooking liquid and process to a purée. Return the peas to the pan, adding ¼ pt (150 ml) of pea stock if the peas have been sieved instead of blended.

1 pt good chicken stock (600 ml)   2–3 sprigs mint

Any remaining pea stock can be used to make up the quantity of chicken stock. Add to the peas. Chop the mint finely or blend with a little stock to chop it. Add to the pan. Bring to the boil and boil gently for a few minutes.

1 egg yolk   ¼ pt double cream (150 ml)
salt and pepper   a little sugar

Mix in a small basin, add a little of the hot soup, mix and add to the pan. Taste for seasoning and serve hot, or cool quickly and then refrigerate. If the stock was a good one this will make the soup set to a jelly. Whisk lightly to break it up.

2 rashers crisply fried or grilled bacon

Chop the bacon and use it to garnish either the hot or cold soup.

5. Cheese

Cheese is generally chosen for its flavour. Some like it very mild, others prefer something with plenty of flavour. A strong flavour is usually the result of long maturing and thus, with some cheeses such as Cheddar, it is possible to buy a fairly new cheese which is mild or a well-matured one which is strong.

To help you when shopping for cheese I give below a rough classification of some of the best-known cheeses. Naturally what some people consider a medium cheese others will consider either mild or strong according to personal taste.

HARD MILD CHEESES

Bel Paese, Caerphilly, Cheshire, Edam, Gouda, New Zealand Cheddar, Port Salut, Provalone, Wensleydale.

SOFT MILD CHEESES

Cottage cheese, cream cheese, curd cheese, demisel, double crème, Fontainebleau, fromage à la crème, Petit Gervais, Petite Suisse, Philadelphia, Pommel, Ricotta (Italian cottage cheese).

MEDIUM CHEESES

Brie, Bresse Bleu, Cheddar, Danish Blue, Derby, Dolce-Latte, Emmental, Gruyère, Lancashire, Tomme au Raisin, Leicester, Pecorino, White Stilton.

STRONG CHEESES

Blue Dorset, Blue Stilton, Blue Vinney, Camembert, Canadian Cheddar, Danish Blue, Double Gloucester, English Cheddar, Gorgonzola, Limburger, La Tomme de Savoie, Pont l'Évêque, Provalone dolce, Roquefort, Samsoe, smoked cheese.

The texture of a cheese is due to the way it is made, to the amount of moisture (whey), which is pressed out of the milk curd during manufacture. So we have *hard-pressed cheeses* such as Parmesan or Cheddar which are very firm cheeses, good for grating; *lightly-pressed cheese* which contains more moisture and is often crumbly in texture, such as Caerphilly; *soft cheeses*, mild in flavour.

Soft cheeses are legally classified according to their butter-fat content and have to carry the appropriate descriptive label. *Skimmed milk soft cheese* has the lowest fat content. Then we have *low-fat soft cheese, medium-fat soft cheese, full-fat soft cheese, cream cheese* and *double cream cheese*, which has the highest fat content and is like cheesy butter.

Buying cheese for cooking

While all cheeses can be used for cooking, the most useful are those which are firm enough to grate easily, and have a flavour that is distinct but not too strong. Cheddar and Cheshire are good ones for this, while Lancashire is an excellent one for toasting.

The Italian cheese Parmesan is considered the finest cooking cheese because it is hard and dry, can be very finely grated, and has a good flavour. It is better to buy this in a piece and grate it yourself as the drums of ready-grated Parmesan often taste very stale.

The Swiss cheeses, Emmental and Gruyère, are both good too, although the former is inclined to become stringy when heated. Other good ones are Dutch Gouda and Italian Mozzarella.

There are many gadgets sold for grating cheese. If you only want small amounts, a simple hand grater is the most practical. If you want fairly large amounts, such as for a reserve in the refrigerator or freezer, a mechanical grater attachment for an electric mixer or an electric blender will save time and effort.

If the cheese is very hard it is better to feed small pieces into a blender with the motor running; softer cheese can be cut in pieces, put in the goblet and processed at slow speed. Most machines will take up to 2 oz (50 g) this way. When the recipe uses liquid or eggs pieces of cheese can be blended with these. If the recipe contains breadcrumbs the cheese can be added to the blender while the crumbs are being made. Very soft cheeses should always be blended with some liquid, otherwise they will make a sticky mass round the blender blades.

Storing cheese

Wrap it loosely in a polythene bag or in foil and keep it in a cool place or in the refrigerator. Remove cheese from the refrigerator about 1 hr before you want to serve it to allow it to come back to room temperature, otherwise it will be lacking in flavour.

Grated cheese can be stored in a jar or other container, loosely covered. Keep it in a cool dry place or in the refrigerator. Shake the jar occasionally.

If cheese is purchased in a box or special wrapper, store it in this.

Keep soft cheese in its container in a cool larder for 24 hrs or in the refrigerator for up to a week.

Cheese can be kept for 4–6 months in a freezer. Freezing gives a crumbly texture to hard cheeses like Cheddar. This does not affect the flavour and the cheese is suitable to use for cooking or in salads or sandwiches. Freezing is a very good way of keeping ripe soft cheeses like Camembert or Valmeuse, when they have reached the right stage of ripeness. Freezing preserves them at this stage without affecting texture or flavour. Before serving, they must be given ample time to thaw (1–2 days in the refrigerator), and then removed and allowed to come to room temperature. If this is not done the cheese will lack flavour. Unsalted cottage cheese is only satisfactory in the freezer for 3–4 months, though other soft cheeses will keep for 4–6 months.

It is best to freeze cheese in small packs of not more than $\frac{1}{2}$ lb (250 g), otherwise the thawing time is very long. If the cheese is already foil-wrapped or in a carton it can be stored like this for a week or so, but for longer storage overwrap with a polythene bag or foil.

Serving cheese

Even if you only serve one kind of cheese at a time, it is useful to have a cheese board. This can be a wooden one or any of the kitchen boards made of laminated plastic. Those shaped like a bat with a handle are the most useful.

On occasions when you provide a fairly large selection and it is not obvious what each cheese is, provide small labels threaded on cocktail sticks stuck in the cheese. Make sure there is room on the board for cutting the cheese and provide suitable knives.

Accompaniments

BREAD

French bread cut in chunks, white or brown bread in slices, dark rye bread in thin slices, crisp breads, rusks, brown or white rolls.

BISCUITS

Plain or semi-sweet such as digestive, also see recipes.

BUTTER

For those who want it. Many think cheese is better without butter.

SALAD VEGETABLES

Arrange these on a large dish or small individual dishes.

Carrot sticks. Scrape young carrots and cut them lengthwise in thin sticks. Put in iced water to keep them crisp.

Celery. Use inside sticks, root ends trimmed but left on, the pieces split in halves or quarters according to size.

Chicory. Washed, drained leaves stood upright in a small jug or jar.

Cucumber. In slices or chunks with the skin left on.

Radishes. Fresh young ones, washed, the roots cut off and the tops trimmed to leave a small tuft. Serve in a small bowl of iced water to keep them crisp.

Spring onions. Trim tops and outer layer and wash well.

Sweet green or red peppers. Wash, cut in half, remove seeds and pith and cut the flesh into strips.

Tomatoes. Wash, dry, leave small ones whole, others cut in halves or quarters.

Watercress. Washed thoroughly, drained and trimmed.

PICKLES

Onions, gherkins, beetroot, mixed pickles or piccalilli, olives (black, green or stuffed).

FRUIT

Apples, pears, grapes, nuts, bananas. Some prefer fruit with cheese in place of bread or biscuits.

Bacon and curd cheese flan

Cooking time 30 mins.
Temperature 220° C (425° F; G7) for 20 mins, then 180° C (350° F; G4) for 10 mins.
Quantities for an 8 in (20 cm) flan.

short-crust pastry using 4 oz (100 g) flour, or use 6 oz (175 g) ready-made

Roll the pastry to line the flan ring, prick the bottom and refrigerate it while the filling is prepared.

6 thin rashers streaky bacon

Remove rinds and grill or fry the bacon, set aside to cool.

4 oz sieved or mashed curd cheese (125 g)	salt and pepper
	¼ pt double cream (150 ml)
3 eggs	1–2 Tbs chopped fresh herbs

Taste the cheese before adding any salt. Whisk the ingredients together to mix them thoroughly. Put the cooked bacon in the bottom of the flan, in rashers or cut in pieces, and pour in the cheese mixture. Bake until the filling is set and lightly browned. Serve warm or cold.

Cheese flan

You can use a mild cheese for this as the yogurt gives it bite and character. The filling is a thick one and will stand a top crust if you prefer it; or you can use the filling for patties or turnovers.

Cooking time 30–40 mins.
Temperature 220° C (425° F; G7)
Quantities for an 8 in (20 cm) flan.

short-crust pastry using 4 oz (100 g) flour, or 6 oz (175 g) ready-made

Roll the pastry to line a flan ring or pie plate. Prick the bottom and refrigerate it while the filling is being prepared.

1 small onion, finely chopped	1 Tbs oil

Heat the oil in a small pan and fry the onion until it just begins to colour. Cool.

2 eggs	¼ pt yogurt (150 ml)
white pepper	

Beat together to mix thoroughly. Add the onion.

8 oz grated mild Cheddar or other cheese (200 g)

Mix with the egg and yogurt and put in the pastry case. Bake until the filling and pastry are lightly browned. Serve warm or cold.

Cheese flan with herb pastry

Cooking time 30 mins.
Temperature 220° C (425° F; G7)
Quantities for a 7 in (18 cm) flan.

4 oz plain flour (100 g)	¼ tsp salt
1 oz butter or margarine (25 g)	1 oz lard (25 g)

Mix the flour and salt in a bowl and rub in the fat.

about 1 Tbs finely chopped fresh herbs

The amount to use depends on how strongly flavoured the herbs are. Use marjoram, tarragon, chervil, thyme or a mixture of the four. Rub the herbs into the flour to distribute them evenly.

1 egg, beaten

Use enough to make a stiff dough. Roll out and line the flan ring, prick the bottom and put it in the refrigerator while the filling is prepared.

2 eggs, beaten, plus any left from the pastry	¼ pt single cream (150 ml) grated nutmeg
4 oz grated Emmental, Edam or Gouda cheese (125 g)	cayenne pepper

Mix together and pour into the pastry case. Bake until the filling is brown and set. Serve warm or cold. The filling may rise a lot during cooking but will shrink somewhat during cooling.

Cheese fondue

Quantities for 4–6.

a cut clove of garlic

Rub the inside of the cooking pot with this. The best kind of pot to use is an enamelled iron pot about 7–8 in (18–20 cm) across. It does not have to be a special fondue pot.

1 lb Gruyère cheese (500 g)

Grate coarsely and put in a bowl.

2–3 tsp potato flour   3 fl oz kirsch (6 Tbs)

Put the flour in a small basin and mix smooth with the kirsch.

½ pt dry white wine (300 ml)   1 Tbs lemon juice, optional

Put these in the fondue pot and heat to boiling. Remove from the heat. Add the cheese and stir with a wooden spoon over a moderate heat until the mixture is smooth and boiling. Add the kirsch mixture and stir until it boils again.

pepper   grated nutmeg

Season to taste and keep the fondue bubbling gently over a spirit lamp, a large candle warmer or some other gentle heat suitable for putting in the centre of the table. Provide each person with a knife and fork and one of the special long-handled fondue forks.

slices of bread cut about 1 in (2½ cm) thick

If preferred, the bread can be cut in cubes, or people can break slices in pieces for themselves. Each spears a piece of bread on the long fork, stirs it round in the fondue in a figure of eight and then transfers it to a plate. The stirring is important to prevent the fondue from becoming stringy.

Fondue is a meal in itself and needs no accompaniments except either a salad or fruit to follow and some kirsch or white wine for drinking with it.

ALTERNATIVES

Instead of the Gruyère cheese use Emmental, or half Emmental and half Gruyère (Neuchâtel or half and half fondue), or use half English Cheddar and half Gruyère.

Cheddar fondue with beer

Quantities for 4–6.

1 cut clove garlic

Rub the fondue pot with this.

½ pt beer (250 ml)

Put in the pot and heat to boiling.

12 oz grated strong English Cheddar (350 g)   1 Tbs flour

Mix together and gradually add to the beer, stirring until smooth.

1 tsp Worcester sauce

Add and bring to the boil. Serve in the same way as above.

Cheese pudding

This makes a good lunch or supper dish. Serve a salad to follow.

Cooking time 30–45 mins.
Temperature 190° C (375° F; G5).
Quantities for 4.

6 oz fresh breadcrumbs (2 c or 175 g)   1 pt hot milk (600 ml)

Soak the crumbs in the milk for a few minutes.

2 egg yolks, beaten   ½ tsp salt
pinch of pepper   4 oz grated strong cheese (125 g)

Add these to the milk mixture.

2 egg whites

Beat these until they stand up in peaks and fold into the cheese mixture. Pour into a well-greased baking dish and cook until the pudding is risen and lightly browned. Serve at once.

Cheese soufflé

Cooking time 30–45 mins.
Temperature 190° C (375° F; G5).
Quantities for 4.

Grease a 2 pt (1¼ l) soufflé dish or other straight-sided baking dish, or use four small soufflé dishes.

2–3 oz butter or margarine (50–75 g)   2 oz flour (6 Tbs or 50 g)

Melt the fat in a small saucepan and stir in the flour. Cook and stir for a minute or so.

½ pt milk (250 ml)

Stir into the pan and whisk or stir until the sauce is smooth and boiling. Cook for 3 mins, stirring frequently.

4 oz grated strong cheese (125 g)   salt
cayenne pepper   French mustard

Add to the sauce, flavouring to taste. Stir until the cheese melts.

3 large egg yolks, or 4 standard   1 Tbs water

Beat these until thick and light and fold into the cheese mixture.

3 large egg whites, or 4 standard

Beat until stiff but not dry and fold into the other mixture. Put in the prepared dish and bake until risen and brown. Serve at once.

Soft cheese with herbs

Use cottage, curd or cream cheese, and fresh chopped herbs.
   Use about 1 tsp herbs for each ounce (25 g) of cheese.
   Suitable herbs are garlic (juice, dried or garlic salt), chopped sage, mint,

marjoram, thyme, chives, basil, dill, tarragon or chervil. Use just one herb or a mixture of several and combine with the cheese. Leave to stand a while before serving to allow the flavours to blend.

Serve in place of other cheese with biscuits or fresh bread, or use as a sandwich filling.

Other recipes using cheese

See the index.

6. Eggs

Unless otherwise stated, the eggs used in my recipes are the standard size of between $1\frac{7}{8}$ oz and $2\frac{3}{16}$ oz, or EEC Grade 4. Large eggs weigh not less than $2\frac{3}{16}$ oz, or EEC Grade 2. In recipes using only two or three eggs, it does not really matter if large eggs are used instead of standard ones, but it can spoil results if you use smaller eggs unless the number is increased to make a total of approximately the same weight. To calculate this take a standard egg as being 2 oz or 56 g.

A shop with a good fast turnover of stock is more likely to sell fresh eggs than one where the eggs are in the shop for some time, particularly if they are not kept cold. If eggs are kept warm they very quickly deteriorate.

At home keep them in a cold larder or a refrigerator. Keep the eggs standing upright in their boxes with the broad end uppermost as this helps to keep the yolk in the middle. Under proper storage conditions the eggs should keep for 1–2 weeks.

Unshelled hard-boiled eggs can be kept for a day in a cold larder or a week in the refrigerator. There is danger of food poisoning if egg dishes are made in advance and kept a long time before serving, even if they are in a refrigerator. For example, stuffed eggs and egg salads should not be kept for more than 2–4 hrs even in a refrigerator. Cooked dishes can be kept for 24 hrs in the refrigerator.

Broken or separated eggs should always be refrigerated, covered closely. Whole eggs or yolks will keep for 1–2 days, whites for about a week. When eggs are kept like this it is wise to use them for cooking rather than in uncooked dishes. When storing yolks alone, put a little cold water on top to prevent a skin from forming.

Whole eggs out of the shell, egg yolks, and egg whites can all be frozen and will keep for 8–10 weeks. This is very useful when using recipes requiring either just yolks or just whites. To prevent yolks from becoming pasty, mix them either with $\frac{1}{2}$ tsp salt or 1 tsp sugar per yolk. Whole eggs frozen in small cake cups can be fried or poached while still frozen, otherwise thaw eggs completely before using them.

When separating whites from yolks it is important to have fresh eggs as stale yolks are very liable to break. If a very small amount of yolk gets into the white, scoop it out with a piece of the shell. Any left in the whites will prevent them from beating up well.

BAKED EGGS

En cocotte

These make an excellent starter for a meal, or two baked eggs per person are enough for a main dish. Single eggs can be baked in special small dishes called cocottes or in any shallow baking dish. For a family meal you can cook all the eggs together in one large shallow dish and then portion them out. The cooking time will depend on the kind of dish used, metal taking least time to heat, thick heat-resistant glass or ceramic longest. The eggs should be served as soon as they are cooked, otherwise the heat of the dish will go on cooking them. It is a good plan to remove them from the oven before the whites are quite set, then by the time they are served and cool enough to eat they will be set firm. The dish can be prepared for cooking a little while in advance and put in the oven 10 minutes or so before serving.

Cooking time about 10–20 mins.
Temperature 200° C (400° F; G6).

Either grease the dishes heavily with butter, or oil them lightly and put in 2 Tbs double cream for each egg. Break the eggs into a saucer and slide each into the dish. Season with salt and pepper, bake until the whites are just set. Serve with fingers of toast or bread.

For a more substantial dish, eggs cooked this way are often served with a garnish such as cooked cocktail sausages, rolls of cooked bacon, or a little tomato or other sauce. The recipes which follow give some of these variations.

Baked eggs with herbs

Follow the above recipe using double or soured cream mixed with 1 tsp chopped fresh herbs for each egg.

Eggs Raymond

Cooking time about 10 mins.
Temperature 190° C (375° F; G5), or use the grill.
Quantities for 4.

1 oz butter (25 g)

Put in a shallow baking dish or in individual dishes and put in the oven until the butter melts.

2 oz shelled shrimps (50 g)　　　　　4 Tbs double cream (60 ml)

Scatter the shrimps over the bottom of the dish and pour in the cream.

4 eggs　　　　　　　　　　　　　salt and pepper

Break each egg into a saucer and slide it into the baking dish. Season.

4 oz grated cheese (100 g)

Sprinkle the cheese over the eggs and bake for a few minutes only, then brown the cheese topping under the grill. If you prefer, this can be cooked entirely under the grill, heating the dishes and melting the butter and then grilling to brown the cheese. This should provide enough heat to set the eggs lightly, which is how they should be cooked. Serve straight away.

Eggs with yogurt and paprika

Cooking time about 15 mins.
Temperature 200° C (400° F; G6).
Quantitites for 2-4.

4 eggs　　　　　　　　　　　　　butter

Grease four small dishes, or one large dish, with butter. Break in the eggs and cook until the whites are just set. Meanwhile prepare the sauce.

1 oz butter (25 g)　　　　　　　　2 tsp paprika pepper

Melt the butter in a small dish in the oven and stir in the paprika.

¼ pt yogurt (150 ml)　　　　　　　salt

Beat the yogurt to make it smooth and add salt to taste.

　　When the eggs are cooked, remove them from the oven and spoon some yogurt over each. Then sprinkle with the butter and paprika mixture and serve with

fingers of toast.

BOILED EGGS

Cooking times
Soft-boiled (soft whites, liquid yolks)
Large   3 mins
Standard   2½ mins
Medium   2 mins

Medium-boiled (firm whites, soft yolks)
Large   4½ mins
Standard   4 mins
Medium   3½ mins

Hard-boiled (firm whites and yolks)
Large   8 mins or more
Standard   7 mins
Medium   6 mins

Put the eggs in cold water to cover. Bring to the boil, turn down the heat to simmering, and cook for the required time. Do not use a lid. Count the time from boiling point.

Hard-boiled eggs should be plunged into cold water as soon as cooked to prevent a dark ring from forming at the junction of yolk and white.

Curried eggs

Cooking time ½ hr. *Quantities* for 4.

1 oz fat (25 g)	1 small onion, chopped

Heat the fat in a small saucepan and fry the onion until brown.

1 oz flour (3 Tbs or 25 g)	1 Tbs curry powder, more or less

Add to the pan, mix and cook for 2–3 mins.

½ pt stock or milk (250 ml)

Add to the pan and stir until the sauce boils.

1 apple, chopped	1 small tomato, chopped
grated rind and juice of ½ small lemon	1 bay leaf
	1 tsp brown sugar
1 Tbs chutney	½ tsp salt

Add to the sauce, cover and boil gently for 20 mins or more. Strain and re-heat.

4–8 hard-boiled eggs   4–8 oz rice (125–250 g)

Boil the rice and eggs while the sauce is cooking. For boiled rice, see page 332. Shell the eggs and cut in half lengthwise. Put in the sauce when it has been strained and re-heat the eggs.

Serve the rice in a circle on a hot dish and put the eggs and sauce in the centre. Serve hot with

chutney.

Eggs with mushrooms

Cooking time 15–20 mins.
Temperature 190° C (375° F; G5).
Quantities for 4.

¼ pt fresh breadcrumbs (150 ml)

Grease a shallow baking dish or four individual dishes. Put a layer of breadcrumbs in the bottom of each.

4 hard-boiled eggs, sliced

Put a layer of egg over the crumbs.

3 rashers streaky bacon

Remove the rinds and cut the bacon in small pieces. Fry until crisp and sprinkle over the eggs.

4 oz sliced mushrooms (125 g)

Fry for a few mins in the bacon fat. Strew over the bacon.

½ pt soured cream (250 ml)   1 Tbs chopped parsley
salt and pepper

Mix parsley and seasonings with the cream and pour it over the eggs.

2 oz grated cheese (50 g)   paprika pepper

Sprinkle cheese over the cream and then a light dusting of paprika pepper. Bake until the cheese has melted and the dish is hot.

Stuffed eggs au gratin

Cooking time about 20 mins. *Quantities* for 4.

4–6 hard-boiled eggs	anchovy essence
lemon juice	

Shell the eggs and cut them in halves lengthwise. Remove the yolks and mash them with anchovy essence and lemon juice to taste. Put back into the whites and put in a shallow fireproof dish.

½ oz butter or margarine (15 g)	½ oz flour (1½ Tbs or 15 g)
½ pt milk (250 ml)	pinch of dry mustard

Melt the fat in a small pan, stir in the flour and stir and cook for a few minutes. Add the mustard and mix in. Add the milk and stir or whisk until the sauce is smooth and boiling. Boil gently for 5 mins.

2 oz grated cheese (50 g)	salt and pepper
grated nutmeg or mace	

Add to the sauce and stir until the cheese melts. Pour it over the eggs. Brown the top under the grill or heat in a hot oven. Serve with

toast or bread and butter.

Stuffed eggs with chervil

Cooking time 20–30 mins. *Quantities* for 4–6.

8 hard-boiled eggs	a little cream
salt and pepper	4 sprigs of chervil

Cut the eggs in half lengthwise, remove the yolks and mash them with salt and pepper and enough cream to moisten. Remove the chervil leaves from the stalks and scissor-chop the leaves. Mix into the egg yolks and re-fill the whites with this mixture.

2 oz butter (50 g)	4 Tbs flour
½ pt single cream (250 ml)	½ pt milk (250 ml)
salt and pepper	pinch of ground mace

Melt the butter in a saucepan, add the flour, mix and cook until crumbly. Stir in the cream and milk and stir or whisk until the sauce is smooth and boiling. Boil gently for 5 mins. Season to taste.

To serve, either heat the stuffed eggs gently in the sauce or put them in a fireproof dish, pour the sauce over and heat them for 15–20 mins in a moderate oven.

FRIED EGGS

Cooking time 3–4 mins.

Heat enough fat to cover the bottom of a frying pan and leave a little for basting the eggs. Do not allow it to become very hot. Break each egg in turn into a saucer and slide it into the hot fat. Cook gently, much more slowly than ordinary frying, basting the top with the fat. When the white is set, lift the egg out on a fish slice and serve it on a hot plate.

Some people like to fry eggs at a high temperature for a shorter time but then the whites tend to be tough round the edges. Others like to turn the egg over when the white is set. This is instead of basting it, but it should only be cooked for a moment after turning unless it is wanted hard-cooked.

The calorie conscious can cut down on the amount of fat used for frying eggs by using only $\frac{1}{2}$ oz (15 g) for cooking 4 eggs and heating this with 2 Tbs water. Instead of basting, the pan is covered with a lid so that the final result is a cross between frying and poaching; the result is very good.

Fried eggs and bacon

Remove rinds from the bacon and fry in a very little fat until it is as you like it, then lift it out and fry the eggs in the same fat, but at a lower temperature.

Fried eggs with bacon and green pea purée

Cooking time 15–20 mins. *Quantities* for 4.

1 lb shelled or frozen peas (500 g)

Boil the peas in a very little lightly salted water until they are tender. Drain, keeping the stock. Rub the peas through a sieve or pulp them in the electric blender, using as much of the cooking liquid as necessary to moisten. Re-heat in the saucepan.

4 Tbs cream (60 ml) 1 oz butter (25 g)
mashed potato powder

Add cream and butter to the purée and enough mashed potato powder to make it a fairly stiff consistency. Put the mixture in four mounds on hot plates and keep hot.

4–8 rashers bacon 4 eggs
fat

Remove the rind and cut the bacon in small pieces. Fry it in a little fat until the bacon is crisp, lift out and keep hot. Fry the eggs in the same fat. Put an egg on each mound of purée and sprinkle the bacon round it.

OMELETS

The two principal types of omelet are the French omelet made with lightly beaten whole eggs and the soufflé omelet made with yolks and whites beaten separately and combined for cooking. There are many variations of these two and many different flavourings are added from which the various omelets derive their names.

It is possible to make family-sized omelets in a frying pan with up to 8 eggs for a 10 in (25 cm) pan. However, omelets cook so quickly that it is quite easy to make individual ones and they look much better than a large one cut in pieces. This certainly applies to French omelets but soufflé omelets and some other varieties which take longer to cook, are more practical made in quantities for 4 or more.

Special omelet pans are useful but any frying pan which is kept smooth and clean will make a perfectly good omelet.

French omelet

Cooking time about 2 mins for single omelets, a little longer for a large one. Use a 5–6 in pan (12–15 cm) for one; a 7 in (18 cm) pan for two; a 10 in (25 cm) pan for four.

Quantities for 4.

8 eggs	pinch of pepper
1 tsp salt	

Beat the eggs just enough to mix yolks and whites thoroughly. Add the seasoning. When making individual omelets it helps to put the eggs in a measuring jug so that about the same amount of egg can be used for each omelet.

1 oz butter (25 g)

This amount of butter is enough for 4 individual omelets or 1 large one. There should be just enough to make a thin layer in the bottom of the pan. When the butter begins to colour, pour in the eggs. Keep a good heat under the pan and use a palette knife to scrape the edges to the centre as they set, letting uncooked egg run into the exposed part of the pan. When it is almost set, but still a little moist on top, fold it away from the handle and tip out on to a hot plate. Serve as soon as possible.

If the omelet is to be stuffed, put the filling on before folding it over.

Bacon omelet

Quantities for 4.

| 2 rashers chopped fried bacon | 1 Tbs chopped parsley |

Add to the eggs before making the French omelet. Cook the bacon in a separate pan from that used to cook the omelet.

Cheese omelet

Quantities for 4.

2 oz finely grated strong cheese (50 g)

Add to the eggs before making the French omelet.

Chicken liver omelet

Quantities for 4.

| 8 oz chicken livers (250 g) | 1 oz butter (25 g) |

Wash and drain the livers. Remove any fibres and cut the livers in small pieces. Heat the butter in a small saucepan and toss the liver in it for a minute, or until just firm.

| 1 Tbs flour | $\frac{1}{4}$ pt stock or wine (150 ml) |
| salt and pepper | |

Sprinkle the flour over the liver, mix and add the liquid. Stir until boiling and season to taste. Set aside to keep hot. As each omelet is made put some of the filling on top before folding it over.

Ham omelet

Quantities for 4.

| 2 oz lean cooked ham, chopped (50 g) | 1 Tbs chopped parsley |

Add to the eggs before making the French omelet.

Kidney omelet

Quantities for 4.

2 sheep's kidneys

Remove skin and core from the kidneys and chop them in small pieces.

½ oz dripping or fat (15 g)

Heat in a small saucepan and fry the kidney for a minute or two. Take care not to over-cook it.

½ Tbs flour   salt and pepper
5 Tbs stock or wine (75 ml)

Sprinkle the flour over the kidney, mix in and then add the liquid, stirring until it boils. Season to taste and keep hot while the omelets are made. Put a little of the filling on each before folding it over.

Mushroom omelet

Quantities for 4.

4–6 oz mushrooms (100–150 g)   2 oz butter (50 g)

Wash, drain and slice the mushrooms. Heat the butter in a small pan and cook the mushrooms in it until tender. Add the mushrooms to the eggs before making the French omelet.

VARIATION

Put the omelets in a fireproof dish and cover with ½–1 pt cheese sauce (300–600 ml). Brown under the grill.

Omelette aux fines herbes

Quantities for 4.

2 Tbs or more of fresh chopped herbs (parsley, tarragon, chervil and chives, mixed)

Add to the eggs before making the French omelet.

Onion omelet

Quantities for 4.

2 small onions or shallots, finely   1 oz butter (25 g)
chopped

Heat the butter in a small pan (not the omelet pan), and fry the onions gently until they are just beginning to brown. Add them to the eggs before making the French omelet.

VARIATION

This omelet is sometimes served with a tomato sauce.

Smoked haddock omelet

Quantities for 4.

8 oz cooked smoked haddock (250 g), flaked	about ¼ pt double cream (150 ml)
French mustard	pepper
	lemon juice

Combine the ingredients, using enough cream to moisten the fish well. Bring to the boil and keep hot. Add some to each French omelet before folding over.

Soured cream omelet

Quantities for 4.

6 Tbs soured cream (90 ml)   chopped herbs, optional

Beat the cream with the eggs and make a French omelet in the usual way, adding herbs for a different flavour. Using cream makes a more moist omelet, improving both the flavour and texture.

Soufflé omelet

Cooking time 15 mins. *Quantities* for 1 large or 4 small omelets.

4 eggs   4 Tbs water

Separate the yolks and whites of the eggs and beat the yolks and water until thick and light.

½ tsp salt   pinch of pepper

Add to the yolks. Beat the egg whites until stiff enough to stand up in peaks.

½ oz butter (15 g)

Use an omelet pan for just one egg; a 10 in (25 cm) frying pan for a large omelet. Heat just enough butter to grease the bottom of the pan. Fold the egg yolks into the whites very gently and pour the mixture into the pan. Cook very slowly for 5 mins, when the omelet should be risen and lightly browned underneath. Be careful not to have too much heat on or the omelet will rise up quickly and then collapse and be tough.

Transfer the pan to a moderate oven or put it under a moderate grill to dry the top slightly, but not enough to toughen and shrivel it. Fold the omelet in half and turn it out on to a hot dish.

The omelet can be served with a sauce such as tomato, cheese or mushroom, or use any of the flavourings already given for French omelets.

Omelet made with egg whites

Cooking time a few mins. *Quantities* for 2.

4 egg whites

Beat until very stiff.

2 Tbs soured cream   salt and pepper

Fold into the egg whites.

½ oz butter (15 g)

This omelet is best cooked in a frying pan, about 9 in (23 cm). Heat just enough butter to cover the bottom of the pan thinly but don't make it hot as for a French omelet. Add the egg mixture and cook slowly until the omelet is brown underneath, then dry the top under a grill or in a moderate oven. Fold over and serve.

Spanish omelet or tortilla

Cooking time about 5 mins. *Quantities* for 4.

8 oz mixed, cooked diced   1 oz butter (25 g) or 2 Tbs oil
  vegetables (250 g)

For the vegetables use any in season but include a little onion and if possible some peas and sweet peppers. Heat the butter or oil in a large frying pan and toss the vegetables in it to heat them without frying, or the omelet will stick.

6 eggs   pinch of pepper
1 tsp salt   2 Tbs chopped parsley

Beat the eggs and add the other ingredients. Pour this over the hot vegetables and cook, without stirring, until the egg is brown underneath. Place in the oven or under the grill to set the top lightly. Fold over and cut in pieces for serving.

Swiss eggs

Cooking time 5–10 mins. *Quantities* for 2–4.

4 eggs, beaten	1 Tbs finely chopped onion
1 Tbs chopped parsley	½ tsp salt
pinch of pepper	1½ oz melted butter or margarine
1½ oz grated Swiss cheese (40 g)	(40 g)

Mix all the ingredients together thoroughly. Heat a knob of butter in a 7–8 in (18–20 cm) frying pan. Pour in the egg mixture and cook it fairly slowly, without stirring, until it is brown underneath and almost set through.

Finish the top by browning it under the grill. If your grill is not suitable for this, continue cooking the mixture until it is set right through. Cut in wedges to serve.

POACHED EGGS

Cooking time 3–5 mins.

Only fresh eggs are suitable for poaching. The whites of stale eggs are watery and do not keep a compact shape. Put about 2 in (5 cm) of water in a frying pan or shallow saucepan, bring to the boil. Remove the pan from the heat. Break each egg in turn into a saucer and slide it gently into the water. Cover the pan and put it over a gentle heat but do not allow to boil again. Leave until the white is lightly set. Use a fish slice for lifting the eggs out, rest it on a clean cloth for a moment to mop up surplus water and then put the egg on hot toast. Serve at once.

For variety of flavour the toast may be spread with savoury butters, see page 57, or with anchovy or other fish paste, or anchovy essence. Other spreads are also useful, for example Marmite, and various sandwich spreads.

Traditional ways of serving poached eggs include buck rarebit (poached egg on Welsh rarebit), and poached egg on smoked haddock.

Eggs Crécy

Cooking time 20–30 mins. *Quantities* for 4.

1 lb carrots (500 g)

Wash, scrape or peel the carrots, cut them in slices and boil in a very little salted water until they are tender. Drain and mash. Alternatively, used drained canned carrots.

1 oz butter (25 g)   salt and pepper

Beat the butter into the hot mashed carrots and season to taste. Arrange the carrots to make a bed for the eggs, either in a large shallow dish or in individual portions.

1 pt parsley sauce (600 ml), page 54   4 eggs, poached

Drain the eggs and put on top of the carrots. Pour the sauce over the top and, if necessary, re-heat in a moderate oven before serving.

VARIATION

Instead of the carrots, use potatoes, parsnips, or cooked chopped spinach.

Eggs Mornay

Cooking time 15–20 mins. *Quantities* for 4.

½ pt cheese sauce (300 ml), page 48   4 eggs

Poach the eggs very lightly and then slip them into cold water to stop further cooking. Drain and put in hot fireproof dishes or one large dish. Pour the hot sauce over the eggs and brown the top either under the grill or in a hot oven. You need a very fierce heat for a short time, otherwise the eggs will become overcooked. Serve at once with

fingers of hot toast.

VARIATION

Florentine eggs are made as above but served on a bed of cooked, well-drained and chopped spinach.

Poached eggs in green sauce

Cooking time about 10 mins. *Quantities* for 3–6.

1 oz butter or margarine (25 g)   2 Tbs flour

Melt the butter or margarine in a small pan, stir in the flour and cook for a minute. Remove from the heat.

¼ pt double cream (150 ml)   ½ pt milk (300 ml)
salt and pepper

Stir in the cream and milk, return to the heat and stir until the sauce boils. Simmer for 5 mins and season to taste.

While the sauce is cooking, poach

6 eggs.

Lift out, drain and put on a hot serving dish or individual dishes.

1 Tbs each of chopped chives, parsley and dill

Add to the sauce, pour it over the eggs and serve with

crisp hot toast or bread and butter.

SCRAMBLED EGGS

Cooking time 5 mins. *Quantities* for 4.

4–5 eggs	pinch of pepper
½ tsp salt	6 Tbs milk (90 ml)

Beat the eggs to mix yolks and whites. Add the seasoning and milk.

1 oz butter or margarine (25 g)

Melt the fat in a small pan but do not make it very hot. Add the egg mixture, cook over a very low heat and stir only once or twice so that the egg sets in large soft clots. Serve as soon as it is set.

4 slices buttered toast

Serve the egg on the toast or with toast fingers served separately.

Scrambled eggs with bacon

Chop 1 rasher of bacon and fry it in the butter before adding the egg mixture.

Scrambled eggs with cheese

Add 1 oz (4 Tbs) grated strong cheese to the eggs before cooking them.

Scrambled eggs Lyonnaise

Chop 1 small onion finely and fry it gently in the butter before adding the eggs.

Scrambled eggs with cheese and parsley

Cooking time about 10 mins. *Quantities* for 4–6.

2 oz butter (50 g) 2 Tbs chopped parsley

Heat the butter in a small saucepan and fry the parsley in it for a few seconds.

4 oz grated strong cheese (125 g) ½ pt dry white wine or cider (250 ml)

Remove the pan from the heat. Add cheese and liquid, heat and stir until the cheese melts.

8 eggs

Break the eggs into the cheese mixture one at a time, mixing each in with a wooden stirrer or small whisk. Combine each thoroughly with the mixture before adding the next. Heat and stir all the time until it thickens.

fingers of toast or fried bread

Serve the egg mixture on hot plates and hand the toast or fried bread separately.

Scrambled eggs with cream cheese

Cooking time 5 mins. *Quantities* for 2–3.

2 oz cream cheese (50 g) 4 Tbs single cream (60 ml)

Beat together until smooth, set aside.

4 eggs salt and pepper
1 tsp finely chopped green herbs

Beat the eggs and add the flavourings.

½ oz butter (15 g)

Melt in a small pan and, when it is fairly hot, add the eggs. Cook slowly until they are just beginning to set, stirring gently once or twice during cooking. Add the cheese mixture, mix and cook until it is hot.

fingers of buttered toast

Serve the eggs in small hot dishes and hand the toast separately.

Scrambled eggs with sweet peppers and tomatoes

Cooking time about 20 mins. *Quantities* for 4–6.

1 large sweet pepper, green or red 2 small onions
1 lb tomatoes (500 g)

Wash the pepper, cut in half, remove seeds and pith and cut the remainder in thin strips. Skin and slice the onions very finely. Skin the tomatoes by pouring boiling water over them, leaving a minute or so and then plunging them into cold water. The skins should then come off easily. Slice them thinly.

1 oz lard (25 g)

Melt in a saucepan and stew the vegetables, with the lid on the pan, for about 15 mins or until tender.

6 eggs							2 tsp salt
¼ tsp paprika pepper

Beat the eggs thoroughly, add the seasoning and pour into the vegetable mixture. Cook gently, stirring occasionally, until the eggs are set. Serve with

fingers of buttered toast.

ALTERNATIVE

When fresh vegetables are out of season, substitute well-drained canned peeled tomatoes and a canned red pepper. Stew the onion in the lard until it is tender and then add the canned vegetables just long enough to heat them through before adding the eggs.

Scrambled eggs with vegetables and cheese

Cooking time about 5 mins. *Quantities* for 4.

6 eggs							2 Tbs cream

Whisk together thoroughly.

1 oz butter (25 g)

Heat in a small pan and add the eggs. Turn down the heat and cook gently.

4 oz cooked diced vegetables (125 g)		chopped chives or other green herbs

When the eggs begin to set, add the vegetables and herbs and stir in gently to mix well.

1 oz butter (25 g)					1 tsp French mustard
2 oz grated cheese (50 g)				salt and pepper

Add to the eggs and mix in, heating until the butter melts, but avoid overcooking.

bread and butter or toast

Serve the egg mixture on small hot plates and serve the bread or toast separately.

EGGS IN PASTRY

Egg and herb quiche

Cooking time 35–40 mins.
Temperature 200° C (400° F; G6) for the pastry; 180° C (350° F; G4) for the filling.
Quantities for an 8 in (20 cm) quiche.

short-crust pastry using 4 oz (100 g) flour, or 6 oz (175 g) ready-made

Roll the pastry to line a flan ring or tin, prick the bottom with a fork and line the pastry with a piece of foil. Refrigerate for 20 mins or so before baking it for about 15 mins. Remove the foil before adding the filling.

1 shallot or ½ small onion, finely chopped
a small knob of butter

Heat the butter in a small pan and cook the onion in it gently until it is soft but not brown. Put it in the bottom of the flan case.

3 eggs
salt and pepper
¼ pt single cream (150 ml)
3 Tbs chopped fresh herbs

For the herbs use a mixture of any of the following: parsley, tarragon, chervil, balm, thyme, savory or mint. Beat the eggs just to break them up and mix with the cream and flavourings. Pour into the pastry case and bake until set and lightly browned, 20–25 mins. Serve hot or cold.

Egg patties

Cooking time about 45 mins.
Temperature 220° C (425° F; G7) for the pastry; 180° C (350° F; G4) for the eggs.
Quantities for 4.

short-crust pastry using 4 oz (100 g) flour, or 6 oz (175 g) ready-made

Roll the pastry thinly and line individual pie tins, 3½ in (9 cm). Prick the bottom of the pastry and line each patty with foil. Refrigerate for a while before baking. Bake until the pastry is set, remove the foil and finish drying the pastry – about 15 min in all. While the pastry is cooking, make the sauce.

1 oz butter or margarine (25 g)
2 Tbs flour

Heat the fat in a small pan, stir in the flour and cook until crumbly.

½ pt creamy milk (250 ml)   salt and pepper

Make up the half pint of milk with a little cream or use half and half. Add to the pan, stir until boiling and cook gently for 5 mins. Season to taste. Keep hot, stirring occasionally to prevent a skin from forming.

4 eggs

Break an egg into each cooked pastry case and bake at the lower temperature until the eggs are just set, about 20 min.

1 Tbs chopped parsley   1 Tbs chopped tarragon

Add to the sauce, spoon some over each egg and serve hot.

7. Fish

Buying

Fresh fish is a very perishable food and it is important to know what to look for when choosing it.

With fillets and steaks, the flesh should be firm and springy to the touch, not collapsed and flabby looking, and the smell should be pleasant, of salt water and the sea.

With whole fish, look for bright red gills and eyes that are full and bright with black pupils. The eyes of stale fish are sunken and dull with grey pupils. The walls of the abdomen of a fresh fish should be firm, not disintegrating.

It is difficult to tell by looking at it whether smoked fish is in good condition, so buy it from a reliable shop and complain if it is stale. It will smell and taste unpleasant. The same is true of shellfish.

Buying frozen fish is more difficult. The quality is affected more by poor storage conditions after it leaves the freezing plant than that of any of the other frozen foods. The visible signs of poor storage conditions are damaged and misshapen packs which show that at some time the fish has been allowed to thaw and then re-frozen. If the airtight cover round the fish has been damaged, moisture will have been lost and the fish may show opaque white patches on the surface. When cooked, this sort of fish is stringy, dry and of poor flavour.

Quantities guide

Most fishmongers will gut, scale and fillet fish for you.

Large whole fish as caught	8–10 oz per portion (250–300 g)
Large whole fish gutted but with the head on	7–8 oz per portion (200–250 g)
Small whole fish	1 fish per portion
Fish steaks	5–6 oz per portion (150 g)

Fish fillets	4–5 oz per portion (125 g)
Crab	1 small per portion
Lobster (in shell)	½–¾ lb per portion (250–350 g)
Mussels (in shells)	1 pt per portion (600 ml)
Prawns (in shells)	½ pt per portion (300 ml)
Frozen or shelled fish such as prawns, scampi, etc.	Allow 3–6 oz per portion (75–150 g), according to the way it will be used.

Yields for shelled fish

½ pt (300 ml) prawns in the shell gives 5 oz (150 g)
½ pt (300 ml) shelled prawns weighs about 6 oz (175 g)
2 lb (1 kg) lobster in the shell gives about ¾ lb meat (350 g)
2 lb (1 kg) crab in the shell gives about 5 oz meat (150 g)

Storing fish

Freshly caught fish will keep for 1–2 days in a cold larder or 3–4 days in the refrigerator. Fish bought from a shop should be stored in a covered dish in the coldest part of the refrigerator and used within 24 hrs. If you want to keep it longer than this it is advisable to freeze it. I find the quality of fish treated this way is often better than when it has been commercially frozen.

Smoked fish, foil-wrapped, will keep 1 day in a cold larder, 2 days in the refrigerator, 1–2 weeks frozen.

Shellfish should be used on the day of purchase, or frozen. If you have no freezer, commercial frozen fish can be kept for 2 days in the refrigerator.

Cooked fish should be stored in a covered dish in the refrigerator. Use within 2–3 days, or the same day if it has been mixed with mayonnaise or other sauce. Fish which has been cooked to serve cold with salad, or to be mixed with a sauce and re-heated, is best stored separately and combined with dressing or sauce just before serving.

Canned fish will keep a year or more if the cans are undamaged but once it has been opened, it should be treated in the same way as cooked fish.

Pickled and salted fish will keep for several days, but it is advisable to keep it in a covered dish in the refrigerator.

Home freezing of fish

If you want to buy fish more than 24 hours in advance it is a good idea to put it in the freezer. Close-wrapping with foil is the best way, though for just 2–3 days the polythene bag in which it was sold will do.

Cooked fish in a sauce is also useful. It can be thawed and heated in a double boiler, over a direct gentle heat, or in a moderate oven. Freeze it in tubs or boxes.

Fish cakes and rissoles can be frozen either before or after frying. Fried ones are heated on trays in a hot oven, un-fried are cooked in a little fat while still frozen.

Scaling, cleaning and filleting fish

When this is being done for you by the fishmonger, ask him for the bones and trimmings to make fish stock for the sauce to serve with it.

SCALING FISH

Put the fish on newspaper and use a small knife to stroke it firmly from tail towards head, scraping the scales off as you go. Then wash well and drain the fish.

CLEANING FLAT FISH

The gut is in a small pocket just behind the head. Cut away the gills, make a small opening just behind the head and pull out the gut. Wash the fish well.

CLEANING ROUND FISH

Slit the belly from head to vent and scrape out the gut. Black skin lining the cavity can be removed by rubbing with a little salt. Wash well. Small fish such as herrings can be cleaned by cutting the head almost off, then pulling it, and the gut will come out still attached. Red mullet and smelts are cleaned by pulling out the gills with the gut attached.

SKINNING FISH

Cut a slit in the skin at the tail end and lever up enough to get a grip on the skin, then hold the fish firmly with one hand while pulling the skin up towards the head with the other hand.

To skin fillets, see page 136.

To skin eels, see page 134.

BONING FISH

For flat fish like plaice or sole, cut along the spine and use a small sharp knife to scrape the flesh from the bone, giving four fillets for each fish.

Large round fish are boned by cutting along the backbone and scraping the flesh off to get two fillets.

Small fish like herrings are slit along the belly and opened out flat; press along the backbone from the outside, turn the fish over and pull the bones out in one piece, starting from the tail end.

Cooking fish

While it is traditional to cook some fish in special ways, most fish can be cooked by any of the usual methods of frying, grilling, poaching, baking, sousing and so on. Below I give a list of the most common fish with the ways they are usually cooked.

I have grouped my recipes in the way I think is most useful for the cook: how to cook small whole fish, large whole fish, fish steaks, fish fillets and shellfish.

COOKING FROZEN FISH

It is usually necessary to thaw this a little in order to separate the pieces without breaking them. If fillets and steaks are completely thawed they tend to lose rather a lot of moisture and flavour, though this is less so with home frozen.

Over-cooking of either fresh or frozen fish makes it dry.

Alphabetical list of fish with recommended cooking methods

The kind of fish available at any one time depends very much on weather conditions. Some fish are more seasonal than others and the seasons given in this list are only approximate.

Anchovy. Fresh ones are available from time to time. Best cooking method is grilling with the heads and tails left on. Canned anchovy fillets are very useful for flavouring other fish, and with eggs, cheese and salads.

Bass. Season May to August. Cook by any method, but one of the best is poached and served with maître d'hôtel or parsley butter.

Bloaters. Available all the year; best in summer. See page 141.

Bream. Season June to December. Boil, steam, grill or bake.

Brill. Season February to April. Poach or steam and serve with a sauce.

Cod. Available all the year; best in winter. Cook by any method.

Coley. Available all the year. Also known as saithe. Cook by any method.

Conger eel. Season March to October. Only young eels are tender; fry or poach.

Crab. Available most of the year; best in summer. See pages 146-8.

Crawfish. Best in summer and autumn. Boil and use as lobster.

Dab. Season June to February. Cook like plaice or sole; boil, steam, fry or grill.

Dog fish, also known as huss or rock salmon. Season October to June. Sold skinned and cut in portions. Cook by any method.

Eels (fresh water). Available all the year. Stew and serve hot; or fry, cut in slices.

Escallops. See scallops.

Flounder. As plaice.

Haddock. Season July to February. Cook by any method. Smoked haddock, see pages 141–4.

Hake. Season June to February. Cook by any method.

Halibut. Season January and February or May to September. Grilled or poached with hollandaise or tartare sauce; or cold for salads.

Herring. Available all the year. Cook any way; grilled, poached or boiled are the best methods. Serve with lemon, mustard sauce or horseradish sauce.

Huss. See dog fish.

Kipper. See pages 144–5.

Lemon sole. Season July to March. Cook in the same way as sole or plaice.

Ling. Available most of the year. Cook as cod.

Lobster. Best in summer. See pages 148–50.

Mackerel. Available most of the year; best in winter. Cook by any method.

Mullet. Grey mullet best in summer; red mullet May to September. Cook grey mullet by any method; red mullet is best fried or grilled with head and tail on.

Mussels. Season March to August. See page 150.

Oysters. Season September to April.

Plaice. Available most of the year; best from May to January. Cook by any method.

Prawns. Best in summer. See pages 150–52.

Red fish. Season June to October. Cook by any method.

Rock salmon. See dog fish.

Saithe. See coley.

Salmon. Season May to August. Whole fish or large pieces boiled and served hot or cold; steaks grilled or en papillote.

Scallops. Available from November to March. See page 152.

Scampi. Available all the year. See page 152.

Shrimps. Best in summer and autumn. See page 152.

Skate. Best in winter. Boil or steam and serve with caper sauce or brown butter sauce; or fry in butter and serve with rémoulade sauce. Use recipes for cooking small whole fish.

Smelt. Season November to February. Fry or grill.

Sole. Available all the year. Cook by any method; best are grilled or steamed and served with melted butter or a sauce such as hollandaise or rémoulade.

Sprats. Season November to February. Leave whole and fry or grill, see page 129.

Trout (river). Available all the year. Grill, fry or poach.

Trout (sea). Season June to August. Poach or steam.

Turbot. Best in winter. Large pieces steamed or baked; cutlets grilled or en papillote.

Whitebait. Season February to July. Leave whole, toss in mixed flour and breadcrumbs and fry in oil for 1 min. Serve with lemon.

Whiting. Season November to February. Cook by any method.

Witch sole. Season August to April. Cook as sole.

HOW TO COOK SMALL WHOLE FISH

Round fish are gutted and scaled but usually cooked with heads and tails still on, though this is not essential. Small flat fish like dabs or small sole, are cleaned, the heads removed or left on, and the dark skin usually removed.

À la Bretonne

Cooking time 20 mins.
Temperature 190° C (375° F; G5).
Quantities for 4 small fish.

Slit the belly of round fish as far down as possible, turn belly side down and press along the backbone to flatten the fish. Wash and drain. The bones can be left in.

Flour   1 tsp salt
$\frac{1}{4}$ tsp freshly ground pepper   2 oz butter (50 g)

Sprinkle the fish with flour to coat it on both sides. Then sprinkle with the salt and pepper. Put the butter in a shallow casserole and put it in the oven for casserole and butter to get hot. Add the fish, skin side up, and cook for a few minutes. Turn the fish over and then put the lid on the casserole and cook until the fish is done (i.e. flakes easily at the thickest part).

1–2 Tbs lemon juice

Sprinkle over the fish and serve hot.

Boiled herrings

Cooking time 6 mins. *Quantities* for 4.

4 fresh herrings   2 oz salt (3 Tbs or 50 g)
$1\frac{1}{2}$ pt water (850 ml)

Clean the herrings and remove heads and tails but do not bone them. Bring the water and salt to the boil, add the fish, and boil with the water at a gallop for 6 mins. Remove the fish, drain, and serve hot with a sauce or cold with salad.
    Suitable sauces are mustard, tomato, onion, parsley or horseradish.

En papillote

Cooking time 30 mins.
Temperature 190–200° C (375–400° F; G5–6).
Quantities for 4 small fish.

For this excellent method, round fish are the best and they usually have heads, tails and fins removed, then are boned and folded back into the original shape. If there are roes, save them to cook with the fish.

4 oz mushrooms, chopped (125 g)   1 tsp lemon juice
salt and pepper   1 Tbs finely chopped parsley or other
1 Tbs butter ($\frac{1}{2}$ oz or 15 g)   herbs

Chop the roes and mix with the mushrooms, then add the other ingredients, using plenty of seasoning and working in the butter to make a smooth mixture. Put some of this inside each fish and press the sides together. Wrap each fish in a loose parcel of foil, put in a baking dish and cook. Remove from the foil and serve with any liquid round the fish. If liked, more lemon or a fish sauce can be served with them, but they are delicious as they are.

Fried in butter

Cooking time about 8–15 mins.

METHOD 1

Dip the fish in milk and then in seasoned flour to coat it well. Fry in hot butter until golden brown. Serve with lemon and parsley.

METHOD 2 (à la meunière)

Coat the fish with seasoned flour and fry in hot butter until brown on both sides. Put on a hot dish and sprinkle with lemon juice, salt and pepper and chopped parsley.

Heat a little more butter until it turns nut brown and pour quickly over the fish. Serve at once.

Fried in deep fat

See page 137, as for fillets.

Grilled

Cooking time about 8–15 mins.

Round fish may be prepared in one of three ways. Split it down the belly and open out flat, pressing along the backbone to make it stay that way. Alternatively, cut several gashes in each side to help the heat to penetrate. The third way is to cut along the backbone to allow heat to penetrate.

For flat fish, remove the dark skin and brush the fish on both sides with oil.

Heat the grill and oil the grid, or the bottom of the grill pan. Add the fish and grill slowly until brown on both sides. Serve with lemon wedges or a sauce such as tartare, brown butter sauce, horseradish sauce, mustard butter, maître d'hôtel butter or mustard sauce.

Grilled sprats

Cooking time 3–4 mins. *Quantities* 1 lb (500 g) for 2–3 portions.

Wash and dry the sprats. Leave them whole and thread them on skewers through the eyes. Grill quickly, turning once. Serve with wedges of lemon and brown bread and butter.

Marinated fish

This method is similar to sousing but less vinegar is used and the flavour is more delicate.

Cooking time 25–30 mins. *Quantities* for 6 small fish.

After cleaning, remove heads and tails and cook the fish with the bones in, or remove the bones and fold the fish back in shape.

1 small onion	1 small carrot
1 bay leaf	

Skin and chop the onion, scrape and slice the carrot and wash the bay leaf.

½ pt white wine or dry cider (250 ml)	¼ pt white wine vinegar (150 ml)
2 tsp salt	½ pt water (250 ml)
	pinch of dried garlic

Put these in a frying pan with the vegetables and bay leaf. Bring to the boil, turn down the heat and boil gently for 15 mins. Use a lid if possible, otherwise you will need to add some more water when the fish is put in. Put in the fish, which should be just covered by the liquid, and boil gently for 10–20 mins or until the flesh flakes easily when tested. Turn the fish once during cooking. Put it in a flat heat-resistant dish and pour the liquid over it, cool, cover and store in the refrigerator. Serve cold with some of the strained liquid as a sauce.

Poached or boiled fish

See page 132. Allow 10–15 mins cooking time.

HOW TO COOK LARGE WHOLE FISH

For most methods, large fish are gutted, scaled and washed thoroughly, but the head and tail are left on.

Baked stuffed

Cooking time ¾–1 hr.
Temperature 190° C (375° F; G5).
Quantities, allow ½ lb per portion (250 g).

Suitable stuffings are lemon stuffing, page 28, or bacon and nut stuffing, page 27.

Fill the belly of the fish, but not too tightly as most stuffings swell during cooking. Sew up the opening with a needle and coarse white cotton.

Brush the fish with melted butter or oil. Heat a little butter or oil in a baking dish, put in the fish and cook until the flesh flakes when tested at the thickest part. Use two fish slices to lift it carefully on to a hot platter, gently pull out the cotton and garnish the fish with parsley or other herbs, wedges of lemon and raw or baked tomatoes.

Serve with boiled or baked jacket potatoes and a suitable sauce such as parsley sauce, fennel sauce or breton sauce.

VARIATION

Use a long skewer and thread it through the fish to fix it in a letter S, with the belly opening at the bottom.

LARGE FLAT FISH

Separate the fillets from the backbone, keeping the edges still together, and push the stuffing under the fillets.

Baked to serve cold

Cooking time 35–45 mins.
Temperature 180° C (350° F; G4).
Quantities for 4–6, or a fish weighing 2–3 lb (1–1½ kg).

Sprinkle the cleaned fish inside and out with salt and pepper. Cut gashes at about 1 in (2½ cm) intervals on one side of the fish. Put it in a shallow, greased baking dish with the cut side uppermost.

4 Tbs olive oil (60 ml)

Pour over the fish.

1 dried bay leaf, crushed, or a good pinch of powdered dried	1 Tbs chopped fennel
1 Tbs chopped parsley	1 Tbs chopped chives
1 sprig thyme, chopped	1 Tbs chopped chervil

Fresh herbs are best but dried may be substituted. Mix the herbs together and rub them into the cuts in the fish.

1 Tbs lemon juice

Sprinkle over the fish. Bake, basting occasionally with the liquid. Allow to cool in the dish.

4 Tbs olive oil (60 ml)   1 Tbs lemon juice

Pour over the fish when it is almost cold. Serve cold with

potato salad, cucumber salad or a mixed salad.

Flambé with tarragon sauce

Cooking time about 45 mins.
Quantities for 4; use a fish weighing 2–3 lb (1–1½ kg), or 4, smaller fish.

The fish should be cleaned in the usual way but the head and tail left on. It can be baked in the oven as for baked stuffed fish, or poached, see below. Avoid over-cooking. Make the sauce while the fish is cooking or make it in advance and keep hot.

a good handful of fresh tarragon leaves	5 Tbs milk (75 ml)

Wash the leaves, warm the milk in a small pan, add the tarragon, cover and leave to infuse.

2 egg yolks	5 Tbs cold milk (75 ml)
1 tsp potato flour	1 oz butter (25 g)

Mix these together in the top of a double boiler or in a basin to go on top of a pan of simmering water. Heat, stirring all the time, until the butter melts and the sauce thickens.

1 oz butter (25 g)

Add and stir until it melts and is blended into the sauce. Strain in the tarragon milk and add

1½ oz butter (40 g) in small pieces.

Mix until this butter has been blended into the sauce.

salt and pepper	lemon juice

Season to taste. Should the flavour of tarragon be insufficient, put back the strained leaves and infuse longer, then strain the sauce before serving. The sauce should be kept warm only, not left over boiling water, or it will spoil.

When the fish is cooked, remove the skin (except from over the head and tail) and put it on a hot metal serving dish or fireproof dish.

4 Tbs warm brandy

Just before serving the fish, pour the warm brandy over it, ignite and baste with the burning liquid. Serve with the sauce handed separately. Plain boiled potatoes are the best vegetable for this, with a salad to follow.

Poached or boiled

This method is suitable for a whole fish with head and tail left on, or for a large piece cut from the middle of a big fish.

Cooking time 10 mins per lb (500 g) plus 10 mins.
Quantities allow ½–¾ lb per portion (250–350 g).

A large oval pan, not very deep, is the best to use, or a proper fish kettle if you have one. Put in the fish and measure in enough cold water just to cover it. Lift out the fish. For each pint (600 ml) of water used add

½ Tbs vinegar	½ bay leaf
1 tsp salt	1 small carrot
2 peppercorns	1 small onion
1 sprig of parsley	

Heat the water and flavourings until hot but not boiling. Put in the fish. A fish kettle will have its own rack for convenient lowering and raising of the fish. Failing this, tie the fish in a piece of muslin. Keep the water just below boiling so that the fish is poached, rather than boiled. The surface of the water should agitate, rather than bubble.

Lift the fish out carefully and test it at the thickest part to make sure it flakes easily. Try not to over-cook the fish or it will be dry and fall to pieces when handled. Drain thoroughly and serve on a hot platter, garnished with lemon and fresh herbs.

Use some of the stock to make a sauce such as parsley, anchovy or fennel; or serve a cold one like salsa verde or Béarnaise.

Salmon

This method is suitable for whole salmon and large trout, or for a large piece cut from a big fish.

Cooking time 10 mins per lb (500 g), plus 10 mins for the first 6 lb (3 kg); 5 mins per lb for the next 6 lb; 3 mins per lb for the next 6 lb; 2 mins per lb for each lb over 18 lb (8 kg).
Quantities ½ lb per portion (250 g).

The fish is washed, gutted and scaled but the head and tail left on. For cooking a large, whole fish a proper fish kettle is essential as the fish should lie out straight. A little space can be saved by skewering it in the shape of a letter S. Large pieces of salmon can be cooked in any convenient pan. Tie the fish in a piece of muslin or other thin white cotton material. It helps if the fish is put on a heat-resistant plate before tying it up.

Put the fish in the pan and measure in cold water to cover. Remove the fish. To each 4 pt (2 l) of water add

1½ oz salt (40 g)	2 sprigs parsley
3 slices lemon	

Bring the water almost to the boil, lower the fish into it and immediately reduce the heat to simmering. Salmon should be thoroughly cooked but not overcooked or it will be dry. Test it at the thickest part to see if the flakes separate easily. Drain well and serve hot or cold.

Serve hot salmon with boiled potatoes and parsley sauce, or hollandaise or tartare, and with cucumber salad. For cold salmon serve mayonnaise or tartare sauce and cucumber salad.

Stewed eels

Cooking time $\frac{1}{2}$ hr. Quantities for 4.

1$\frac{1}{2}$ lb eel (700 g)	2 cloves
1 bay leaf	$\frac{1}{2}$ tsp salt

To skin the eel hold the head in a cloth or piece of paper and cut through the skin round the neck. Turn back about 1 in (2$\frac{1}{2}$ cm) of the skin and then pull the head with one hand and the skin with the other and it should strip off easily. Cut the eel in 2 in (5 cm) slices. Put in a pan with the flavourings and $\frac{1}{2}$ pt (250 ml) water. Bring to the boil and simmer gently for 20 mins. Lift out the eel and keep it hot.

1 oz butter (25 g)	$\frac{1}{2}$ tsp anchovy essence
1 oz flour (3 Tbs or 25 g)	5 Tbs milk (75 ml)
$\frac{1}{2}$ pt eel stock (300 ml)	1 Tbs chopped parsley
salt and pepper	

Melt the butter and add the flour, stirring and cooking until crumbly. Add the stock and stir until it boils, then boil gently for 5 mins. Add the anchovy and milk and re-heat. Taste for seasoning and add the chopped parsley. Put the eel in the sauce and heat well.

1$\frac{1}{2}$ lb mashed potatoes (700 g)

Serve the fish and sauce in a border of mashed potato.

HOW TO COOK FISH STEAKS

The best methods are baked, grilled or en papillote, but any of the recipes given for cooking fillets are also suitable if a little longer cooking time is allowed.

Baked to serve cold

Cooking time about 1 hr.
Temperature 180° C (350° F; G4).
Quantities for 4.

2 tomatoes skinned and chopped roughly, or use an equivalent amount of canned tomatoes
1 medium-sized onion, chopped
1 clove of garlic or a pinch of dried
4 Tbs oil (60 ml)

Heat the oil in a small pan and add the vegetables.

2 tsp sugar
salt and pepper
a pinch of fresh thyme leaves

Add to the pan and simmer for 15–20 mins until the onion is tender and the sauce thick. Remove the clove of garlic when the sauce is sufficiently flavoured.

5 Tbs white wine or dry cider (75 ml)

Add and simmer for a couple of minutes.

4 fish steaks
salt and pepper

Put these in a shallow casserole or baking dish, pour the sauce over the fish and cover with a lid or with foil. Bake for 30 mins or until the fish is cooked. Cool as quickly as possible and store in a covered dish in the refrigerator.

chopped parsley

Sprinkle plenty over the fish before serving.

Grilled

Cooking time 10–15 mins depending on the thickness. *Quantities* for 4 steaks.

2 Tbs oil
¼ tsp salt
1 tsp anchovy essence
1–2 tsp lemon juice
pinch of pepper

Mix these together and brush them over the fish before and during cooking. Heat the grill and cook the fish under a moderate heat until it is brown on one side with the flesh showing opaque half-way through. Turn, brush with the sauce, and grill the other side until brown and cooked through.

Serve with lemon wedges, potatoes and a salad, or with grilled mushrooms or tomatoes. If you want a sauce use a savoury butter or tartare sauce, or one of the other cold savoury sauces.

Alternative basting sauces, see pages 24–6.

Grilled salmon steaks or cutlets

About 1 in (2½ cm) thick is ideal for grilling; middle cut looks best.

Cooking time 20–25 mins. *Quantities* 1 steak per person.

melted butter or oil

Use this to brush the fish on both sides. Cook under a moderate heat, turning once or twice, and cooking until the flesh easily separates from the bone when tested with a fork.

salt and pepper tartare or rémoulade sauce
boiled potatoes cucumber salad

Sprinkle the salmon with seasoning and serve with the hot potatoes. Serve the sauce and salad separately.

En papillote

Cook in the same way as for small whole fish en papillote, see page 128, or for salmon steaks, see below. Alternative flavouring for the steaks could be a squeeze of lemon juice, salt and pepper and some chopped dill or fennel.

Salmon steaks en papillote

Wrap each steak in a loose parcel of foil, folding the ends to make a good seal. Either cook the parcels in a steamer, poach in water, or bake in a moderate oven.
Cooking times: 35 mins for slices 1 in (2½ cm thick); 45 mins for slices 1½ in (4 cm) thick; 50 mins for slices 2 in (5 cm) thick.

If the fish is to be served cold, leave it to cool in the wrapping and then store in the refrigerator. Serve with cucumber salad and tartare or rémoulade sauce. Serve hot with boiled potatoes, cucumber salad and hollandaise sauce, or a cold sauce as for the cold fish.

HOW TO COOK FILLETS OF FISH

If the fillets have a dark or rough skin it is best, though not essential, to remove this before cooking them. To do this, place the fillet, skin side down, on a board or bench top. Use a piece of kitchen paper to help you get a good grip on the tail end or narrowest end and use a knife in the other hand to scrape the fish from the skin, rolling it off in one piece.

Fricassée

Cooking time about 30 mins. *Quantitites* for 4.

1–1½ lb fish fillets (450–700 g)   lemon juice
salt

Wash and dry the fish. Put it on a flat dish and sprinkle liberally with salt and lemon juice. Leave it for ½ hr, preferably covered and in the refrigerator. Drain off any liquid and pat the fish dry with paper towels. Cut it into convenient pieces.

1½ oz butter or margarine (40 g)   2 oz flour (6 Tbs or 50 g)

Melt the fat in a frying pan and stir in the flour, cooking and stirring until it turns crumbly.

1 pt fish stock or water mixed with a little dry white wine or cider (600 ml)

Add to the pan, stirring or whisking until the sauce is smooth. Boil gently for 5 mins. Add the pieces of fish and cook gently until they are opaque all through, about 10–15 mins. Remove and keep hot.

1 tps capers

Add to the sauce.

1–2 egg yolks   2 Tbs cold water
1 Tbs lemon juice

Mix together and stir into the sauce.

salt and pepper   chopped fennel or other herbs

Season the sauce and serve the fish and sauce sprinkled with chopped herbs.

Fried in deep fat

COATING BATTER

4 oz flour (¾ c or 125 g)   1 tsp salt
pinch of pepper

Put in a mixing bowl and make a well in the centre.

1 egg   about ¼ pt milk (150 ml)

Break the egg into the well in the flour and mix round, working from the centre outwards, adding milk gradually until a thick batter is formed. Beat until smooth.

Alternatively, put all ingredients in the goblet of the electric blender and process for one minute.

FRYING

For general notes on deep-fat frying, see page 31. Wash the fish fillets and dry them thoroughly on paper towels. Frozen fillets can be used thawed and dried, or frozen. Dip the fish in flour to coat it well and then dip it in the batter. Drop the fish into the hot oil. A pint of oil will fry 2 or 3 fillets at a time provided you keep a good heat under the pan. Small, thin fillets will take 2–3 mins, large fillets 5–10 mins at 190° C (375° F).

Drain the fish on absorbent paper and keep it hot. Serve as soon as possible.

ACCOMPANIMENTS

Potato chips and/or salad, lemon wedges, tartare or rémoulade sauce.

Fried in butter

See method for small whole fish, page 129.

Grilled

See method for fish steaks, page 135.

Poached with cheese sauce

Cooking time 15–20 mins. Quantities for 4.

8 small plaice or sole fillets, or other similar fillets

Poach these for 5 mins either in fish stock made with the bones and trimmings or in water flavoured with a bay leaf, peppercorns, salt, a slice of onion and a dash of cider or wine vinegar. Drain the fish, reserving the liquid, and put the fish in a fireproof dish to keep hot.

1 oz butter (25 g)   1 oz flour (3 Tbs or 25 g)

Melt the butter in a small pan, stir in the flour and cook for a minute.

½ tsp dry mustard   cayenne pepper
5 Tbs strained fish stock (75 ml)

Remove the pan from the heat, stir in the seasonings and then the stock. Return to the heat and stir until it boils.

5 Tbs soured cream (75 ml)   5 Tbs dry cider (75 ml)
½ oz grated Parmesan cheese (15 g)

Add to the sauce, mix and heat. Pour over the fish.

1 oz grated Parmesan cheese (25 g)

Sprinkle on top of the sauce and grill until the cheese has lightly browned. Serve hot.

Poached with mushrooms and cream sauce

Cooking time ½ hr. *Quantities* for 4.

1–1½ lb fillets (500–750 g)

Cut the fish in portions and poach it gently in salted water to cover. Keep the water just under the boil. Cook until a thick cut end looks opaque all through, about 10–15 mins. Drain and keep hot. While the fish is cooking begin making the sauce.

1 small onion, finely chopped	1 oz butter (25 g)

Heat the butter in a small saucepan and fry the onion until it just begins to colour.

½ pt fresh double or soured cream (250 ml)	6 oz mushrooms, sliced (175 g)
1–2 Tbs chopped fresh marjoram or 1–2 tsp dried	2 Tbs lemon juice
	salt and pepper
	½ tsp paprika pepper

Add to the onions, mix and boil gently for 15 mins or until the sauce begins to thicken. Pour it over the fish and serve hot.

Portuguese baked fish

Cooking time 20 mins.
Temperature 200° C (400° F; G6).
Quantities for 4.

1–1½ lb fillets (500–750 g)	1 small onion, chopped
1 tsp salt	pinch of pepper
4–6 tomatoes	1 oz butter or margarine (25 g)

Cut the fish into four portions. Grease a shallow baking dish large enough to allow the fish to lie in a single layer. Sprinkle the fish with salt and pepper. Strew the chopped onion over the fish. Skin and chop the tomatoes, or use an equivalent amount of canned tomatoes. Add to the fish and dot with pieces of butter or margarine. Bake. Test the centre of a thick piece to make sure it is cooked.

3 oz grated cheese (1 c or 75 g)

Sprinkle the cheese over the fish and either put it under the grill to melt the cheese or put the dish in the top of the oven. Serve with

boiled potatoes or boiled rice.

Sole Véronique

Cooking time 30 mins. *Quantities* for 4.

4 large or 8 small fillets of sole   about ½ pt dry white wine (250 ml)

Put the fillets in a frying pan or other shallow pan with enough wine barely to cover.

1 small onion, very finely chopped   a sprig of parsley

Add to the fish and cook very gently for about 6 mins or until the fish is opaque all through. Use a fish slice to lift it out carefully, put the fish in a hot serving dish and keep hot.

salt and pepper

Season the liquid and boil it hard until it is reduced to about half. Strain it through a fine sieve. Return it to the pan.

8 oz white grapes (250 g)   ½ pt double cream (250 ml)

Wash the grapes, skin, and remove the pips. Add to the wine together with the cream and boil gently until the sauce thickens.

1 oz butter (25 g)

Add to the sauce in small bits. Mix well and pour over the fish. Serve at once.

Stuffed fillets

The best fillets for stuffing are fairly thin ones like plaice or sole.

Cooking time 30 mins.
Temperature 190° C (375° F; G5).
Quantities for 4.

lemon stuffing, page 28 or bacon and   1 lb fillets (500 g)
  and nut stuffing, page 27

Skin the fillets and spread them on a flat surface with the skinned side uppermost. Spread with stuffing and roll up firmly. Put in a casserole or baking dish small enough to hold them snugly so that they keep each other in shape.

¼–½ pt fish stock, wine or cider   2 oz chopped mushrooms (50 g)
  (150–250 ml)

Sprinkle the mushrooms over the fish and add enough liquid to come about a quarter of the way up the fish. Cover and bake for 20 mins. Pour the liquid into a small saucepan and put the fish to keep hot.

¼ pt fresh double cream or soured cream (150 ml)

chopped parsley or other herbs

Add the cream to the stock and boil until the sauce thickens a little. Pour it over the fish, sprinkle with herbs and serve.

HOW TO COOK SMOKED FISH

Bloaters

Split them along the belly and open out flat. Grill for about 5 mins or until well heated through. Season with pepper and serve with a small knob of butter on each.

An alternative method is to poach them in water, then drain, remove from the bone and serve the fillets on hot buttered toast. Serve with lemon wedges.

Haddock, cod and similar fish

Smoked haddock is sold as fillets or on the bone. Smoked cod and other similar fish are usually sold as fillets. They are all cooked in the same way, see below.

Smoked Finnan haddock are small whole fish which are opened out and flattened before smoking.

Smokies or Arbroath smokies are small haddock cured and smoked whole.

Baked smoked haddock

Cooking time 20–30 mins. *Temperature* 220° C (425° F; G7).

Butter a casserole and put in the haddock, skin side down. Heat equal quantities of milk and water and when it is boiling pour it over the fish, using enough to cover. Put on the lid and cook until the fish is done enough to flake easily when tested at the thickest part.

Serve the fish with some of the cooking liquid poured over it and with a knob of butter on top. Serve with brown bread and butter or hot mashed potatoes.

Grilled smoked haddock

Brush the fish with melted butter, margarine or oil and grill until the flesh separates easily when tested. Spread with softened butter and serve hot with oatcakes and butter, or pour over it a sauce made by melting equal quantities of French mustard and butter.

Poached smoked haddock

Put the fish in a pan with milk just to cover, or use a mixture of half milk and half water.

Bring to the boil and then cook gently below boiling until the flesh flakes easily when tested. Lift out and keep hot.

Use the liquid to make a parsley sauce, or poach eggs in it and serve one on each portion of fish.

Smoked haddock flan

Cooking time about 1 hr.
Temperature 200° C (400° F, G6), then 190° C (375° F; G5).
Quantities for an 8 in (20 cm) flan.

short-crust pastry using 4 oz flour (100 g), or 6 oz (175 g) ready-made

Roll the pastry to line a flan ring or pie plate. Prick the bottom with a fork and line the flan with a piece of foil. Refrigerate for about 20 mins before baking at the higher temperature for about 20 mins, removing the foil for the last 5 mins.

4 oz smoked haddock fillet (125 g)

Remove any skin and cut the fish in slices.

1 medium-sized onion, finely chopped   1 oz butter (25 g)

Heat the butter in a small pan and fry the onion gently until it is tender but not browned. Spread in the bottom of the cooked flan case and put the fish on top of it.

lemon juice

Sprinkle over the fish.

2 eggs, lightly beaten $\frac{1}{4}$ pt milk (125 ml)
salt and pepper

Mix together and pour over the fish. Bake until the custard is set (about 40 mins). Serve warm or cold, garnished with

sliced tomato or olives.

Smoked haddock pancakes

Quantities for 8 pancakes (see recipe, page 37).

8 oz cooked smoked haddock fillets (250 g)

Remove any skin and flake the fish.

2 oz butter or margarine (50 g)   2 oz flour (50 g)

Melt the fat in a small saucepan and stir in the flour, cooking and stirring until it looks crumbly.

1 pt milk, or milk plus fish stock (600 ml)

Add to the pan and stir or whisk until the sauce is smooth and boiling. Boil gently for 5 mins.

2 cooked or canned sweet peppers   4 or more Tbs cream
salt and pepper   lemon juice

Remove any seeds and chop the peppers finely. Add to the sauce with cream and seasoning. Divide the sauce in two, keeping both halves hot. Add the fish to one half and heat to boiling, then keep hot while the pancakes are made. Pile the pancakes on top of one another, keeping them hot. To serve, put a spoonful of the filling on each, roll up and pack close together in a shallow baking dish. Pour the remaining sauce over the top and put the dish in a moderate oven for 15–20 mins to make sure the pancakes are hot. Garnish with

strips of red pepper, paprika pepper or chopped herbs.

Smoked haddock pie

Cooking time about 15 mins for the filling (prepare in advance); 30 mins for the pie.
Temperature 220° C (425° F; G7).
Quantities for 4.

1 lb smoked haddock fillets (500 g) $\frac{1}{2}$ pt milk (250 ml)

Poach the fish in the milk for about 10 mins, drain, keeping the milk. Make it up to $\frac{1}{2}$ pt (250 ml) with water. Flake the fish.

1 oz butter or margarine (25 g)   2 Tbs flour
1 tsp dry mustard

Heat the fat in a saucepan and add the flour. Mix and cook until it looks crumbly. Stir in the mustard. Add the milk and water mixture and stir or whisk until the sauce is smooth and boiling. Boil gently for 5 mins.

4 oz lean bacon rashers, chopped   1 Tbs chopped parsley
   (125 g)   pepper
1 hard-boiled egg, roughly chopped   1 tsp lemon juice

Add to the sauce together with the fish. Allow to cool. Put the mixture in a $1\frac{1}{2}$ pt (1 l) pie dish with a pie funnel in the centre. The funnel is advisable because something is needed to hold the pastry up. Do not fill the pie dish to the top with the fish mixture or it will boil over during baking.

8 oz puff pastry (250 g)   milk or beaten egg for brushing

Roll the pastry very thinly. Cut strips for the edge of the dish. Stick them on with egg or milk, brushing the top side as well. Put on the main piece of pastry, trim and slash the edges with a knife. Cut a slit in the centre, decorate with pastry trimmings, brush with milk or egg and bake until the pastry is brown and well risen. Serve hot.

Kippers or kippered herrings

The best kippers are a smoky golden colour and are usually known as 'oak smoked' kippers. Others are coloured bright brown; these are cured and smoked more quickly and consequently are cheaper and easier to buy. Kippers are sold on the bone or as fillets.

Boiled kippers

Place the kippers in a jug deep enough to take them with a little room to spare at the top. Pour in boiling water to cover them. Put a saucer on the jug, or some other lid, and stand the jug in a warm place for 5–10 mins, depending on the size of the kippers. Pour off the water and serve the kippers on hot plates with a small knob of butter on each and with lemon wedges.

Grilled kippers

To make the kippers plump and juicy, put them in a dish, pour hot water over them and leave 1–2 mins. Line the grill pan with foil (optional), put in the kippers skin side down and grill for 5–8 mins. Sprinkle with pepper, put a knob of butter on each and serve with lemon wedges.

The idea of the foil is to have a less smelly pan to wash up.

Kipper pasties

Cooking time 30 mins.
Temperature 220° C (425° F; G7).
Quantities for 4 pasties.

2 medium-sized kippers or the equivalent in fillets

Grill or boil the kippers. Cool and flake, removing all bones.

1 oz butter or margarine (25 g)   1 oz flour (3 Tbs or 25 g)
¼ pt milk (150 ml)

Melt the fat in a small pan, add the flour, mix and cook until it looks crumbly. Stir or whisk in the milk until the sauce boils.

2 oz grated cheese (50 g)   ½ Tbs lemon juice
pinch of pepper

Add to the sauce together with the flaked kipper. Leave to become cold.

short-crust pastry using 8 oz flour (250 g), or 12 oz (350 g) ready-made

Divide the pastry into four pieces, form each into a round and roll out to a circle about 6 in (15 cm) in diameter. Cover one half of each round with some kipper filling. Moisten the edges with water, fold over and press the edges together to seal well. Bake until the pastry is well browned. Serve hot or cold.

Kipper quiche

Cooking time 35 mins.
Temperature 220° C (425° F; G7).
Quantities for a 7 in (18 cm) quiche.

short-crust pastry using 4 oz flour (100 g), or 6 oz (175 g) ready-made

Roll the pastry and line a flan ring or pie plate. Put it in the refrigerator while the filling is being prepared.

8 oz kipper fillets (250 g), or 1 lb on the bone (500 g)

Boil the kippers. Remove all skin and bone and flake the flesh. Cool and then put it in the pastry case.

1 egg   4 Tbs milk or cream (60 ml)
1 Tbs French mustard   pinch of cayenne pepper

Whisk together and pour over the kippers.

2 oz grated strong cheese (50 g)

Sprinkle over the top of the filling and bake until set. Serve hot or cold.

ALTERNATIVE

After sprinkling on the cheese, add a few stoned black olives.

LEFTOVERS

If there are one or more complete portions of fish in a sauce this can be frozen for future use. Small amounts of plainly cooked fish can be used in many ways. The following suitable recipes will be found in the index:

Egg and haddock toasted sandwiches
Fish cocktail
Fish mousse
Open sandwiches
Sandwich fillings
Smoked haddock flan
Smoked haddock omelet
Smoked haddock pancakes.

SHELLFISH

Crab

Crabs can be up to 12 in (30 cm) across, but a medium-sized one of about 8 in (20 cm) is usually considered the best buy. Buying by weight is the best way; they should be heavy for their size. About 2 lb (1 kg) is a good weight and enough for 3 people, while 2½–3 lb (1½ kg) will serve 4 people. Crabs are usually sold cooked, but it is quite easy to cook them for yourself. Frozen crab meat is good value.

BOILING

Put the crab in plenty of fast boiling salted water and do not allow the water to stop boiling. Allow 15 mins per lb (½ kg). Remove from the water and put in a cool place to cool rapidly.

PREPARING

Put the cooked crab on its back and pull off the claws and legs. Crack these with a small hammer or nutcrackers and extract the meat. Still with the crab on its back, take hold of the centre and pull it right out of the surrounding shell. This part will be found to have the gills attached to it, looking like long, hairy fronds. These should be discarded. The mouth and stomach will still be attached to the back shell. Remove and discard these. Use a spoon to scoop the meat from the shell. Pick out the brown meat and the meat from the leg sockets. Put all together in a basin.

If the shell is required for serving dressed crab, break away the inner part, leaving just a rim round the outer edge, like a dish. Wash and dry.

Dressed crab

Quantities for 3.

1 medium-sized crab, about 2 lb (1 kg)	2 Tbs oil
hard-boiled egg	2 Tbs vinegar
lemon and parsley	salt, mustard and cayenne pepper

Prepare the crab as described above. Mix the flesh with the vinegar and oil and season well. Wash and dry the shell and put the meat back in it, decorating with lines of chopped hard-boiled egg and chopped parsley, and finally with pieces of lemon.

ALTERNATIVE

Instead of serving the crab in the shell, arrange it in individual nests of lettuce leaves or in small scallop shells.

Crab fondue

Cooking time a few mins. *Quantities* for 4.

8 oz Caerphilly cheese, coarsely grated (250 g)	1 tsp lemon juice
5 Tbs dry white wine	3–4 oz canned, fresh or frozen crab meat (75–125 g)

Drain and flake the crab meat, removing any bony bits. Frozen crab meat may be used frozen or partially thawed. Put all the ingredients in a pan and heat slowly, stirring until the cheese melts. Serve in small hot dishes.

bread, rolls or toast

Serve separately, the fondue to be eaten with the aid of a fork and pieces of bread or toast. Follow with a salad.

Crab, hot buttered

Cooking time 5 mins. *Quantities* for 3.

1 medium-sized crab, about 2 lb (1 kg), or 5–6 oz of crab meat (150–175 g)	2 tsp lemon juice
2 tsp vinegar	pinch of cayenne pepper
	2 tsp chopped parsley

1 Tbs cream
½ tsp anchovy essence

3 Tbs fresh breadcrumbs
½ oz butter (15 g)

Remove the crab meat from its shell as described on page 146. Combine the meat with the other ingredients and heat it in a saucepan.

3 slices hot toast   paprika pepper

Serve the crab in small hot dishes, decorate with paprika pepper, and serve the toast separately.

Lobster

When lobsters are caught the shell is blue-black in colour, sometimes brownish, but when they are cooked it turns bright red.

A variety of spiny lobster is less frequently caught. This has a shell thickly covered with spines of varying sizes. It is equally good to eat.

The average size of lobster sold in Britain is 1-4 lb (½-2 kg), though many think the smaller 12-14 oz (350-400 g) ones have the finest flavour of all.

A lobster weighing 1-1½ lb (½-¾ kg) is sufficient for two portions; for larger ones allow 1 lb (½ kg) per portion. Whether they are sold raw or cooked, they should be heavy in relation to their size. The large claws are the tastiest part of any lobster.

Lobsters are most frequently sold ready cooked but are also sold 'live', though the latter are nearer dead than alive by the time they reach city shops.

The method of judging the freshness of a cooked lobster is to test the curled up tail, which should be stiff to straighten out and should spring back sharply when released.

Imported canned lobster is useful for making salads, cocktails, patties and similar dishes. The flavour is not the same as that of a fresh lobster but it makes appetising dishes.

TO BOIL LOBSTER

Live lobsters should be handled by lifting them by the back of the thoracic shell and keeping well away from the claws. Boil enough water to cover the lobster generously, about 1 gallon (4 l) per lobster. Drop the lobsters in one at a time and see the water comes back to boiling each time. Use wooden tongs or spoons to keep them immersed for the first couple of minutes. Remove from the water and put in a cold place to cool quickly.

COOKING TIMES

After the water boils allow 20 mins for a 1 lb (½ kg) lobster, up to 45 mins for a 3-4 lb (1½-2 kg) size. Avoid over-cooking as this makes the meat stringy and tough. If it is to have further cooking before it is served, for example in a sauce, it is better to err on the side of under-cooking.

Lobster, cold or dressed

Wipe the lobster thoroughly with a clean damp cloth. Twist off the legs and claws. With the back of a strong knife knock off the tips of the claws and drain away any water. Then tap several times round the broadest part of each claw and the shell should fall apart. Hold the pincers with the mobile claw facing away from you and cut the cartilage between them, using the point of a sharp knife. This will enable the meat to be drawn out in one piece. When serving cold lobster it is usual to leave the meat in the claws for the diner to remove, which is easy if the claws have been prepared properly. The legs are also served intact. Place the body on a board with the back uppermost and use a strong, sharp knife to cut along the centre of the body from the junction of head and body to the tail. Turn the lobster round and cut the head in half.

Remove the intestinal cord from the body, then the stomach, and discard these. Remove and discard the gills but keep the green liver.

To serve, arrange the halves of lobster on a bed of lettuce or other salad greens and arrange the claws round them. Serve with mayonnaise or French dressing, and French bread or rolls.

Lobster vol-au-vents

Cooking time about 30 mins.
Temperature 230° C (450° F; G8).
Quantities for 4 vol-au-vents.
4 good-sized vol-au-vent cases

These can be baked in advance and re-heated for service, but are best when freshly cooked. They can be ready-made ones from the baker or from the freezer, or make your own from puff pastry. For shaping and baking, see page 43.

FILLING

5–6 oz cooked or canned lobster meat (150–175 g)

If canned lobster is used, drain, keeping the liquid. Cut the large pieces of flesh in slices and put all the flesh on a dish. Refrigerate until you are ready to make the filling.

½ oz butter (15 g)
¼ pt double cream (150 ml)
2 Tbs fish stock

1–2 egg yolks
2 Tbs brandy, warmed

Put the butter in a small frying pan. Beat the egg yolks and cream, using 2 egg yolks for a thickish sauce. Heat the butter and cook the pieces of lobster gently until they are heated through. Ignite the brandy and pour it over the lobster. When the flames have died down add the fish stock and bring to the boil. Then add the cream and egg yolk and cook very gently until the sauce thickens. Fill the hot vol-au-vents and put on the caps. If there is any surplus sauce, pour it over the vol-au-vents.

ALTERNATIVE

Instead of lobster use crawfish tails or a mixture of cooked mussels and prawns.

Mussels à la marinière

Cooking time 15 mins. *Quantities* for 4.

4 pt mussels (2¼ l)

Discard any shells which are even slightly opened. Wash the mussels in several changes of water, scrubbing off as much sand and weed as possible.

To open the shells, put them in a large pan with a very little water, just enough to make some steam. Put the lid on and cook gently until all the shells have opened. Avoid over-cooking or the mussels will shrivel. Strain the liquid through a piece of clean white cloth and keep it for the sauce. If there is any weed inside the shells remove it. It is usual to serve the mussels still in the shells. Make the strained stock up to ¾ pt (400 ml) with water.

1 Tbs chopped parsley	2 oz butter (50 g)
1 tsp chopped chives or finely chopped onion	3 Tbs fine fresh breadcrumbs

Put these in a pan with the liquid and mussels, bring to the boil and simmer for 2 mins.

brown bread and butter or rolls and butter to serve with it	2 Tbs lemon juice or white wine

Sprinkle the lemon or wine over the mussels and serve them in soup plates, with the liquid. Provide plates for the empty shells and a soup spoon for the last of the liquid.

Prawns

These are usually sold cooked and unshelled, canned or frozen. Raw prawns are cooked by boiling in sea water or heavily salted water (see boiled herrings), for 2–3 mins or longer for large ones. Have the water boiling, drop in the live prawns and do not allow to go off the boil. Drain and leave to cool.

Fresh prawns, cooked or raw, have a distinct sea-clean smell and do not attract flies. Stale prawns are pale and clammy with a pungent smell.

The best way of serving prawns is plain, with brown bread and butter and possibly pepper and some lemon juice; but they can be served in a variety of ways, including fish cocktail, page 74, and the following recipes.

Prawns or scampi flambé with cream sauce

Cooking time a few mins. *Quantities* for 4.

2 oz butter (50 g) 12 oz shelled prawns or scampi (350 g)

Melt the butter in a frying pan and heat the fish in it.

4 Tbs brandy (60 ml)

Pour into the pan and give it a few seconds to warm up. Ignite the brandy and shake the pan.

pepper grated nutmeg
2 Tbs lemon juice

When the flames have died down season the fish and add the lemon juice.

½ pt double cream (250 ml)

Add to the fish and simmer until the sauce thickens.

boiled rice, page 332, using 8 oz raw rice (250 g)

Serve the prawns or scampi on a bed of rice, garnished with parsley or other herbs.

Prawn pancakes

Cooking time 15–20 mins.
Quantities for 8 pancakes, see page 37.

8 oz shelled prawns (250 g) grated nutmeg
¼ pt soured cream (150 ml) salt and pepper
2 tsp lemon juice

Put all in a small pan and bring slowly to the boil.

2 tsp potato flour 2 Tbs sherry

Blend to a smooth cream and stir into the prawn mixture. Stir until it thickens and put to keep hot while the pancakes are made. Fill each as it is made and put to keep hot, in a fireproof dish.

melted butter

When all are ready, brush the tops with melted butter and crisp them under the grill or in a hot oven.

Scallops, baked

Scallops are usually sold already opened, but if this has not been done, prepare them either by heating gently until the shells open, or by cutting off the flat shell. Remove any black parts and the beard, leaving only the white and orange parts.

Cooking time 30 mins.
Temperature 180° C (350° F; G4).
Quantities Allow 2 scallops per person.

Season the scallops with salt and pepper, leaving them in the concave shell or putting them in a small shallow baking dish. Sprinkle them with lemon juice and cover the tops with fresh breadcrumbs. Dot with butter, cover with a piece of foil and bake. Serve with wedges of lemon and bread and butter.

Scampi

These are sold cooked, in the shells or shelled, and also frozen. The fleshy tails are the part eaten and, when cooked, are pale pink. Frozen raw scampi should be thawed before separating and then poached 3–4 mins in salted water, avoiding over-cooking. Serve in the same way as prawns, or coat with batter and fry in oil, or serve in a curry sauce.

Shrimps

There are two kinds of shrimps: the pink shrimp is reddish-grey when raw, bright pink when cooked, and looks very like a small prawn. The brown shrimp is grey speckled with brown when raw and becomes pinkish, speckled brown, when cooked.

They are usually sold cooked and shelled, also canned, frozen and as potted shrimps.

Raw shrimps are cooked by putting them live into boiling sea water or heavily salted water (see boiled herrings), and boiling rapidly for 2–3 mins. Drain and cool. Shelling these tiny fish requires experience and is easier when they are fresh. Fresh shrimps have a clean smell and do not attract flies.

One pint (600 ml) of shrimps yields about 3½–4 oz (100 g) when shelled. They are usually served plain in the same way as prawns; or on an open sandwich; or cooked by any of the methods used for prawns. They are also excellent to use as a garnish for any white fish dish or added to the sauce served with it.

See also avocado pear, page 71; eggs Raymond, page 105.

Shellfish flan

Cooking time about 45 mins.
Temperature 220° C (425° F; G7) for the pastry; 190° C (375° F; G5) for the filling.
Quantities for an 8 in (20 cm) flan.

short-crust pastry made with 4 oz flour (100 g), or use 6–8 oz (175–250 g) ready-made

Roll the pastry thinly to line a flan ring or pie plate. Press a layer of foil inside and refrigerate for about 20 mins before baking for 15–20 mins. Remove the foil when the pastry is set to allow the inside to dry a little.

1 oz butter (25 g)   2 Tbs finely chopped onion

Heat the butter in a small pan and cook the onion in it until tender.

4 oz cooked, canned or frozen crab, shrimps, lobster, or prawns (100 g) or a mixture

Add to the onion and cook gently for a couple of minutes.

2 Tbs sherry or dry white wine

Add and mix in. Remove from the heat and cool a little.

2 eggs, beaten   6 Tbs cream (90 ml)
1 Tbs concentrated tomato purée   ¼ tsp salt
pinch of pepper

Combine with the fish mixture and pour into the cooked flan case.

1 oz grated Parmesan cheese (25 g), or 2 oz other cheese (50 g)

Sprinkle this on top of the filling and bake until it is set and lightly browned, about 25 mins.

Serve hot or cold.

8. Meat

Although most kinds of meat are available throughout the year, some have seasons when they are at their best. These are:

English beef – October to March
English lamb – July to September
New Zealand lamb – January to June
Scotch beef – September to December
Scotch lamb – July to October
Welsh lamb – July to September.

To know which cuts to buy for which method of cooking is important, particularly if you want to buy and cook as economically as possible. As a guide in helping you to choose suitable cuts I have listed these at the beginning of each recipe section. It is very difficult for the shopper to tell whether a particular cut is good quality so the choice of butcher is very important. It is usually worth while paying a little more for reliable quality rather than to risk sometimes being disappointed in the final result. This applies particularly to the more expensive cuts for roasting, frying and grilling. If you are going to do long, slow cooking in a casserole the quality of the meat you start with is less important.

Buying frozen meat and meat for the freezer

For owners of freezers there are three types of meat available. First, the small pieces of quick frozen meat such as steaks and chops, sold for cooking without thawing and usually with cooking instructions supplied. This meat will have been properly matured before freezing and should be tender when cooked.

Then there is the meat frozen in carcass form and cut up for sale either by the vendor of bulk foods for the freezer, or by the butcher, who sells it either still frozen or thawed. This meat is frozen soon after killing and has not had the usual hanging and maturing. It is best completely thawed before cooking and if kept in the refrigerator for 2–3 days after thawing it will improve in quality.

The third possibility is to buy well-hung meat from a good butcher and freeze it yourself in the cuts and sizes you want. Wrap it in foil or put it in freezer bags. Most butchers offer suitable meat for freezer owners. This sort of matured meat can be cooked with or without thawing, though it is usually better to thaw large pieces before cooking them.

Thawing frozen meat

The ideal method is to thaw the meat in its original wrapper and in the refrigerator. This takes considerably longer than thawing at room temperature but slow thawing gives better results because there is less loss of juice.

When thawed at room temperature joints of meat can appear to be thawed while the inside is still frozen and this makes it difficult to assess the cooking time required. Always thaw meat for longer than you estimate is needed, rather than skimp the time. It will not harm the meat to keep it in the refrigerator for a while after it has thawed completely, and sometimes it is definitely beneficial.

APPROXIMATE THAWING TIMES

	Steaks and Chops 1 in ($2\frac{1}{2}$ cm) thick	Joints
in the refrigerator	12–18 hrs	3–5 hrs per lb ($\frac{1}{2}$ kg) up to 4lb (2 kg); 5–7 hrs per lb if larger
at room temperature approx. 15° C (60° F)	2–3 hrs	1–2 hrs per lb ($\frac{1}{2}$ kg) for small joints; 2–3 hrs per lb if larger

In an emergency joints can be thawed in running cold water or in front of an electric fan, when the time for thawing will be approximately $\frac{1}{2}$–$\frac{3}{4}$ hr per lb ($\frac{1}{2}$ kg).

Storing meat

Always keep fresh or thawed meat in the coolest possible place, preferably in a refrigerator. Put the meat on a plate with a loose piece of foil or polythene on top. Wrap cooked meat closely in foil or polythene or put it in a polythene box.

A GUIDE TO SAFE STORAGE TIMES

Naturally these depend on how fresh the meat is when purchased, and also on the kind of meat; lamb and beef keep better than pork, veal or offal.

Raw joints. 2 days in a cold larder; 4–5 days in the refrigerator.

Steak and chops. 1 day in the larder; 3–4 days in the refrigerator.

Stewing meat. 1 day in the larder; 2–3 days in the refrigerator.

Minced meat. Use the same day or keep 1 day in the refrigerator.

Offal. Use the same day or keep 1–2 days in the refrigerator.

Sausages. Use the same day, or keep 3–4 days in the refrigerator.

Sliced bacon. 2–3 days in the larder; 7–10 days in the refrigerator.

Cooked joints. 2–3 days in the larder; 3–5 days in the refrigerator. Remove in time to let the meat come to room temperature before serving.

Sliced cooked meat (from the shop and not date-stamped). Use the same day or keep 1 day in the refrigerator.

Sliced cooked meat (home-cooked). 2–3 days in the refrigerator.

Cooked casseroles or leftovers. 2–3 days in the refrigerator. Boil up before serving.

Pâtés and spreads. 1–2 days in the refrigerator, depending on the kind; pâtés keep better than spreads containing sauces and salad dressings. Remove from the refrigerator some time before serving.

Meat pies (from the shop). Use the same day.

Meat pies (home-made). 2–3 days in the refrigerator.

As meat can be a source of food poisoning the way it is cooked and the way it is handled and stored after cooking is very important. Any under-done meat, but especially boned and rolled meats, pork or sausages are a potential hazard. For safety, meat should be cooked right through to the centre. When meat is to be served cold, it should be put in a cool place (not the refrigerator), until it is quite cold, then stored in the refrigerator and not brought out until half an hour or so before it is to be served, just long enough to let it come back to room temperature.

If cooked meat, including a casserole, is being re-heated it must be brought up to boiling point to make it safe, and preferably kept boiling for 10–15 mins. Just warming up is very dangerous.

Once canned meat has been opened it should be treated in the same way as other cooked meat.

Freezing cooked meat dishes

Frozen meat can be used to make cooked dishes and then re-frozen.

Stews and casseroles are amongst the most satisfactory for home freezing, most recipes being suitable for storing for up to a month. Be careful with the quantities of seasoning, including garlic and onion; these tend to become stronger in flavour with storage. Avoid over-cooking meat before freezing; it will have more cooking during thawing and re-heating. To reduce the original cooking time by about ½ hr is sufficient.

After cooking, cool the meat as quickly as possible, but not in the refrigerator. It is better to freeze the mixture in smallish containers, maximum 2 pt (1 l); amounts larger than this take too long to thaw. Use polythene bags or boxes for freezing.

When thawing and heating casseroles and similar dishes, small quantities of not more than a pint (½ l) can be heated over a direct gentle heat, stirring frequently and bringing right up to the boil, which will take about 45 mins. Alternatively, heat the meat in a casserole in a hot oven – 200° C (400° F; G6) – for ¾–1 hr for 1–2 pt sizes (½–1 l). Heat until bubbling.

Sliced cooked meat should be wrapped to exclude air. To thaw it, remove from the freezer to the refrigerator 3–4 hrs before serving.

Meat cakes and rissoles can be frozen either before or after frying; in the latter case heat for 20–30 mins in a hot oven before serving; raw ones fry while still frozen, 5–10 mins depending on thickness.

For freezing meat pies, see page 39.

Carving

To become a good carver requires a certain amount of experience, but to start right is important. The knife should be really sharp, the kind being less important than the sharpness. Many people use a medium-sized cook's knife rather than a traditional carving knife. Always sharpen the knife before starting to carve. Some people find it easier to carve well with an electric carving knife.

Joints are always easier to carve if they have been allowed to rest for about 15 mins after cooking to allow a certain amount of firming up to take place.

Meat is usually more tender if it is cut across the fibres. If cut with the fibres their shape can be easily seen and this way makes tougher chewing.

Carving should be a sawing action, with long, light strokes backwards and forwards, done as evenly as possible to give complete slices. Use a fork with a thumb guard and, if possible, do the cutting away from yourself.

Exceptions to the rule of cutting across the grain are: *saddle of mutton* which is carved parallel with the backbone; *leg of lamb or mutton* which is sometimes carved parallel with the bone.

ROAST BEEF

SUITABLE CUTS

For high-temperature roasting use sirloin or a large piece of rump or fillet steak.

For low-temperature roasting use topside, thick flank, top rib, fore rib, back rib, leg of mutton cut, brisket, and all anonymous boned and rolled cuts.

HIGH-TEMPERATURE ROASTING 220° C (425° F; G7).

Times: 15 mins per lb ($\frac{1}{2}$ kg) and 15 mins over for rare meat; 20 mins per lb ($\frac{1}{2}$ kg) and 20 mins over for medium done.

LOW-TEMPERATURE ROASTING 160° C (325° F; G3).

Times: unboned ribs and thin pieces 40 mins per lb ($\frac{1}{2}$ kg) for medium or well-done; boned and rolled and thick pieces 45 mins per lb ($\frac{1}{2}$ kg) for medium or well-done.

QUANTITIES

With bone, allow $\frac{1}{2}$–$\frac{3}{4}$ lb (250–350 g) per person; no bone, allow 4–6 oz (125–175 g) per person.

METHOD

Calculate the cooking time so that the meat will be done about $\frac{1}{4}$–$\frac{1}{2}$ hr before you want to serve it. It is easier to carve if allowed to rest for a while and this gives you time to cook the Yorkshire pudding which needs a higher temperature than the meat and allows time to finish browning roast potatoes, often necessary when low-temperature roasting is used; there is also the gravy to be prepared.

For roasting, put the meat on a rack, fat side uppermost so that it becomes self-basting. Use either a rack in the roasting pan or put the meat on one of the oven racks with a pan below for the drippings. Vegetables for roasting can either be placed in the pan or cooked in a separate pan, see Vegetables. To prevent fat from splashing the oven when high-temperature roasting is used, the meat can be wrapped in polyester cooking film, or use a roasting bag. This is not necessary with low-temperature roasting.

There is no need to baste the meat unless for purposes of flavour, for example, basting with wine or a herb marinade.

ACCOMPANIMENTS

Thin or thickened gravy, see Sauces. Fresh grated horseradish or horseradish sauce; mustard; Yorkshire pudding; roast potatoes, roast parsnips, a green vegetable or salad.

Yorkshire pudding

Cooking time 30–45 mins.
Temperature 230° C (450° F; G8).
Quantities for 4–6.

4 oz plain flour (¾ c or 100 g)   ½ tsp salt

Put in a basin and make a well in the centre.

2 eggs   about ½ pt milk (250 ml)

Break the eggs into the well and start stirring from the centre, gradually working in the flour and adding half the milk. Beat very thoroughly and then add the rest of the milk to make a thin batter.

ALTERNATIVE METHOD

Put all the ingredients in the goblet of the electric blender and process at high speed for one minute.

1 oz dripping or other fat (25 g)

The pudding can be cooked in one large pan, a shallow pan about 8 × 10 in (20 × 25 cm), or in large patty tins. Put the dripping or fat in the tin and put it in the oven to get really hot. Pour in the batter and put the tin near the top of the oven; bake until risen and brown. The cooking time can be varied to give a soft inside or one crisp all through.

FRIED AND GRILLED BEEF

SUITABLE CUTS

Fillet, rump or sirloin. Châteaubriand steak is a thick slice of fillet.
Entrecôte steak is from the upper part of a sirloin, without the bone.
Tournedos is a small, thick piece of fillet.
Minute steaks are very thin pieces of steak.

QUANTITIES

Allow 6–8 oz per portion (175–250 g): 4 oz for a thin steak (125 g).

Grilling

COOKING TIMES

	Rare	Medium	Well-done
½ in thick (1 cm)	7 mins	9 mins	11 mins
1 in thick (2½ cm)	10 mins	12 mins	14 mins
Frozen steaks			
½ in thick (1 cm)	9 mins	11 mins	13 mins

These times are only a guide and will vary with the type of grill you have. If there are no manufacturer's instructions use the above times to begin with and adjust them as necessary.

TO GRILL

Score the fat round a sirloin steak to keep the meat flat, taking the cuts right through to the beginning of the meat itself; alternatively, remove the fat. Brush the steaks with oil or a basting sauce and pre-heat the grill. Cook the steak under a fierce heat for 1 minute each side, then reduce the heat slightly or move the meat further away from the grill and continue cooking, turning the meat every 2 minutes. Season with salt and pepper and serve.

Frozen steaks should be cooked under a moderate heat until they have thawed, then put them closer to a fierce heat for the final browning.

ACCOMPANIMENTS

Grilled tomatoes and mushrooms; watercress; chip potatoes; green salad, baked jacket potatoes, maître d'hôtel butter; anchovy butter; garlic butter; grated fresh horseradish or horseradish sauce; French or English mustard; Worcester sauce; Béarnaise sauce.

Frying

COOKING TIMES

2 mins for a very thin steak; 5–15 mins for others, depending on the thickness of the steak and whether you like it rare, medium or well-done.

TO FRY

Heat a little butter, other fat or oil in a heavy frying pan and when it is hot put in the steak. Brown for about 1 min on each side. Keep cooking over a high heat, turning the meat every minute or two, but avoid over-cooking or the meat will be tough and dry. Even when well-done it should still feel springy when pressed gently with the back of a fork. Serve on a hot dish.

Swill out the pan with a little liquid such as stock, wine or lemon juice. Let the liquid boil for a minute or two to dissolve all the tasty sediment from the bottom of the pan and pour this over the meat.

Beef Strogonoff

Cooking time 10–15 mins. *Quantities* for 4.

1 lb thinly sliced rump, sirloin or fillet steak (500 g)

Beat the steak well to flatten it. Cut it into strips about 2 in (5 cm) long and $\frac{1}{4}$ in (6 mm) wide.

1 medium-sized onion   6 oz button mushrooms (175 g)

Skin the onion and slice it very finely. Wash, dry and slice the mushrooms.

2 oz butter (50 g)

Heat half the butter in a frying pan and cook the onions, stirring frequently until they are lightly browned. Add the mushrooms and fry for a few minutes. Remove the onions and mushrooms and keep hot. Add the remaining butter to the pan and when it is melted add the beef and fry it for 3–5 mins, stirring frequently. Put back the onions and mushrooms and mix.

$\frac{1}{2}$ pt soured cream (250 ml)   salt and pepper

Add the cream and season well. Cook for 1 min and serve with rice or noodles and a green salad.

Fondue Bourguignonne

Quantities for 4.

1–1$\frac{1}{2}$ lb lean steak (500–700 g)

Use either fillet, rump or sirloin steak, well hung. Trim off any fat (allow for this when buying the steak). Cut the meat in $\frac{1}{2}$–$\frac{3}{4}$ in (1–2 cm) cubes and arrange it on small plates or on a fondue plate. Garnish with any greenery available, or with pickles.

1–1$\frac{1}{2}$ pt peanut or groundnut oil ($\frac{3}{4}$–1 l)

Put oil in the fondue pot to make it just less than half full. Heat to 190° C (375° F). Transfer the pot to the fondue burner or hotplate on the dining table. This must be able to supply enough heat to keep the oil up to temperature.

Provide fondue forks for each person, and a knife and fork. The cubes of meat are speared with the fondue fork and put in the oil until browned; then transfer them to the plate and put another piece of meat in the oil.

ACCOMPANIMENTS

Worcester sauce or soy sauce; horseradish sauce; Béarnaise sauce; garlic butter; fresh French bread or crisp rolls; mixed green salad or tomato and sweet pepper salad.

Put a portion of the chosen sauces into small dishes, one of each for each. The diners dip their meat into the chosen sauce.

Grilled marinated beef steak

For each pound (500 g) of steak allow 1 Tbs olive oil, 1 Tbs vinegar and pepper. Mix these together and let the steak soak in them for 24 hrs, turning the meat over once or twice. Then grill as for plain steak, page 160.

Kebabs

Cooking time about 10 mins. *Quantities* for 4.

1 lb sirloin or fillet steak (500 g)	salt and black pepper
sugar	2 cloves garlic or garlic salt

Cut the meat in cubes of a suitable size for your kebab skewers and grill, about 1 in (2½ cm) is an average. Sprinkle the meat with salt and pepper. Rub this in and rub well with the crushed garlic cloves or garlic salt. Sprinkle with sugar.

1 oz butter (25 g)	2 small onions finely chopped
2 Tbs lemon juice	2 Tbs sugar
1 tsp soy sauce	

Melt the butter and lightly fry the onion until it begins to brown. Add the remaining ingredients and heat without boiling.

Thread the meat on skewers, put it in a shallow dish and pour the sauce over it, basting to coat well, then grill. Remove from the skewers as each portion is served.

ACCOMPANIMENTS

Potatoes and a salad. Béarnaise sauce or any of the basting liquid left over.

Steak Diane

Cooking time 5 mins. *Quantities* for 4.

1 lb fillet steak (500 g) cut ¼ in (6 mm) thick	1 oz butter (25 g)
	2 Tbs oil

Heat the butter and oil in a frying pan until the butter begins to change colour.

Fry the steaks for 1–2 mins each side. Remove from the pan and put to keep hot. Turn the heat down under the pan.

| 2 Tbs Worcester sauce | 1 Tbs lemon juice |

Add to the pan, stir well and heat.

| 1 Tbs very finely chopped onion | 2 tsp chopped parsley |

Add to the pan and simmer for a minute. Pour over the steaks and serve with

potatoes or fresh rolls, and a salad.

Steak Mirabeau

Cooking time 8–10 mins. *Quantities* for 4.

| 1 oz butter (25 g) | ½ tsp anchovy essence |

Soften the butter, without melting, and work in the anchovy essence, using a pestle and mortar if possible. Form into a small pat and divide into four pieces. Put in the refrigerator until required.

| 8 anchovy fillets | stoned green olives |
| fresh tarragon leaves | |

Rinse the anchovy fillets in warm water and drain them well. Wash and drain the tarragon leaves.

| 4 small steaks, fillet, rump or sirloin | olive oil |

Brush the steaks with oil and grill them under a fierce heat, turning once to brown both sides. Cook until done to your liking. Serve on hot plates with a pat of the anchovy butter on each steak. Garnish with the anchovy fillets, olives and tarragon leaves. Serve with

boiled or sauté potatoes and a salad.

BEEF CASSEROLES, STEWS AND PIES

SUITABLE CUTS

Blade, chuck, leg, shin, shoulder steak, skirt, thin flank or anonymous stewing or braising steak.

Beef Bourguignon

Cooking time $2\frac{1}{4}$ hrs. *Quantities* for 4.

2 oz butter (50 g)
1 medium-sized onion, sliced
3 rashers bacon, chopped

Heat the butter in a saucepan or casserole and fry the onion and bacon in it gently until brown.

1 lb beef (500 g)

Trim off excess fat and cut the meat in small pieces. Use a perforated spoon to remove the bacon and onion from the pan. Add the meat and fry brown.

2 Tbs flour

Sprinkle over the meat and cook until it browns.

$\frac{1}{2}$ pt stock (250 ml)
2 oz mushrooms (50 g)
1 tsp salt
1 Tbs red wine
a bouquet garni
$\frac{1}{4}$ tsp freshly ground pepper

Slice large mushrooms, leave small ones whole. Stir the stock into the meat, return the bacon and onion, and add the other ingredients. Cover and cook slowly for 2 hrs, on top or in a slow oven.

Braised steak with soured cream

Cooking time $1\frac{1}{2}$ hrs. *Quantities* for 4.

4 portions chuck steak
1–2 oz lard (25–50 g)
2 onions, chopped

Use a sauté pan with a lid or a shallow saucepan or similar cooking utensil. Heat the lard and brown the meat in it. Remove and fry the onions until they begin to brown.

salt and pepper
1 Tbs French mustard
$\frac{1}{4}$–$\frac{1}{2}$ tsp grated nutmeg
water or stock

Add to the pan using enough water or stock to half cover the onions. Return the meat. Cover and cook slowly until the meat is tender, adding more liquid as required, but avoid making much gravy. If preferred, the cooking may be done in a slow to moderate oven.

1 Tbs flour
$\frac{1}{4}$ pt soured cream (150 ml)

Lift out the meat and keep it hot. Mix the flour smoothly with the cream. Add to the pan and stir until the sauce boils. Boil gently for a few minutes. Return the meat to make sure it is well heated before serving.

Casserole with olives

Cooking time 1½–2 hrs.
Temperature 150° C (300° F; G2).
Quantities for 4.

1½ lb stewing steak (700 g)   1 clove garlic, skinned
1 oz fat (25 g) or 2 Tbs oil

Trim off surplus fat and cut the meat in small pieces. Heat the fat or oil in a casserole or frying pan and fry the garlic for a couple of minutes. Lift out the garlic and discard it. Add the meat and fry until brown.

3 oz stuffed olives, sliced (75 g)   1 tsp salt
½ a red or green pepper, fresh or   about ½ pt tomato juice (250 ml)
  canned, sliced   2 sprigs fresh thyme or 1 tsp dried
                                          thyme

For the olives use ones stuffed with pimentos or with anchovy. Add to the meat together with the other ingredients. If sprigs of thyme are used, tie these in a bunch using white cotton and remove before serving the casserole. Add dried thyme about ½ hr before the end of cooking time. Use enough tomato juice almost to cover the meat. Put on the lid and cook gently until the meat is tender.

Casserole with seven herbs

Cooking time 3 hrs or longer.
Temperature 120–150° C (250–300° F; G½–1).
Quantities for 4.

1 lb lean stewing steak, cut in pieces   3 Tbs flour
  (500 g)   1 tsp salt
pepper

Mix the flour and seasoning and toss the meat in this until it is coated well. Set aside.

2 oz fat (50 g) or 4 Tbs oil   1 clove garlic, skinned

Heat the fat or oil in a casserole or frying pan and fry the garlic for a minute, remove and discard. Add the meat and fry until it is well browned all over.

1 lb mixed vegetables (500 g)

This can be made up with any vegetables available, carrots, onions, turnips (not too much), celery, sweet peppers, mushrooms, fresh peas or beans, to mention some possibilities. The vegetables should be washed, peeled when necessary and cut fairly small, either slicing or dicing them according to the kind. Add to the meat and fry for a minute or so longer, stirring all the time.

½–¾ pt stock or water (250–400 ml), or use some beer, wine or cider with water or stock	1 bay leaf (small or half a large) 1 sprig each of thyme, parsley and marjoram

Stir the liquid into the meat and vegetables, adding just enough to moisten well, remembering that more liquid will come from the vegetables during cooking. Tie the herbs in a bunch, or in muslin, and add to the centre of the mixture. If a frying pan has been used, now transfer the mixture to a casserole. Cover and cook slowly until the meat is tender. The longer the cooking the better the flavour. If you are going to cook the casserole for more than 3 hrs, use the lower temperature.

chopped basil or chervil	chopped lemon balm or lovage leaves

Mix the chosen herbs and sprinkle them over the top of the casserole at serving time.

If you are using dried herbs, do not add at the beginning of cooking but stir them in about ½ hr before the end of the cooking time. Remove herb sprigs before serving the casserole.

Curry

This looks a mess when you start cooking it but by the end it has a thick creamy sauce, the cottage cheese having thickened it without the need for any flour.

Cooking time 1½–2 hrs. *Quantities* for 4.

1½ lb stewing steak (700 g)

Trim off surplus fat and cut the meat in pieces, not very small.

4 Tbs oil	3 onions, sliced

Heat the oil in a saucepan and fry the onions until they begin to brown.

1 crushed clove of garlic 1½ tsp salt	2 Tbs curry powder, more or less 4 Tbs lemon juice

Stir in the curry powder and then the other ingredients and the meat.

8 oz cottage cheese (250 g)

Stir in, cover and cook slowly until the meat is tender. This can be done on top or in the oven. Avoid adding any liquid if you can, as the curry makes its own liquid during cooking.

Goulash

Cooking time 2–3 hrs. Quantities for 3–4.

1 lb lean stewing steak (500 g)   1 oz fat (25 g) or 2 Tbs oil

Cut the meat in 1 in (2½ cm) cubes and fry it brown in the hot fat, in a saucepan or casserole.

2 onions, sliced

Add to the meat towards the end of browning and continue cooking until the onions begin to brown.

¼ pt stock (150 ml)   2 tsp paprika pepper, or more
1 tsp salt   a good pinch of caraway seeds
2 Tbs concentrated tomato purée

Add these to the meat, cover and simmer for 2–3 hrs adding a little more stock if needed. Cooking can be done on top or in a slow oven.

4–6 medium-sized potatoes.

Peel and quarter and boil for 15–20 mins in a little salted water. Add them to the goulash for about the last 10 mins of cooking time. Serve on a hot dish accompanied by

boiled cabbage.

Steak and kidney pie

Many people today make this pie by cooking the steak and kidney in advance and then just giving it a short cooking period with the pastry on top. While this makes a perfectly adequate pie it cannot compare with the old-fashioned method, which is the one below.

Cooking time 2 hrs.
Temperature 230° C (450° F; G8) for the first 10 mins, then reduce to 150° C (300° F; G2) for the remainder of the time.
Quantities for 6–8.

8 oz flour (1½ c or 200 g) made into short-crust pastry using half lard and half butter or margarine

Make the pastry first and put it in a cold place to rest while the filling is prepared.

2 lb skirt or chuck steak, or a mixture   8 oz kidney, any kind (250 g)
    (1 kg)   ½ tsp freshly ground pepper
1 tsp salt   water or stock
1 Tbs flour

Skirt steak is used because it gives the best gravy and is not a gristly cut. Cut the steak in small pieces, removing most of the fat. Cut the kidney in small pieces, removing skin and any tubes or central core. Mix the flour and seasoning and put in a clean paper bag, shake the meat in this to coat it with flour. Pack the meat into a 1½ pt (850 ml) pie dish but do not press it down, rather pile it up towards the centre to help hold the pastry up. Add water or beef stock to three-quarters fill the dish.

Roll the pastry and cover the pie in the usual way, see page 43. Cut a slit in the centre of the crust. Put the pie on a baking tray, brush the top with beaten egg and water or with milk and bake. If the pastry becomes as brown as you like it before the meat is cooked, cover the top with a piece of foil put on loosely. Serve the pie hot or cold.

Steak and kidney pudding

Cooking time 4 hrs. *Quantities* for 4-6.

1 lb chuck, shoulder or skirt steak (500 g)	8 oz ox or veal kidney (250 g)
1 tsp salt	¼ tsp freshly ground pepper
	1 oz flour (3 Tbs or 25 g)

Cut the meat in cubes and the kidney in small pieces. Mix flour and seasoning and put in a clean paper bag with the meat and kidney. Shake together to coat the meat with flour.

2 small onions

Peel and slice finely or chop coarsely.

8 oz self-raising flour (1½ c or 200 g)	½ tsp salt
3 oz prepared suet (⅓ c or 75 g)	

Mix together in a basin.

about 5 Tbs cold water (75 ml)

Add the water quickly and use a knife to mix to a soft dough. Cut off a quarter of the pastry and roll the rest into a circle big enough to line a 1½-2 pt (1 l) pudding basin. Lift the pastry into the basin and mould it to fit the bottom and sides with a little overhanging the top. Add the meat and onion in layers and enough cold water to come half-way up the meat. Do not pack the meat down tightly. Roll the remaining piece of pastry into a circle to fit the top of the basin and place it on top of the meat. Turn the surplus pastry over this and press to seal the two together. Cover the top of the basin with foil, pressing the sides close to the basin. Put it in a saucepan with boiling water coming half-way up the sides of the basin. Put on the lid and boil steadily. Look at it occasionally to make sure it is not boiling dry and, if necessary, add a little more boiling water.

The pudding is served in the basin. Any left over can be steamed again for 1 hr to re-heat it; but it should be kept in the refrigerator and used within 24 hrs.

Boiled salt beef (silverside)

Cooking times: 1 lb ($\frac{1}{2}$ kg) or less, 1 hr; 2–3 lb (1–1$\frac{1}{2}$ kg), 2–3 hrs; 4–5 lb (2–2$\frac{1}{2}$ kg), 3–4 hrs; more than this, 20 mins per lb ($\frac{1}{2}$ kg) plus 20 mins. Large pieces of meat are always more succulent than small pieces, specially for serving cold.

Quantities: allow 4–6 oz (125–175 g) per portion, raw weight. Soak the meat in cold water to cover for 3–4 hrs, or overnight.

1 onion	1 bay leaf
3 or 4 cloves	6 peppercorns
1 sprig parsley	

Skin the onion and stick the cloves into it. Wash the herbs. Put the meat and flavourings in a pan and cover with cold water. Bring to the boil, turn down the heat and keep the water just off the boil but with the surface agitated occasionally.

4 oz carrots per person (125 g)

Peel or scrape and cut large ones in half. Add them to the pan an hour or so before the end of cooking. Young ones will need less than an hour, old ones may need longer.

ACCOMPANIMENTS

Other vegetables can be added with the carrots, for example, potatoes, parsnips or celery sticks. Cook green vegetables separately and cook the traditional dumplings separately, see page 37. For a sauce, serve some of the cooking liquid or use a mustard, parsley or salsa verde sauce.

PRESSED BEEF

Put the cooked meat in a basin with stock to cover and put a plate and weight on top. Cool as quickly as possible and then store in the refrigerator.

MINCED BEEF

Butcher's mince is usually made from trimmings left when a carcass has been cut up. The price varies according to the amount of fat the mince contains, so it is worth while buying the more expensive. There are few methods of cooking mince where it is an advantage to have fatty meat and many recipes can be spoiled if the mince is too fat.

Most butchers will mince a piece of lean steak for you if you ask them; or you can buy lean stewing steak and mince it yourself, easiest to do with an electric mincer.

Mince should be used up as soon as possible because it very quickly goes bad. For short periods, store it in the refrigerator, spread out thinly on a plate with a piece of foil on top. It can also be frozen, either made up into beef burgers or as plain mince frozen in a flat slab.

Burgers

Cooking time 20–25 mins. *Quantities*: allow 4 oz mince (125 g) per portion.

PLAIN BURGERS

Season the mince with salt and pepper and shape it into flat cakes about 3 in (8 cm) in diameter and ¾–1 in thick (2 cm). Either grill under a moderate heat or fry in a very little hot fat or oil until they are brown on both sides and cooked through. If you are not sure of the timing, cut one to see if it is done. Avoid over-cooking or too fast cooking as this makes the burger shrink and become dry and tough.

Burgers can be served with a variety of accompaniments, including sauces, savoury butters, grilled or fried tomatoes or mushrooms, watercress or other salad, potatoes, green vegetables, or grill the burgers and put a thin slice of cheese on top, grilling to melt it.

ALTERNATIVE MIXTURE

Quantities for 4–6.

1 lb lean mince (500 g)	4 oz minced lean bacon (125 g)
4 oz stale bread soaked in milk and squeezed dry (125 g)	salt and pepper
	fresh chopped or dried herbs

Mash the bread to make it smooth and mix with the other ingredients. Shape and cook as above.

These are sometimes served on fried or baked onion rings.

Sausage to serve cold

This sausage has a firm, close texture not unlike salami.

Cooking time 2 hrs either boiled, steamed or baked.
Temperature 150° C (300° F; G2).
Quantities for 8–10. Sliced surplus sausage freezes very well.

1 lb lean minced beef (500 g)	1 small onion, minced or finely
8 oz streaky bacon (250 g)	chopped

Remove the rinds and mince or chop the bacon. Mix with the meat and onion. Home-minced meat should be put through the mincer more than once to make it fine.

4 oz rolled oats (1 c or 125 g)	1 Tbs Worcester sauce
1 egg, beaten	1 tsp salt
¼ tsp freshly ground pepper	

Add these to the meat and mix well. Shape the mixture into a long, thick sausage something like a breakfast sausage. Wrap it in foil, sealing the ends carefully. If it is to be baked, place the sausage on a baking tray or in a shallow tin. To boil, put it in boiling water to cover and reduce the heat to a very slow boil.

Remove the foil carefully and roll the sausage in

dried breadcrumbs.

Leave until cold and then wrap and store in the refrigerator. Serve thinly sliced.

Zucchini moussaka

This can be made with baby marrows instead of zucchini.

Cooking time ¾–1 hr preparatory cooking; ¾ hr final baking.
Temperature 190° C (375° F; G5).
Quantities for 4.

Start preparing the three mixtures for this well in advance of the final cooking.

MIXTURE 1

8 oz raw minced beef (250 g)	1 oz butter (25 g)
1 small onion, finely chopped	

Heat the butter in a saucepan and cook the onion and beef for a few minutes.

1 tomato, skinned and chopped, or 1 canned tomato
pinch of pepper
1 tsp salt
a small piece of crushed garlic

Add to the meat, cover and cook over a low heat for ½ hr. Remove from the heat.

2 Tbs dried breadcrumbs, or use crumbs from dry biscuits
1 Tbs chopped parsley
1 egg, beaten

Add half the egg and the crumbs and parsley to the meat mixture and set aside.

MIXTURE 2

1 lb zucchini, courgettes or small marrows (500 g)

Wash, remove stem ends and cut the zucchini in ¼ in (6 mm) slices.

2–4 Tbs olive oil

Use as large a frying pan as possible and heat enough oil to make a film on the bottom. Fry the zucchini in relays, lightly browning both sides and adding more oil as needed.

MIXTURE 3

¼ pt béchamel sauce (150 ml)
1 oz grated Parmesan or other hard cheese (25 g)
3 oz cottage cheese (75 g)

Mix these together with the other half of the egg.

butter
dried breadcrumbs

Grease a 2 pt (1 l) baking dish and sprinkle a layer of crumbs in the bottom. Put in alternate layers of zucchini slices and the meat mixture. Pour the sauce over the top and bake until the top is browned and the moussaka hot all through. Serve hot, either in the dish or turned out and cut in wedges.

BEEF LEFTOVERS

Good ways of using up small quantities of cooked beef include cutting it in dice and adding it to a salad of mixed vegetables, or a potato salad. Alternatively mince or chop it finely, mix with some bottled sauce and use for plain or toasted sandwiches.

Hash, to serve hot with vegetables or to make a potato pie, can be very good if it is mixed with a well-flavoured sauce as in the recipe on page 173.

Beef cakes

Cooking time 10 mins. *Quantities* for 4 cakes.

2 oz fresh breadcrumbs (50 g)
4 oz minced cooked beef (125 g)
about 3 Tbs wine or stock
shake of garlic salt or dried garlic

1 egg, beaten
salt and pepper
$\frac{1}{2}$ tsp paprika pepper

Mix all together thoroughly, divide into four and shape into flat cakes. Fry brown on both sides in a very little hot oil or butter.

ALTERNATIVE FLAVOURINGS

Add a little grated lemon rind and/or some chopped fresh or dried herbs.
   Add a little grated cheese to the mixture.
   Instead of all beef, use a mixture of beef and cooked ham or bacon.

Fricadelles

Cooking time 10–15 mins. *Quantities* for 4.

8 oz minced cooked beef (200 g)
1—2 Tbs very finely chopped onion
salt and pepper

4 oz mashed potato (100 g)
1 egg, beaten
grated nutmeg

If no mashed potato is available use potato powder instead. Make up 1 oz (25 g) of the powder with $\frac{1}{4}$ pt (150 ml) milk or water. Allow it to become cold before adding it to the other ingredients.

   Combine all the ingredients thoroughly. If any more liquid seems to be needed to moisten the mixture, add a little wine or bottled sauce. It should be soft enough to mould easily. Turn the mixture on to a floured board and divide it into four pieces. Shape each into a large round flat cake. Fry slowly in hot oil or butter until well browned on both sides. Serve hot with a well-flavoured gravy or sauce and a green salad or green vegetable.

Hash

Cooking time about 20 mins. *Quantities* for 4–6.

1 medium-sized onion, finely chopped   1 oz dripping or other fat (25 g)

Heat the fat in a saucepan and fry the onion gently until it begins to brown.

1 oz flour (3 Tbs or 25 g)

Stir into the onion and stir and cook for a few minutes.

¾ pt stock (400 ml)

Stir into the pan and stir until it boils. Boil gently for 5 mins.

1 lb minced or finely chopped cooked beef (500 g)	1 small gherkin, chopped, or 1 Tbs capers
fresh chopped or dried herbs or horseradish	Worcester sauce or mushroom ketchup
salt and pepper	gravy browning if liked

Add the meat and seasoning to taste and boil gently for 10 mins. Serve hot with potatoes, rice or spaghetti and a salad.

Layered pancakes

Cooking time about 25 mins. *Quantities* for 4.

8 oz minced or finely chopped cooked beef (250 g)	½ pt Espagnole sauce (300 ml), or use a canned soup
pinch of grated nutmeg	1 Tbs lemon juice
salt and pepper	dried garlic or garlic salt

Heat the sauce or soup and flavouring and then add the meat. Boil gently for 10 mins and then put it to keep hot while the pancakes are made, see page 37. Make these not less than 8 in (20 cm) in diameter.

As the pancakes are cooked, put the first one on a hot serving dish, spread with a layer of the meat mixture and repeat the layers, placing the top pancake with its good side uppermost. To serve, cut in wedges like a cake. Serve with

salad or a green vegetable.

ROAST LAMB

SUITABLE CUTS

Leg, shoulder, loin, best end of neck, breast (boned, stuffed and rolled). Both shoulder and leg are sometimes boned and stuffed before roasting, see Stuffings.

TEMPERATURE AND TIME 180° C (350° F; G4); 45 mins per lb (½ kg).

QUANTITIES: leg, allow ½–¾ lb (250–350 g) per portion; shoulder and loin, allow 1 lb (½ kg) per portion; best end of neck and breast, allow ½–¾ lb (250–350 g) per portion.

METHOD

Time the cooking so that the meat can rest for 15 minutes after cooking and before carving.

To enhance the flavour, herbs can be added to the meat. This can be done in several ways. If you like garlic, either rub the meat all over with a cut clove or insert a few fine slivers of garlic near the bone, for example, at the cut end of a leg. Alternatively, rub the meat with dried crushed herbs or with a herb seasoning. The best herbs for lamb are rosemary, fennel, tarragon and lemon thyme.

Either put the meat on a rack in the roasting pan or put it on an oven rack with a pan beneath to catch the drippings.

ACCOMPANIMENTS

Thin or thickened gravy; red currant jelly; mint sauce; onion sauce; roast, boiled or mashed potatoes; green peas or beans; carrots; turnips; haricot beans; spinach; sweet peppers; aubergines.

Roast shoulder of lamb with herb marinade

Cooking time 45 mins per lb ($\frac{1}{2}$ kg), after marinating.
Temperature 180° C (350° F; G4).
Quantities for 4-6.

1 small shoulder of lamb

Put the meat in a shallow dish, choosing one just large enough to take the joint. Alternatively, the meat can be boned and tied in a smaller shape.

1½ tsp chopped fresh rosemary, or ½ tsp dried
1½ tsp chopped fresh tarragon
1½ tsp chopped fresh thyme, or ½ tsp dried
8 Tbs olive oil (120 ml)

Heat these together enough to bring out the flavours without actually frying the herbs, then cool the mixture.

¼ pt lemon juice (150 ml)

Add to the cold oil and herbs and pour the marinade over the meat. Cover, and keep either at room temperature for several hours or overnight in the refrigerator. Lift the meat out of the marinade and put it on a rack in the roasting pan or on an oven rack with a pan below. Use surplus marinade to baste the joint every ¼–½ hr during cooking.

The liquid used for basting has a sharp flavour from the lemon so you may prefer to dilute it with some stock when making the gravy in the usual way.

FRIED AND GRILLED LAMB

SUITABLE CUTS

Loin chops and best end of neck cutlets; boned slices of leg.

Grilling

COOKING TIME

Cutlets 7–10 mins; chops and slices of leg 10–20 mins depending on the thickness and whether you like the meat well-done or still a little pink in the middle. Frozen: cutlets 12–15 mins; chops 15–25 mins.

TO GRILL

Trim off surplus fat. With cutlets it is customary to trim the fat and meat from the bones up to the thick meaty bit at the top.

Brush the meat with oil or a basting sauce and pre-heat the grill. Grill under a moderate heat, turning the meat frequently so that browning and cooking finish together.

ACCOMPANIMENTS

Savoury butter (parsley, tarragon or garlic); mushroom sauce; onion sauce; fried potatoes; grilled tomatoes and mushrooms; grilled aubergines; salad.

Those who like meat and fruit together can put a slice of orange or pineapple on top of the meat when it is almost cooked, brush the fruit with oil and finish cooking.

Grilled lamb chops with herbs

Cooking time 15–20 mins, plus 1 hr marinating. *Quantities* for 4.

4 lamb chops	1 tsp salt
1 tsp dried rosemary	1 tsp dried marjoram
1 tsp dried thyme	

Pound the herbs and salt together to make a fine mixture. Use a pestle and mortar for this or process them in the electric blender. Rub the mixture thoroughly into the meat on both sides. Put in a covered dish in the refrigerator to marinate. Grill as described above, but omit the brushing with oil.

Meat 177

Kebabs with yogurt marinade

Cooking time 20–30 mins, plus 3 hrs marinating. *Quantities* for 4.

1–1½ lb lean boned lamb, preferably from the leg (500–750 g)

Trim the meat and cut it in convenient sizes for your grill. Put the meat in a dish with a lid.

¼ pt yogurt (150 ml)	1 Tbs finely chopped onion
1 Tbs lemon juice	½ tsp salt

Combine and pour over the lamb, stir to mix and cover. Store in the refrigerator for 3 hrs, turning the meat over once or twice. Drain from the marinade and thread on kebab skewers with any of the following:

pieces of bacon next to the meat to help baste it	mushrooms
small or halved firm tomatoes	pieces of blanched green pepper

If you are not using bacon, baste the meat during cooking with a little oil or melted butter. To blanch the pepper, pour boiling water over it to soften a little but not make it floppy.

Cook until the meat is done to your taste. The marinade tends to restrict browning so use a slightly higher heat than you would normally, or cook a little longer. Serve the kebabs on a bed of

boiled or fried rice flavoured with herbs.

Fried minute lamb cutlets

Cooking time a few mins. *Quantities* for 4.

8 lamb cutlets	garlic
freshly ground pepper	

Carefully remove the 'eye' of meat from each cutlet. Flatten the meat to about ¼ in (½ cm) thick, using a cutlet bat or a wooden rolling pin. Season the meat, either using dried garlic or rubbing with a cut clove.

1 oz butter (25 g)

Heat the butter in a frying pan and, when it begins to colour, add the meat and fry it quickly until brown on both sides.

1–2 Tbs lemon juice   chopped parsley

Put the meat on a hot serving dish and add the lemon juice to the pan, stirring to dissolve the sediment. Add the parsley, pour the liquid over the meat and serve with

potatoes or rice and a salad.

Fried lamb with cinnamon and soured cream

Cooking time 40-50 mins. Quantities for 4.

2 medium-sized onions, finely chopped	2 Tbs olive oil
	1 oz butter (25 g)

Heat the butter and oil in a frying pan and when the butter begins to colour, add the onion and fry until it just begins to brown.

1-1½ lb boneless leg of lamb (500-700 g)	½ tsp ground cinnamon

Cut the meat in 1 in (2½ cm) cubes and sprinkle it with the cinnamon. Add to the onions and mix. Turn down the heat, cover the pan and continue to cook gently until the meat is tender, about 30 mins.

½ pt soured cream (250 ml)   salt and pepper

Add to the meat and turn up the heat to make the cream boil. Stir well and boil gently for a few minutes. Season to taste and serve with

rice or noodles and green beans, peas or a salad.

LAMB CASSEROLES, STEWS AND PIES

SUITABLE CUTS

Chump chops; best end or middle neck cutlets; the shank or knuckle end of a leg; boned shoulder or leg.

Baked chops au gratin

Cooking time 1½ hrs.
Temperature 160° C (325° F; G3).
Quantities for 4.

4 chump chops cut about 1 in (2½ cm) thick	1 oz fat (25 g), or 2 Tbs oil

Trim fat from the chops and cut out the bones. The fat can be used for frying the chops; cut it in small pieces and heat in the frying pan. When the fat begins to run, add the chops and brown them on both sides. Transfer to a shallow casserole large enough to take the meat in a single layer.

2 onions, sliced	¾ lb canned tomatoes (350 g)
½ tsp salt	¼ tsp freshly ground pepper
1 tsp sugar	a little basil, marjoram or garlic

Put the slices of onion on top of the meat, spoon the tomatoes over the top and add the seasoning.

2 oz grated cheese (½ c or 50 g)   2 oz fresh breadcrumbs (⅔ c or 50 g)

Mix together and sprinkle over the meat. Cover and bake.

Braised lamb shank

Cooking time 2¼ hrs.
Temperature 150° C (300° F; G2).
Quantities for 4.

the shank or knuckle end of a leg of lamb	2 oz fat (50 g), or 3–4 Tbs oil

A large casserole in which you can both fry and cook the meat is ideal for this recipe. Heat the fat or oil and brown the meat all over. Lift it out and pour off any remaining fat or oil.

1 onion, sliced	1 tsp chopped tarragon
1 tsp chopped thyme	salt and pepper
¼–½ pt white wine or dry cider (150–300 ml)	

Put the onion in the bottom of the casserole with the meat on top. Sprinkle the meat with the herbs and seasoning. Pour in wine or cider to the depth of about ½ in (1 cm). Cover the casserole and cook for 2 hrs or until the meat is tender. Remove the meat and carve it, arranging the slices on a hot dish. Put to keep hot. Carefully pour off the fat from the onion and juices in the casserole.

¼ pt yogurt (150 ml)   2 Tbs capers

Rinse the capers in cold water and add them to the casserole with the yogurt. Stir and heat until boiling. Pour the sauce over the meat.
  If preferred, the onion can be strained out before adding the other ingredients.

Casserole of cutlets

Cooking time 1–1½ hrs.
Temperature 180° C (350° F; G4).
Quantities for 4.

8 best end of neck cutlets   1 oz fat (25 g) or 2 Tbs oil

Trim surplus fat from the cutlets. Heat the fat or oil in a frying pan and brown the cutlets. Transfer them to a casserole.

1 onion, sliced, or 1 whole clove of   1 rasher bacon, chopped
  garlic, skinned

Add to the fat in the frying pan and cook for a few minutes. Remove and discard the clove of garlic if used.

8 oz canned tomatoes (250 g)   salt and pepper
½ fresh or canned sweet pepper, sliced

Add to the frying pan and bring to the boil. Pour over the cutlets.

1 bay leaf   2 Tbs chopped mint

Add to the casserole. Cover and cook until the meat is tender. Remove the bay leaf and serve.

Devilled neck of lamb

Cooking time 1½ hrs.
Temperature 160° C (325° F; G.3).
Quantities for 4.

2 lb middle neck of lamb cutlets   1 oz fat (25 g), or 2 Tbs oil
  (1 kg)

Heat the fat or oil in a saucepan or fireproof casserole and fry the meat in it until it is brown.

2 stalks celery, chopped   1 onion, chopped
2 tomatoes, skinned and chopped

Add to the meat and continue frying for a few minutes.

2 tsp dry mustard   2 tsp salt
1 tsp Worcester sauce   ¼ tsp freshly ground pepper
¼ pt vinegar (150 ml)   ¼ pt stock (150 ml)

Mix the seasonings and sauce to a smooth paste and add the vinegar and stock.

Pour over the meat, turning it over to coat it with the sauce. Cover and cook on top or in the oven until the meat is tender. Serve with

boiled potatoes or rice and a green vegetable or a salad.

Lamb and apple pie

Cooking time 1½ hrs.
Temperature 230° C (450° F; G8) for 10 mins, then 150° C (300° F; G2) for the rest of the time.
Quantities for 4.

4 oz flour made into short-crust pastry (100 g), or use 6 oz ready-made (175 g)

Make the pastry and put it in a cool place to rest while the filling is prepared.

1 lb lean lamb or mutton without bone (500 g), or about 2 lb (1 kg) with bone	8 oz cooking apples (250 g) 3 oz onion (75 g) salt and pepper

Cut the meat in small pieces. Peel, core and slice the apples, skin and slice the onions. Put these into a 1 pt (600 ml) pie dish in layers, seasoning well with salt and pepper. Make sure the dish is well filled with meat and apple, or pile it towards the centre to hold the pastry up. Add cold water to half fill the dish.

Roll the pastry and cover the pie in the usual way, see page 43. Cut a slit in the top of the crust. Bake until the meat is tender. If the pastry browns before this, cover the top loosely with a piece of foil. Serve the pie hot or cold.

Lamb with tarragon

Cooking time 1¼–1½ hrs. *Quantities* for 4.

2–2½ lb middle neck of lamb in one or two pieces (1 kg)	1 tsp salt a sprig of tarragon

Boil enough water to barely cover the meat. Add the meat and flavourings and simmer gently for one hour or until the meat is tender. Lift it out and cut the meat off the bone. Cut it in small pieces and put it to keep hot. Strain the stock.

1 oz flour (3 Tbs or 25 g) 2 Tbs tarragon vinegar	1 Tbs soured cream

Mix the flour to a smooth paste with the cream and vinegar and gradually add to it about ½ pt (250 ml) of the strained stock. Put in a pan and stir until it boils, adding more stock as needed to give the sauce a pouring consistency. Boil gently for 5 mins.

1 egg yolk
salt and pepper
4 Tbs soured cream (60 ml)

Beat these together to mix well. Remove the sauce from the heat and stir in the egg mixture. Bring to the boil, taste for seasoning and add more stock if needed. Return the meat and heat long enough to make sure it is hot.

chopped parsley or tarragon

Serve the meat and sauce liberally garnished with the chopped herb.

Navarin of lamb

Cooking time 2 hrs on top or in the oven.
Temperature 150° C (300° F; G2).
Quantities for 4.

1½ lb lamb without bone (700 g) (shoulder or shank end of leg)
¼ tsp freshly ground pepper
1½ oz fat (40 g), or 3 Tbs oil
pinch of sugar
1 tsp salt

Remove the fat and cut the meat into pieces of about 2 oz (50 g) each. Heat the fat or oil and fry the meat until it is brown, adding the seasoning and sugar during frying. When it is well browned pour off excess fat, keeping it for later use.

2 Tbs flour

Sprinkle it over the meat and continue frying until the flour begins to brown.

1 pt water (½ l)

Add to the meat and stir until it boils.

1 clove garlic (optional)

Skin and crush the garlic and add it to the meat. Cover and simmer for 1 hr.

8 small onions or shallots, skinned

Fry these brown in the oil or fat left from the first frying. Drain them well on kitchen paper and add to the meat.

1½ lb small potatoes, new if possible (700 g)

Peel or scrape and add to the meat. Simmer until the vegetables are cooked, about another ¾ hr. Before serving the navarin, skim off any fat from the top.

Pilau

Cooking time about 1 hr. *Quantities* for 4–6.

8 oz rice (250 g)

Special rice is sold for making pilaus, but a good quality pudding rice will do. Wash the rice if necessary and drain well.

1½ lb lean lamb without bone, shoulder or leg (700 g)
2 Tbs lemon juice

Cut the meat in small pieces and sprinkle it with the lemon.

2 oz butter (50 g)

Heat it in a large heavy saucepan, add the rice and cook gently for about 10 mins, without browning. Stir frequently.

¼ pt double cream (150 ml)
½ pt lamb stock (250 ml)
pinch of ground cloves
pinch of ground cinnamon
¼ pt thick yogurt (150 ml)
1 Tbs chopped fennel
pinch of ground cumin seeds
salt and pepper

Add to the rice, mix, cover and cook gently for 15 mins, on top or in the oven – 180° C (350° F; G4).

2 oz butter (50 g)

Heat in a frying pan. Drain any liquid from the meat and fry until it changes colour. Add it and the drained liquid to the rice, mix and continue cooking until the meat is tender, about ½ hr. Remove the lid and let the rice dry for a few minutes before serving the pilau.

Ragout of lamb

Cooking time 2 hrs. *Quantities* for 4.

4 oz butter beans (125 g)

Wash the beans and soak them overnight with cold water to cover. Alternatively, cover with boiling water and soak for 4–5 hrs.

about a 2 lb piece of shoulder of lamb or mutton (1 kg)

Cut the meat off the bones (about 1–1½ lb meat (500–700 g)). Then cut it in small pieces.

1 tsp salt
1 tsp paprika pepper

Sprinkle these over the meat.

2 Tbs oil

Heat the oil in a saucepan or casserole and fry the meat until brown.

6 shallots or small onions, chopped 2 Tbs chopped parsley
¾ pt canned tomatoes (400 ml)

Add to the meat together with the drained soaked beans. Cover and simmer until the meat and beans are tender.

¼ pt yogurt, cream or evaporated 1 Tbs cornflour
   milk (150 ml)

Blend the cornflour to a cream with a little cold water and stir it into the meat. Bring back to the boil and simmer for 5 mins. Stir in the yogurt, cream or evaporated milk and serve.

Spiced lamb casserole

Cooking time 1½ hrs.
Temperature 180° C (350° F; G4).
Quantities for 4.

2 lb best end of neck cutlets (1 kg)

Trim off excess fat and put the cutlets in a casserole.

1 medium-sized onion, finely chopped   salt and pepper
2 tsp curry powder   ½ tsp ground cloves
½ tsp ground ginger   ½ tsp ground cinnamon

Sprinkle over the meat.

6 oz curd cheese (175 g)

Beat with a little water to give it a spreading consistency. Spread on top of the meat and spices, cover and cook until the meat is tender, turning it once or twice during cooking so that the spices, juices and curd are well blended with the meat. No additional liquid should be needed as the curd and meat juices will make enough sauce.

LAMB LEFTOVERS

Serve lean cold roast lamb with a salad of cucumber, watercress and a little finely chopped onion or spring onions; or with a potato salad flavoured with mint. Other good accompaniments for cold lamb are mint sauce, red currant jelly, sweet pickled fruit or chutney.

Burgers

Cooking time 10–15 mins. *Quantities* for 4 burgers.

8 oz lean minced cooked lamb (250 g)	1 small onion, finely chopped
	2 tsp flour
1 Tbs chopped parsley	beaten egg to bind (about ½ egg or 1 yolk)
pepper	

Mix all the ingredients together, using enough egg to bind to a stiff mixture. Shape into four round cakes about 1 in (2½ cm) thick.

4 rashers streaky bacon

Remove the rinds and wrap a rasher round each burger, fastening with a wooden cocktail stick.

Fry the burgers in a little fat or oil or grill them until brown on both sides. Serve hot with

sauce or gravy and a vegetable or salad.

Lamb pie

Cooking time about 45 mins.
Temperature 220° C (425° F; G7).
Quantities for a 7 in flan ring or pie plate (18 cm).

short-crust pastry using 6 oz flour (175 g), or use ½–¾ lb ready-made (250–375 g)

Roll the pastry thinly to line the flan ring or pie plate and roll another piece for the lid. Refrigerate these while the filling is being prepared.

6 oz cold cooked lean lamb (175 g)

Cut the meat in dice or thin slices.

1 Tbs chopped fresh mint	salt and pepper
6 oz cottage cheese (175 g)	

Put a layer of cottage cheese in the bottom of the pie, then the meat, seasoning it and adding the mint. Cover with the rest of the cheese.

2 Tbs cream   milk or egg for brushing the top

Pour the cream over the filling. Cover with the pastry lid, sealing the edges together. Cut a slit in the centre top and brush the top with milk or egg. Bake the pie until the pastry is brown. Serve hot or cold.

ALTERNATIVE

Instead of using mint, flavour the meat with ground cumin and sprinkle the brushed pastry with sesame seeds.

Shepherd's pie

Cooking time $\frac{1}{2}-\frac{3}{4}$ hr.
Temperature 200–220° C (400–425° F; G6–7).
Quantities for 4.

12 oz lean minced cooked lamb or mutton (350 g)	1–1½ lb old potatoes (500–700 g)

Mince the meat. Peel the potatoes and put in boiling salted water. Boil until tender. Meanwhile make the sauce.

2 medium-sized onions, chopped	1 oz flour (3 Tbs or 25 g)
1½ oz fat (40 g)	¾ pt stock (400 ml)

Heat the fat in a saucepan and fry the onions until they begin to brown. Add the flour, stir and cook until crumbly. Add the stock and stir until the sauce boils. Boil gently until the onions are tender.

salt and pepper	chutney or ketchup
chopped gherkins or capers	fresh or dried herbs

Flavour the sauce to taste, add the meat and bring to the boil.

1 oz butter (25 g)	1–2 Tbs milk

Drain and mash the potatoes with the butter and milk. Put the meat mixture in an ovenproof dish and spread the potato over the top, roughing the top with a fork. Bake or grill until the potatoes are brown on top. The meat and potatoes must be hot when the dish is assembled, otherwise it will need to be cooked in a hot oven for ½ hr to heat through.

ROAST PORK

SUITABLE CUTS

Loin, leg, spare ribs, hand and spring, blade.

TEMPERATURE AND TIME

190° C (375° F; G5). Pieces under 3 lb (1½ kg) weight, calculate as 3 lb. Spare ribs and loin 35 mins per lb (½ kg); leg, hand and spring or blade 40 mins per lb (½ kg). Pork must be thoroughly cooked; err on the side of over-cooking rather than under-cooking.

QUANTITIES

With bone, ½–¾ lb per portion (250–350 g); no bone, 4–6 oz per portion (125–175 g).

METHOD

Time the cooking to allow the pork to rest for 15 mins before carving.

To get crisp crackling make sure the rind is above the level of the drippings in the pan, that is, put the meat on a rack and do not cover it. It helps to make crisp crackling if the rind is rubbed with salt or brushed with oil before cooking. Extra flavour can be added by rubbing herbs into the slits in the rind before roasting. The best herbs to use are sage, marjoram, basil, rosemary, thyme, garlic, caraway or ground coriander. Alternatively, the meat can be boned and stuffed, see Stuffings, pages 28–9.

ACCOMPANIMENTS

Boiled, mashed or roast potatoes; gravy; apple sauce; lemon and sage sauce; onion sauce; celery; onions; green vegetables; red cabbage; roast parsnips; roast pumpkin.

Roast loin of pork with apple and prunes

for about 3 lb loin (1½ kg), allow 6 large prunes and 1 apple

Pour boiling water over the prunes and leave them to stand until soft enough to remove the stones.

Peel, core and chop the apple.

Using a small sharp knife, separate the meat from the thin rib bones for part of the way down to make a pocket for the fruit. Put in the prunes and apples and sew or tie up the opening to keep the fruit in place. Remove the ties before serving the meat. Roast as described above.

Roast spare ribs with sage and ginger

2–3 lb spare ribs (1–1½ kg)
2 tsp crushed dried sage, marjoram, caraway or thyme
¼–½ tsp salt
½ tsp ground ginger
pinch of pepper

Mix the flavourings together and rub well into the non-bony meat and into the cuts in the rind. Brush the rind with oil and roast as described above.

Pork cooked this way has an excellent flavour both hot and cold.

FRIED AND GRILLED PORK

SUITABLE CUTS

Loin chops, spare rib cutlets, fillet or tender loin.

QUANTITIES

Allow 1 chop, 1–2 cutlets, or 4–6 oz fillet or tender loin (125–175 g) per portion.

Fried and grilled chops

Cooking time 15–20 mins or more depending on the thickness. Trim off surplus fat before cooking.

TO GRILL

Cook fairly slowly under a moderate heat so that browning and cooking finish together. Turn the meat once during cooking. Pork should be thoroughly cooked, but if the heat is too fierce the meat will become hard and dry in the process.

TO FRY

Heat just enough lard or oil to cover the bottom of the frying pan with a thin layer. Brown the chops quickly on each side and then reduce the heat to continue the cooking. To cover the pan with a lid at this stage helps to keep the meat moist. When the chops are cooked, remove them to a hot dish. Pour off the fat, swill the pan out with stock or wine and use this as a gravy. Season the gravy with salt and pepper and add chopped parsley or other fresh herbs.

ACCOMPANIMENTS

Grilled or fried tomatoes or mushrooms; apple sauce; red currant jelly; grilled halves of canned peaches; grilled slices of pineapple; mashed potatoes; green beans; spinach.

Marinated chops with cider sauce

Cooking time 20–25 mins after 1 hr marinating. *Quantities* for 4.

4 thick pork chops

Use a small, sharp knife to score the flesh in two or three places on either side.

2 Tbs chopped green herbs   oil
salt and pepper

Mix the herbs with plenty of seasoning and enough oil to make a paste. Rub this into the cuts in the meat. Leave for an hour or more in a cold place. Then fry the chops. Put to keep hot. Pour surplus fat from the pan.

¼ pt cider (150 ml)

Add to the pan, bring to the boil and stir to dissolve all sediment.

1 Tbs chopped gherkins   1 Tbs chopped capers

Add to the sauce and heat for a minute. Pour over the chops and serve.

Pork chops with sauerkraut

Cooking time ½–¾ hr. *Quantities* for 4.

4 pork chops   1 oz lard (25 g)

Heat the lard in a sauté pan or deep frying pan and brown the chops on both sides. Remove from the pan.

1 medium-sized onion, finely chopped

Brown in the lard.

paprika pepper   salt
part of a crushed clove of garlic, or   caraway seeds
  some garlic salt

Sprinkle into the pan, using flavourings to taste, turn down the heat, return the chops and moisten the whole with a very little water. Cover the pan and cook slowly for about 20 mins or until the meat is cooked. Remove the chops and keep them hot.

1 lb sauerkraut (500 g), rinsed and drained

Add to the pan and heat through for about 10 mins.

¼–½ pt soured cream (150–250 ml)

Add to the sauerkraut, mix and heat to boiling. Serve with the chops.

Fried pork and green peppers

Cooking time about 20 mins. *Quantities* for 4-6.

1½ lb fillet of pork (700 g)

Cut the meat in thin strips 1½ in long (3½ cm) and about ¼ in thick (6 mm).

½–1 oz lard (15–25 g)
2 cloves garlic, skinned and crushed
3 spring onions or 1 shallot, finely chopped

Heat the lard in a sauté pan or frying pan, using enough to give a thin layer. Fry the onion and garlic for a minute.

2 green sweet peppers

Remove stem, seeds and core and dice the flesh. Add to the pan and fry gently for 5 mins. Add the pork and fry, stirring and turning, until it changes colour.

1 Tbs flour
1 Tbs brown sugar
2 Tbs soy sauce

Mix to a paste and add to the pan with enough stock or water to moisten the meat. Stir until it thickens and simmer for a few minutes. Test a piece of pork to make sure it is cooked through. Serve with

rice or noodles and a green vegetable salad.

Sauté of pork fillet

Cooking time 20–30 mins. *Quantities* for 4.

1 lb pork fillet (500 g)
½ oz lard (15 g)

Cut the fillet into slices about ¾ in (2 cm) thick. Heat the lard in a sauté pan or deep frying pan. Add the slices of pork and fry until brown on both sides and cooked through. Remove from the pan and keep hot.

1 small onion, chopped

Add more lard if necessary and fry the onion gently until it is almost tender.

6 sage leaves, finely chopped
½ pt dry cider (250 ml)
salt and pepper
1 Tbs concentrated tomato purée

Add to the onions and stir and cook until the sauce has thickened a little. Return the pork and re-heat it. Serve with

rice or noodles and green beans or peas.

Meat 191

Kebabs with pineapple

Cooking time about 30 mins. *Quantities* for 4.

a basting sauce, pages 25–6, or Cumberland sauce, page 58.

Prepare the sauce in advance.

1–1½ lb lean boneless pork, fillet is best but other tender pork will do (500–700 g)	1 lb can of pineapple cubes (454 g), or use pineapple rings cut into pieces 8 small very firm tomatoes, or 4 large

Cut the pork in pieces about ½ in cubed (1 cm), or thinner pieces if preferred; these will cook in less than 30 mins. Drain the pineapple. Wash the tomatoes and cut them in pieces a little bigger than the meat. They must be firm tomatoes or they will over-cook in the time it takes to cook the pork. Thread the pork, pineapple and tomatoes on the kebab skewers putting either pineapple or tomato between each pair of pieces of meat. Brush with the Cumberland sauce or basting sauce and grill, basting two or three times during cooking. The pork must be cooked right through. Heat any remaining sauce and serve it with the kebabs. Serve plain or on a bed of boiled rice.

PORK CASSEROLES, STEWS AND PIES

SUITABLE CUTS

Belly, spare ribs, hand and spring; for leaner but more expensive casseroles use fillet or trimmed chops.

Belly of pork casserole

Cooking time 3 hrs.
Temperature 160° C (325° F; G3).
Quantities for 4.

2 medium-sized onions, skinned and sliced	1 large cooking apple, peeled, cored and sliced

Put in layers in a casserole.

1½ lb sliced belly of pork (700 g)	2 carrots, peeled and sliced

Trim surplus fat from the pork and put it on top of the onions and apples with the carrots on top of the pork.

½ pt brown stock (250 ml), or use a mixture of stock and red wine
salt and pepper

1 Tbs mushroom ketchup
2 tsp chopped fresh sage, or 1 tsp dried

Combine and add to the casserole. Cover and cook. If desired, thicken the gravy with 1–2 Tbs blended flour.

Casserole of spare ribs

Cooking time 1½ hrs.
Temperature 200° C (400° F; G6).
Quantities for 4.

4 thick spare rib cutlets

Put the cutlets in a wide, shallow casserole and bake without covering, for about 30 mins or until the meat is well browned.

1 small onion, skinned and chopped   ½ oz butter (15 g), or 1 Tbs oil

Heat the butter or oil in a small pan and fry the onion until brown.

1 stalk celery, chopped
1 Tbs brown sugar
2 tsp dry mustard
1 tsp salt
1 Tbs vinegar

2 tsp concentrated tomato purée
1 Tbs Worcester sauce
¼ pt water (150 ml)
½ tsp paprika pepper
2 Tbs lemon juice

Add the celery to the onions. Combine the other ingredients and add to the onions and celery. Pour off any fat surrounding the pork and pour the sauce over the top. Cover with a lid and continue cooking for about ¾ hr or until the meat is tender and the vegetables cooked. Serve with

baked jacket potatoes.

Pork and apple pie

Cooking time 1½–2 hrs.
Temperature 230° C (450° F; G8) for 10 mins, then 160° C (325° F; G3) for the rest of the time.
Quantities for a 1½ pt (850 ml) pie dish.

1¼ lb fillet of pork, or other lean pork without bone (600 g)
pinch of ground nutmeg

1 tsp salt
pinch of pepper

Cut the pork in thin slices and sprinkle it with the seasonings.

1 lb apples (500 g)

Peel, core and slice and put them in the pie dish in layers with the meat, piling it up in the centre.

| 1 tsp brown sugar | ¼ pt white wine or cider (150 ml) |
| 1 oz butter (25 g) | |

Add sugar and wine to the pie and dot the top with small pieces of the butter.

8 oz ready-made puff pastry (250 g)

Cover the pie in the usual way, see page 43. Bake until the meat is tender. Serve hot or cold.

Pork goulash

Cooking time 1½ hrs. *Quantities* for 4–6.

2 lb boneless pork (1 kg)	2 tsp paprika pepper, more or less
2 medium-sized onions, skinned and sliced	2 oz chopped bacon (50 g)
	1 oz lard (25 g)
1 tsp vinegar	salt

Trim excess fat from the meat and cut it in pieces. Heat the lard in a saucepan or casserole and fry the bacon and onion until they begin to brown. Add the meat and other ingredients and continue frying for a few minutes longer.

stock or water

Add enough to come about half-way up the meat, cover and simmer on top or in a slow oven until the meat is tender, about 1 hr.

| 1 Tbs potato flour or arrowroot | ¼ pt yogurt (150 ml) |

Blend together and stir into the meat. Stir until the sauce thickens.

| ½ oz butter (15 g) | 1 tsp paprika pepper |

Melt the butter in a small pan, stir in the pepper and add a little warm water. Pour over the goulash and serve. Serve with

boiled potatoes or noodles and cabbage or spinach.

Cutlets or chops with sweet corn

Cooking time about 1¾ hrs.
Temperature 180° C (350° F; G4).
Quantities for 4.

| 4 pork chops or 4–8 spare rib cutlets | 1 Tbs oil |

Trim surplus fat from the meat. Heat the oil in a frying pan and brown the meat;

transfer to a casserole or baking dish large enough to take the meat in a single layer.

4 Tbs evaporated milk

Pour the fat from the frying pan, add the milk and mix to incorporate all the brown bits from the pan. Set aside.

2 oz fresh breadcrumbs (50 g)
1 egg, beaten
1 small onion, finely chopped
1 small green sweet pepper
6 oz canned sweet corn kernels or niblets (175 g)
1 tsp salt

Remove stem and pith from the pepper and chop the flesh. Combine all these ingredients with the milk from the frying pan and spread the mixture on top of the meat. Cover and bake for 1½ hrs or until the meat is tender.

Serve hot with a green vegetable or cold with salad.

BOILED PORK, HAM OR BACON

SUITABLE CUTS

Salt or pickled belly of pork is the cut most frequently boiled, but hand and spring and other cuts may be used too. A whole ham or piece of gammon is useful for serving a number of people on special occasions but small pieces of gammon or small bacon joints are more practical for the family. Today these are often sold vacuum-packed and with cooking instructions.

Boiled salt or pickled pork

Cooking time: pieces under 1 lb (½ kg) need 45 mins; 1–2 lb (½–1 kg), 1–1½ hrs; 2–3 lb (1–1½ kg), 1½–1¾ hrs; over 3 lb (1½ kg), allow 30 mins per lb (½ kg). Pressure cooking, allow 12 mins per lb (½ kg).
Quantities 6–8 oz raw weight per person (175–250 g).

Soak small pieces in cold water to cover for 1 hr; larger pieces, soak for 4–5 hrs or more. Then put the meat in a saucepan with fresh cold water to cover and bring to the boil. Remove any scum from the top.

1 skinned onion or 6 peppercorns
1 bay leaf
4–5 cloves or whole allspice

If the onion is used, stick the cloves in it. Add the flavourings to the pan, cover and simmer for the required time. The water should not bubble continuously, just an occasional bubble on the agitated surface of the liquid.

carrots, turnips, parsnips, potatoes, celery, onions or leeks

Any of these can be cooked with the meat, adding them for the last ½–1 hr of cooking. Prepare them in the usual way for boiling, cutting large ones in pieces.

chopped parsley or other herbs

When cooked, lift out the vegetables with a perforated spoon or strainer and remove the meat. Remove the rind from the meat and cut meat in slices. Put the slices on a hot platter with the vegetables and a little stock to moisten. Sprinkle it with plenty of chopped herbs. Alternatively, make a sauce using stock and herbs.

Cold salt pork is suitable for serving with salad or as a sandwich filling.

Hot boiled salt pork is a traditional accompaniment to roast veal and roast or boiled chicken, when it supplies the fat which these meats lack.

PRESSURE COOKER METHOD

Soak the meat first. Allow ½ pt (250 ml) water for each 15 mins of cooking time. Put the meat on a trivet in the bottom of the pan with its fat side uppermost. Add 3 or 4 cloves and 1 Tbs brown sugar with the water. Bring to pressure. When cooking is finished allow the pressure to drop slowly.

Boiled bacon or pieces of gammon

Cook and serve in the same way as for salt pork, above.

SAUCES

Suitable sauces are parsley, mustard, salsa verde, Espagnole sauce.

Boiled whole ham or gammon

Cooking times: 12 lb (5 kg), 3¼ hrs; 14 lb (6 kg), 3½ hrs; 16 lb (7 kg), 4 hrs; 18 lb (8 kg), 4¼ hrs; 20 lb (9 kg), 4½ hrs.
Quantities: allow 4–6 oz per portion (125–175 g).

Soak in cold water to cover: ham for 24 hrs, gammon for 8–12 hrs. Scrub off any 'bloom' or mould. Place the meat in a large pan with fresh cold water to cover. Bring the water slowly to the boil, reduce the heat and simmer for the required time. Turn off the heat and leave the ham in the water for another hour.

TO SERVE HOT

Remove the skin, sprinkle the fat with dried breadcrumbs. Dress the knuckle with a paper ham frill.

TO BAKE

After removing the skin from the boiled ham, score the fat in a criss-cross fashion to form diamond-shaped cuts. Stick a whole clove in each diamond, sprinkle the fat with brown sugar and bake until brown, 20–30 mins at 230° C (450° F; G8).

TO SERVE COLD

Put the cooked ham in a cold place for 24 hrs, but not in the refrigerator until after this. Remove the skin, sprinkle the fat with crumbs as for hot ham, above, and put a paper ham frill on the bone. Ham is most easily carved with a special long, thin ham knife.

ACCOMPANIMENTS

With hot ham serve parsley sauce, pease pudding, boiled potatoes and vegetables. With cold ham serve salad and sweet pickled fruit or apple or cranberry sauce or jelly.

Ham or bacon in madeira sauce

This is an excellent way of making a hot meat dish from cold sliced ham or boiled bacon.

Madeira sauce; use the Espagnole sauce recipe, page 50, adding madeira for the wine

Use enough sauce to cover the slices of meat. Put in a frying pan or other shallow pan and bring to the boil. Boil gently for 5 mins and serve hot.

ACCOMPANIMENTS

Noodles; braised celery; green beans; broad beans; cooked chicory; leaf spinach; rolls or bread and a salad.

Cooking bacon rashers

There is an enormous variety of types and grades of bacon and no clear system of labelling, so the best thing to do is find a shop that keeps the kind of bacon you like and stick to it.

Bacon can be roughly divided into heavily salted and lightly salted, and again into smoked and green, or unsmoked. Smoked has a dark rind and tends to be heavily salted. Green has a pale rind and is often lightly salted, but not always. Smoked bacon keeps better than green bacon.

After cutting, bacon dries quickly so either buy bacon from a shop which has a quick turnover or buy it vacuum-packed. Stale bacon has discoloured fat and smells unpleasant with a rancid flavour.

Keep bacon wrapped in polythene or foil in the refrigerator.

Salty rashers can be made less so by soaking them in warm water for ½ hr; drain and dry before frying or grilling.

Bacon and eggs

See page 109.

Bacon rolls

These are used as a garnish for many savoury dishes or as part of grills such as kebabs. Streaky bacon, cut thinly, is the best to use. Trim off the rinds and roll the rashers up.

Secure them with cocktail sticks or thread them on metal skewers. Either grill them for about 6–8 mins under a moderate heat, turning once; or bake them for about 30 mins in a moderate oven, 190° C (375° F; G5), until the outside fat is crisp. If possible, put the rolls on a rack so that the fat can run away from them.

Baked bacon rashers with cider

Cooking time 30 mins, after 2 hrs soaking.
Temperature 190° C (375° F; G5).
Quantities for 4.

4 thick, lean bacon rashers, preferably gammon	¼ pt dry cider (150 ml)

Remove the rind from the bacon and put the rashers in a shallow fireproof dish. Pour in the cider and leave to soak for 2 hrs, turning the rashers over at half-time.

Bake, and serve with the liquid as a sauce. Serve with

boiled potatoes and a salad.

Fried gammon in sweet mustard sauce

Cooking time 10–15 mins. *Quantities* for 4.

4 portions of gammon about ¼–½ in thick (½–1 cm)	lard or other fat

Remove any rind from the gammon and snip the fat at intervals to make the slices stay flat during cooking. Heat the lard in a frying pan and cook the gammon for 5–10 mins or until cooked through, turning two or three times during cooking as this helps to keep the gammon slices flat. Remove and keep hot. Turn the heat down, and pour off some of the fat if there seems to be rather a lot in the pan.

2 Tbs French mustard	1 oz brown sugar (2 Tbs or 25 g)
¼ pt water, stock, cider or wine (150 ml)	1 tsp paprika pepper

Mix these together and add them to the fat in the pan. Cook and stir the sauce for a few minutes. Return the gammon, cover the pan and cook for another 5 mins. Serve hot with

boiled potatoes, rice or noodles, and a salad.

PORK LEFTOVERS

Serve cold roast pork or boiled ham and bacon with potato salad, sweet pickled fruit, beetroot, mixed pickles or chutney, cole slaw, mixed green salad.

Cold pork also makes a good potato pie, see shepherd's pie, page 186, or hash, page 173. For ham, see ham or bacon in maderia sauce, page 196, ham mousse, page 199, or noodles with ham and soured cream, page 328.

Ham and egg pie

Cooking time ½–¾ hr.
Temperature 220° C (425° F; G7).
Quantities for 4.

short-crust pastry using 4 oz flour (100 g), or 6–8 oz (175–250 g) ready-made puff or short-crust pastry

Make the pastry and put it in a cold place to rest while the filling is prepared.

1 oz butter or margarine (25 g)	1 oz flour (3 Tbs or 25 g)

Melt the fat in a small pan and stir in the flour. Cook gently until crumbly.

½ pt chicken stock (250 ml)

Add to the pan and whisk until the sauce is smooth, thickened and boiling. Boil for about 3 mins.

salt and pepper
1 tsp chopped marjoram
1 tsp chopped tarragon

pinch of ground mace or grated nutmeg

Add to the sauce and set aside to cool.

8 oz cold cooked ham or boiled bacon (250 g)
3 hard-boiled eggs

8 oz drained canned or cooked vegetables (250 g)

Remove the fat from the ham or bacon and cut the meat into small cubes. Shell the eggs and cut them in quarters. Drain the vegetables. Mix the sauce with the meat and vegetables and put it in a flat pie plate, 1 pt size (½ l). Press the eggs into the surface. Cover with pastry, brush the top with beaten egg or milk and bake until the pastry is brown and the filling bubbling. Serve hot.

Ham mousse

Quantities for 4–6.

½ oz gelatine (1½ Tbs or 15 g)   3 Tbs hot water

Sprinkle the gelatine into the water and stir to dissolve it.

8 oz lean cooked ham, minced (250 g)
¼ pt evaporated milk (150 ml)
¼ pt mayonnaise (150 ml)

1 Tbs lemon juice
½ tsp paprika pepper

Mix together and add the gelatine. Alternatively, instead of mincing the ham put it in the blender with the liquid and process in several lots until smooth.

1 egg white, beaten

Fold this into the ham mixture. Pour into a 1½ pt (850 ml) mould. Cover and put in the refrigerator to set. Before adding the mousse the mould may have a layer of aspic jelly set in the bottom, which gives the mousse a better appearance when it is turned out.

ROAST VEAL

SUITABLE CUTS

Boned, stuffed and rolled breast; boned top of the leg (fillet); leg; loin; boned and rolled shoulder (oyster); or a small shoulder on the bone.

TEMPERATURE AND TIME

160° C (325° F; G3). Pieces with bone, allow 30 mins per lb (½ kg); boned and rolled joints, allow 40 mins per lb (½ kg); pieces under 3 lb (1½ kg), allow 1½–2 hrs.

QUANTITIES

With bone, allow ½–¾ lb (250–350 g) per person; without bone, allow 4–6 oz, per person (125–175 g).

METHOD

As veal is a very lean meat it needs some special treatment to prevent it from becoming dry. There are several ways of doing this. Either baste with fat at 15 min intervals, or cover the top of the meat with strips of fat bacon which add flavour as well as fat (barding), or cover with a loose lid of foil, or use a roasting bag. If foil is used it should be removed for the last ½ hr of cooking to allow the meat to finish browning. If the veal is completely wrapped in foil it will need to be roasted at a higher temperature, 230° C (450° F; G8). Veal should be thoroughly cooked as it is unpalatable and indigestible if served under-done.

Place the meat on a rack or directly in the roasting pan.

Being one of the less highly flavoured meats, veal is very much improved by the addition of herbs during cooking or in an accompanying sauce or gravy. The best ones are fines herbes, rosemary, marjoram, lemon thyme or savory.

ACCOMPANIMENTS

Stuffing, or balls of stuffing baked separately from the joint, see Stuffings; boiled or grilled bacon or boiled salt pork; roast or mashed potatoes; spinach; green beans; chicory; young carrots; sweet peppers.

Roast stuffed veal

To stuff breast of veal, it should be boned, spread with stuffing and rolled up, then securely tied with fine white string at about 1 in (2½ cm) intervals. An alternative method is, after boning, to cut a pocket in the meat, stuff and sew up using coarse white cotton.

Leg and shoulder are stuffed where the bone has been removed. Shoulder is usually rolled in a neat shape and tied.

Loin is stuffed by separating the flesh from the thin rib bones sufficiently to make a pocket for the stuffing, then sewing up the opening.

The best stuffings to use are lemon stuffing, page 28, or cheese and rosemary stuffing, page 27.

FRIED VEAL

SUITABLE CUTS

Loin or chump chops, loin cutlets, escalopes, best end of neck cutlets.

Fried chops or cutlets

Cooking time 15–25 mins depending on size and thickness.
Quantities: allow 1 chop or 2 small cutlets per portion.

Fry the veal in a hot mixture of half butter and half lard or oil. Brown quickly each side and then reduce the heat, cover the pan, and finish cooking slowly. If you are not sure of the timing, cut one to make sure it is cooked right through.

Swill the pan out with a little stock, lemon juice, wine, cider or cream and pour the gravy over the chops. Garnish with chopped parsley or other fresh herbs and a little finely chopped onion.

ACCOMPANIMENTS

Mashed potatoes or boiled noodles; spinach; fried tomatoes or mushrooms; green beans; sweet peppers; aubergines; young carrots; or a green salad.

Fried escalopes

Cooking time 3–4 mins.
Quantities 1 escalope per person (about 3–4 oz or 75–125 g).

Escalopes should be neat slices of meat, in one piece. Poor-quality escalopes are often ragged bits of meat. If they have not already been beaten flat and thin, ask the butcher to do this for you, or else do it yourself using a wooden rolling pin.

ESCALOPES WITH LEMON

Fry them in hot butter. By the time they are brown on both sides they are usually cooked through. Remove from the pan and keep hot. Add a very little water to the pan and boil it hard for a minute or two to dissolve the sediment in the pan.

For every 4 escalopes add 1 Tbs lemon juice and pour the gravy over the escalopes.

Serve with mashed or fried potatoes and a lettuce salad.

WIENER SCHNITZEL

Coat the escalopes with beaten egg and then fine fresh breadcrumbs. Fry for 3–4 mins in oil, preferably in a deep fat fryer. Drain on absorbent kitchen paper and serve as soon as possible, garnished with anchovy fillets and wedges of lemon.

Serve with mashed or fried potatoes and a green salad.

Chops or cutlets à l'hongroise

Cooking time about 30 mins. *Quantities* for 4.

4 good-sized loin chops, or 8 cutlets   salt
paprika pepper

Sprinkle the meat with salt and plenty of paprika pepper, rubbing it in.

1 oz butter (25 g)

Heat the butter in a frying pan and brown the meat on both sides.

2 Tbs finely chopped onion

Sprinkle into the pan, turn down the heat, cover and cook slowly until the meat is cooked through, about another 15–20 mins.

½ pt double cream or soured cream   ¼ pt dry white wine (150 ml)
(250 ml)

Remove the meat from the pan and keep it hot. Add the wine to the pan, turn up the heat to make it boil rapidly and stir to incorporate the sediment in the pan. Boil for a minute or so to reduce it a little and then add the cream. Continue boiling until the sauce thickens a little. Return the meat, make sure it is hot and serve with

noodles or saffron rice and a mixed green salad.

Chops or cutlets with mushrooms

Cooking time 20–30 mins. *Quantities* for 4.

4 veal chops, or 8 cutlets
2 Tbs olive oil
1 oz butter (25 g)

Heat the butter and oil in a frying pan or sauté pan until the butter just begins to colour. Fry the meat quickly to brown it on both sides. Reduce the heat, cover the pan and cook slowly for 15–20 mins more.

8 oz sliced mushrooms (250 g)

Add these to the pan when the meat is half cooked. Stir occasionally. Lift out the meat and keep it hot.

¼ pt dry sherry (150 ml)
salt and pepper
¼ pt double cream (150 ml)

Add the sherry and bring to the boil, stirring all the time. Add the cream and boil until the sauce thickens a little. Season to taste. Return the meat to the sauce, re-heat and serve with

boiled potatoes or noodles and spinach, green beans or carrots.

Escalopes flambées

Cooking time about 5 mins. *Quantities* for 4.

4 veal escalopes
1 oz butter (25 g)
salt and pepper

Season the escalopes and heat the butter in a frying pan. Fry the escalopes quickly until they change colour on both sides.

2 Tbs warm brandy

Pour over the veal and ignite.

½ pt double cream (250 ml)
2 canned or cooked red peppers, chopped
2 tsp concentrated tomato purée

When the flames have died down, add the cream and boil until it begins to thicken. Add the tomato purée and sweet pepper, stir and heat for a few seconds and serve with

noodles, boiled potatoes or spaghetti dressed with butter and tomato purée; and green beans or salad.

Escalopes Parmesan

Cooking time 10–15 mins. Quantities for 4.

4 escalopes of veal	small piece of finely chopped garlic,
1 oz butter (25 g)	or use garlic salt

Heat the butter in a frying pan and add first the garlic and then the veal.

2 Tbs grated Parmesan cheese	2 tsp paprika pepper
salt and pepper	

Sprinkle this over the meat and fry it gently until brown on both sides. Lift out and keep hot. Swill out the pan with a little stock, lemon juice or white wine and pour the liquid over the meat. Serve with

spaghetti or noodles and a green salad.

VEAL CASSEROLES AND STEWS

SUITABLE CUTS
Boned shoulder, breast, hock, knuckle, neck and cutlets, also pie veal.

Blanquette of veal

Cooking time 2 hrs. Quantities for 4.

1½ lb breast or shoulder of veal weighed without bone (700 g), cut in small pieces	1 stick celery, chopped
	1 carrot, chopped
	½ Tbs salt
1 clove, stuck in the onion	pinch of mixed dried herbs or a sprig of lemon thyme
1 onion, skinned	

Put all the ingredients in a saucepan with 1 pt (600 ml) of water and bring to the boil. Simmer for an hour or until the meat is tender. Strain and put the meat aside to use later.

1 oz butter (25 g)	½ pt veal stock (250 ml)
2 Tbs flour	

Rinse out the saucepan, dry it and melt the butter in it. Add the flour and stir and cook for a minute. Add the stock and stir or whisk until the sauce is smooth and boiling.

2 oz button mushrooms, sliced (50 g)   pinch of pepper
6 small onions or shallots, skinned

Add these to the sauce, cover the pan and boil gently for about 45 mins or until the onions are tender, adding more stock if the sauce becomes too thick.

1 egg yolk   2 Tbs cream
1 Tbs lemon juice

Mix these together and stir into the sauce, stirring until it thickens some more. Add the meat and allow to become hot, but do not boil.

grilled bacon rolls and lemon wedges   2 Tbs chopped parsley
  (optional)

Serve the dish sprinkled with chopped parsley and garnished with the bacon rolls and lemon wedges. Serve with

mashed potatoes and spinach or a green salad.

Casserole with rosemary or thyme

Cooking time about 1½ hrs.
Temperature 150° C (300° F; G2).
Quantities for 4.

1–1½ lb pie veal (500–700 g)   1 Tbs flour
1 tsp salt

Trim the meat and cut it in small pieces, toss in the flour and salt to coat it well.

1 Tbs olive oil

Heat in a casserole or frying pan and brown the meat well. Remove from the pan.

1 Tbs olive oil   1 medium-sized onion, finely chopped

Add the oil to the pan and fry the onion until it just begins to brown.

8 oz canned tomatoes (250 g)   pinch of pepper
2 oz sliced mushrooms (50 g)   1 tsp chopped fresh rosemary or
¼ pt dry white wine or cider (150 ml)   thyme, or ½ tsp dried

Add to the pan, mix to dissolve the sediment, return the meat, cover and cook until the veal is tender.

¼ pt soured cream or fresh double   1 Tbs flour
  cream (150 ml)

Mix the cream gradually into the flour and stir this into the casserole. Stir until it thickens and boil gently for 1-2 mins.

Italian veal stew

Cooking time 30-40 mins. *Quantities* for 4.

8 small veal cutlets	4 Tbs olive oil

Heat the oil in a sauté pan or shallow saucepan and fry the cutlets brown on both sides.

1 stalk celery, chopped	1 medium-sized carrot, chopped
1 medium-sized onion, chopped	

Add to the pan, lower the heat, cover with a lid or with foil and cook slowly until the vegetables are tender, about 10 mins.

1 Tbs concentrated tomato purée	salt and pepper
¼ pt dry sherry (150 ml)	

Add to the pan and continue cooking until the meat is tender, about 20 mins, adding a little water if the pan begins to get dry.

chopped parsley	mashed potatoes

Serve the stew sprinkled liberally with parsley and accompanied by creamy mashed potatoes.

Osso buco

Cooking time 1½-2 hrs. *Quantities* for 4.

2 veal hocks	2 onions, chopped
1 large carrot, chopped	flour

Ask the butcher to saw the hocks into 3 in (8 cm) pieces. Coat the pieces of hock with flour.

2 oz butter (50 g), or 4 Tbs olive oil

Heat the fat or oil in a deep stew pan or casserole and fry the meat and vegetables in it until they are brown.

¼ pt red wine (150 ml)	1 pt stock (600 ml)
2 Tbs concentrated tomato purée	1 tsp salt
a bouquet garni	¼ tsp freshly ground pepper

Add to the pan, using enough stock just to cover the meat. Simmer until the meat is tender, on top or in a slow oven. Remove the bouquet garni.

a little grated lemon rind   chopped parsley

Serve the sauce and meat sprinkled with lemon and parsley. Serve with boiled potatoes or boiled rice.

OTHER VEAL RECIPES

Galantine

Cooking time 2–3 hrs. *Quantities* for 12 or more.

3 lb breast of veal in one piece (1½ kg)

The veal should be boned, but keep the bones for stock.

8 oz gammon or lean bacon (250 g)   1 lb pork sausage meat (500 g)
3 hard-boiled eggs

Remove the rind and chop the bacon. Mix it with the sausage meat. Put the veal on a board, skin side down. Spread half the sausage meat mixture on top of it. Shell and slice the eggs and put them on top of the sausage meat, then cover with the rest of the sausage mixture. Roll the meat up and wrap it firmly in foil, making the joins secure.

½ tsp salt   ½ bay leaf
sprig of parsley   sprig of thyme

Put the veal bones in a pan with enough water just to cover them and the galantine. Bring to the boil and simmer for a few minutes, add the galantine and simmer for 2–3 hrs.

Lift it out of the stock, remove the foil and press the galantine between two plates, with a weight on top. Put in a cool place and when it is quite cold, cover and store in the refrigerator. Before serving, glaze it as follows:

2 Tbs gelatine   1½ pt stock (850 ml)

Heat the stock, sprinkle in the gelatine and stir to dissolve it, then boil the stock hard to reduce to about ½ pt (250 ml).

gravy browning

Colour the stock and leave it to cool. When it begins to thicken, brush it thickly over the galantine. Leave to set. To serve, slice the galantine thinly and serve with salad.

Terrine

Cooking time 2 hrs.
Temperature 160° C (325° F; G3).
Quantities for 6.

1 lb sliced boneless veal, any cut (500 g)	2 oz liver (50 g)
	1 shallot or small onion
8 oz belly of pork (250 g)	

Keep about 4 oz (125 g) of the veal and mince the rest with the other meats and the onion, mincing twice to make a fine mixture.

1 Tbs chopped parsley	1 tsp salt
½ tsp mixed spice	pinch of pepper

Add to the meat and mix well.

8 oz thinly sliced streaky bacon (250 g)	1 bay leaf

Remove the rinds from the bacon and wash the bay leaf. Put the leaf in the bottom of a 6 in (15 cm) soufflé dish or cake tin. Line the dish with some of the bacon rashers, put in a layer of the minced meat and then a layer of veal slices, then bacon rashers and repeat these layers until all the ingredients have been used, finishing with a layer of bacon. Cover with a piece of foil pressed down on top of the dish. Bake the terrine.

Remove the cover, put a flat plate or a lid, a little smaller than the dish, on top of the meat and put a weight on this. Put the terrine in a cold place and when it is quite cold store it in the refrigerator.

To serve, turn out of the mould and slice. If a layer of fat has collected on top of the terrine, remove this just before unmoulding it. Serve with salad, or as a starter.

Veal and ham plate pie

Cooking time about 1¼ hrs.
Temperature 190° C (375° F; G5) for 40 mins, then 180° C (350° F; G4) for about 30 mins.
Quantities for an 8–9 in (20–25 cm) pie plate.

short-crust pastry using 4 oz flour (100 g), or use 6 oz ready-made (175 g)

Make the pastry and put in a cold place while the filling is prepared.

1 lb boneless veal (500 g), cut in small pieces
¼ pt stock or water (150 ml)
salt and pepper
4 oz bacon (125 g), cut in strips
1 tsp grated lemon rind, or use a mixture of chopped lemon thyme, chervil and parsley

Put all these in a bowl and mix well. Turn into the pie plate.

1 hard-boiled egg

Shell and cut the egg in 8 sections. Press into the meat, white uppermost.

Brush the edges of the pie plate with water and roll the pastry thinly to make a lid a little bigger than the top of the pie. Trim the edges, put on the pie and turn the over-hanging pastry under to make a double edge. Press down and mark with a knife or fork to decorate the edge. Brush the pie with beaten egg and water or with milk and bake. Serve hot or cold.

Veal leftovers

Serve cold sliced veal with a plain orange salad or with chicory and orange salad; with a plain tomato salad or tomato and sweet pepper salad. Small cubes of cooked veal are very good in a Parisian salad.

For using veal leftovers in hot dishes, chicken recipes are suitable and so are beef recipes.

All these will be found in the index.

KIDNEYS

Devilled kidneys

Cooking time 1 hr. *Quantities* for 3-4.

6 sheep's kidneys

Remove fat and skin and cut the kidneys in half. Cut out any hard core. Wash and drain well, or dry on paper towels.

1 onion, chopped
1 oz fat (25 g), or 2 Tbs oil
1 small carrot, chopped

Heat the fat or oil in a small pan and fry the vegetables until they begin to brown.

1 oz flour (3 Tbs or 25 g)

Add to the pan and stir in. Cook until it browns, stirring occasionally, for about 15 mins. Remove from the heat.

½ pt stock (250 ml)

Gradually add to the pan and stir until well blended. Return to the heat and stir until it boils.

small piece of bay leaf   sprig of parsley

Add to the sauce and simmer for ½ hr, stirring occasionally and adding water if the sauce tends to become too thick. Strain and re-heat.

1 Tbs made mustard   1 Tbs Worcester sauce
1 tsp curry powder   1 tsp anchovy essence

Mix the curry powder to a smooth paste with the other ingredients and add to the sauce in the pan. Season with salt and pepper and keep hot.

1 oz fat (25 g), or 2 Tbs oil

Heat in a frying pan and cook the kidneys in it until small beads of blood begin to appear on the top, turn and cook the other side. Put on a serving dish and pour the sauce over them or put them in the sauce to keep hot until required. Serve with one of the following:

fingers of toast; mashed potatoes; boiled rice, macaroni or spaghetti; and a salad.

Grilled kidneys (lamb's or pig's) and bacon

Cooking time about 10 mins.

Remove rinds from the bacon rashers, one or two per portion. Allow two lamb's or one pig's kidney per portion. Remove the skin, cut kidneys in half and remove the hard white core using scissors.

Put the kidneys in the grill pan with the bacon on top. Grill until the bacon is cooked, remove and keep it hot. Grill the kidneys, turning when beads of blood begin to show on the surface, turn and grill until blood appears again. Serve with any juices in the grill pan and with

salad, spinach, or grilled tomatoes   boiled or fried potatoes
  and watercress.

Kidney pancakes

Quantities for 8 pancakes, see page 37.

4 lamb's kidneys, 2–3 pig's or ½–¾ lb   2 oz chopped bacon (50 g)
  calf's (250–350 g)   2 oz sliced mushrooms (50 g)

Remove fat, fibres and core from the kidneys, wash and drain them. Cut into small pieces and set aside.

| 1 oz fat (25 g) | 1 oz flour (3 Tbs or 25 g) |

Heat the fat in a small pan and fry the bacon in it until almost cooked. Add the kidney and fry quickly until it changes colour. Use a perforated spoon to remove the bacon and kidney from the pan. Sprinkle in the flour and mix well.

| ½ pt stock (300 ml) | salt and pepper |

Stir in the stock and bring to the boil, stirring all the time. Add the mushrooms and seasoning and simmer for 5 mins. Return the kidney and bacon to the sauce and simmer for a few minutes longer. Put to keep hot while the pancakes are made.

As each is completed put a spoonful of the kidney mixture on it, roll it over and put in a large shallow baking dish. Any mixture left over can go on top or round the pancakes.

grated cheese

Sprinkle thickly on top of the pancakes and put them under a moderate grill to crisp and brown the cheese.

LIVER

Casserole of ox liver

Cooking time 1¼ hrs.
Temperature 180° C (350° F; G4).
Quantities for 4–6.

| 1 lb thinly sliced ox liver (500 g) | seasoned flour |

Wash and drain the liver. Remove any coarse tubes and dust the liver with seasoned flour.

1 oz butter (25 g), or 2 Tbs oil, or a mixture

Heat in a frying pan and brown the liver quickly on both sides, lift out and set aside.

| 2 rashers streaky bacon, diced | 1 small onion, finely chopped |

Add to the pan and fry until the onion begins to colour.

| 2 Tbs chopped fresh herbs, sage, tarragon or fennel or use 1 tsp dried powdered sage or rosemary
pinch of garlic salt | salt and pepper
2 Tbs lemon juice
5 Tbs stock or water (75 ml) |

Add to the pan and just bring to the boil. Put half the sauce in a shallow casserole, add the slices of liver and pour the rest of the sauce over it. Cover and cook until the liver is tender, about 1 hr.

Liver and bacon with red wine

Cooking time about 10 mins. *Quantities* for 4.

¾–1 lb calf's, lamb's or pig's liver (350–500 g)   4–8 rashers streaky bacon

Ask the butcher to slice the liver very thinly or buy it in a piece and slice it yourself. If you have a supply of liver in the freezer you will find it very easy to slice thinly when it is partially thawed. It can be cooked before it is completely thawed and is more juicy this way. Remove rinds from the bacon.

lard or oil

Heat enough to cover the bottom of the frying pan. Add the bacon and fry until done according to your taste. Remove and keep hot. Add the liver and cook it quickly on both sides until browned. Avoid over-cooking as this makes it hard and tough. Remove the liver and keep it hot.

¼–½ pt red wine, or a mixture of wine, stock and lemon juice (150–250 ml)

Add to the pan, using enough liquid to make the amount of gravy you like. Stir and boil to dissolve all the sediment in the pan. Season to taste. Return the liver and make sure it is hot before serving with the bacon and

sauté or boiled potatoes and a green salad.

Liver loaf

Cooking time ¾ hr.
Temperature 200° C (400° F; G6).
Quantities for 6.

8 oz any kind of liver (250 g), in one piece   2 oz onion (50 g or 1 small), chopped
½ oz fat (15 g), or 1 Tbs oil

Wash the liver, drain and dry it on paper towels. Heat the fat or oil and brown the liver and onion in it quickly. Remove the pan from the heat.

2 oz bacon (50 g or 2 rashers)

Remove the rinds and mince bacon, liver and onion together. Put in a bowl.

4 oz pork sausage meat (125 g)	1 egg, beaten
2 oz fresh breadcrumbs (⅔ c or 50 g)	1 Tbs lemon juice
1 tsp Worcester sauce	1 tsp celery salt
pinch of pepper	5 Tbs water or red wine (75 ml)

Mix all ingredients with the liver to make a smooth soft consistency. Put in a greased 1 lb (½ kg) loaf pan and cover with a lid of foil. Bake.

To serve hot, turn out of the tin, slice and serve with tomato or Espagnole sauce and vegetables.

To serve cold, allow the loaf to cool in the tin, cover, and store in the refrigerator. Slice and serve as cold meat.

Liver Veneziana

Cooking time 5–8 mins. *Quantities* for 2–3.

8 oz calf's or lamb's liver (250 g)

Have the liver sliced very thinly and then cut the slices into pieces about 1 in (2½ cm) square.

2 medium-sized onions   olive oil

Skin the onions and slice them very finely. Heat a little oil in a frying pan and cook the onions until they brown. Add the liver and cook for 2 minutes, stirring all the time.

salt and pepper	2 tsp chopped parsley
3 or more leaves of finely chopped fresh sage, or a pinch of dried	2–3 Tbs red wine or stock

Add to the liver and cook for ½ min longer, stirring to dissolve the sediment in the pan. Serve with

boiled or sauté potatoes and a salad.

TONGUE

Boiled ox tongue

Cooking time 2½–3 hrs.
Quantities: allow 4 oz (125 g) per portion. One tongue will weigh 4 lb, more or less (2 kg).

Usually the tongue will be sold after some days in a pickling solution, but whether fresh or pickled, it needs to be soaked in cold water to cover. Leave overnight in a cool place.

2 bay leaves
1 onion
1 carrot
1 Tbs salt, for fresh tongue
6 peppercorns
1 piece of turnip
2 stalks celery

Skin the onion, scrape or peel the carrot, peel the turnip, wash the celery. Put the tongue in a large pan with fresh cold water to cover, bring to the boil, and simmer for 5 mins. Drain away the water, add fresh cold water to cover and then the vegetables and flavourings. Bring to the boil and simmer until tender. Remove any scum as it rises to the top.

When it is tender, drain and plunge the tongue in cold water. When it is cool enough to handle, remove the skin and any bones and pieces of gristle at the root end. Serve in one of the following ways:

PRESSED TONGUE

Coil the tongue up tightly in a straight-sided basin or cake tin to make a tight fit. Add a little of the stock to fill the crevices. Put a flat plate, slightly smaller than the container, or a smaller cake tin, on top of the tongue with a heavy weight on top. Leave until cold and store in the refrigerator. Turn out of the mould and slice horizontally.

HOT TONGUE

Put the tongue on a board and slice it thinly, from the tip towards the root, and serve it in a sauce such as tomato, parsley or Espagnole. Serve potatoes and vegetables with it.

GLAZED TONGUE

Put the tongue on a board or large flat serving dish and arrange it straight as in the mouth. Leave to become cold. Brush the cold tongue with aspic jelly which is on the point of setting. Garnish with salad vegetables. Slice thinly as for hot tongue.

Boiled calf's tongue

These usually weigh between 1 and 2 lb ($\frac{1}{2}$–1 kg). Cook the same way as above for ox tongue, allowing 2 hrs cooking time.

Boiled sheep's tongues in onion sauce

Cooking time $2\frac{1}{2}$ hrs. *Quantities* for 4.

1 large onion
2 tsp salt
1 pt water ($\frac{1}{2}$ l)
4 fresh tongues
a bouquet garni

Skin the onion and slice it thinly. Put in a pan with the other ingredients. Boil gently for 1½ hrs or until the tongues are tender. Remove them from the stock, plunge them in cold water and when they are cool enough to handle, peel off the skin and remove any small bones at the base of the tongues. Strain the stock and cool it.

½ oz butter or margarine (15 g) ½ oz lard (15 g)
1 oz flour (3 Tbs or 25 g)

Melt the fats in a small saucepan, add the flour and stir and cook gently for a few minutes. Add 1 pt (600 ml) of the cold stock to the roux, stirring until the sauce is smooth and boiling.

4 small onions or shallots

Skin and add to the sauce, together with the tongues, and simmer for 30 mins or until the onions are tender.

chopped parsley or other green herbs

Serve the tongues and onions liberally sprinkled with the herbs.

BOILED PICKLED TONGUES

Soak in cold water for 12 hrs before cooking as above.

TRIPE

Tripe au gratin

Cooking time 1¼ hrs. *Quantities* for 4.

1 lb dressed tripe (500 g)

Cut the tripe into fingers and cover it with cold water. Bring to the boil and boil for 2 mins. Strain.

1 large onion ½ lemon
1 tsp salt

Skin the onion and put it in a pan with the tripe, salt and cold water just to cover. Add a squeeze of lemon juice. Bring to the boil, cover, and simmer for 1 hr.

1 oz butter (25 g) ¼ pt milk (150 ml)
1 oz flour (3 Tbs or 25 g) ¼ pt tripe stock (150 ml)

Melt the butter in a saucepan and stir in the flour, cooking and stirring for a minute or so. Remove from the heat and stir in the milk and stock, whisking or stirring until smooth. Bring to the boil, stirring all the time. Boil gently for a few minutes.

salt and pepper

Season the sauce to taste and add the tripe and the onion, chopped. Pour into a hot fireproof dish.

1½ oz grated strong cheese (4 Tbs or 40 g)
½ oz butter (15 g)
1½ oz fresh breadcrumbs (½ c or 40 g)

Melt the butter in a small pan and add the crumbs. Stir to coat them and then add the cheese. Sprinkle on top of the tripe and brown under the grill.

SAUSAGES

The variety of sausages available is enormous, especially of continental types.

Most of them are meant for serving cold as starters or as part of a cold meat platter. Most popular among these are liver sausage, mortadella, salami, garlic sausage and ham sausage, but there are many others.

Some sausages are for serving hot or cold. Chief among those served hot are black pudding, frankfurters, saveloys, Strasbourg sausages and boiling rings. Most of these need to have about 10 mins cooking in simmering water before serving them, usually with mashed potatoes and often with sauerkraut. They may also be sliced and heated in a vegetable soup to make a good lunch or supper dish.

Many sausages are now vacuum-packed and date stamped, often with cooking and serving instructions included.

English beef and pork sausages

FRIED SAUSAGES

Cooking time 30 mins, or less for small sausages.

Heat a little fat in a frying pan and cook the sausages very slowly until they are well browned. If cooked too fast they will tend to burst but some like them this way. These however, should be given thorough cooking as it is important to have them cooked right through.

GRILLED SAUSAGES

Cooking time 20–30 mins.

Grill them fairly slowly under a moderate heat, turning them frequently until they are well browned and cooked right through. Grilled bacon rolls, apple rings, tomatoes and mushrooms can be cooked at the same time.

BAKED SAUSAGES

Cooking time 30 mins.
Temperature 220° C (425° F; G7).

Put the sausages in a single layer in a shallow baking tin or fireproof dish and bake until they are well browned. This is one of the best ways of cooking sausages as it is rare for them to burst and they get a thorough cooking. Baked tomatoes, mushrooms and other foods can be cooked at the same time.

Norfolk pork sausages

Cooking time 25–30 mins. *Quantities* for 3–4.

1 small onion or shallot, finely chopped   ¾ pt milk (400 ml)

Heat all but 2 Tbs of the milk in a fairly large saucepan. Add the onion and bring to the boil.

1 lb pork sausages (500 g)

Separate the sausages and prick each in several places, using a fork. Drop them into the boiling milk and boil gently for 30 mins. Lift them out and keep them hot.

1 Tbs cornflour   1 tsp dry mustard

Mix these to a smooth paste with the 2 Tbs of milk, add to the hot milk, stirring quickly to blend. Boil for 3 min.

salt and pepper   chopped parsley

Season the sauce to taste, return the sausages and heat for a minute or so. Serve with plenty of parsley and with

boiled potatoes and a green vegetable or salad.

Smothered sausages

Cooking time 5–10 mins grilling, followed by ½ hr baking.
Temperature 200° C (400° F; G6).
Quantities for 3–4.

1 lb pork sausages (500 g)

Make the grill very hot and brown the sausages quickly all over. They do not need to cook through.

bacon rashers, as many as there are sausages

Remove the rinds and wrap a rasher round each sausage. Pack them side by side in a casserole just big enough to take them in a single layer.

1 or 2 large cooking apples

Peel, core and slice in rings. Put in an overlapping layer on top of the sausages.

¼ pt stock (150 ml)

Pour into the dish, cover with a lid, and bake until the apples and bacon are cooked. Serve in the casserole.

Frankfurters with paprika potatoes

Cooking time 40–50 mins. *Quantities* for 4–6.

1 oz fat (25 g)	4 oz chopped onion (125 g)

Heat the fat in a saucepan and fry the onion until it begins to brown.

1 oz flour (3 Tbs or 25 g)	1 tsp paprika pepper

Add to the onion and mix well.

1 Tbs wine vinegar	½ pt stock (250 ml)
2 tsp salt	

Add to the pan and stir until boiling.

1½ lb potatoes, preferably new ones (700 g)

Scrape or peel and cut in pieces the size of an egg. Add them to the sauce. Cover the pan and cook over a gentle heat until the potatoes are tender. Occasionally stir gently to prevent the potatoes from sticking to the pan but do not break them in the process.

1½ lb frankfurters (700 g)

Put on top of the potatoes for the last 10 mins of cooking to allow them to heat through. Serve the potatoes with the sausages on top. Serve with a salad.

9. Poultry and Game

POULTRY

Oven-ready birds with a well-known brand name are usually a safe buy. They may be labelled as spring chickens or poussins (small ones giving 1–2 portions); frying or roasting chickens; and boiling fowls (long, slow cooking required). The largest and finest roasting chicken is a capon. A small duck or duckling weighs about 3 lb (1½ kg), a duck 4 lb (2 kg) upwards. A small goose will weigh about 6 lb (3 kg), a large one up to 20–24 lb (9–11 kg). Turkeys come in much the same size range.

When buying unbranded fresh poultry, it is wisest to buy from a shop you know sells good-quality food.

If the poultry is frozen make sure the skin is not discoloured over the breast, as this shows the birds have not been stored carefully and the quality may be poor. The discolouring shows as brownish patches instead of the white skin of a fresh bird.

Storing

Fresh poultry will keep for 2–4 days in a cold larder. In the refrigerator (in a polythene bag), a chicken or duck will keep 3–4 days and a goose or turkey for a week. In the freezer, poultry will keep for 10–12 months.

APPROXIMATE THAWING TIMES FOR FROZEN POULTRY

	In refrigerator or cold larder	At room temperature 15° C (60° F)
Whole chicken	24–36 hrs	6–8 hrs
Chicken joints	6 hrs or more	3 hrs
Small turkey, goose or capon	2 days	Not recommended
Large turkey or goose	3–4 days	Not recommended
Duckling and ducks	24–36 hrs	6–8 hrs

STORING COOKED POULTRY AND ADVANCE PREPARATION

Poultry which is being prepared to serve cold should be thoroughly cooked and carefully stored, otherwise it can be a source of food poisoning.

Stuffing can be a cause of trouble. If it is being prepared in advance it should not be put in the bird until just before cooking and if the stuffed bird is to be served cold, the stuffing should be removed after cooking and cooled and refrigerated separately. Stored like this it can be safely kept for a couple of days.

If casseroles are cooked in advance for re-heating, they should be cooked thoroughly for the full time, cooled quickly, and when quite cold, stored in the refrigerator. When re-heating, bring to the boil and boil gently for 20–30 mins to make sure the meat is thoroughly heated through. Just warming up is dangerous.

Carving

First remove the legs at the joint nearest the body. The simplest way is to hold the end of the leg in one hand and pull the leg slightly away from the body while severing the joint with a knife or poultry scissors. Each leg may be cut into two portions at the joint. Next remove the wing together with a small portion of the breast. Then remove the wishbone by slicing down across the breast at the neck end. Then the breast is cut in slices, carving downwards.

Home freezing poultry and game

Young poultry and game are the best for freezing.

Poultry should be killed not more than two days before freezing; game birds should be hung first to give the condition you prefer; hares and rabbits should be hung for 24 hrs; venison should be well hung and then frozen in the same way as meat.

Prepare the poultry and game as you would for cooking and freeze it whole or in joints, first chilling the meat for 12 hrs in the refrigerator. It is advisable to freeze stuffing separately and usually more convenient to freeze giblets separately. Polythene bags are suitable for poultry or game but first protect any sharp bones with a cap of foil.

Cooked poultry or game can be frozen whole, jointed or sliced; first removing stuffing from whole birds. Casseroles and other cooked dishes are treated in the same way as meat.

For approximate thawing times for poultry, see page 219, and for game, page 241.

CHICKEN

Roast chicken

Oven-ready roasting chickens are usually from 3 lb (1½ kg) up to 6–8 lb (3–4 kg) for a capon. The larger birds usually have more flavour than younger ones and those which are well hung before drawing have most flavour. Frozen birds are usually young, drawn and frozen immediately after killing and have least flavour. They should be completely thawed before cooking and need the help of herbs and other flavourings to compensate for their immaturity.

COOKING TIMES

For birds up to 3½ lb (1½ kg), allow 20 mins per 1lb (½ kg) plus 20 mins. For larger birds, allow 25 mins per lb (½ kg).

TEMPERATURE

190° C (375° F; G5) for birds up to 3½ lb oven-ready weight (1½ kg); 180° C (350° F; G4) for larger birds.

QUANTITIES

Allow ½ lb (250 g) oven-ready weight per portion.

METHOD

If the bird has a parcel of giblets inside, remove these, rinse them well and use them to make stock. Rinse the chicken inside and out and drain well. If stuffing is being used (see Stuffings, pages 26–9, for recipes), fill the chicken from the crop end to make it plump. Fasten the flap of neck skin over the stuffing and secure to the back of the bird with a small skewer or cocktail stick. Surplus stuffing can be put in the body of the bird, or formed into small balls and cooked separately to use as a garnish. Instead of stuffing, a knob of butter can be put inside with a small peeled onion, or put a sprig of fresh herb such as rosemary or tarragon inside.

Brush the breast with oil or melted butter and put the chicken on a trivet in the roasting pan, or on an oven rack with a pan below. To keep the breast moist, cover it with a piece of fat bacon or foil, removing these for the last 20 mins of cooking to allow the breast to brown. An alternative method is to cook the bird in a polyester film roasting bag.

Some chopped vegetables can be put in the roasting pan to help flavour the gravy. Use stock made from the giblets for making the gravy.

ACCOMPANIMENTS

Bread sauce; grilled or baked bacon rolls; chipolata sausages; sliced boiled ham or pickled pork; stuffing; mashed, roast or fried potatoes; a green vegetable, or serve watercress or a lettuce salad.

Braised chicken

Cooking time 2–3 hrs.
Temperature 160° C (325° F; G3).
Quantities for 4–6.

1 chicken (3 lb or 1½ kg)	2 oz butter (50 g)
salt and pepper	

Season the chicken inside and out. Heat the butter in a casserole or saucepan large enough to take the chicken. Brown the chicken in the butter, turning it occasionally to brown it all over.

4 oz chopped bacon (125 g)	8 small onions, or 2 medium-sized
1 lb of other vegetables (500 g)	salt
(potatoes, celery, carrots, peas)	

Skin the onions and cut medium-sized ones in pieces. Prepare the other vegetables and cut them in small pieces. Put these round the chicken and sprinkle the vegetables with salt. Cover and cook until the chicken is tender, either on top of the cooker or in the oven.

Serve the chicken with the vegetables as a garnish and the liquid as a sauce.

Chicken in a pot

This is a very good way of cooking chicken to serve cold. It can be done with a whole chicken or with a carcass after the legs have been removed for another dish, very useful for a small family. Then, if you prefer, the chicken breast and wings can be served hot with a good sauce such as onion, mushroom, or Espagnole.

Cooking time 1–1½ hrs.
Temperature 180° C (350° F; G4).
Quantities for 4–6.

3 lb roasting chicken (1½ kg)	¼ pt water (150 ml)
salt and pepper	2 Tbs white wine

Wash the chicken and giblets and put the giblets in the bottom of a saucepan or casserole with the chicken on top. Season with salt and pepper and add the water and wine. Cover and cook until the thick part of the thigh is done. (When pierced with a fork no red liquid runs out.)

Use the cooking liquid for a sauce if the chicken is served hot, or add it to stock for a soup, made with the carcass.

ALTERNATIVE

Put either a bay leaf, a sprig of rosemary or a sprig of tarragon inside the chicken or on top.

FRIED AND GRILLED CHICKEN

Small, young chickens are the best for frying or grilling, though roasting chicken joints are suitable for sautés, that is, fried and then finished in a sauce.

The best chickens for grilling are spring chickens or poussins; these are either cut in half along backbone and breast bone or, for very small ones, cut through the backbone and opened out flat to make one portion. Small, young roasting chickens will also supply joints suitable for grilling.

Fried chicken joints

Cooking time 20–25 mins. *Quantities* for 4.

4 portions of frying chickens	2 tsp salt
1 oz flour (3 Tbs or 25 g)	$\frac{1}{4}$ tsp freshly ground pepper

Mix the flour and seasonings and put them in a paper bag. Wash and dry the pieces of chicken, put them in the bag and shake to coat them thoroughly with the flour, using more flour if necessary.

oil for frying

Use a frying pan large enough to allow the pieces of chicken to lie flat in a single layer. Alternatively, cook the pieces in relays and keep hot in a slow oven or in a warming cupboard.

Put oil in the pan to the depth of about $\frac{1}{4}$ in (6 mm). Make it hot and then brown the chicken pieces all over, reduce the heat and continue cooking for another 15–20 mins or until the chicken is tender. Drain well on absorbent kitchen paper.

raw quartered tomatoes	watercress or lettuce

Serve these as a garnish or as a tossed salad.

Fried chicken flambée, with cream

Cooking time about 45 mins. *Quantities* for 4.

4 portions of frying chicken	1 oz butter (25 g)

If you are buying chicken joints rather than a whole chicken, try to have them all the same as this simplifies the cooking.

Wash and dry the chicken and season it with salt and pepper. Heat the butter in a frying pan and then fry the chicken until it changes colour, but do not allow it to brown. Turn down the heat, cover the pan and cook slowly until the chicken is tender. This will take less time for breast pieces than for legs, so remove the former as soon as they are cooked and keep them hot. When all are tender, return to the pan to keep hot. The cooking can be completed at table on a spirit burner, or in the kitchen just before serving.

4 Tbs warm brandy

Ignite and pour over the chicken pieces, basting them with the burning liquid. When the flames have died down put the chicken on a hot serving dish. Keep hot.

½ pt soured cream or double cream (250 ml)

Add to the pan and stir well to incorporate the juices in the pan. Boil it rapidly until reduced by about half. Pour it over the chicken and serve, with

noodles or new potatoes; a vegetable or a green salad.

Chicken fondue

Quantities for 4.

4 chicken breasts

These can be fresh or frozen breasts. If frozen chicken is used, thaw it completely and allow to come to room temperature before serving. Wash the chicken and dry it carefully on paper towels.

Cut the chicken in small pieces ½–¾ in thick (1–2 cm). Arrange the pieces on a small plate or in a fondue dish and garnish with parsley, chervil or other green stuff available.

1–1½ pt peanut or groundnut oil (600–800 ml)

Put oil in the fondue pot to make it just less than half full. Heat to 190° C (375° F) and transfer the pot to fondue burner.

Provide fondue forks for spearing the meat for cooking and a plate, knife and fork for eating the cooked meat. The pieces of chicken will take about 2 mins to cook.

ACCOMPANIMENTS

Béarnaise sauce; Breton sauce; curry mayonnaise; softened savoury butters; fresh French bread or crisp rolls; saffron or herb rice; salad.

Barbecue chicken

Cooking time 25–30 mins. *Quantities* for 4.

4 portions of frying chicken

Wash the chicken and dry well. Place it on the grill rack, skin side down.

1 tsp dry mustard	1½ oz melted butter or margarine
2 tsp Worcester sauce	(40 g)
2 Tbs vinegar	

Mix together and brush the chicken with it. Pre-heat the grill and cook the chicken under a moderate heat, brushing occasionally with the remaining sauce. Turn once during cooking. Serve garnished with

tomatoes and watercress.

Spatchcock chicken

Cooking time ½–¾ hr.
Quantities: allow 1 poussin or small spring chicken per portion.

salt and pepper ½ Tbs lemon juice per portion
½ oz (15 g) melted butter per portion

Split each chicken in half down the backbone. Flatten the bird and secure it in position by passing a fine skewer through the legs. Sprinkle with salt and pepper and lemon juice. Set aside for ½ hr.
   Pre-heat the grill and cook the chicken, brushing it with butter during cooking. Cook under a high heat for 5 mins each side or until brown and then reduce the heat for the rest of the cooking time. Serve with

fried or sauté potatoes; grilled tomatoes, mushrooms, sweet peppers or
   aubergines; mixed salad; grilled bananas; a cold sauce such as Breton.

ALTERNATIVE

Instead of making a spatchcock of the chicken cut it completely in two through the backbone and the breast bone, then grill the two halves as above.

Sauté of chicken with herbs and olives

Cooking time 45 mins. *Quantities* for 4.

| 4 portions of frying or roasting chicken | 1 clove of garlic
4 Tbs olive oil (60 ml) |

Heat the oil in a sauté pan or deep frying pan, add the garlic and chicken and fry until brown. Remove the chicken and discard the garlic.

2 Tbs flour

Add to the oil remaining in the pan and mix well. Cook for 2–3 mins.

1 Tbs each of chopped fennel, chives and parsley

Add to the pan and cook for a minute longer.

½ pt dry white wine or cider (250 ml)

Stir into the pan and stir until it boils.

| ¼ pt soured cream or thick yogurt (150 ml) | salt and pepper
12 stoned black olives |

Add to the pan, mix and return the chicken. Cover the pan and cook slowly until the chicken is tender.

Sauté of chicken with tarragon sauce

Cooking time 1 hr. *Quantities* for 4.

Begin by making the sauce.

| ½ oz butter (15 g)
1 rasher bacon, chopped | 1 small onion, finely chopped |

Heat the butter in a small pan and fry bacon and onion until they begin to brown.

1 Tbs flour

Add and mix and cook until just beginning to brown.

| ½ pt chicken stock (250 ml)
2 tsp concentrated tomato purée | salt and pepper |

Add to the pan and stir until boiling. Put to boil gently while the chicken is cooked.

| 4 portions of frying chicken | 1 oz butter (25 g) |

Heat the butter in a sauté pan or deep frying pan and fry the chicken until golden on both sides, lower the heat, cover the pan and cook slowly for about 30 mins or until the chicken is tender. Remove from the pan and put to keep hot.

| 2 Tbs chopped fresh tarragon | ¼ pt dry white wine (150 ml) |

Add the tarragon to the sauce and the wine to the pan in which the chicken has been cooked. Stir until the wine is boiling and boil until reduced by half. Add the tarragon sauce and mix. Return the pieces of chicken and turn them over in the sauce to coat them well. Make sure they are hot before serving with

Boiled or mashed potatoes or boiled noodles; green beans; or mixed green salad.

Spanish chicken

Cooking time 1 hr. *Quantities* for 4.

| 4 portions of frying or roasting chicken | salt and pepper |
| 1 clove of crushed garlic | 4 Tbs olive oil |

Season the chicken with salt and pepper. Heat the oil and garlic in a sauté pan or shallow saucepan. Remove the garlic when it is brown. Put in the chicken and fry it, turning it often.

| 8 oz lean gammon, cut in strips (250 g) | 2 fresh or canned sweet red peppers, chopped |
| 1 medium-sized onion, finely chopped | |

When the chicken begins to brown add these ingredients, cover the pan, turn down the heat and cook slowly until the chicken is tender. Serve with

rice or pasta.

CHICKEN CASSEROLES

Casseroles can be made with joints of roasting chicken, in which case the cooking time will be about 1½–2 hrs. If they are made with joints of older chicken or boiling fowl, they usually need 3–4 hrs cooking.

Unless otherwise specified, either kind of chicken can be used in these recipes, selecting the appropriate cooking time and temperature.

Casserole with curd cheese and spicy sauce

Cooking time 1½–3 hrs.
Temperature 160–180° C (325–350° F; G3–4).
Quantities for 4.

4 portions of chicken	¼ tsp ground cloves
¼ tsp ground black pepper	½ tsp salt
¼ tsp ground ginger	¼ tsp ground cinnamon

Remove the skin from the chicken. Mix the spices and salt and rub the mixture into the chicken.

2 onions, finely sliced	olive oil

Heat oil in a frying pan or casserole using just enough to make a thin film on the surface. Fry the onions until brown.

8 oz curd cheese (200 g)	1 Tbs lemon juice
½ tsp turmeric	

Mix together, add to the onion and mix, adding water to moisten if the mixture is very dry. Add the chicken, turn it over to coat with the sauce and turn once during cooking. Put in a covered casserole and cook slowly until the chicken is tender. This is meant to be a fairly dry dish but if you prefer more liquid, add some stock. Serve with

boiled rice and a salad.

Casserole with green peppers

Cooking time 1½ hrs.
Temperature 180° C (350° F; G.4).
Quantities for 4.

4 joints of roasting chicken	1 oz butter (25 g)

Heat the butter in a frying pan or casserole and fry the chicken until brown.

2 green peppers, chopped	1 small onion, chopped

Remove seeds, pith and stem before chopping the peppers. Add peppers and onion to the chicken and cook for a few minutes longer.

¼ pt chicken stock (150 ml)	¼ pt double cream or evaporated milk
salt and pepper	(150 ml)

Add to the chicken. Cook in a covered casserole until the chicken is tender. If a

Poultry and Game 229

smooth sauce is preferred, lift out the chicken and put the sauce in the electric blender to make it smooth. Then pour it over the chicken and serve.

Casserole with herbs and lemon

Cooking time 1½ hrs.
Temperature 180° C (350° F; G4).
Quantities for 4.

| 4 portions of chicken | 1 oz butter (25 g) |

Heat the butter in a frying pan or casserole and brown the chicken on both sides. Remove the chicken.

| 2 tsp flour | 6 fl oz soured cream (175 ml) |

Add the flour to the remaining butter in the pan, mix and then add the cream, stirring until all the sediment in the pan has been dissolved.

½ tsp salt	pepper
2 oz sliced mushrooms (50 g)	2 Tbs chopped fennel
2 Tbs chopped parsley	2 Tbs chopped chives

Add to the sauce and mix. If the frying has been done in a casserole return the chicken, if in a frying pan put the chicken and sauce in a casserole, cover and cook until tender.

| 2 tsp lemon juice | grated rind of ½ lemon |

Remove the chicken to a serving dish, add the lemon to the sauce and pour it over the chicken.

Chicken à la Marengo

Cooking time 1½–3 hrs.
Temperature 160–180° C (325–350° F; G3–4).
Quantities for 4.

| 4 portions of chicken | 2 Tbs olive oil |

Heat the oil in a casserole or frying pan and cook the chicken quickly until it is brown all over. Remove the chicken.

| 1 Tbs flour | 4 Tbs white wine (60 ml) |
| 4 Tbs stock (60 ml) | |

Add the flour to the oil and mix and cook for a few minutes. Stir in the stock, mixing until smooth and then add the wine.

½ clove garlic, chopped
a bouquet garni
1 tsp salt
¼ tsp freshly ground pepper
1 Tbs concentrated tomato purée
4 oz mushrooms, sliced (125 g)

Add these to the sauce and either return the chicken to the casserole or transfer chicken and sauce to a casserole. Cover and cook until the chicken is tender. Remove the bouquet garni. Serve the chicken with

boiled potatoes and spinach, green beans or a green salad.

Chicken goulash

Cooking time 1½–3 hrs.
Temperature 160–180° C (325–350° F; G3–4).
Quantities for 4.

1 oz lard (25 g)
1 medium-sized onion, finely chopped

Heat the lard in a frying pan or casserole and stew the onion in it until it begins to soften.

4 portions of chicken
2 Tbs paprika pepper

Add the pepper to the onion and mix in, then add the chicken, turning it over to coat it with the onion mixture.

1 large tomato, fresh or canned, or use 1–2 tsp concentrated tomato purée
¼ tsp or more of caraway seeds
salt
½ pt chicken stock (250 ml)

Cut up the tomato and add it with the other ingredients. Put in a covered casserole and cook until the chicken is tender. Lift out the chicken and keep it hot.

2 Tbs flour
¼ pt soured cream or yogurt (150 ml)

Blend the flour to a smooth paste with the cream or yogurt and stir this into the chicken liquid. Stir until it boils and boil gently for a few minutes. Return the chicken and make sure it is hot before serving. Serve with

potatoes or noodles and cabbage or other green vegetable or a salad.

Curried chicken

Cooking time 2–4 hrs.
Temperature 160–180° C (325–350° F; G3–4).
Quantities for 4.

4 portions of chicken	1 oz flour (3 Tbs or 25 g)
2 tsp salt	

Coat the chicken with the seasoned flour.

2 medium-sized onions, chopped	1 tomato, chopped
2 small apples, chopped	a small piece of garlic, crushed
3 Tbs oil	

Heat the oil in a frying pan or casserole and fry the chicken until brown. Remove and fry the vegetables.

2 Tbs curry powder, more or less

Add with any of the flour left over from coating the chicken. Mix and cook for a few minutes more.

½ pt chicken stock (250 ml)	1 Tbs desiccated coconut
grated rind and juice of ½ lemon	1 tsp brown sugar
2 Tbs raisins or sultanas	

Add the stock to the curry mixture and stir and mix until smooth and boiling. Add the other ingredients and put the chicken and sauce in a casserole. Cover and cook until the chicken is tender. Serve with

boiled rice, chutney and green salad.

RECIPES USING COOKED CHICKEN

These are for leftover chicken from a roast or other cooked chicken, or chicken can be cooked in advance specially for making them.

Chicken à la King

Cooking time 10–15 mins. *Quantities* for 4–6.

12 oz cooked chicken, without bone (350 g)

Remove all skin and cut the chicken into dice. Refrigerate until required.

7½ oz can sliced mushrooms in water (225 g)

Drain, keeping the liquid to add to the stock.

| 1 oz butter or margarine (25 g) | 3 Tbs chopped green pepper |

Melt the fat in a small pan and cook the pepper and mushrooms in it for about 5 mins, stirring frequently.

| 1 oz cornflour (3 Tbs or 25 g) | ½ tsp salt |

Add to the pan and mix well.

| ½ pt chicken and mushroom stock (300 ml) | ½ pt milk (300 ml) |

Add this to the pan, stirring until the sauce is smooth and boiling.

2 canned red peppers or pimentos, sliced

Add the red pepper and the chicken and mix well. Simmer until the chicken is well heated. Serve with

cooked rice or mashed potatoes, sweet corn, green beans or peas.

Chicken and ham turnovers

Cooking time 25–30 mins.
Temperature 230° C (450° F; G8).
Quantities for 4 large turnovers.

| ½ pt milk or chicken stock, or a mixture (300 ml) | 1 oz butter or margarine (25 g) |
| | 1 oz flour (3 Tbs or 25 g) |

Melt the butter or margarine in a small saucepan, add the flour and stir and cook for a few minutes. Stir in the liquid and whisk or stir until the sauce is smooth and boiling. Boil gently for 5 mins. Set aside to cool.

| 4 oz minced or finely chopped cooked chicken (125 g) | salt and pepper |
| 4 oz minced or finely chopped cooked ham (125 g) | 1 Tbs chopped mixed tarragon, parsley, chervil and chives |

Add to the cold sauce, seasoning to taste.

12 oz puff pastry (350 g)

Roll the pastry into an oblong not more than ⅛ in thick (3 mm). Cut it into four pieces and put some of the mixture on one half of each. Moisten the edges of the pastry with water or milk, fold in half and seal the edges. Put on a baking tray, brush with egg and water or with milk and cut a small slit in the top of each turnover. Bake until the pastry is crisp and brown. Serve hot or cold.

Chicken pie

This should not be a sloppy filling and thus is suitable for a conventional pie made in a pie plate or for small pies made in patty tins or for turnovers or Cornish pasties. The directions below are for making one large pie and you will naturally need to increase the quantity of pastry for small pies or pasties and somewhat reduce the cooking time.

Cooking time 30 mins.
Temperature 230° C (450° F; G8).
Quantities for a 7 in pie plate (18 cm).

6 oz puff or flaky pastry (175 g)

Roll the pastry to fit the top of the pie plate and set it aside in a cool place to rest while the filling is prepared.

½ small onion, finely chopped   1 oz butter (25 g)
2 oz thinly sliced mushrooms (50 g)

Heat the butter in a frying pan and cook the onion in it until it just begins to colour. Then add the mushrooms and cook for a minute or so longer.

½ Tbs flour   salt and pepper
¼ pt soured or single fresh cream   pinch of grated nutmeg or mace
  (150 ml)

Add the flour to the pan and mix in, then stir in the liquid and stir until the sauce thickens, season to taste and cook for 5 mins. Set aside to cool.

2 hard-boiled eggs, chopped   8 oz diced cooked chicken (250 g)
2 Tbs chopped parsley or other herbs

Mix with the cooled sauce and put in the pie plate. Cover with the pastry lid, cutting a strip off to make a double edge in the usual way, see page 43, and decorating the edges with a knife. Cut a slit in the centre of the pie and bake until the pastry is browned and the filling bubbling. Serve hot or cold.

Fricassée

Cooking time about 20 mins. *Quantities* for 4.

1 oz butter (25 g)   2 Tbs flour
½ pt chicken stock or stock and milk   pinch of ground nutmeg
  (300 ml)   salt and pepper

Melt the butter in a small saucepan and add the flour, stirring and cooking for a couple of minutes. Add the liquid and whisk or stir until the sauce is smooth and boiling. Boil gently for 5 mins. Season to taste.

12 oz diced cooked chicken (350 g)

Add to the sauce and bring to the boil. Keep hot until ready to serve.

2 egg yolks

Beat a little and add to the chicken mixture, mixing in carefully.

1 Tbs lemon juice   1 Tbs chopped parsley

Add to the sauce.

4 rolls of grilled or fried bacon

Use these to garnish the fricassée. Serve with

mashed potatoes and spinach, peas or carrots.

Stuffed chicken pancakes

Quantities for 8 pancakes, see recipe page 37.

1 oz butter (25 g)   2 oz finely sliced mushrooms (50 g)

Melt the butter in a small saucepan, add the mushrooms, cover and stew gently for 3–4 mins.

2 Tbs flour $\frac{1}{4}$ pt chicken stock (150 ml)

Add the flour to the mushrooms and mix well, then stir in the stock and stir until the sauce boils.

4 oz diced cooked chicken (125 g)	2 finely chopped hard-boiled eggs
1 tsp chopped parsley	salt and pepper
1 tsp chopped tarragon	1 Tbs cream

Add these to the sauce, seasoning to taste. Bring to the boil and then put over simmering water to keep hot while the pancakes are made. As each is cooked, turn it out on to a piece of greaseproof paper, add a spoonful of filling, roll up and put in a hot fireproof dish. Keep hot.

When all the pancakes are made put the dish in a hot oven to crisp the pancakes, or sprinkle them with grated cheese and put under the grill until the cheese melts.

DUCK AND DUCKLING

For most people duck is a luxury food eaten occasionally and then preferred either roasted or served cold with salad. It can, however, be cooked in any of the ways already given for cooking chicken, though the final dish will be more fatty than when made with chicken.

Domestic ducks are sold fresh or frozen, the latter usually being of a consistently good quality. Buy fresh duck from a shop you know sells good-quality, properly labelled poultry or one which sells the ducks with their head and feet on. By looking at these you can get a good idea of the age of the duck. A duck young enough for roasting will have a bright yellow bill and feet.

QUANTITIES TO BUY

The tendency today is for more ducklings and smaller ducks to be marketed and these 3–3½ lb birds (1½ kg) will usually only provide 4–5 good portions each. For larger ducks, reckon at least ½ lb (250 kg) oven-ready weight per person.

Roast duck or duckling

COOKING TIMES AND TEMPERATURES

Small duck or duckling, 1 hr at 180–190° C (350–375° F; G4–5); or 1¼–1½ hrs at 160° C (325° F; G3).
Large duck, 15 mins per lb (½ kg) at the higher temperature, 25 mins per lb at the lower temperature.
Frozen birds should be thawed completely before cooking.

METHOD

The duck is often stuffed with sage and onion stuffing but prune and apple or lemon stuffing are good alternatives. Alternatively, stuff it with a peeled onion and a sprig of sage, or with an unpeeled orange.

Rub a little salt into the skin to make it crisp and place the bird on a trivet in the roasting pan or on an oven rack with a pan below for the drippings. Because of the fat in the bird neither the addition of fat nor basting is necessary.

When the bird is cooked, lift out and make gravy in the pan. Orange juice and/or red wine are frequently added to the gravy.

OTHER ACCOMPANIMENTS

Duck with roast potatoes and green peas is traditional with or without apple sauce. Instead of apple sauce serve an orange salad or a tart jelly like red currant

Serve boiled potatoes and other green vegetables as alternatives to roast potatoes and peas.

Duck with mint

This recipe is a change from straight roasting and makes the flesh very succulent and full of flavour but hardly fatty at all.

Cooking time 1½ hr for the duck; ¼–½ hr for the sauce.
Temperature 220° C (425° F; G7).
Quantities for 4–6.

4 lb duck, oven-ready weight (2 kg)	salt
1 oz softened butter (25 g)	1 tsp chopped mint

Begin cooking the duck about 2 hrs before serving time. If the skin is at all damp pat it dry with paper towels, then sprinkle with salt and rub it in. Work the mint into the softened butter and spread this over the breast of the duck.

2 small carrots, chopped	2 medium-sized onions, chopped
2 sticks celery, chopped	1 rasher bacon, chopped
1 sprig of thyme	½ bay leaf, crushed
1 oz butter (25 g)	2 Tbs madeira or sherry

Use a covered roasting pan or a large casserole for cooking the duck. Melt the butter in it and add the wine, bacon, vegetables and herbs. Put the duck on top of the vegetables, breast up. Cover and cook for 1½ hrs or until the duck is tender when tested in the thick part of the thigh. By this time the lower half of the duck will be surrounded by melted fat and juices from duck and vegetables, the upper half will be brown like roast duck. Transfer the duck to a dry baking tin and put it back in the oven to dry and crisp the skin, then keep hot. Meanwhile, prepare the sauce.

¼ pt stock made from the giblets (150 ml), or use chicken stock

Add this to the vegetables and liquid in the pan and boil for 5 mins. If more convenient, do this in a saucepan. Strain the sauce into a basin and use a spoon or ladle to remove as much of the fat as possible. Return the sauce to the pan and re-heat, adding more stock if you want more sauce.

1–2 Tbs lemon juice	2 Tbs chopped mint
pepper	

Add to the sauce, taste for seasoning and serve in a sauce boat. Alternatively, carve the duck and pour the sauce over it.

GOOSE

Several varieties of domestic geese are bred, some being small (about 6 lb or 3 kg) while others average about 10 lb and can be as big as 20–24 lb (9–11 kg).

In Britain, the goose has always been a bird for special occasions, chiefly Michaelmas and Christmas, and it is usually simply stuffed and roasted. Stuffings are sage and onion or apple and prune.

Roast goose

Cooking times for oven-ready weights

6 lb (3 kg)	1 hr 40 mins
12 lb (5 kg)	2 hrs 20 mins
18 lb (8 kg)	3 hrs 10 mins
24 lb (11 kg)	4 hrs

Temperature 160° C (325° F; G3).
Quantities: allow about $\frac{3}{4}$ lb oven-ready weight per person (350 g).

METHOD

Stuff the bird from the crop end and fasten the skin flap securely at the back. Put surplus stuffing in the body. Put the goose on a trivet in the roasting pan or on an oven rack with a pan below to catch the drippings. Put a piece of foil lightly over the breast. Remove this for the last $\frac{1}{2}$ hr of cooking.

ACCOMPANIMENTS

Gravy; apple sauce; roast or boiled potatoes; red cabbage; green vegetable.

COLD ROAST GOOSE

Slice and serve with salad; watercress is very good, or use chicory and beetroot.
Any of the recipes given for using cooked chicken can also be used for goose.

TURKEY

A small turkey weighs 6–8 lb (3–4 kg) and a large one can be 20–25 lb (9–11 kg) or occasionally even bigger, but these will not go in any but a very large oven, so be careful when buying a big one that your oven is large enough to take it. They may be fresh or frozen and are usually sold plucked and drawn or oven-ready.

They are most often roasted though turkey joints can be cooked in the same way as chicken joints, with a little longer cooking time. Leftover cooked turkey can be cooked in any of the ways given for using cooked chicken.

Frozen turkey should always be completely thawed before cooking.

Roast turkey

COOKING TIMES AND TEMPERATURES

Cooking times are calculated either on the undrawn weight or on the drawn or oven-ready weight before stuffing. In fact, when a bird is stuffed it weighs approximately the same as it did before drawing and cleaning.

Cooking times also vary with the temperature used and whether the bird is wrapped in foil. In my opinion, it is better to forget the foil wrapping and roast the turkey at a fairly low temperature, see below.

It is always wiser to allow plenty of time for cooking. It does not matter if the bird is ready a bit too soon. It will keep hot without harm. To test if the bird is done, take the end of a leg in a paper towel and move it up and down. If cooked enough, it should move easily at the joint.

QUANTITIES

Undrawn weight, allow approximately $1\frac{1}{2}$ lb ($\frac{3}{4}$ kg) per person; oven-ready weight, allow approximately $\frac{3}{4}$ lb per person (350 g).

METHOD

Stuff the turkey just before roasting it, allowing about 4 oz (125 g) of stuffing per lb ($\frac{1}{2}$ kg) of turkey. If the ingredients for the stuffing are prepared in advance, store any perishable items such as the giblets and sausage meat in the refrigerator and combine them just before stuffing the bird.

Rinse the turkey in cold water and pat it dry with paper towels. Use chestnut stuffing, page 27. Stuff it first from the crop end to make a good plump shape and then cover the opening with the flap of neck skin and fasten this skin to the back with a small skewer. Spoon the rest of the stuffing into the body but do not pack it tightly. Cross the legs and tie them to the tail. Brush the bird with oil or melted butter.

Temperature 160° C (325° F; G3).

Place the turkey on an oven rack with a pan below to catch the drippings. Put a cap of foil over the breast but do not let it come down the side and do not press it close to the breast as this interferes with heat transfer to the meat.

When the bird has cooked for about two-thirds of the required time, cut the string holding the legs together to allow the heat to penetrate the inside of the thigh, which is the part that takes longest to cook. If necessary, remove the foil for the last ½ hr of cooking to allow the breast to brown.

Lift the bird on to a serving dish and put back in the oven to keep warm. Use the drippings to make gravy.

COOKING TIMES

	When weighed undrawn or after stuffing	*Oven-ready weight before stuffing*
lb	Hrs	Hrs
6–8 (3–4 kg)	2½–3	3½–3¾
8–10 (4–5 kg)	3–3½	3¾–4¼
10–14 (5–6 kg)	3½–4	4¼–4¾
14–18 (6–8 kg)	4–4½	4¾–5¼
18–20 (8–9 kg)	4½–5½	5¼–6¼
20–24 (9–11 kg)	5½–6	6¼–7

ACCOMPANIMENTS

Boiled, roast or fried potatoes; onions, brussels sprouts, peas or pumpkin. Garnishes: small sausages and grilled or fried bacon rolls. Sauces: brown gravy, cranberry sauce, bread sauce.

Devilled turkey

Cooking time about 10 mins after 1 hr or more marinating. *Quantities* for 4.

the meat from 2 legs of cooked turkey

Divide the turkey into four pieces suitable for serving and remove the skin. Score the flesh deeply with a small sharp knife.

1 oz butter (25 g)
¼ tsp freshly ground black pepper
¼ tsp curry powder
pinch of cayenne pepper
pinch of ground ginger

Soften the butter slightly and work in the flavourings. Spread the mixture over the turkey, working it into the cuts. Leave it in a cold place for at least 1 hr.

Grill until crisp and brown on the outside. Serve with

cranberry sauce.

Turkey paprika with caraway seeds

This can be used as a pie or flan filling, to make a potato pie, to serve in a border of mashed potatoes, or with rice or pasta.

Cooking time about 30 mins. *Quantities* for 4.

1 medium-sized onion, chopped	1 small green pepper or 2 sticks celery, chopped
3 Tbs oil	

Heat the oil in a saucepan and fry the vegetables slowly until they are soft. Remove from the heat.

1 Tbs flour	1 Tbs or more of paprika pepper
1 Tbs concentrated tomato purée	1 tsp sugar

Add to the pan and mix in.

½ pt turkey stock (250 ml)

Blend in, return to the pan and stir until it boils.

½ tsp salt   ½ tsp or more of caraway seeds

Add, cover the pan and simmer for 15 mins.

12 oz cooked turkey cut in small pieces (350 g)   ¼ pt yogurt, beaten smooth (150 ml)

Add to the sauce and boil gently for 5 mins longer. Serve straight away.

GAME

Game includes all wild birds and animals which are hunted for food. Some of these are covered by the game laws and can only legally be hunted at certain times of the year, though nowadays many are available from the freezer at all times of the year. Because of its relative scarcity, game is usually expensive when compared with poultry and other meats.

Tame pigeons and rabbit are usually classed with game for cooking purposes, although when young and tender they can be cooked in the same ways as chicken.

Fresh game birds are usually hung up by the feet in a cool place for a week or more until they develop a strong flavour and the flesh becomes more tender. Only then are they plucked and drawn. This can be an unpleasant operation, but if you purchase game from a butcher it will be done for you.

Game purchased ready for cooking will keep for 3-4 days in the refrigerator.

If it is smelly it is best to wrap it closely in foil or polythene to protect the other food in the cabinet.

Frozen game should be completely thawed before cooking, the time required depending on the size.

THAWING TIMES

	In the refrigerator	At room temperature
Birds	24–36 hrs	6–8 hrs
Hare and rabbit joints	6–12 hrs	3 hrs
Venison steaks	6–12 hrs	3 hrs
Venison joints	3–5 hrs per lb (½ kg) up to 4 lb (2 kg); 5–7 hrs per lb if larger	1–2 hrs per lb (½ kg) up to 4 lb (2 kg); 2–3 hrs per lb if larger

For home freezing, see home freezing poultry and game, page 220.

Game which has been cooked for serving cold should be cooled quickly (not in the refrigerator), then covered closely and stored in the refrigerator, where it will keep for 2–3 days. Game pies and pâtés purchased from a shop are best used the same day.

Roasting is the favourite method of cooking most game. Unless you know the bird is a young one or has been well hung it is better to roast it fairly slowly at a low temperature, rather than the traditional method of fast roasting at a high temperature. The same applies to other types of game.

All game can be used for casserole cooking. For game birds and rabbit use recipes for chicken casseroles; for hare and venison use recipes for beef casseroles, particularly those containing red wine, herbs and spices.

Blackcock or black grouse (female greyhen)

SEASON

20 August to 10 December.

QUANTITIES

Average weight 3½ lb (1½ kg), sufficient for 3–4 portions.

COOKING

They are usually well hung before cooking. Young ones can be split, skewered out flat and grilled for 25–30 mins, turning them occasionally and brushing with melted butter. Serve with a brown sauce such as Espagnole.

Larger birds are cleaned and trussed like a chicken. Roast for $\frac{1}{2}$–$\frac{3}{4}$ hr at 220° C (425° F; G7) or 1–1$\frac{1}{2}$ hrs at 180° C (350° F; G4).

Blackcock tend to be dry birds so should be basted with melted butter or else have a piece of mild fat bacon tied over the breast. Remove this towards the end of cooking. The usual way of serving is to put the bird on a piece of buttered toast and serve gravy, bread sauce and fried breadcrumbs with it.

Grouse

SEASON

12 August to 10 December, after which it is too old to be palatable for roasting.

QUANTITIES

Average weight 1$\frac{1}{4}$ lb (600 g), sufficient for 2–3 portions.

COOKING

It needs to be hung for 3–4 days but some people like it left until high.

Put a piece of butter inside the bird with some lemon juice and roast it at 220° C (425° F; G7) for about 30 mins, or more slowly at 180° C (350° F; G4) for 40–50 mins.

The liver is usually cooked separately, pounded to a paste, and spread on a piece of toast on which the bird is served. Other accompaniments are fried or grilled bacon or bacon rolls, potato crisps, watercress, and gravy made from the drippings in the pan.

ALTERNATIVE METHOD

Cover the breast of the bird with a piece of fat bacon, put the bird on a piece of toast and baste frequently during cooking. A few minutes before the end of cooking, remove the bacon, dredge the breast with flour, return to the oven to brown. Serve on the toast with gravy made from giblet stock, bread sauce and fried breadcrumbs.

Grouse are also good served cold.

Guinea-fowl

SEASON

From January to June. Both the flesh and the eggs are eaten.

QUANTITIES

Average weight 3 lb (1$\frac{1}{2}$ kg), sufficient for 3–4 portions.

COOKING

Cook in the same way as chicken.

Partridge

SEASON

From 1 September to 1 February.

QUANTITIES

It is a small bird, one being usually only enough for 2 portions.

COOKING

Tie a piece of fat pork or bacon over the breast and roast at 220° C (425° F; G7) for about 30 mins. Remove the bacon or pork for the last 5 mins. Serve with bread sauce and a salad garnish.

Pheasant

SEASON

From October to February.

QUANTITIES

One bird will serve 2–4 people, depending on the size. They are very often sold in pairs (a brace), which serves 5–6 people. The hen pheasant is considered better eating than the cock and is distinguished by a shorter tail and duller plumage.

COOKING

Pheasants are hung for varying lengths of time to develop a good flavour. Some people like them to be almost decomposing. Pheasant is cooked in the same way as chicken. Walnut stuffing, page 29, is very good with it. Cooking time will be 40 mins–$1\frac{1}{2}$ hrs depending on the temperature used.

Cover the breast with a piece of mild bacon or fat pork and remove this for the last 10 mins. Roast the giblets round or under the bird to provide a good gravy. Serve with bread sauce and brown gravy, garnish with watercress and serve with potatoes and vegetables.

Pigeon

QUANTITIES

One bird is enough for 1-2 portions, domestic pigeons being smaller than wood pigeons.

COOKING

If the birds are young they can be roasted like a small chicken, but if older are best made into a casserole or jugged like a hare.

Plover

SEASON

From 1 September to 31 January.

QUANTITIES

Allow 1 bird per portion.

COOKING

Roast for about 30 mins in a hot oven, 220° C (425° F; G7).

Quail

SEASON

Available in the summer months.

QUANTITIES

Allow 1-2 birds per portion.

COOKING

The traditional method of roasting is to wrap each bird in vine leaves and cook it in a hot oven for about 30 mins.

Snipe

SEASON

12 August to 31 January.

Poultry and Game 245

QUANTITIES

Allow 1 bird per portion.

COOKING

Roast in a hot oven, 230° C (450° F; G8), for 15–20 mins, depending on whether it is preferred rare or well done. Serve on toast with a thin gravy or with melted butter and lemon. Some insist on having it cooked undrawn and underdone.

Teal

SEASON

1 September to 31 January.

QUANTITIES

Allow 1 bird per portion.

COOKING

Young teal may be split open and grilled like a spatchcock chicken, see page 225, or roasted for 20 mins in a hot oven, 230° C (450° F; G8). Add lemon juice to the gravy.

Widgeon

SEASON

1 September to 31 January.

QUANTITIES

One bird will serve 2 portions.

COOKING

Roast in a hot oven, 230° C (450° F; G8), for 15 mins if liked underdone; 20–25 mins well done.

Wild duck

SEASON

From September to January.

QUANTITIES

Average size 2 lb (1 kg), sufficient for 4 portions; small duck, allow 1 per portion.

COOKING

Large ones, stuff with sliced apples and roast as for domestic duck, page 235. Small ones, roast unstuffed in a hot oven, 230° C (450° F; G8), for 20–30 mins. Serve with orange salad, watercress and gravy; also roast potatoes or potato crisps.

Woodcock

SEASON

1 October to 31 January.

QUANTITIES

One bird gives 1–2 portions.

COOKING

Roast in a hot oven, 230° C (450° F; G8), for 20–25 mins. Serve on a slice of fried bread with any of the accompaniments served with roast chicken.

HARE

SEASON

September to February.

QUANTITIES

One will give 5–6 portions.

COOKING

Young hares are tender and may be roasted but older hares are very tough and only suitable for long, slow cooking as in jugged hare, or for making into soup.

Hare needs to be well hung before cooking, up to a week for an old one, 3–4 days for a young one.

A young hare has soft ears which are easily torn, the paws are slender and the claws not easily seen, the coat is smooth.

Hare purchased by the pound, cut up, is best treated as old hare.

When you buy a whole hare from the butcher he will skin and prepare it for you.

Roast hare

Cooking time 1½–2 hrs.
Temperature 160° C (325° F; G3).
Quantities for 5.

1 young hare	rashers of fat bacon
lemon stuffing or sage and onion stuffing	light ale or cider

Wash the hare and dry the inside with paper towels. Line the cavity with slices of fat bacon and put in the stuffing. Sew up the opening with a needle and coarse white cotton. Put the hare in a roasting pan with a little beer or cider and cook gently, basting from time to time. Serve the liquid in place of gravy, thickening it with flour or cornflour if desired. Serve with

red currant jelly, boiled or baked onions, boiled carrots and any green vegetable.

Jugged hare

Cooking time 3–4 hrs.
Temperature 150° C (300° F; G2).
Quantities for 5–6.

1 hare, or 3–4 lb joints (1½–2 kg)   1 oz fat (25 g), or 2 Tbs oil

Wash and dry the pieces of hare. Heat the fat or oil in a casserole or frying pan and brown the hare all over. Remove from the pan or casserole.

2 onions, sliced	3 whole allspice
a bouquet garni	½ tsp freshly ground pepper
6 cloves	2 tsp salt
1 tsp grated lemon rind	

Tie the bouquet garni and spices in a piece of muslin. Add onions and flavourings to the hare.

1 oz butter (25 g)	1 oz flour (3 Tbs or 25 g)
¼ pt wine or cider vinegar (150 ml)	½ pt red wine, dry cider, or beer (250 ml)

Melt the butter in the pan in which the hare was fried, add the flour and stir and cook for a few minutes. Add the liquid gradually and stir until smooth and boiling. Pour this over the hare or return the hare to the casserole. Cover and cook very slowly until the hare is tender.

lemon stuffing made into balls and fried, page 28
a green vegetable
red currant jelly
boiled potatoes

Serve these with the hare, first removing the bag of flavourings.

RABBIT

Wild rabbit and tame rabbit differ in flavour and tenderness. Tame rabbit is almost indistinguishable from chicken when it is cooked with flavourings. Wild rabbit has a much stronger flavour. This can be removed to a certain extent by soaking the rabbit for ½ hr in salted water and then blanching it for 1 minute in boiling water.

SEASON

Wild rabbit is in season from September to February.

QUANTITIES

A young rabbit or leveret will give 3 portions; an adult rabbit will give 4–5 portions; rabbit purchased as joints, allow ½ lb per portion (250 g).

COOKING

Rabbit joints can be used in the same recipes as chicken joints, older rabbit being more suitable for casserole cooking; young rabbit and tame rabbit can be used in any recipe.

VENISON

This is the flesh of deer of all kinds but chiefly the stag of red deer, roebuck and fallow deer.

SEASON

October to December.

QUANTITIES

As for veal.

COOKING

The leg and loin are considered the prime cuts and together make the haunch, which is a very large joint. Venison is usually roasted, though venison steaks and cutlets are grilled, and the meat from the shoulder sometimes stewed.

Grilled venison cutlets

Cooking time 20–25 mins. *Quantities*: allow 1 per person.

Cutlets from the neck are used, cut 1 in (2½ cm) thick. Season with salt and pepper and turn them every 2 mins during grilling. Serve with a knob of butter on top, grilled mushrooms and baked jacket potatoes.

Grilled venison steaks

Cooking time 20–25 mins. *Quantities*: allow 1 per person.

Steaks are cut 1 in (2½ cm) thick from the top of the leg or the loin. Turn them every 2 mins during cooking. Heat a baking dish and put in it 1 oz butter for each lb (25 g for each ½ kg) of meat. Add the cooked steak and turn it over in the butter to coat it well. Serve at once.

Jugged venison

See jugged hare, page 247. Substitute 2 lb (1 kg) venison shoulder meat for the hare.

Roast venison

Cooking times and temperatures, see roast veal, page 200.

A 6 lb (3 kg) haunch of venison needs 3–4 hrs roasting. The meat can be cooked in a roasting bag, or baste it frequently with equal quantities of red currant jelly, butter and water. Serve with brown gravy and red currant jelly.

10. Vegetables

In this chapter I have listed vegetables in alphabetical order and included hints on selecting, preparing, storing and cooking each one.

Ideal storage conditions are lacking in many homes, particularly flats, and the cook who wants to serve fresh vegetables either has to buy them frequently in small quantities or use refrigerated storage.

All vegetables keep fresh longest if they are stored in a cool place in the dark. Potatoes and root vegetables will keep well in a cold larder or shed, but the refrigerator is better for the more perishable kinds. Before putting them in the refrigerator they should be washed and trimmed of roots, damaged leaves and so on, drained very thoroughly and then stored in the special compartment provided in the refrigerator, or store in polythene bags or boxes. The thorough draining after washing is very important for if they sit in a pool of water in the refrigerator, they will soon rot. I always put a folded paper towel in the bottom of polythene boxes, to soak up excess water. It is, of course, important not to have refrigerated storage cold enough to freeze the vegetables.

To me, the advantage of refrigerated storage is not only that it keeps vegetables fresher for longer, but that the often time-consuming washing and preparation can be done well in advance of cooking. I leave peeling, chopping and slicing until just before cooking thus preserving maximum flavour and food value. Most vegetables will keep for up to a week, some longer. Thin and delicate leaves which are easily bruised keep the shortest time.

Avoid deliberately cooking vegetables in advance for re-heating because flavour and vitamin content deteriorate a lot with this sort of treatment.

When there are vegetables left from a meal the best way of using them up is in salads or to make soup. Store them in covered containers in the refrigerator. If they are mixed with a sauce or dressing use them within 1–2 days; dry, they will keep longer.

Home freezing guide

Most vegetables need to be blanched (scalded) before packing. Begin measuring the scalding time when the water comes back to the boil after the vegetables have been added. After scalding plunge them in ice-cold water until they are cold right through, drain and pack.

Asparagus. Grade according to the thickness of the stalks. Wash and scrape the lower ends. Cut in even lengths to fit the containers. Scald 4 mins for thick pieces, 2 mins for thin.

Beans, broad. Pod and grade. Use only very young beans. Scald 3 mins.

Beans, French or runner. Use only young and stringless beans. Leave French beans whole, slice or cut other beans. Scald 2–3 mins.

Beetroot. Use small young ones only, or cook larger ones until tender, peel and cut up. Scald young ones 20 mins or until the skin will rub off.

Broccoli, sprouting. Use only young tender stalks. Cut in lengths to fit the container. Scald 3 mins.

Brussels sprouts. Use only small firm ones, trimming off any loose outer leaves and the stalks. Wash, scald 3 mins.

Carrots. Leave very small ones whole, slice or dice others. Remove tops and wash the carrots well. Scald 5 mins and rub off the skins. Then cut up large ones.

Cauliflower. Break into flowerets 2 in (5 cm) across. Scald 3 mins.

Celery. When frozen is only suitable for cooking. No need to blanch.

Mushrooms. Wash and drain. Freeze button ones whole, slice large ones.

Onions. Skin, chop and freeze in small packs.

Parsnips. Peel and slice ½ in (1 cm) thick. Scald 2 mins.

Peas. Use young ones only. Shell and scald 1–2 mins.

Potato chips. Fry, drain well, cool and freeze. To heat, spread on baking trays in a hot oven, 200° C (400° F; G6) for 5–10 mins. Sprinkle with salt and serve.

Spinach. Scald 2 mins.

Sweet Peppers. Wash, remove seeds and stem. Halve, slice or dice and freeze in small packs without scalding.

Tomatoes. Freeze as stewed tomatoes, purée or juice.

Using frozen vegetables

Frozen cooked beetroot can be thawed and used as fresh cooked beetroot.

Vegetables such as onions, celery, mushrooms, tomatoes and sliced or diced sweet peppers which are to be used for flavouring purposes can be fried or added to a casserole or sauce without thawing.

Other vegetables are cooked without thawing. Put them in a very little boiling salted water and cook until just tender, which will take less time than when cooking fresh vegetables.

ARTICHOKES, GLOBE

These decorative plants belong to the thistle family and it is the flower head which is eaten, while in the bud stage. Home-grown ones are in season in the summer, imported ones are available for most of the year.

Artichokes must be fresh and the leaves should be green, without any brown tips or any horny appearance, as this makes them old and stale and unpleasant to eat.

Use them as soon as possible after picking or buying and if they have to be kept a while, stand them in a bowl with the stalks in water and keep in a cool place.

Boiled globe artichokes

Cooking time 15–45 mins depending on age and size.
Quantities: allow 2 small or 1 average size per person.

Cut off the stalks and remove the outer row of tough leaves. Use kitchen scissors to trim the tops of the other leaves to a neat shape. Soak the artichokes for an hour in plenty of cold water to which has been added some salt and 1 Tbs of vinegar. This is to draw out any insects in the leaves. Drain them upside down.

Cook them stem end down, in a little boiling salted water until an outside leaf pulls out easily when tested. Avoid over-cooking or the flavour will be lost.

Drain them upside down, squeezing gently to remove some of the water. They may be served warm or cold, usually with French dressing or hollandaise sauce handed separately.

To eat them, the leaves are torn off one by one, the base of each being dipped in the dressing or sauce and the soft end pulled off by the teeth. When all the outer leaves have been eaten the small inner ones and the fluffy centre are discarded leaving the bottom, the best part, which is eaten with a knife and fork.

ARTICHOKES, JERUSALEM

These look like very knobbly potatoes; the small ones are extremely difficult to peel but they must be peeled as the skins are very thick and fibrous. They have a very distinctive flavour and texture which not everyone likes and many find them rather indigestible.

They are in season from October to March and can be dug from the garden as required. Those bought from a shop will keep several days in a cool place or in the refrigerator. If stored in a warm, dry place they very quickly shrivel and become unusable.

Boiled Jerusalem artichokes

Cooking time 20–30 mins. *Quantities:* allow $\frac{1}{2}$ lb (250 g) per person.

Prepare the artichokes by scrubbing and peeling, cutting off the very small knobs to make them a more even shape. As you peel them, put them in a bowl of cold water containing 1 Tbs vinegar for each 2 pt ($1\frac{1}{4}$ l). This helps to keep them a good colour. Leave them in the water for $\frac{1}{2}$ hr.

Put them in boiling salted water to cover, and boil until they are tender when tested with a fork.

They need a sauce, such as béchamel sauce. The artichokes can be cooked in a mixture of milk and water and this stock used for making a sauce.

Artichokes with cheese

Cooking time $\frac{1}{2}$–$\frac{3}{4}$ hr.
Temperature 220° C (425° F; G7) for 10 mins only, or use the grill.
Quantities for 4.

2 lb artichokes (1 kg)   2 onions, sliced

Prepare the artichokes as in the previous recipe and boil until tender, with the onions. Drain.

$\frac{1}{4}$ pt milk (150 ml)   grated cheese
salt and pepper

Mash the vegetables with the milk, and season to taste. Put them in a greased baking dish and cover the top with a generous layer of grated cheese. Heat in the oven for 10 mins to melt the cheese, or cook under the grill. Serve hot.

ASPARAGUS

Asparagus loses it flavour very quickly after being cut and should preferably be used the same day. It is always an expensive vegetable and stale asparagus is not worth buying. You can tell whether it is fresh by looking at the cut ends which have a hard dry look when it has been cut a long time. It is best to buy bundles with even-sized heads, otherwise some will be under-cooked and some over-cooked. If necessary, the bundle should be sorted out into sizes for cooking.

When frozen, asparagus retains its flavour fairly well. Canned asparagus has a very different flavour from the fresh, but it is a very pleasant vegetable and useful in cooking.

Home-grown asparagus is at its best from May to June but imported asparagus is available both earlier and later than this.

Boiled asparagus

Cooking time 15–30 mins depending on the age and thickness of the stalks.
Quantities: allow 6–8 medium-sized pieces per person.

Wash the asparagus, scrubbing the white ends and scraping downwards with a sharp knife. Place in bundles of about a dozen pieces, or in portions, and tie with white string, keeping the heads level. Trim the cut ends to an even length. Use these for vegetable stock or cook them with the heads to add flavour to the water.

If you cook asparagus often it is worth while buying an asparagus boiler which is made tall enough to take the stalks standing upright. It is important to try and improvise something of this sort, otherwise it is very difficult to get the thick lower parts of the stalks cooked at the same time as the delicate heads.

Use the deepest pan you have and, for a lid, use an inverted basin, preferably heat-resistant glass, so you can see what is going on. Heat enough water in the pan to cover the thick ends of the stalks. Add salt and bring to the boil. Stand the bundles upright and put on the lid. Boil gently until the tips are tender. Do not over-cook or flavour will be lost and the heads will fall off as the asparagus is lifted out of the pan.

Drain it in a colander and serve hot with melted butter, brown butter sauce or hollandaise sauce. Serve cold with French dressing.

Vegetables 255

Asparagus mould

This is for serving cold as a lunch or supper dish or for a buffet meal.

12–15 oz can of asparagus (375 g)   ½ oz gelatine (1½ Tbs or 15 g)

Drain the asparagus. Heat the liquid, sprinkle in the gelatine and stir to dissolve it. Rub the asparagus through a sieve or pulp it in the electric blender with a little of the liquid. Add to the gelatine mixture.

¼ pt evaporated milk or cream   salt
  (150 ml)   cayenne pepper

Add to the asparagus, seasoning to taste. Pour into a 1–1½ pt mould (½–1 l) and leave to cool. Cover and store in the refrigerator. Unmould on to a serving dish and garnish with

chopped cooked ham or small rolls of ham.

Serve with brown bread and butter or fresh rolls and butter.

Asparagus quiche

Cooking time 40 mins.
Temperature 200° C (400° F; G6) for 10 mins, then 180° C (350° F; G4) for 25–30 mins.
Quantities for an 8 in (20 cm) quiche.

short-crust pastry using 4 oz flour (100 g), or use 6 oz ready-made (175 g)

Roll the pastry fairly thinly and line a flan ring or pie plate with it. Prick the bottom with a fork and put the case in the refrigerator while the filling is prepared.

4 rashers bacon

Remove the rinds and fry or grill the bacon until crisp. Cool, chop and set aside.

15 oz can of asparagus (425 g)

Drain and cut the asparagus into 1 in pieces (2½ cm). Set aside.

2 eggs, beaten   1 Tbs finely chopped onion
¼ pt single cream or evaporated milk   2 oz grated strong cheese (50 g)
  (150 ml)   1 tsp salt
1 tsp sugar   pinch of grated nutmeg
pepper

Mix all the ingredients together. Remove the pastry case from the refrigerator and strew in the bacon, then add the asparagus pieces and gently pour in the egg mixture.

grated Parmesan cheese

Sprinkle a layer on top of the filling and bake until the filling is set and the top lightly browned. Serve warm or cold.

AUBERGINES

A fresh aubergine should have a full, shining skin, be firm to the touch and unwrinkled. They are not worth buying if they are stale. Use as soon as possible but if they are purchased in advance, store them in a cool, dry place.

The main season for aubergines is in summer and autumn but they are imported throughout most of the year.

Quantities: allow 1 per person, or half a large one.

Fried aubergines

Wash and remove the stalks. Cut the aubergines in ½ in slices (1 cm). Dip the slices in a frying batter or in egg and breadcrumbs. Fry in hot fat and serve plain or with a tomato sauce.

Grilled aubergines

METHOD 1

Cooking time 15–20 mins. *Quantities* for 4.

2–4 aubergines	salt and pepper
olive oil	

Wash and dry the aubergines and remove the stem end. Cut them in half lengthwise, and put them in a single layer, cut side up, in a shallow dish. Sprinkle with salt and pepper and brush with olive oil to coat them well. Leave to marinate for 1 hr or more.

Grill them under a moderate heat until they are tender and browned on top. When they are beginning to brown, brush with more oil. Serve as a garnish for fried or grilled meat.

METHOD 2

Wash, remove stem end and cut the aubergines in $\frac{1}{2}$ in (1 cm) slices. Mix oil and seasonings in the proportions of 1 Tbs oil with $\frac{1}{4}$ tsp salt and a pinch of pepper. Dip the slices of aubergine in this and grill them for about 3 mins on each side or until tender. Serve plain or with grated cheese sprinkled on top.

Stuffed aubergines

Cooking time $\frac{1}{2}$ hr.
Temperature 190° C (375° F; G5).
Quantities for 4.

| 4 aubergines | oil |

Wash the aubergines and cut them in half lengthwise. With the point of a sharp knife criss-cross the flesh to within 1 in (2$\frac{1}{2}$ cm) of the skin. Fry them in oil, cut side down, for about 7 mins. Cool, remove the pulp leaving enough round the edge to retain the natural shape of the aubergine. Rub the pulp through a sieve or purée it in the electric blender.

| 8 oz chopped mushrooms (250 g) | $\frac{1}{2}$ oz grated cheese (15 g) |
| 1 egg, beaten | salt and pepper |

Put in a basin with the aubergine pulp.

| dry breadcrumbs | grated cheese |

If the filling is very sloppy add a few breadcrumbs, but avoid making it stodgy. Put the aubergine shells in a baking dish and put in the filling. Sprinkle the tops liberally with more breadcrumbs and grated cheese and bake for about 20 mins or until the tops are lightly browned. Serve hot.

BROAD BEANS

When buying broad beans you should be able to see the shape of the bean clearly in the pods, but the pods should be a fresh green in colour and not too large. If the pods are losing their fresh look and becoming grey-green the beans are probably over-mature and will be mealy with tough skins. They are then only suitable for making a purée. On the other hand, tiny bright green pods which don't show the shape of the beans probably have none inside, but the pods can be sliced and boiled like green beans.

Broad beans are in season from June to August. They tend to lose flavour when frozen but are very good canned.

If you are not going to use fresh beans straight away, shell them, put them in a polythene bag and store in the refrigerator.

Boiled broad beans

Cooking time 10–30 mins depending on the age.
Quantities: allow ½–1 lb per portion (250–500 g). If the pods are well filled with beans ½ lb (250 g) should be enough for one portion.

Shell the beans. Put about 1 in (2½ cm) of water in a pan and add 1 tsp salt per 4 portions. When the water is boiling add the beans and boil gently until tender when tested with a fork. Strain, keeping the liquid for a sauce or for stock. Toss the beans in a little melted butter or margarine and sprinkle them with chopped parsley or a little chopped savory. Alternatively, serve them with a white sauce made with half milk and half bean water. Flavour the sauce with chopped parsley or savory.

For a supper dish, garnish the beans with rolls or fried or grilled bacon.
Serve cold for salads or hors d'œuvre.

Broad bean and bacon stew

Cooking time 20–30 mins. *Quantities* for 4.

2 oz butter or margarine (50 g)	1 oz flour (3 Tbs or 25 g)
3–4 lb young broad beans (1½–2 kg), or 1 lb frozen (½ kg)	¾ pt stock or water (400 ml)

Shell the beans. Melt the fat in a large saucepan and stir in the flour. Cook for few minutes and then add the stock. Stir until the sauce boils. Add the beans.

2–4 oz bacon (2–4 rashers or 50–100 g)

Remove rinds and cut the bacon in small pieces. Add to the pan and boil gently until the beans are tender.

salt and pepper	1 tsp sugar
2 Tbs chopped parsley	2 Tbs vinegar

Season to taste. Add sugar, parsley and vinegar and serve hot.

Broad beans in fennel sauce

To serve with bacon, ham, pork, veal, lamb or chicken.

Cooking time 20–30 mins. *Quantities* for 4.

2–4 lb beans (1–2 kg), or 1 lb shelled or frozen beans (½ kg)

Shell the beans and boil them in a little lightly salted water until they are tender, 10–20 mins, depending on their age. Drain, keeping the liquid. Put the beans to keep hot.

½ pt bean stock, or stock plus milk or cream (250 ml)
½ oz butter or margarine (15 g)
½ oz flour (1½ Tbs or 15 g)

Melt the butter or margarine in the saucepan in which the beans were cooked. Stir in the flour and cook for a minute. Add the liquid and stir or whisk until the sauce is smooth. Boil gently for 5 mins.

salt and pepper 2 or more Tbs chopped fennel

Season the sauce, add the fennel and return the beans. Allow them to become hot before serving.

DRIED BEANS

There are many different kinds of dried beans used for human food and a lot of them are sold in shops in Britain. The most commonly used are haricot beans (small white ones) and butter beans (large white ones). Butter beans are sold canned but the most popular are baked beans. All dried beans are cooked in the same way, by boiling, either plain or with flavouring materials and other ingredients to make traditional dishes.

Boiled dried beans

Cooking time 2–3 hrs, or 20–30 mins pressure cooking.
Quantities: allow 2 oz (50 g) dried weight, which will give about 4 oz (100 g) cooked weight, per portion.

Unless they are very old stock, dried beans do not need to be soaked before cooking, and even then they should not be soaked more than 1–1½ hrs or they may begin to ferment.

To boil them heat 1 pt (½ l) water for every 4 oz (100 g) of beans to be cooked. When the water boils, drop in the beans, cover and boil gently until they are tender when tested with a fork. Drain, keeping any liquid for stock. Season to taste with salt and pepper and chopped green herbs. For extra flavour add an onion stuck with a few cloves and cook with the beans; or add a few bacon rinds or a bacon or ham bone.

When using a pressure cooker for beans be sure it is not more than half filled with beans and water. Only a third full is safer as they have a tendency to froth and can block the steam vent.

Dried beans à la Bretonne

Boiled dried beans are drained and mixed with the following flavourings.

For each lb (½ kg) of beans being cooked fry 2 sliced medium-sized onions in oil or fat until the onions are browned, add the cooked and drained beans and mix well. Sprinkle with chopped parsley and serve hot.

Italian beans

Cooking time 2 hrs, or 25–30 mins pressure cooking. *Quantities* for 4.

8 oz haricot or butter beans (200 g)

Boil the beans until tender and then drain well; or use 1 lb (450 g) drained canned beans.

4 Tbs oil	2 Tbs concentrated tomato purée
2 fresh sage leaves, chopped	salt and pepper

Heat the oil and sage together and, when hot, add the drained beans and cook until the oil is absorbed. Add the tomato purée and mix well, seasoning to taste.

Beans and mushrooms

Suitable for a lunch or supper dish.

Cooking time 10 mins. *Quantities* for 3.

2 Tbs finely chopped onion	1½ oz butter or margarine (40 g)
8 oz sliced mushrooms (250 g)	

Heat the butter or margarine in a large frying pan. Fry the onion and mushrooms until the onion begins to brown.

16 oz can baked beans in tomato sauce (454 g)	1 Tbs Worcester sauce
1 tsp soy sauce	salt
	dried marjoram

Add to the pan and simmer until heated. Season to taste.

chopped parsley   toast or brown bread

Serve sprinkled with plenty of chopped parsley and hand the toast or bread separately.

GREEN BEANS

These include many kinds of French, dwarf or kidney beans and runner beans. Home-grown French beans are in season in the summer but are imported for most of the year. Runner beans are in season from July to October.

Good quality beans should be firm-looking and the shape of the seed inside should not be very pronounced, the flatter the better, provided they are not too young to have any flavour.

New kinds of runner beans are less inclined to be stringy than the older varieties, but even so, don't buy runner beans which are showing the shape of the bean inside. They will almost always be too mature for good eating.

Green beans keep well for a few days if they are washed, drained well and put in the refrigerator in polythene bags or boxes. They also freeze very well, and are much better than canned green beans.

Boiled green beans

Cooking time 15-20 mins. *Quantities:* allow 4-6 oz (100-150 g) per portion.

Wash the beans. French beans should be left whole, simply cutting off the tips and stem end. Many people slice runner beans very finely but the flavour is better if they are cut across in several largish pieces.

Put them in 1 in (2½ cm) of water in a pan with 1 tsp salt per lb (½ kg) of beans. When the water boils, add the beans, cover and boil rapidly until they are tender. Drain thoroughly, return to the pan with a little butter and stir or toss the beans to coat them with butter.

French beans in cream sauce

Cooking time about 1½ hr. *Quantities* for 4.

1 lb French beans (500 g)

Wash, drain and cut off tops and tails. Cut each bean in three pieces. Cook them in a little boiling salted water until tender. Drain, reserving the stock. Put the beans to keep hot.

1 oz butter or margarine (25 g)   1 Tbs finely chopped onion

Melt the butter or margarine in a small pan and cook the onion in it until tender.

1 oz flour (3 Tbs or 25 g)   about ¼ pt of the bean stock (150 ml)

Add the flour to the pan and mix and cook for a minute. Add stock to make a thick sauce.

salt and pepper   pinch of sugar
1 Tbs chopped parsley or dill   lemon juice

Add and simmer for 5 mins.

6–8 Tbs soured cream (90–120 ml)

Add to the sauce and heat, then pour over the beans and serve.

Runner beans Béarnaise

Cooking time 15–20 mins. *Quantities* for 4.

1 lb runner beans (500 g)   2 tomatoes, chopped
1 Tbs butter   salt and pepper
1–2 oz chopped bacon (25–50 g)

Boil the beans as described above for boiled green beans. Drain and keep hot. Fry the bacon and tomatoes in the butter for a few minutes. Add the beans and mix well. Season to taste and serve hot.

BRUSSELS SPROUTS

The best sprouts are the very small tight ones which unfortunately are rather hard to buy. They look best and have a lovely nutty flavour. Failing this try to buy graded ones, not a mixture of tiny, medium and large, because the small ones overcook before the large ones are tender. Do not buy blighted ones as they are almost impossible to wash, nor any which look wilted and have yellow outside leaves, as these will undoubtedly be stale. Very loose open sprouts are a bad buy as they often have bad centres and become mushy when cooked.

Sprouts will keep fresh and crisp for several days if they are washed, drained and stored in a polythene bag or box in the refrigerator. They are in season from summer to spring but are at their best in the winter.

Boiled brussels sprouts

Cooking time about 15 mins. *Quantities:* allow 4–6 oz per person (100–150 g).

Prepare the sprouts by cutting off any damaged leaves and cutting a cross in the bottom of the stem to help speed up cooking. Wash quickly in plenty of cold water. If they vary widely in size grade them into two lots. Heat about 1 in (2½ cm) of water in a saucepan and add 1 tsp salt for each lb (½ kg) of sprouts. Bring the water to the boil and add the larger sprouts; when the water boils again gradually drop in the smaller sprouts. Put on the lid and boil rapidly until they are only just tender. Avoid over-cooking as this spoils both the colour and flavour. They are nicest to eat if still slightly firm. Drain well, return to the pan with a knob of butter and toss until it is melted and coats the sprouts.

Brussels sprouts Lyonnaise

Cooking time 20 mins. *Quantities* for 4.

1½ lb sprouts (700 g)

Prepare and boil as in the recipe above. Drain well.

1 oz butter (25 g)   2 Tbs finely chopped onion

Heat the butter in the pan and fry the onion in it until it begins to brown. Add the sprouts and cook for a minute longer, then serve.

CABBAGE

Many varieties are cultivated, maturing at different times of the year so that some variety is in season all the year round. Some cabbages have round heads or hearts, some pointed, some are large varieties and some very small. One variety of red cabbage matures in the summer and another in the autumn.

Cabbage keeps well and transports well so if you see one looking tired and wilted you may be sure it is either pretty stale or has been left lying in a warm place. In any case it is a bad buy. Cabbages with large white hearts are nutritionally not as good a buy as the smaller and greener ones, though for cabbage salads the large white hearts are more tender.

Do not buy cabbage which has been cut in half for display purposes because you do not know how long it has been cut and it may have lost its freshness and some of its nutritive value.

In a cool, dark place cabbage will keep fresh for many days. For refrigerator storage, trim off damaged outer leaves and surplus stalk, wash in cold water, drain and put the whole cabbage in a polythene bag.

Because cabbage is available fresh all the year, there is not much point in freezing it, with the possible exception of cooked red cabbage which makes a useful emergency store. White cabbage is fermented to make sauerkraut and red cabbage made into vinegar pickles.

Boiled cabbage

This is not a recipe for the traditional wet and smelly cabbage of catering establishments but is for making cabbage taste fresh and delicious.

Cooking time about 15 mins. *Quantities:* allow 6–8 oz per person (175–250 g).

Remove any very coarse or damaged leaves and cut off any stalk. Cut the cabbage in halves or quarters and remove the hard inside stalk.

Wash the cabbage, drain and cut it in ½ in (1 cm) strips.

Put about 1 in (2½ cm) of water in a saucepan with 1 tsp salt to each lb (½ kg) cabbage. When the water boils, add the cabbage, put on the lid and boil rapidly until it is just tender when tested with a fork. Avoid cooking to the collapsed and soggy stage.

Drain it and return it to the pan with a knob of butter. When the butter melts, stir the cabbage to coat it. Serve as soon as possible.

For variety, flavourings can be added, for example herb seeds such as fennel, dill and caraway cooked with the cabbage, or fresh chopped herbs sprinkled over at serving time; or try the recipe below for fried cabbage.

Fried cabbage

Cooking time 15 mins. *Quantities* for 4.

1½ lb cabbage (700 g)	pinch of ground mace or nutmeg
1 medium-sized onion, chopped	½ tsp salt
1 rasher bacon, chopped	fat or oil

Remove the tough outer leaves and the centre core of the cabbage. Wash and drain. Cut it into thinner slices than for boiling, about ¼ in (6 mm).

Heat enough fat or oil to make a thin layer in the bottom of a saucepan and when it is hot, but not smoking hot, add the other ingredients. Stir, cover the pan, turn down the heat and cook gently until the cabbage is just tender. Serve as soon as possible.

Cabbage with cream sauce

Cooking time about 15 mins. *Quantities* for 4.

1 lb white cabbage (500 g)

Wash, drain and shred the cabbage fairly finely, removing the core and any coarse ribs.

1 oz butter or lard (25 g)

Heat this in a saucepan and add the cabbage. Cover the pan and stew the cabbage gently until it is tender, but do not allow it to brown.

salt and pepper   1 Tbs lemon juice
1 Tbs sugar

Add and cook a few minutes longer.

¼ pt soured cream (150 ml)   pinch of grated nutmeg

Add, mix well and make sure it is hot before serving.

ALTERNATIVES

Beat the cream with 1 egg yolk and add chopped dill in place of the nutmeg.
  Cook some finely chopped bacon with the cabbage.

Stuffed cabbage leaves

Cooking time ½–1 hr depending on the cabbage. *Quantities* for 4.

8 oz cooked cold meat (25 g)

Remove any fat or gristle and either mince, chop finely or shred the meat in the blender. Tip into a basin.

1 Tbs finely chopped onion   salt and pepper
1 Tbs chopped parsley   1 egg, beaten
fresh or dried thyme or marjoram

Instead of chopping the onion and herbs, these can be blended with the meat, seasonings and egg. Mix the ingredients thoroughly with the meat.

4 large cabbage leaves or 8 smaller ones

Do not use very small leaves, you need large enough ones to accommodate the filling. Put the leaves in a bowl and cover them with boiling water. Leave for 2–3 mins or until they are pliable. Drain and spread out flat. If the ends of the ribs are very thick, remove and lap the cut ends. Put some filling on each leaf and roll up from the stem end folding in the sides to make a neat parcel. Pack the rolls close together in a saucepan.

2 Tbs concentrated tomato purée	2 Tbs brown sugar
¼ pt soured cream (150 ml)	white stock or water

Mix the tomato, sugar and cream and pour over the cabbage. Add enough stock or water just to moisten the pan and prevent burning. Cover closely and boil gently until the cabbage is tender. This should only take 30 mins if the cabbage is young, but considerably longer if the leaves are tough. Lift out the rolls on to a hot dish and keep hot.

1 egg yolk	2 Tbs lemon juice

Mix together and stir into the liquid in the pan. Stir and heat until it just comes to the boil. Taste for seasoning, pour over the cabbage and serve.

White cabbage with herb seeds

Cooking time about 15 mins. *Quantities* for 4.

1 lb finely sliced white cabbage (500 g)	1 oz lard (25 g)
	1 onion, finely chopped

Put in a saucepan with just enough boiling water to prevent burning. Cover and cook gently until the cabbage is tender.

2 Tbs lemon juice	1 tsp caraway, dill or fennel seeds
salt and pepper	

Stir into the cabbage.

1 tsp flour

Sprinkle over the cabbage, mix in and cook for a few minutes longer. Serve hot.

Red cabbage

Cooking time ½–¾ hr. *Quantities* for 4.

1 lb red cabbage (500 g)	1 large onion
1 large apple	

Remove any discoloured outer leaves from the cabbage, cut it in half, and remove the centre stalk. Wash and drain well and cut in slices ¼ in (6 mm) thick or less. Alternatively, slice the cabbage, onion and apple in a mechanical shredder. Otherwise, peel and slice the onion and apple as well.

1 oz lard (25 g)
2 Tbs water
2 Tbs vinegar
1 tsp salt
pinch of pepper
1 Tbs brown sugar

Melt the dripping in a saucepan and add all the other ingredients. Cover, bring to the boil and boil gently until the cabbage is tender, stirring occasionally. If it seems in danger of boiling dry, add a little more water, but the pan should be practically dry by the time cooking is finished. If more convenient, put the cabbage in a casserole and cook in a slow oven as for a stew.

Serve with pork or sausages.

Sauerkraut

This is usually served with sausages, smoked meats, ham and bacon, and with boiled salt beef and other salted meats.

Sauerkraut is sold by the pound in some shops and is also available canned. If you are not using up a whole can at once the surplus can be stored for a week or so in a covered dish in the refrigerator, longer in the freezer.

The simplest way of cooking it is to rinse it and put it in a pan with just enough cold water to prevent burning and to boil it for ½ hr. Drain and serve hot. Or use the recipe below.

Sauerkraut with caraway or capers

Cooking time ½–1 hr. *Quantities* for 4.

1 oz lard (25 g)
1 onion, chopped

Heat the lard in a saucepan and cook the onion until it begins to brown.

1 lb sauerkraut (500 g), rinsed and drained

Add to the pan and cook for a few mins.

¼ pt white wine or cider (150 ml)
¼ pt water (150 ml)

Add to the pan, bring to the boil, cover and boil gently until the sauerkraut is tender.

1 tsp potato flour blended with a little cold water
salt and pepper
½ tsp sugar
1 tsp caraway seeds or 1 Tbs capers or to taste

Thicken the liquid in the pan with the blended potato flour and add seasonings to taste. Serve hot.

CARROTS

Carrots are one of the root vegetables which are in season all the year round and in mild places can be left in the ground all winter. There are two main types, the long-rooted and the shorter or stump-rooted, also known as the horn type.

Buy carrots which are a good even shape and a moderate size. Very small ones are a nuisance to prepare and very large ones are sometimes woody inside and inclined to be dry and tasteless. Avoid any which show signs of worm infection because there will be a great deal of wastage, the whole carrot often being useless.

Some of the best carrots are sold ready washed in polythene bags; this is a good way of buying them for you can see clearly what you are getting and it is worth paying a little more not to be landed with a high proportion of useless carrots.

To prepare very young carrots all you need do is wash them thoroughly and cut off the tops, then cook them whole. Older ones need to be scraped and those which are really old need to be peeled thinly. Cut out any damaged parts, cut off the tops and trim the roots. For quick cooking, cut large carrots in rings or in slices lengthwise.

Carrots keep very well in any cool dark place. For refrigerator storage, wash, drain and put in a polythene bag or box.

Boiled carrots

Cooking time about 20 mins. *Quantities:* allow 4–6 oz per person (125–175 g).

Prepare the carrots (see above), and cut large ones into slices or rings. Boil about 1 in ($2\frac{1}{2}$ cm) of water in a pan and add 1 tsp salt for each 1 lb of carrots ($\frac{1}{2}$ kg). When the water is boiling, add the carrots, cover the pan, and boil until they are tender but not soft. Drain, keeping the water for stock. Return the carrots to the pan with a knob of butter and shake to coat them with the melted butter. Serve with chopped parsley, chives or other fresh herbs sprinkled on top.

ALTERNATIVE

Use some milk and some of the carrot stock to make a parsley sauce. Combine with the carrots.

Vegetables 269

Carrots and celery

This makes a change and is useful when there are some outside sticks of celery to be used up.

Cooking time about 20 mins. *Quantities* for 4.

3–4 medium-sized carrots 4–5 large sticks of celery

Scrape and slice the carrots. Scrub and slice the celery. Cook them together in a little boiling salted water until they are tender. Drain.

pinch of sugar 1 Tbs chopped parsley
1 oz butter (25 g)

Return the vegetables to the pan with these ingredients and toss to mix well.

Casserole of carrots

Cooking time $\frac{1}{2}$–1 hr.
Temperature 160–190° C (325–375° F; G3–5).
Quantities for 4.

1 lb carrots (500 g) pinch of pepper
$\frac{1}{2}$ oz butter or other fat (15 g) $\frac{1}{2}$ tsp salt
1–2 Tbs stock or water

Scrape or peel the carrots. Either cut them in rings or lengthwise in sticks, not too thin. Put in the casserole with the other ingredients, cover and cook until they are just tender. Serve with any liquid left in the dish.

chopped parsley or other fresh herbs

Sprinkle on generously just before serving.

Vichy carrots

Cooking time 15–20 mins. *Quantities* for 4.

1 lb young carrots (500 g)

Wash and, if necessary, scrape the carrots. Remove the tops and cut the carrots in slices.

1 oz butter (25 g) 1 tsp sugar
$\frac{1}{2}$ tsp salt

Melt the butter in a saucepan or casserole and add the other ingredients with the carrots. Cover and cook until the carrots are just tender.

1 Tbs chopped parsley

Sprinkle over the carrots and serve hot.

Carrots and cheese quiche

Cooking time 30 mins.
Temperature 220° C (425° F; G7).
Quantities for a 7 in (18 cm) quiche.

short-crust pastry using 4 oz flour (100 g), or use 6 oz ready-made (175 g)

Roll the pastry thinly and line a flan ring or pie plate with it. Prick the bottom and put it in the refrigerator while the filling is prepared.

4 oz finely grated raw carrot (100 g)
1 tsp finely chopped onion
salt and pepper
3 Tbs cream
pinch of ground mace or nutmeg

2 oz strong cheese, coarsely grated (50 g)
1 egg, beaten
3 Tbs milk

Mix all the ingredients together and put in the prepared pastry case. Bake until the filling is set and lightly browned. Serve warm or cold.

Carrot mould with green peas

This is suitable for a main dish for lunch or supper, or serve it as a dinner-party vegetable.

Cooking time $\frac{1}{2}$–$\frac{3}{4}$ hr.
Temperature 180° C (350° F; G4).
Quantities for 4–6.

8 oz cooked or drained canned carrots (250 g)

Rub the carrots through a sieve or pulp them in the electric blender.

salt and pepper
1 Tbs finely chopped onion
1 egg, beaten

$\frac{1}{4}$ pt single cream or evaporated milk (150 ml)

Add to the carrot purée and mix well. Pour into a well greased or oiled border mould, $\frac{3}{4}$ pt size (400 ml). Stand this in a baking tin with hot water coming half-way up the sides of the mould. Cook until set. Remove the mould from the water and leave it to stand for a few minutes before turning it out on to a hot dish.

8 oz shelled fresh or frozen green peas   a knob of butter
(250 g)

Boil the peas, drain and toss with the butter to coat them. Pile them in the centre of the mould and serve hot.

ALTERNATIVE

Moisten the peas with a little béchamel or other sauce.

CAULIFLOWER

Either cauliflower or white broccoli, which looks very like cauliflower, is available all the year round. Choose one with a firm compact head surrounded by green leaves. Stale and yellow-leaved cauliflowers have a poor flavour and the stems may be flabby instead of crisp. If the leaves have all been trimmed away it is quite likely that the vegetable is not as fresh as it should be.

Provided a fresh cauliflower has been purchased it can be kept in good condition for several days if it is first washed and drained, and then put in a polythene bag in the refrigerator. If you don't want to use it all at once, cut off the quantity of sprigs you want and return the rest to the refrigerator.

Boiled cauliflower

Cooking time 15–20 mins. *Quantities* 1 medium-sized head for 4.

Remove the stalk and all except the smallest leaves. The stalk may be sliced and cooked with the rest. The cauliflower may be boiled in small pieces, in individual flowerets, or left whole. When boiled whole it takes longest to cook and has a stronger flavour but many prefer the appearance of a whole cauliflower. I much prefer it cooked in sprigs for the minimum possible time so that it still has firmness.

Boil about $\frac{1}{2}$ in (1 cm) of salted water in a pan. Add the cauliflower (flower side up if it is whole). Cover and boil until just tender. Avoid over-cooking or it will have a very strong flavour and will fall to pieces when handled. Drain well. Serve with a white or béchamel sauce, hollandaise or brown butter sauce.

Cauliflower Milanaise

Cooking time 20–30 mins. *Quantities* for 4.

1 medium-sized cauliflower

Wash the cauliflower and divide it into sprigs. Put it in a little boiling salted water and boil until it is barely tender. Drain and keep hot.

2 oz grated cheese (½ c or 50 g)   2 oz butter or margarine (50 g)

Grease a shallow baking dish and sprinkle a layer of cheese over the bottom. Add the cauliflower and sprinkle it with the rest of the cheese. Add half the butter cut in small pieces. Place in a hot oven or under the grill to brown the cheese. Meanwhile heat the rest of the butter in a small pan until it turns light brown, pour it over the cauliflower and serve.

Cauliflower with walnuts

Cooking time 20–30 mins. *Quantities* for 4.

1 oz fresh breadcrumbs (25 g)   1 oz chopped walnuts (25 g)
a small knob of butter or margarine

Melt the fat in a small pan and stir in the crumbs to coat them well. Mix with the walnuts.

1 oz butter or margarine (25 g)   1 oz flour (3 Tbs or 25 g)
½ pt milk (300 ml)   salt and pepper

Tip the walnut mixture on to a plate, rinse out the pan and melt the butter or margarine in it. Stir in the flour and cook for a minute or two. Add the milk and stir or whisk until it boils. Boil for 5 mins and season to taste. Keep it hot.

1 medium-sized cauliflower in sprigs

Cook in a little boiling salted water until just tender. Drain and arrange in a baking dish. Mask with the sauce and sprinkle with the nut mixture. Brown under the grill or in a hot oven.

CELERIAC

(turnip-rooted celery)

This is a variety of celery with a large edible root. It is in season in the autumn and winter.

To prepare, wash it thoroughly and peel fairly thickly. Cut in slices or chunks. Cook and serve like celery.

CELERY

Although imported celery is available most of the year it is at its best in the autumn and winter when the home-grown celery has had the benefit of frosty weather, which makes it specially crisp.

When buying celery look at the colour of the small leaves. If these are browning, the celery is probably stale. The sticks should be firm and crisp, and there should be a good proportion of small inner ones, showing a good heart. If all the top leaves have been cut off and some of the outside stalks trimmed off as well, this shows poor quality.

Only the inner stalks are tender enough to serve with cheese; the next layer is suitable for chopping up for salads and the outer leaves are best used for soups, stews and casseroles.

To prepare celery, trim the tops, keeping good small leaves for use in salads, soups, stews or to dry and use for flavouring. Leave only the small inner stalks attached to the root. Trim this and when serving the celery with cheese slit in half lengthwise. Scrub the stalks if necessary. Very large outside stalks may need to be scraped with a small knife to remove coarse outside fibres.

To keep celery in good condition, after washing, put it in a polythene bag or box in the refrigerator.

Braised celery using a whole head

Cooking time 30 mins. *Quantities* for 4.

1 large head of celery or 2 smaller heads

Separate the outer stalks and wash them well. Cut them in even lengths to fit in the saucepan. Cut the inner stalks if necessary, and cut the heart in quarters lengthwise.

1 carrot, sliced	2 rashers bacon, chopped
1 small turnip, sliced	a sprig of parsley
1 onion, sliced	a piece of bay leaf
salt and pepper	stock

Put these in the bottom of a saucepan with enough stock just to cover. Put in the celery, cover and boil until it is just tender.

1 Tbs arrowroot or potato flour to ½ pt stock (250 ml)

Lift the celery into a serving dish. Strain the stock, return to the pan and thicken it with the starch blended to a cream with a little cold water. When it thickens, pour it over the celery and serve hot.

Celery and mustard sauce

Cooking time about 30 mins. *Quantities* for 4.

1 lb celery (500 g)

Scrub the celery stalks and cut them in 1 in (2½ cm) pieces. Boil in a little salted water until they are tender. Drain and keep hot.

2 oz butter (50 g)   1 tsp made mustard
pepper

Melt the butter and mix with the mustard and pepper. Add the hot celery and mix well before serving.

Celery with yogurt

Cooking time about 20 mins. *Quantities* for 4.

8 large sticks celery, or equivalent amount of canned celery

Scrub the celery and cut it in 1 in (2½ cm) pieces. Boil it in a little salted water until just tender. Drain.

1 egg   ¼ pt yogurt (150 ml)

Beat the egg in a small basin and beat in the yogurt. Place the basin over boiling water and beat the sauce with a wooden spoon until it is hot and has thickened a little. The yogurt will thin to begin with and then thicken up again.

pepper   chopped chives and/or parsley

Add to the sauce. Put the celery in a hot serving dish and pour the sauce over it.

CHICORY

Chicory is in season in the autumn and winter. The tips of good quality chicory should be a pale yellow. Stale chicory has greenish or even browning tips, and the edges of the outer leaves may be beginning to discolour.

Washed and drained chicory will keep in good condition for several days if stored in a polythene bag or box in the refrigerator.

To prepare it for cooking, use a pointed vegetable knife to remove a cone-shaped piece from the base of each head of chicory. This is to allow the hot water to penetrate the thick end more easily and help the cooking.

Boiled chicory

Quantities: allow 1 lb (500 g) for 4.

Cook the chicory for about 20 mins in a little boiling salted water to which some lemon juice has been added to keep the chicory white. Serve it either plain, or chopped and re-heated in a little melted butter to which a pinch of sugar has been added.

Chicory Polonaise

Cooking time ½ hr. *Quantities* for 4.

1 lb chicory (500 g)	2 Tbs milk
½ oz fat (15 g) or 1 Tbs oil	4 Tbs stock
½ tsp salt	

Wash and prepare the chicory and put it in a pan with the other ingredients. Cover and boil gently for ½ hr.

1 hard-boiled egg

Shell and chop finely. Serve the chicory with the egg sprinkled over it.

Chicory with cheese and ham

Cooking time about 1 hr.
Temperature 190° C (375° F; G5).
Quantities for 4.

1 lb chicory (500 g)	1 Tbs lemon juice

Boil the chicory until tender in a little water with the lemon juice. Drain, keeping the liquid.

1 oz butter (25 g)	2 Tbs flour
½ pt cooking liquid and milk mixed (250 ml)	salt and pepper
	2 oz grated strong cheese (50 g)

Melt the butter in a small pan, stir in the flour and cook for a minute. Add the liquid and whisk or stir until the sauce is smooth and boiling. Boil for a few minutes, stirring all the time. Add the cheese. Season with salt and pepper.

4 oz sliced boiled ham (100 g)

Put the chicory in a baking dish in layers with the sauce and ham; or wrap each piece of chicory in a piece of ham and pour the sauce over the top.

4 Tbs buttered breadcrumbs

Sprinkle over the top and bake for about 20 mins, or until well heated and brown on top.

COURGETTES

See Marrow.

KOHL RABI

In season during the autumn and winter. They are at their best when small and freshly gathered, and are cooked in the same way as turnips, though they have a milder flavour. They need to be peeled fairly thickly. They are specially good boiled in a little water and served with a parsley sauce using the stock from cooking them, and are also good for salads, either raw shredded or sliced cooked.

LEEKS

Leeks are in season from September to May but the season may be extended with imported ones. During the cold weather they keep well left in the ground and are dug as required. Medium-sized leeks are the best to buy and any tops left on should be green; yellowing tops show the leeks are stale. Only the white part is normally used so if you buy leeks with a lot of green in proportion to the white, there will be a lot of wastage.

If leeks are trimmed and washed they will keep in good condition for up to a week if stored in polythene bags or boxes in the refrigerator.

During the growing period, leeks are usually earthed up to keep them white, and soil becomes lodged between the top leaves. Careful washing is needed to make sure all this is removed. Begin by cutting off the green tops either entirely down to the white or leaving about 2 in (5 cm) of the green, according to taste. Remove any coarse outer leaves or any damaged parts. Cut off the roots, being sure to leave enough of the base to hold the white leaves together. Slit each leek about a third of the way down from the top and wash them under running water, opening the slit leaves back well to remove all dirt. Drain upside down.

Very large leeks may be cut in half lengthwise and very small ones can be tied in bundles before cooking to make them easier to manage.

Boiled leeks

Cooking time 10-20 mins depending on size.
Quantities: allow 2 leeks per portion, more or less according to the size.

Prepare the leeks as described above. Use a pan large enough to let them lie flat. Heat about 1 in (2½ cm) of water with 1 tsp salt for each pound of leeks.

When it is boiling, add the leeks, cover and boil gently until they feel tender when pierced with a fork at the root ends. Drain them upside down in a colander to remove as much water as possible. Serve plain or with melted butter or a sauce (using some of the cooking water), for example a white or béchamel sauce, cheese, caper or tomato sauce.

Leeks with cheese and cream

Cooking time 45 mins.
Temperature 190° C (375° F; G5).
Quantities for 4.

2 lb leeks (1 kg)

Prepare and boil the leeks until tender, then drain.

4 oz grated cheese (1 c or 100 g)

Sprinkle a layer of cheese in a shallow baking dish. Arrange the leeks on the cheese and sprinkle with some more cheese.

6 Tbs double cream (90 ml)   salt and pepper

Put on top of the leeks and cheese and add a final layer of cheese. Bake until golden brown and hot. Serve as a separate course or as a vegetable with chicken, veal or fish.

Leek purée with grilled bacon or gammon

Cooking time 20 mins. *Quantities* for 4.

2 lb trimmed leeks (1 kg)

Cut the leeks in halves lengthwise and wash them carefully under a running cold tap. Boil in a little salted water until they are tender. Drain and rub through a sieve or pulp them in the electric blender.

1 egg, beaten
pinch of grated nutmeg
pepper

¼ pt double cream or evaporated milk (150 ml)

Add these to the purée and mix well.

½ oz butter (15 g)

Melt in a pan, add the purée mixture and heat gently until it thickens, stirring all the time. Taste for seasoning. If necessary add mashed potato powder to thicken the purée.

4 gammon rashers, grilled or fried

Serve with the purée.

Leek and cottage cheese quiche

Cooking time 8 mins preparatory cooking; 45 mins baking.
Temperature 220° C (425° F; G7).
Quantities for an 8 in (20 cm) quiche.

short-crust pastry using 4 oz flour (¾ c or 100 g), or use 6 oz ready-made (175 g)

Roll the pastry thinly to line a flan ring or pie plate. Refrigerate while the filling is prepared.

¾–1 lb trimmed leeks (300–500 g)   ½ oz butter (15 g)

Wash the leeks carefully and slice them coarsely. Melt the butter in a saucepan and stew the leeks in it for about 3 mins.

¼ pt milk (150 ml)

Add to the leeks and simmer for 5 mins.

1 egg   3 oz cottage cheese (75 g)
salt and pepper

Beat together and then add the leeks. Set aside to cool. Put it in the flan case.

grated nutmeg

Sprinkle a thin layer on top of the filling and bake until the pastry is lightly browned and the filling set. Serve hot or cold.

MARROW AND COURGETTES

Courgettes, also known as zucchini, belong to the same family as the vegetable marrow but are smaller and are usually not allowed to grow more than 3–4 in long (8–10 cm) before being gathered. Marrows, picked when small and young, can be sliced and cooked in the same way as courgettes. At this stage they need no peeling and the whole of the vegetable can be eaten. When marrows become larger, they need to be peeled and the seeds and pulp removed from the middle. The resulting marrow has much less flavour than a courgette or marrow eaten young. A small marrow is about 9 in (24 cm) long.

Courgettes are at their best from May to September, marrows from June to October. Be careful when buying courgettes and make sure they are fresh, shown by tight shining skins; stale ones look jaded and wrinkled and will taste bitter. If washed, drained and stored in a polythene bag in the refrigerator they will keep fresh for several days. Small marrows are treated in the same way: large, mature ones can be kept in a cool, dry place, often for weeks or even months.

Marrow or courgettes cooked in butter

Cooking time 15–20 mins. *Quantities* for 4.

1 lb courgettes or young marrow (500 g)

Wash and trim off any stalk, drain. Leave small courgettes whole but cut larger ones (4 in (10 cm) or more long) in pieces and cut marrow in pieces. Large marrow, peeled and with seeds and pith removed, can be cut in pieces and cooked the same way.

about 1 oz butter (25 g)   salt and pepper

Melt enough butter to make a thin layer on the bottom of a saucepan, add the vegetables and seasoning, cover and cook over a gentle heat, or in a moderate oven, until tender. Shake the pan occasionally or stir gently with a wooden spoon.

chopped parsley or other fresh herbs such as mint, thyme or chives

Serve the vegetables with any liquid in the pan and sprinkle them with chopped herbs.

Courgettes with cheese and cream

Cooking time 5 mins frying; 30 mins baking.
Temperature 220° C (425° F; G7).
Quantities for 4.

| 1 lb courgettes or small marrow (500 g) | 2 Tbs seasoned flour |

Wash the courgettes or marrow and cut in slices about $\frac{1}{4}$ in (6 mm) thick. Toss the slices in seasoned flour.

1 oz butter (25 g), or 2 Tbs olive oil

Use a large frying pan and heat the butter or oil, or a mixture. Add the courgettes and toss and cook for 5 mins. Put half of them in a shallow baking dish.

| 1 Tbs very finely chopped onion | 4 oz grated cheese (100 g) |

Sprinkle the onion over the courgettes and then half the cheese. Add the remaining courgettes.

| $\frac{1}{2}$ pt soured cream (250 ml) | 4 tomatoes, sliced |

Pour the cream over the courgettes, top with tomato and finally the remaining cheese. Bake until the top is brown and the courgettes are tender when tested with a fork. Serve hot.

Marrow Lyonnaise

Cooking time 20–30 mins. *Quantities* for 4.

| 1 lb prepared weight (500 g) of mature marrow butter or oil for frying | 1 large onion, chopped or finely sliced |

Cut the marrow in small pieces and boil it in a little salted water until barely tender. Drain well. Heat some butter or oil, enough to make a thin layer in the saucepan, and fry the onion until it is tender. Add the drained marrow, mix carefully and allow to become hot before serving.

chopped parsley

Sprinkle on generously just before serving.

Marrow or courgettes stewed with tomatoes

Cooking time 35 mins. Quantities for 4.

2 lb marrow (1 kg), or 1 lb courgettes (500 g)

Wash the courgettes, trim the ends and cut in slices about an inch (2½ cm) thick. Peel marrow and remove the skins before cutting the flesh in small pieces.

8 oz tomatoes (250 g) 1 oz fat (25 g), or 2 Tbs oil
1 medium-sized onion, chopped

Wash and slice the tomatoes. Heat the fat or oil in a saucepan and fry the onion and tomatoes for about 5 mins. If oil is used the dish is suitable for serving cold as salad or hors d'œuvre.

salt and pepper ½ tsp sugar
¼ pt stock (150 ml) 2 tsp chopped basil, marjoram or
a little crushed or powdered garlic thyme

Add to the pan together with the prepared marrow or courgettes, cover and cook gently until the vegetables are just tender.

chopped parsley or some more of the herbs used in cooking

Serve garnished with the chopped herbs.

Marrow or courgettes in paprika sauce

Cooking time 15–20 mins. Quantities for 4.

1–1½ lb courgettes or small marrow (500–700 g)

Wash and trim off stem ends. Cut in 2 in (5 cm) slices.

½ oz lard (15 g) 2 tsp paprika pepper

Heat the lard in a saucepan. Add the marrow or courgettes and sprinkle with pepper. Cook slowly for about 5 mins, turning occasionally. Do not allow to brown.

2 tsp flour ¼ pt soured cream (150 ml)
salt

Mix the flour to a paste with some of the cream. Add the remainder and then stir into the marrow. Add salt to taste. Continue to cook slowly until the marrow is tender. Serve hot.

Roast or baked marrow

This is one of the best ways of cooking mature marrow. It can be cooked with the skin on, but cut it in large pieces and remove the seeds and pulp. It can either be cooked in the hot fat round or under a joint or in a separate pan with a little fat or dripping. Baste it occasionally with the melted fat and cook until it feels tender when pierced with a fork. Cooking time will depend on the temperature of the oven; in a hot oven it takes about 40 mins, when roasting at low temperatures, about 1 hr.

Season with salt and pepper before serving it.

If the marrow has been peeled, the pieces can be turned over at half time instead of basting.

MUSHROOMS

Most of the mushrooms on sale are cultivated, though in some places field mushrooms are also sometimes available. Cultivated mushrooms need not be skinned, simply wash and dry them and trim the stalks level with the sides or gills of the mushrooms. These trimmings should not be wasted but chopped and used either with the tops or in a separate dish, or for flavouring sauces, stock and soups. Mushroom stalks are sometimes sold separately much more cheaply than whole mushrooms and are useful to buy for flavouring purposes.

Mushrooms which have been gathered from the fields should be skinned in order to see if they have any worms in them, shown by holes in the white part under the skin. These mushrooms should be discarded. A very large number of fully grown field mushrooms are infested and it is often a waste of time to gather any but the very small button field mushrooms.

Button mushrooms are used for adding whole to a dish, for garnishing purposes, and for use in dishes where a light colour is required. Fully grown mushrooms darken the cooking liquid but have more flavour and are the best for serving as grilled or fried mushrooms. Avoid over-cooking as this causes loss of flavour.

Fresh mushrooms should keep for 24 hrs in a cold larder spread out in a single layer on a large dish. In a covered container in the refrigerator they should keep for 2–3 days, but don't wash them before storing or they will rot. Button mushrooms or sliced larger mushrooms freeze very well and are a useful store for flavouring purposes, as are canned or dried mushrooms. Dried ones can be added to sauces, stews and soups without any previous soaking. Frozen mushrooms can be cooked without thawing.

Baked mushrooms

Cooking time about 10 mins.
Temperature 190° C (375° F; G5).
Quantities 1–4 oz per person (25–100 g), depending on how they are used.

Wash the mushrooms and remove the stalks. Grease a shallow baking dish liberally with butter and put in the mushrooms, preferably in a single layer. Sprinkle with salt and pepper and cover with a lid or with foil. Bake until the thick centres are just tender and serve with any juices in the dish.

Fried mushrooms

Wash the mushrooms and remove the stalks. Drain very thoroughly. The stalks may be sliced and fried as well. Heat a little butter or oil or use fat from fried bacon and fry the mushrooms, gills uppermost, until they are just tender.

Grilled mushrooms

Wash and drain thoroughly and remove the stalks. If the mushrooms are to be cooked alone, put them gill sides up in the grill pan and put a knob of butter in each one. Grill gently until they are just tender. If they are being cooked with bacon, put them under the bacon so that the bacon fat bastes them instead of using butter.

On skewers for kebabs use medium-sized ones as the skewers are likely to split button mushrooms.

Creamed mushrooms

Cooking time a few mins. *Quantities* for 4.

1 oz butter (25 g)	8 oz mushrooms (250 g)

Wash the mushrooms and slice them, not too finely. Heat the butter in a frying pan and fry the mushrooms for one minute, stirring with a wooden spoon. Turn the heat down a little.

½ tsp salt   pinch of freshly ground pepper
2 Tbs flour

Sprinkle these over the mushrooms and mix quickly.

¼ pt milk (150 ml)   ¼ pt double cream (150 ml)
1 Tbs lemon juice or sherry

Add to the mushrooms, stir until boiling, and serve in small hot dishes with fingers of hot buttered toast or brown bread and butter.

Mushroom flan

Cooking time 30–35 mins.
Temperature 220° C (425° F; G7).
Quantities for a 7–8 in flan (18–20 cm).

short-crust pastry using 4 oz flour (100 g), or use 6 oz ready-made (175 g)

Roll the pastry thinly to line a flan ring or pie plate. Prick the bottom with a fork and put the flan in the refrigerator while the filling is prepared. Roll any trimmings of pastry and cut these in strips to use for a lattice top after the filling has been added.

1 medium-sized onion, finely chopped   1½ oz butter (40 g)

Melt the butter in a small pan and cook the onion in it until it is tender but not brown.

½ pt milk (300 ml)   1 bay leaf

Heat together in a separate small pan, remove from the heat when the milk boils and set aside to infuse for about 5 mins.

1 oz flour (3 Tbs or 25 g)

Remove the pan containing the onions from the heat and stir in the flour. Strain the milk and stir it in gradually until the sauce is smooth. Return to the heat and stir until the sauce boils.

1 egg yolk   2 Tbs double cream

Mix together. Remove the sauce from the heat and stir in the egg mixture. Put on one side.

4–6 oz mushrooms (100–150 g)   1 oz butter (25 g)

Cut large mushrooms in quarters, halve medium-sized ones, leave small ones whole. Heat the butter in a frying pan and cook the mushrooms for 2–3 mins. Add them to the sauce.

salt and pepper   pinch of ground nutmeg

Season to taste and put in the pastry case. Cover the top with a lattice-work of pastry strips. Bake until the pastry is lightly browned. Serve hot or cold.

ONIONS

Onions are available all the year round but in late winter and early spring it is often difficult to find ones of good quality. Spring onions are the thinnings from the sowings for a new crop.

Good quality mature onions should look dry and bright and feel firm. Damp-looking, soft onions are usually rotten in the centre.

The most important condition for storing onions to last the winter is to keep them dry and for this reason they are often hung up in strings or bundles in the kitchen or some other dry room.

They are frequently used chopped and the easiest way to do this is to slice a skinned onion downwards almost through to the root end in thin layers and then to slice again at right angles. Finally slice horizontally when the onion will fall away in small dice. If very finely chopped onion is required, chop these dice with a cook's knife. Onions can also be chopped in water in an electric blender or liquidizer, then strained before use; or they can be put through a mincer or shredder.

Baked onions

METHOD 1

Wrap the unpeeled onions in foil, singly, and stand them on a baking shelf. Cook in a moderate oven until they are soft when squeezed, about 45–60 mins.

METHOD 2

Skin the onions and cook them in a little fat in a moderate or hot oven until they are tender. They may be baked round or under a joint of meat or cooked in a separate pan.

Baked stuffed onions

Serve these as a dish on their own or to accompany meat – for example, roast lamb or pork.

Cooking time about 20 mins to boil the onions, then 40–45 mins for baking.
Temperature 200° C (400° F; G6).
Quantities for 4.

4 large Spanish onions

Remove the skins and boil the onions in a little salted water until they are almost tender but still firm enough to keep their shape. Drain and cool.

Using a small pointed knife remove most of the centre of the onions, keeping just enough of the original to hold its shape. Put the onions in a baking dish. Chop the centres finely and put in a basin.

1 oz fresh breadcrumbs (25 g)	salt and pepper
2 oz grated strong cheese (50 g)	¼ tsp ground mace
½ tsp paprika pepper	8–10 large leaves sage, finely chopped

Add to the chopped onion and mix well.

½ pt soured cream (250 ml)

Use a little of the cream to bind the stuffing together. Fill the onions, piling up the top. Pour remaining cream round and over the onions and bake until they are quite tender. Serve with the cream as a sauce.

Onion and cheese quiche

Cooking time 40 mins.
Temperature 200° C (400° F; G6).
Quantities for a 7 in (18 cm) quiche.

short-crust pastry using 4 oz flour (100 g), or use 6 oz ready-made (175 g)

Roll the pastry thinly and line a flan ring or pie plate. Prick the bottom with a fork and put the pastry in the refrigerator while the filling is prepared.

1 small onion, finely chopped	3 oz strong cheese, grated (75 g)
3 fresh sage leaves, finely chopped, or use other herbs	1 egg, beaten
salt and pepper	¼ pt milk (150 ml)

Mix together and pour into the pastry case. Bake until set and lightly browned. Serve warm or cold.

PARSNIPS

Parsnips are in season from September to April and are one of the root vegetables which can be left in the ground during the winter and dug as required.

Buy small to medium-sized ones as large ones can have woody centres. Avoid any which look shrivelled. To keep them fresh, wash, drain and store in a polythene bag in the refrigerator.

To prepare them for cooking, scrub well, remove any small rootlets and the top bit where the leaves grew. Then peel them using a vegetable knife or potato peeler. If peeled in advance, keep them in cold water to prevent discoloration.

Baked or roast parsnips

Cooking time $\frac{1}{2}$ hr or more, depending on size of pieces and temperature of the oven.
Temperature 180° C (350° F; G4) upwards.
Quantities: allow 4–6 oz per person (100–175 g).

Peel the parsnips and cut them in halves or quarters. Melt some fat in a baking tin and roll the parsnips in this to coat them. Alternatively, roll them in the fat from a joint being roasted. Bake until they are tender and browned, turning once during cooking. Parsnips contain some sugar and this caramelizes on the outside to give a delicious flavour.

Parsnips cooked in butter

Cooking time 15–20 mins.
Quantities: allow 4–6 oz per person (100–175 g).

Peel the parsnips and cut them in thick slices. Melt enough butter to make a thin layer on the bottom of the saucepan. Add the parsnips, sprinkle with salt and pepper, cover and stew slowly, shaking the pan occasionally or stirring gently. By the time they are tender they should be golden brown and most of the butter should be absorbed. Sprinkle with chopped parsley and serve hot.

If more convenient, do the cooking in a moderate oven.

Parsnips with carrots

Cooking time about 30 mins.
Quantities: allow 4–6 oz mixed vegetables per person (100–175 g).

This mixture looks attractive and has a more interesting flavour than either vegetable cooked alone.

Peel the parsnips and cut them in pieces. Scrape the carrots and cut them in slightly smaller pieces. Heat about 1 in (2$\frac{1}{2}$ cm) water in a pan, add salt and when boiling add the vegetables. Cover and boil steadily until they are tender. Drain and mash together with a knob of butter or margarine and some pepper.

PEAS

Fresh green peas are in season from May to October. Unless you grow your own it is difficult to obtain really top quality peas and many prefer to use frozen ones. When buying green peas, look for ones with rounded and full pods of a good fresh green. Lots of very flat pods among them means you are buying pods and not peas, while light-coloured dryish-looking pods show the peas inside will be too mature to make pleasant eating.

If you buy peas in advance of using them either leave them in the pods and keep in a cool place, or shell them and put the peas in a polythene bag in the refrigerator. In general, though, peas should be cooked as soon as possible after gathering as the flavour deteriorates fairly quickly.

French method of cooking peas

Cooking time ½ hr. *Quantities* for 4.

4 or 5 outside leaves of a large lettuce

Wash and use to line the bottom of the saucepan; either leave whole, or shred them if the lettuce is a coarse one.

2 lb well-filled pods (1 kg), or	pinch of pepper
1 lb frozen peas (500 g)	2 rashers mild bacon
1 oz butter or dripping (25 g)	½ tsp salt
2 or 3 Tbs water	4-5 spring onions, white only

Shell the peas, remove bacon rinds and chop the bacon. Skin the onions. Put all the ingredients in the saucepan, cover, and cook gently until the peas are tender, adding more water if needed to prevent burning, but do not make a lot of liquid. Serve the peas with the liquid and the other ingredients.

Green pea purée with eggs and bacon

Cooking time 15-20 mins. *Quantities* for 4.

1 lb frozen peas or shelled fresh peas (500 g)

Boil the peas in a little lightly salted water until they are tender. Drain, reserving the stock. Either rub the peas through a sieve or blend them to a purée in the electric blender, using as much of the cooking liquid as is needed for this purpose. Re-heat the purée in the saucepan.

4 Tbs double cream (60 ml)	1 oz butter (25 g)
mashed potato powder	

Add cream and butter to the purée and sprinkle in enough potato powder to make the peas a fairly stiff consistency. Put the mixture in four mounds on hot plates or on a serving dish and put to keep hot.

8 oz bacon rashers (250 g) 4 eggs

Remove the rinds and cut the bacon in small pieces. Fry until it is crisp. Poach the eggs. Put an egg on each portion of purée and sprinkle the bacon round it.

Peas and peppers

Cooking time 5–10 mins. *Quantities* for 4.

1 lb fresh or frozen peas (500 g)

Boil in a little salted water until the peas are tender. Drain and keep hot.

1 oz butter (25 g)

Put in the pan and heat.

½ a red or green sweet pepper, chopped salt and pepper

Cook the chopped pepper in the butter for a few minutes until it is softened. Add the peas, season to taste and serve hot.

Pease pudding

Cooking time: dried peas, about 2 hrs; split peas, $\frac{1}{2}$–$\frac{3}{4}$ hr, plus 1 hr steaming in each case.

Quantities for 4.

8 oz dried or split peas (200 g)

Wash the peas and tie them in a piece of muslin. Cooking time is reduced if they are soaked in cold or boiling water for an hour or more before cooking, but this is not essential. Use 2 pt (1 l) water for soaking and/or cooking.

1 onion cloves

Skin the onion and stick 4–6 cloves in it. Put the bag of peas in the water with the onion and boil gently until the peas are soft. Lift out the bag and rub the peas through a sieve, or pulp them in the electric blender.

1 oz butter or margarine (25 g) 1 egg
salt and pepper

While the purée is still warm beat in the fat and then the egg with seasoning to taste. Put the mixture in a greased pudding basin, cover with a lid of foil and steam for 1 hr. Unmould and serve with meat such as pork, ham or bacon, or serve as a separate dish with a sauce such as

tomato or Espagnole sauce.

PEPPERS, SWEET

(also known as capsicums or sweet pimentos)

These are at their best in the summer and autumn but are in the shops for most of the year. The ripe red and yellow peppers are usually less plentiful than the green ones, but all are cooked the same way.

When in good condition sweet peppers have a taut, smooth, shiny skin and are firm with no soft patches. If dull, soft, or wrinkled they are stale and then can be very hot and bitter. It is wise to taste a tiny piece before using them.

To keep peppers fresh, wash and drain and store in a polythene bag or box in the refrigerator where they will keep for several days. They can also be cut in pieces or sliced, and frozen.

To prepare them for serving or cooking, wash, dry, cut in half, scrape out all the seeds, and cut out the white pithy parts. The flesh can be used raw for salads or hors d'œuvre, or cooked as flavouring for casseroles, rice dishes, or to make a dish on its own.

Fried sweet peppers

To serve as a garnish for meat, fish or poultry.

Cooking time 8–10 mins. *Quantities* for 4.

4 sweet peppers, green or red

Wash, cut in half, remove seeds and pithy white bits. Cut the flesh in small pieces.

2 Tbs oil

Heat the oil in a saucepan, add the peppers, cover and cook over a gentle heat until the peppers are almost tender but not soft. Season with salt and pepper and serve hot.

Grilled sweet peppers

Wash the peppers, cut in half lengthwise, remove seeds and white pith. Leave in halves or cut in smaller pieces according to taste. Brush with oil and grill until just tender, turning once during cooking.

When grilling peppers as part of a kebab it is often a good idea to blanch the peppers first in a little boiling water to soften them slightly, otherwise they may be rather too raw for many tastes.

Italian dish of green peppers

Cooking time ½–¾ hr. *Quantities* for 4.

1 medium-sized onion, chopped	2 Tbs olive oil

Heat the oil in a sauté pan or saucepan and cook the onion in it gently until it is just beginning to colour.

4 large green peppers	1 lb tomatoes (500 g)
garlic to taste	salt and pepper
1 Tbs finely chopped fresh rosemary	

Cut the peppers in half, remove seeds and white pith and cut the halves in pieces about 1 in (2½ cm) square. Skin the tomatoes and cut them in halves or quarters. Add all these ingredients to the onions, cover and cook gently until the peppers are just tender. Serve hot or cold.

Sweet peppers with yogurt

Suitable for an hors d'œuvre or to serve with hot or cold meat or poultry.

Cooking time 10–15 mins. *Quantities* for 2–4.

2 large green peppers, or 4 small ones

Cut the peppers in half lengthwise, remove seeds and stem end. Cut large ones in half again. Put under a hot grill, skin side up, and cook until the skin wrinkles and begins to burn. Remove from the grill and cool. Peel off the skin.

2 Tbs olive oil

Heat in a frying pan and cook the peppers both sides, until they are tender. Put them in a shallow dish.

about ¼ pt yogurt (150 ml), beaten smooth	salt

Use enough yogurt to cover the peppers. Sprinkle with salt and drizzle the oil from the pan over the top. Serve hot or cold.

Stuffed sweet peppers

Cooking time 30 mins, after 5 mins boiling.
Temperature 200° C (400° F; G6).
Quantities for 4.

4 medium to large green peppers

Cut each in half lengthwise and remove core and seeds but be careful not to remove too much of the stem end, retaining a case suitable for filling. Boil about an inch (2½ cm) of salted water in a pan, add the peppers, cover and boil for 5 mins. Drain. Put in a greased shallow baking dish.

8 oz cottage or curd cheese (250 g)	salt
about 6 oz chopped cooked ham or other cooked meat (175 g)	1–2 eggs
	garlic or garlic salt to taste

Mash the cheese and beat in the egg, then the flavourings and meat. Divide between the pepper halves and bake until the filling is set. If necessary, colour the tops under the grill. Serve hot.

POTATOES

Home-grown new potatoes are in season from the end of April to the beginning of September but imported new potatoes are available during the whole year. Old potatoes are in season from September until the new ones come into the shops in large quantities; but the old ones are often of poor quality at the end of their season and it is worth paying more to have new ones.

If potatoes still have the earth on them it is difficult to tell the quality; best to buy them from a reliable shop and complain if the quality is poor. If you want to store potatoes for more than 2 or 3 days it is always better to buy those with the earth still on as this helps to prevent them from going green. Potatoes with green patches should be discarded as unsafe to eat. If buying washed potatoes in polythene bags examine them carefully to make sure they are not beginning to turn green and buy only enough to last a couple of days.

Store potatoes in a place which is cool and dark, but not wet or frosty. They can be washed, dried and stored in polythene bags in the refrigerator, but not many have room for this.

When preparing potatoes for cooking, scrub well to remove the dirt. For boiling and baked jacket potatoes no further preparation is needed unless there are damaged bits to be cut out. Potatoes can be boiled with the skins on and served like that, or skinned before serving. When peeling, do this as thinly as possible and if a machine is used, run it for the least possible time. This is to conserve flavour and food value.

Sometimes it is convenient to peel potatoes in advance, when they should be covered with cold water. An alternative, and better for long storage, is to put the peeled potatoes in a polythene bag in the refrigerator. Either of these procedures means a loss of flavour and food value so they are to be avoided if possible.

Creamed or mashed potatoes

Cooking time 20–40 mins, depending on size. *Quantities* for 3–4.

1 lb old potatoes (500 g)

Choose potatoes of an even size or cut large ones. Boil in the skins and skin before mashing, or peel before boiling.

Boil about 2 in (5 cm) water in a saucepan with 1 tsp salt and add the potatoes. Cover and boil very gently until they are tender when pierced with a fork. Drain. To skin hot potatoes hold them on a fork and use a small vegetable knife for peeling. Either put the potatoes through a potato ricer, or a sieve, or break up with a fork or potato masher. Using a sieve or ricer naturally gives a smoother product. Put the potatoes back in the saucepan over a very low heat.

1 Tbs milk	1 oz butter (25 g)
salt and pepper	chopped fresh herbs, optional

Beat these into the potato, beating until well blended and smooth, and make sure the potatoes are hot before serving them. Use as soon as possible.

Baked jacket potatoes

Cooking time 45 mins or longer, depending on the size.
Temperature 200–300° C (400–450° F; G6–8).
Quantities: allow 1 large or 2 small potatoes per portion.

Potatoes can be baked at a lower temperature than this for very much longer times, but they do not have the crisp skins and floury insides of those baked faster.

Choose potatoes without blemishes and scrub well. Dry in paper towels and rub the skins all over with oil. This is not essential but gives a better flavoured skin. Put on a baking sheet or straight on the oven rack and bake until one feels soft when squeezed gently in a cloth.

When cooked they should be pricked with a fork to let the steam out and ensure a floury inside. Prick a cross on the top of each, using a table fork. Gently squeeze the potato at the bottom, using both hands, and the cross will open out in four leaves. Put in some salt and pepper and a knob of butter and serve as soon as possible.

Alternative flavouring can be a herb butter, pages 57–8, instead of plain butter.

Baked stuffed potatoes

Quantities for 4.

4 medium-sized potatoes	8 oz cottage cheese (250 g)
1 Tbs finely chopped onion or chives	½ oz soft butter or margarine (15 g)
1 tsp salt	pepper

Bake the potatoes as above. Cut a slice from the longest side of each. Scoop the potato into a hot bowl, leaving enough to maintain the shape of the shells. Mash the potato. Add the other ingredients and mix thoroughly. Stand the potato shells on a baking tray and pile the potato back in them.

butter or margarine   paprika pepper

Put a knob of butter or margarine on each one and a good sprinkling of paprika pepper. Put back in the oven to heat well and brown the tops.

ALTERNATIVE

Beat 1 egg with the potato and other ingredients.

New potatoes with cream

Cooking time 15–20 mins. *Quantities* for 4.

1 lb small to medium new potatoes (500 g)

Wash well and put in boiling salted water to half cover. Boil until tender. Drain, cool a little and skin. Return the potatoes to the saucepan.

¼ pt soured cream (150 ml), or use fresh double cream with a little lemon juice

chopped dill, parsley, chives or mint

Add to the potatoes, mix well and re-heat. Serve hot.

Ofentori potatoes

This is a very good way of using up mashed potatoes. Serve it as a dish on its own with green salad or as an accompaniment to meat, poultry or fish.

Cooking time 40 mins.
Temperature 200° C (400° F; G6).
Quantities for 4–6.

6 oz streaky bacon (175 g)

Remove the rinds and chop the bacon, dividing it into two portions and setting one aside for a topping. Put the other half in a mixing bowl.

1 lb cooked mashed potato (500 g)	¼ tsp salt
pepper	pinch of grated nutmeg
2 Tbs milk or cream	2 eggs, beaten

Add to the bacon in the mixing bowl and combine thoroughly. Put in a greased pie dish or other baking dish and smooth the top. Sprinkle the remaining bacon on top and bake until the potato is browned on top and the bacon cooked. Serve hot.

Potato chips

Cooking time 8–10 mins.
Frying temperature 190–200° C (375–390° F).
Quantities 6–8 oz raw potato (150–200 g) per portion.

Majestics are the best of the ordinary potatoes, but a waxy variety is even better as it soaks up less fat. Use large potatoes, wash and peel them. A potato chipping device is a time saver if you make chips often. Otherwise slice the potatoes lengthwise about ⅜ in (9 mm) thick and then again the other way to make the chips. Cover with cold water and soak for about 1 hr. Drain and dry thoroughly on a clean towel.

For general notes on deep-fat frying, see page 31.

A frying basket is a convenience for lifting the chips in and out of the oil, but any metal strainer can be used. The quantity of chips you can safely put in at a time depends on the size of the pan and the amount of oil as well as the amount of heat under the pan. It is much better to cook a few chips perfectly in several lots than to have a large quantity of soggy chips. When they are crisp and brown, lift them out on to a piece of absorbent paper on a tray and put them to keep hot. Sprinkle with salt and serve as soon as possible.

Potato crisps or game chips

Wash and peel the potatoes. Cut them into thin shavings on a vegetable slicer or shredder and soak in cold water for an hour. Drain, dry and fry like chips, but they will take only about 1 minute to cook. Sprinkle with salt before serving.

Sauté potatoes

boiled potatoes	butter, fat or oil for frying
chopped parsley or other green herbs	salt and pepper

The potatoes can be leftover boiled ones or cooked specially. They should be cooked gently so that the outsides are not crumbly.

Slice them about ¼ in (6 mm) thick. Heat enough butter, fat or oil to make a thin layer in a frying pan and fry the potatoes until they are brown on both sides, turning once during frying. Serve on a hot dish and sprinkle them with parsley or other green herbs and with seasoning.

ALTERNATIVE

When the potatoes are almost done, sprinkle the top with grated cheese and heat just to melt it. Fried chopped bacon and/or onion can be added for extra flavour.

Scalloped potatoes

To serve as an accompaniment to roast or other meat.

Cooking time 1–1½ hrs.
Temperature 200° C (400° F; G6).
Quantities for 3–4.

1 lb potatoes (500 g)	1 medium-sized onion, finely chopped
2 rashers streaky bacon, chopped	
salt and pepper	

Peel the potatoes and slice them thinly. Use the onion raw or soften it by frying in a little fat. Oil a baking dish or pie dish about 1 pt size (½ l). Put a layer of potato in the bottom, sprinkle with salt and pepper, onion and bacon and repeat the layers, finishing with potato.

¼ pt soured cream (150 ml)	½ Tbs flour

Blend the flour and cream and pour the mixture on top of the potatoes. Bake until the potatoes are soft and the top browned. Serve hot.

PUMPKIN OR WINTER SQUASH

This vegetable is in season in the late summer and autumn, but a really ripened pumpkin will keep well in a dry cool place for use during the winter months.

There are several varieties of edible pumpkin, most of them large, round, and deep yellow to orange in colour. They need plenty of sun to mature and ripen them to give a good flavour, otherwise they are a very disappointing vegetable.

To prepare pumpkin for cooking, cut it in pieces, and remove the seeds and pulp. The tough outer skin may either be removed now or else after cooking; when the skin is very tough the latter is the simpler method.

Pumpkin seeds are edible and contain a fair amount of protein, fat and B vitamins.

Baked or roast pumpkin

Cooking time 45–60 mins.
Temperature 190–200° C (375–400° F; G5–6).
Quantities for 4.

2 lb pumpkin (1 kg)　　　　　　　salt and pepper
melted butter, margarine or oil

Cut the pumpkin in about 8 pieces, removing seeds and skin. Put in a baking dish and brush with fat or oil. Sprinkle with salt and pepper and bake until tender and brown. It may also be cooked round meat being roasted.

Boiled pumpkin

Cooking time 20–30 mins. *Quantities* for 4.

2 lb pumpkin (1 kg)　　　　　　　1 oz butter (25 g)
salt and pepper

Cut the pumpkin in pieces and remove skin and seeds. Boil about 1 in (2½ cm) water with 1 tsp salt. Add the pumpkin, cover, and boil until tender. Drain well and mash with plenty of butter and pepper.

SPINACH

There are very many different varieties of spinach, one or another of them being in season for most of the year.

It is a vegetable which wilts very quickly so a fresh green look is a good indication of age and quality. Wilted spinach is just not worth buying. If bought in advance fresh spinach can be kept in good condition by washing, draining thoroughly and then putting in a polythene bag in the refrigerator.

Spinach needs very thorough washing, especially the small-leaved varieties which grow close to the ground and are usually cultivated in sandy soil. Pick over, removing any decayed leaves or weeds, and wash in several changes of water until the last water is clean. Lift the spinach out each time to allow the sand to collect in the water. Discard the water, run in fresh, and add the spinach. Drain in a colander.

Some varieties such as spinach beets have large stems. It is better to remove these before cooking and cut them in small pieces. Boil a very little salted water, add the stems and bring back to the boil before adding the leaves.

The thick white stems of Swiss chard can be treated in the same way or cooked as a separate vegetable and served with parsley or other sauce.

Boiled leaf spinach

Cooking time 10–15 mins.

Quantities: allow ½ lb (250 g) per person.

Wash and drain the spinach and put it in a large pan without any water. Add 1 tsp salt per lb (½ kg) of spinach, cover and bring to the boil. Boil until tender. Drain in a colander, pressing the spinach to remove as much moisture as possible. Put it back in the pan with a knob of butter or margarine, mix and heat until all free moisture has evaporated. If liked, add a pinch of pepper and ground mace or nutmeg.

Spinach au gratin with mushrooms

Suitable for a main dish in a light meal.

Cooking time 30–40 mins.
Temperature 200° C (400° F; G6).
Quantities for 4–6.

2 small onions, finely chopped	1 Tbs oil

Heat the oil in a frying pan or small stew pan and cook the onions in it until they are tender and beginning to soften.

4 oz sliced mushrooms (125 g)	salt and pepper

Add to the onions and continue cooking gently until the onions are quite tender. Keep warm.

2 lb spinach (1 kg) 1 oz butter (25 g)
1 Tbs oil

Wash and drain the spinach and put it in a large pan with the oil and butter. Cover and cook until it is just tender. Drain and chop roughly.

6–8 oz firm mature cheese (175–250 g)

Grate the cheese. Grease a baking dish and put the spinach, onion mixture and cheese in it in layers, finishing with a topping of cheese. Dot the cheese with butter and bake near the top of the oven for about 20 mins to brown the cheese. Serve hot.

Spinach pie

Cooking time 40–45 mins.
Temperature 200° C (400° F; G6).
Quantities: for a tin about 10 in (25 cm) by 6 in (15 cm) and about 2–3 in deep (5–8 cm). This will cut into about 8 pieces.

1 lb fresh spinach (500 g) 2 tsp salt

Wash the spinach carefully and remove the thick stalks. Drain it well and chop coarsely or slice finely. Put it in a large bowl. Sprinkle the salt over it and toss with the hands to distribute the salt evenly. Leave to stand for an hour.

8 oz puff pastry (250 ml)

Roll it out as thinly as you possibly can without breaking it, about $\frac{1}{16}$ in (2 mm). Cut off about two-thirds and use to line the tin. Put this and the remaining piece in the refrigerator.

Squeeze the spinach in a colander to remove surplus moisture and compress it. Put in a bowl.

6 oz cottage cheese (175 g) 1 egg, beaten
1½ Tbs olive oil pepper

Add to the spinach and mix vigorously to distribute the cheese evenly. Put this in the lined tin, cover with pastry, pressing the edges together well.

beaten egg or milk sesame seeds (optional)

Brush the pastry with egg or milk and sprinkle with sesame seeds. Bake until the pastry is well browned, by which time the spinach will be cooked. Serve hot.

SWEDE OR SWEDE TURNIP

This is a winter vegetable which keeps in good condition until the spring. It is a large root vegetable with yellow flesh which turns orange when cooked. It should be peeled thickly and cut into chunks, then boiled in a little salted water for 20–30 mins, drained and mashed with a generous piece of butter and plenty of pepper. Finely grated raw swede is good in a winter salad and has a sweetish taste.

SWEET CORN OR MAIZE

In season in late summer and early autumn; also available canned as kernels or as creamed corn. I think canned corn has more flavour than fresh corn grown in our climate.

To cook corn-on-the-cob, first remove the leafy sheath and the silky threads underneath. Boil the cobs in a small quantity of water. If they take more than 20 mins to become tender it is an indication that the corn is too mature for serving this way. Pressure cooking is the best way of softening older corn. When it is tender, drain and serve with plenty of melted butter. Alternatively strip the corn off the cob and mix it with melted butter and seasoning.

Pressure cooking takes about 4 mins.

Creamed corn

Cook the corn by boiling or pressure cooking and strip it off the cob. Mix with a béchamel sauce.

Corn and tomatoes

Cooking time ½ hr. *Quantities* for 4.

1 oz butter or margarine (25 g)	a sprig of parsley
1 pt chopped tomatoes (600 ml)	½ bay leaf, chopped
1 small sprig thyme, chopped	

Heat the fat in a saucepan and cook the tomatoes and herbs in it for 10 mins.

1 pt cooked or canned corn kernels (600 ml)	1 tsp sugar
	salt and pepper

Add to the tomatoes and simmer for 20 mins. Serve hot as a vegetable.

TOMATOES

Home-grown are in season from April to October, imported ones throughout the year. A 'small' tomato is usually taken as weighing about 1 oz (25 g); a 'medium' one 2 oz (50 g), and a 'large' one 3–4 oz (75–100 g) or more.

When buying tomatoes firmness is the important thing to look for. Such a tomato has a shiny skin, taut and light in colour. As they become riper the skin darkens and loses its shine. Only buy the very ripe ones if they are cheap and if you are going to use them for cooking right away.

Keep tomatoes in a cool place. In a polythene bag or box in the refrigerator they will keep for several days.

The only preparation needed is to wash them and remove the stems. For some recipes it is desirable to remove the skins; to do this the tomatoes should be immersed in boiling water for a minute and then plunged in cold water, when the skins will come off easily.

The simplest ways of cooking tomatoes are baking in a moderate oven for about 20 mins, or frying or grilling for about 10 mins. Small tomatoes are cooked whole, larger ones cut in half. Cut tomatoes can be sprinkled with salt and pepper and some fresh chopped or dried herbs.

Stuffed tomatoes

Cooking time 20 mins.
Temperature 190° C (375° F; G5).
Quantities for 4.

8 medium-sized tomatoes, firm and ripe, or use 4 large ones

Wash and cut a slice off the stem end. With a small spoon scoop out the pulp, taking care not to break the skin. Season the insides with salt and pepper, including a little garlic salt if liked. Put the tomatoes in a shallow, greased baking dish.

2 oz breadcrumbs (50 g)
2 anchovy fillets, rinsed and chopped
1 tsp chopped parsley
½ oz grated cheese (15 g)
2 oz chopped minced ham (50 g)
pepper

Mix all together and use the mixture to stuff the tomatoes. Put the slice on top as a lid. Bake until the tomatoes are cooked but not broken. Serve hot.

Tomato flan

Cooking time 20–30 mins.
Temperature 200° C (400° F; G6).
Quantities for a 7 in flan (18 cm).

short-crust pastry using 4 oz flour (100 g), or use 6 oz ready-made pastry (175 g)

Roll the pastry thinly to line a flan ring or pie plate. Prick the bottom with a fork and put the flan in the refrigerator while the filling is prepared.

14 oz can peeled whole tomatoes (400 g)

Drain and slice or cut up the tomatoes.

chopped fresh thyme or marjoram, or use powdered dried herbs   2 oz strong cheese (50 g)

Cut the cheese in small dice. Put the tomatoes in the pastry case and sprinkle them with the herbs and cheese.

1 oz anchovy fillets (25 g)   1 oz stoned black olives (25 g)

Put the anchovy fillets on top of the tomatoes in a lattice or other pattern and put the olives in between the anchovies. Bake until the pastry is lightly browned and the cheese melted. Serve warm or cold.

TURNIPS

Turnips are in season for most of the year, though towards the end of the winter and in early spring the old ones become pithy inside and are not much use. Young spring turnips are delicious, cooked, or raw grated in salads. The flavour is strong and when they are used with other root vegetables, they should be in the minority or their flavour will predominate. The flavour of turnips goes well with lamb and mutton. Young green turnips can be cooked like spinach.

Young turnips can be kept fresh and crisp for several days if washed and stored in a polythene bag or box in the refrigerator, as can mature turnips.

Most turnips have a thick skin which must be peeled off before cooking, the exception being very young tender turnips which should not need to be peeled at all.

They can be boiled in salted water for about 20 mins, but there are more interesting ways of cooking them.

Turnips cooked in butter

Cooking time 15–20 mins.
Quantities: allow 4–6 oz per person (100–175 g).

Peel the turnips and cut large ones in pieces. Heat enough butter to make a thin layer on the bottom of a saucepan, add the turnips and ½ tsp salt per lb (½ kg). Cover the pan and stew gently until the turnips are tender, shaking the pan occasionally. Serve, sprinkled with chopped parsley.

Turnip ragout

Cooking time 45 mins. *Quantities* for 4–6.

16–20 small young turnips

Wash, peel if necessary.

1 oz dripping (25 g)	1 pt stock (600 ml)
1 oz flour (3 Tbs or 25 g)	1 tsp salt
pinch of pepper	1 Tbs sugar

Melt the dripping in a stew pan and stir in the flour, stirring and cooking until it turns yellow. Remove from the heat and stir in the stock. Return to the heat and stir until it boils. Add the flavourings and the turnips, cover, and cook gently until the vegetables are tender.

chopped parsley

Sprinkle with plenty of parsley and serve as an accompaniment to lamb or pork.

11. Salads

I have divided the recipes in this chapter into those for serving as accompaniments to hot or cold meat, poultry, game or fish, and those suitable for a main dish. Main dish salads can make a very adequate light meal, served with bread or rolls and possibly soup to start with.

The preparation of salads can be time-consuming but is made very much simpler if a supply of suitable vegetables is kept washed and ready in the refrigerator. Other ingredients can be prepared in advance and kept refrigerated. It is better to store prepared ingredients separately, leaving the assembly until meal time. With a few exceptions such as cucumber or cooked vegetables, most salads deteriorate rapidly after they have been dressed; but a bowl of raw salad vegetables can be mixed and stored covered in the refrigerator to be dressed at the last minute. Meat, poultry, game and fish can be dressed in advance, but do not store them for more than about 4 hrs.

List of salad ingredients

Artichokes, cooked or canned bottoms or hearts of globe artichokes, cooked Jerusalem artichokes

Asparagus, cooked or canned

Aubergines, cooked or canned and sliced

Avocado pears, raw, skinned and sliced or diced

Beans, any kind, cooked or canned

Beetroot, fresh cooked, canned or pickled

Brussels sprouts, finely shredded raw

Cabbage, raw crisp heart, finely sliced

Carrots, raw grated, or cooked or canned sliced or diced

Cauliflower, raw sliced flower or cooked sprigs

Celeriac, peeled and shredded

Celery, raw sliced

Chicory, raw as leaves or sliced
Corn, sweet, cooked or canned kernels
Corn salad, raw
Courgettes, cooked, sliced
Cucumber, raw sliced or diced
Endive, raw
Florence fennel, raw sliced or shredded
Fruit, any kind raw, the best being oranges, grapefruit, apple, pear, melon; dried fruit such as raisins, dates; canned pineapple or fresh
Kohl rabi, raw grated or cooked diced
Leeks, very finely sliced raw, or cooked whole or sliced
Lettuce, outdoor-grown the best
Mushrooms, raw button, cooked or canned
Mustard and cress, anyone can grow it anywhere
Nuts, any kind, coarsely chopped
Onions, spring and Spanish raw, the latter finely sliced, others cooked
Potatoes, cooked and dressed while hot, new potatoes or waxy kinds best
Radishes, raw, sliced or as a garnish
Sorrel, raw leaves removed from stalks
Spinach, tender raw with other salad greens
Swedes, raw grated
Sweet peppers, raw sliced, cooked or canned
Tomatoes, firm ones best, sliced or stuffed, in halves or quarters
Turnip, young ones raw grated
Watercress, raw as sprigs or roughly chopped.

Salad dressings

See Salad Dressings, pages 61–4.

Herbs and other flavourings

Any fresh herbs can be added to salads singly or mixed. Whole leaves such as lemon balm can be used but it is better to chop or scissor-snip others. Dried herbs can be used to flavour dressings, as can herb vinegars or herb oils and mustards.

Herb flowers make attractive garnishes and are edible, the best ones being *Anchusa italica*, bergamot, borage, chives, marigold petals, marjoram, nasturtium, rosemary or sage.

Those who like garlic will appreciate it in salad dressings; strain out fresh garlic before using the dressing, or use garlic salt or dried garlic for flavouring. Finely chopped chives, raw onion or Welsh onion are all good in small amounts. Pickled vegetables and fruits are all good but specially gherkins, capers, olives, pears, red cabbage and beetroot.

SALADS FOR ACCOMPANIMENTS

Apple and chicory

Quantities for 4.

2 small apples, peeled, cored and diced	4 Tbs yogurt
salt and pepper	2 Tbs lemon juice

Mix together to coat the apple with the dressing.

2 carrots, grated	grated rind of ½ an orange
2 heads of chicory, sliced	

Combine with the apple and serve.

Apple, carrot and orange salad

Quantities for 4.

2 medium-sized grated or shredded raw carrots	1 orange

Skin the orange, divide in sections and cut it in small pieces, discarding pips and pith. Put in a bowl with the carrots.

4 Tbs yogurt or yogurt dressing

Add salt and pepper and a little vinegar to plain yogurt and mix with the carrot and orange.

2 red apples

Wash, core and cut in dice or slice finely. Add to the carrot mixture, combine well and serve.

Beetroot salad with horseradish and fennel

Quantities for 4–6.

1 lb cooked beetroot (500 g)

Skin and slice thinly, arranging the slices in a serving dish.

¼ pt wine vinegar (150 ml)	¼ pt water (150 ml)
1 tsp salt	2 Tbs oil
2 oz sugar (4 Tbs or 50 g)	

Mix to dissolve the sugar.

2 oz grated horseradish (50 g)   2 tsp chopped fresh fennel

Sprinkle these over the beetroot and then add the vinegar mixture.

Beetroot, apple and potato salad

Quantities for 3–4.

4 oz sliced pickled beetroot (125 g)	1 small apple, peeled, cored and sliced
4 oz cold boiled potatoes, sliced (125 g)	pinch each of ground coriander seeds and caraway seeds
3–5 Tbs French dressing	
1 tsp grated horseradish	

Add the horseradish and herb seeds to the dressing. Use this to mix with the salad ingredients. Leave it to stand for about ½ hr for the flavours to blend. Garnish with

sprigs of watercress or other salad greens.

Brussels sprouts and celery salad

Quantities for 4.

8 brussels sprouts	4 sticks celery
salad dressing, any kind	

Wash the sprouts and slice them as finely as possible, discarding the stem end. Wash and chop the celery. Combine these with enough dressing to moisten well and put the salad in a bowl. Garnish with

sliced hard-boiled egg and/or sliced beetroot.

Brussels sprouts and orange salad

Quantities for 4.

8 oz brussels sprouts (250 g) 2 large oranges

Wash and drain the sprouts and slice them as finely as possible, discarding the stem. Peel the oranges, remove all pith and divide them in segments. Mix sprouts and oranges together, reserving a few orange segments to garnish the top of the salad.

mayonnaise or yogurt dressing

Combine the salad with enough dressing to moisten, and garnish with orange segments.

Cabbage, celery and apple salad

Quantities for 4.

2 sticks celery, chopped	1 carrot, grated
6 oz very finely shredded raw cabbage (2 c or 175 g)	1 dessert apple, peeled and chopped salad dressing
1 Tbs chopped chives	1 Tbs chopped marjoram

Mix all the ingredients together with enough dressing to moisten and serve in a salad bowl.

Cauliflower salad

Quantities for 4.

1 medium-sized cauliflower mayonnaise
8 canned anchovy fillets

Separate the cauliflower into small sprigs and put them in about $\frac{1}{2}$ in (1 cm) boiling salted water. Cover and cook until they are barely tender. Drain and allow to become cold.

Arrange the cauliflower in a shallow serving dish with the flower heads uppermost. Mask the whole top with mayonnaise and decorate with a criss-cross of rinsed and drained anchovy fillets.

Celery, apple and beetroot salad with fennel

Quantities for 4.

2 sticks celery, chopped
1 medium-sized beetroot, diced
French dressing, about 3 Tbs
2 apples, peeled, cored and chopped
1 Tbs chopped fennel

Combine the salad ingredients with dressing and sprinkle with the chopped fennel.

Chicory and olive salad

Quantities for 4.

6 medium-sized pieces of chicory
2–3 Tbs French dressing
chopped fresh tarragon
8 large green olives, stoned and chopped

Wash and drain the chicory. With the point of a small vegetable knife cut a cone-shaped bit from the bottom of each piece. Slice the chicory finely, or chop it and mix with the olives and dressing. Serve sprinkled with the chopped tarragon.

If no fresh tarragon is available, use tarragon vinegar to make the dressing and garnish the salad with chopped parsley.

Chicory and orange salad

This uses just the orange rind, leaving the flesh for a fruit salad or other dish.

Quantities for 4.

6 medium-sized pieces of chicory
2 oranges

Wash and drain the chicory. Scrub the oranges and peel off the orange part of the skin very thinly. Cut this in fine strips and boil them in plenty of water for 5–6 mins. Drain and allow to become cold.

½ Tbs French mustard
¼ pt soured cream or fresh double cream (150 ml)
salt and pepper
cayenne pepper
lemon juice, optional

Mix the mustard and cream and season the dressing well, adding lemon juice to sharpen it if fresh cream is used. Cut the heads of chicory in half lengthwise and remove the hard core at the base. Cut the leaves in pieces of a suitable size to eat with a fork. Put them in a serving dish, sprinkle with the orange rind and serve the dressing separately.

Chicory and beetroot salad

Quantities for 4.

4 small heads of chicory   1 medium-sized cooked beetroot

Wash the chicory and slice it. Skin and dice the beetroot and mix with the chicory.

1 hard-boiled egg
1 Tbs tarragon vinegar
4 Tbs yogurt

salt and pepper
1 Tbs lemon juice

Mash the egg yolk and mix it with the other ingredients to make a dressing. Pour it over the salad and decorate with the chopped egg white.

Cole slaw with walnuts

Quantities for 4.

8 oz crisp white cabbage heart (250 g)   4 oz shelled walnuts (125 g)

Wash the cabbage and drain well. Shred it finely by hand or in a mechanical shredder. Alternatively use the electric blender and chop the cabbage with cold water to cover, then drain and squeeze out moisture. Chop the walnuts coarsely.

4 Tbs mayonnaise   salt and pepper

Mix the cabbage and nuts with the mayonnaise and add seasoning to taste.

ALTERNATIVE

Instead of walnuts use a little finely chopped onion or sweet green pepper; or a small chopped dessert apple.

Courgette salad with mint and chives

Cooking time 20 mins. *Quantities* for 4–6.

1 lb courgettes (500 g)

Wash, trim the ends and boil the courgettes in a little salted water until they are barely tender. Drain and allow to become cold. Cut in diagonal slices about $\frac{1}{4}$ in ($\frac{1}{2}$ cm) thick and arrange them in a shallow serving dish.

4 Tbs olive oil
1 tsp sugar
pepper
1 Tbs chopped chives

3 Tbs lemon juice
$\frac{1}{2}$ tsp salt
1 Tbs chopped mint

Mix these together and pour over the courgettes.

VARIATION

Use young marrow cut in pieces, skin and all.

Cucumber salad, Swedish style

Quantities for 4–6.

1½ lb cucumber (1 large or 700 g)

Peel the cucumber and slice it as thinly as possible, the thinner the better. Arrange it in layers in a shallow dish.

1 Tbs salt

Sprinkle this over the cucumber and leave for 2 hrs for the moisture to be drawn out. Pour away the liquid and rinse the cucumber to remove surplus salt. Drain well.

| 4 Tbs wine vinegar | 1 Tbs sugar |
| 1 Tbs water | freshly ground pepper |

Mix these and pour them over the cucumber in a serving dish.
Sprinkle on top before serving the salad.

2 Tbs chopped parsley or dill

Sprinkle on top before serving the salad.

Cucumber and melon salad

Quantities for 4–6.

4 Tbs French dressing made with lemon juice (60 ml)	1 pt peeled diced cucumber (½ l)
4 Tbs chopped mixed dill, mint and tarragon in equal quantities	1 pt peeled diced melon (½ l)
	a sprinkling of caster sugar

Combine the cucumber and melon with the dressing and sugar. Sprinkle the salad with the chopped herbs.

Cucumber and nasturtium salad

| cucumber, peeled and sliced very thinly | French dressing made with a herb vinegar |

Put the cucumber in a shallow serving dish and add a generous quantity of dressing. Leave to marinate for at least ½ hr.

nasturtium flowers   small nasturtium leaves

Be sure to wash the flowers well under a running cold tap and wash the leaves. Drain both thoroughly.

Just before serving the salad put the flowers and leaves in a garland round the cucumber. Both flowers and leaves are edible.

Grapefruit and beetroot salad

Quantities for 4.

2 large grapefruit

Peel and remove all pith. Divide into segments or slice the flesh in circles, removing pips.

2 medium-sized cooked beetroot,   1 lettuce
  sliced   French dressing

Wash and dry the lettuce and use it to line a salad bowl or arrange on a flat dish. Put the grapefruit and beetroot in alternate layers on the lettuce. Pour the dressing over it just before serving.

Green bean and apple salad

Quantities for 4.

8 oz cooked whole French beans, or use sliced green beans (250 g)

Cut the whole beans in pieces and put them in a bowl.

1 small dessert apple, peeled, cored   1 stick of celery, chopped or sliced
  and cut in pieces   salt and pepper
mayonnaise or other dressing

Mix all the ingredients together with enough salad dressing to moisten well. Season to taste.

Green leaf salad

For this use any green leaves available – shredded brussels sprouts or cabbage, corn salad, endive, lettuce, mustard and cress, sorrel, spinach or watercress – with fresh green herbs. The larger the mixture, the more interesting the salad. Just before serving, toss the salad with a good French dressing made with wine vinegar or lemon juice according to taste.

Leeks vinaigrette

Boil leeks in the usual way, see page 277, cutting large ones in half lengthwise. Drain them thoroughly and allow to become lukewarm. Dress with French dressing. Sprinkle with chopped herbs or with capers and serve warm or cold.

Mixed salad

This is made from a mixture of any salad ingredients available, see the list on pages 304–5. Use six or more different ingredients according to what is available. Tear leaves in small pieces or shred them, grate root vegetables and cut others in small pieces. Dress with a French dressing and add chopped fresh herbs.

Mushroom salad, raw

raw button mushrooms	chopped parsley
French dressing made with lemon juice	finely chopped garlic or garlic salt, optional

Wash and drain the mushrooms. Slice them very thinly and dress with plenty of French dressing and chopped parsley. Add garlic to taste.

Mushroom salad, cooked

Cooking time 5 mins. *Quantities* for 4.

8 oz mushrooms (250 g)

Wash and drain, remove stalks and boil mushrooms in a little salted water until they are barely tender. Drain and cool, then slice thinly.

2 thin slices of raw onion	2 tsp sugar
2 Tbs double cream	freshly ground pepper
salt	1–2 Tbs lemon juice

Chop the onion very finely and mix it with the other ingredients, seasoning to taste. Add the sliced mushrooms and combine gently. Serve in a salad bowl and sprinkle the top of the salad with

chopped parsley, mint, marjoram or tarragon.

Orange salad

Quantities for 4.

4 oranges

Peel the oranges and remove all pith. Slice into thin rounds, removing the pips.

chopped fresh tarragon and chervil

Sprinkle over the oranges.

2 Tbs olive oil   1 Tbs wine vinegar
2 tsp lemon juice

Mix together and pour over the oranges, leave for a while to marinate. Serve the salad on individual dishes, garnished with

sprigs of watercress.

Orange, apple and celery salad

Quantities for 4 or more.

3–4 oranges

Peel the fruit, removing all pith. Either slice the oranges in rounds or divide into segments, removing the pips.

1 small lettuce, washed and dried

Arrange the lettuce on individual plates or on a large platter and put the orange in the centre.

1 or 2 dessert apples   4 small stalks of crisp celery

Peel, core and chop the apples. Wash and chop the celery. Have approximately equal quantities of apple and celery. Combine and put on top of the orange.

1 Tbs chopped nuts   mayonnaise or French dressing

Sprinkle the nuts over the apple and celery and serve the dressing separately.

If this is prepared in advance mix the apples with a little of the dressing or with lemon juice, to prevent discoloration.

Potato salad

Use either new potatoes or a waxy variety. Floury potatoes tend to crumble and spoil the look of the salad. If they are the only kind available, boil them in their skins until they are just tender, and allow them to become cold before peeling.

Quantities for 4–6.

- 1½ lb freshly boiled potatoes (700 g)
- 1 Tbs chopped green herbs (dill, fennel, parsley or mixed)
- 1 Tbs finely chopped onion or chives
- 6 Tbs French dressing or mayonnaise (90 ml)

If new or waxy potatoes are used, dress them while they are still warm, using French dressing. If you must have mayonnaise with your potato salad, dress the warm potatoes with half the quantity of French dressing and, when they are cold, add mayonnaise.

Cut the cooked potatoes in cubes and mix them with the onion and dressing. Serve with the green herbs sprinkled on top.

ALTERNATIVE

Boil the potatoes with 2 bay leaves and a small skinned onion. To allow the flavours to penetrate during boiling, cut off a strip of skin from each potato.

Potato salad with yogurt dressing

Quantities for 3–4.

- 1 lb freshly cooked, diced potatoes (500 g)
- 1 tsp caraway seeds
- 2 Tbs finely chopped onion
- ½ pt thick yogurt (300 ml)
- 1 tsp curry powder or to taste
- 1 tsp salt
- 2 Tbs chopped mint

Combine the yogurt with the flavourings and pour this over the potatoes. Mix gently and then refrigerate until the salad is well chilled.

Sauerkraut salad with capers

To serve with cold ham, pork or sausages.

Quantities for 2–4.

8 oz sauerkraut (250 g)

Put in a sieve or colander and squeeze the sauerkraut gently to extract as much moisture as possible. Chop it finely and put in a bowl.

- 2 or more Tbs mayonnaise or salad oil
- pinch of sugar
- lemon juice
- salt

Mix with the sauerkraut, seasoning to taste. Put in a serving dish.

1–2 Tbs capers

Sprinkle over the salad.

Sorrel and lettuce salad

Use equal quantities of sorrel leaves and lettuce leaves.

French dressing, 3–4 Tbs for a salad for 4   fines herbes, 1–2 Tbs for a salad for 4

Wash and drain the sorrel and lettuce. Pick the sorrel leaves from the stalks, tearing the larger pieces of English sorrel into small pieces, or shred them.

Tear the lettuce leaves in small pieces and combine with the sorrel. Dress the salad just before serving, adding the herbs at the same time.

Sweet pepper salad

Use green, red or yellow sweet peppers.

RAW

Wash the peppers, cut in half lengthwise and remove seeds, stalk and white pith. Slice the flesh very thinly and dress with French dressing; or mix the peppers with other salad vegetables to make a mixed salad.

COOKED

Wash the peppers, cut in half lengthwise and remove stem, seeds and white pith. Grill them skin sides up until the skin can easily be peeled off. This takes only a few minutes. Then slice the peppers and dress as before. Some people find completely raw peppers a little indigestible and this amount of cooking, combined with removal of the skin, makes them more acceptable.

Sweet pepper and tomato salad

canned red peppers	ripe tomatoes
French dressing	finely chopped onion, optional

Drain the peppers and slice them. Wash and slice an equal quantity of tomatoes. Pour French dressing over them and sprinkle with the onion; or use fresh chopped herbs instead.

Tomato salad

There are a number of ways of making this simple salad. Some people insist on skinning the tomatoes first, which is a pity as it makes them lose flavour and shape.

Use firm, ripe tomatoes, remove the stalks and wash and drain. Using a very sharp knife, slice the tomatoes thinly and arrange them in a shallow dish in overlapping layers. They can be dressed with an ordinary French dressing to which a little sugar has been added; or sprinkle the tomatoes with a little sugar before adding the dressing.

Alternatively, dress with olive oil, salt, pepper and sugar and omit any vinegar or lemon juice.

Sprinkle the salad with chopped fresh herbs such as parsley, basil, chervil, chives, savory, tarragon or a mixture of several herbs.

Tomato and cucumber salad

This is very good for serving with fish. Arrange a row of overlapping slices of cucumber beside a row of tomato, dress, and sprinkle with herbs.

Turkish cucumber salad

To serve with fried or grilled fish and hot or cold chicken or lamb.

Quantities for 4.

1 cucumber, peeled and diced   salt

Put the cucumber in a colander and sprinkle it with a little salt. Leave it for ½ hr to drain.

1 clove crushed garlic   1 Tbs vinegar
½ pt yogurt (250 ml)

Mix these together, combine with the cucumber, cover and refrigerate until well chilled.

ALTERNATIVE

Instead of vinegar use lemon juice, and if liked, add a little olive oil. Add 3 Tbs chopped fresh mint or 1 Tbs dried powdered mint.

White bean salad

Quantities for 4.

1 lb cooked or canned butter or   4 Tbs olive oil (60 ml)
  other white beans (500 g)   1 Tbs lemon juice
salt and pepper

Drain the beans thoroughly and put them in a serving dish. Mix the oil, lemon juice and seasoning and pour over the beans. Sprinkle liberally with

chopped fresh mint or dill.

MAIN DISH SALADS

Banana and cheese salad

Quantities for 4.

2 hard-boiled eggs   4 oz cheese (100 g)

Shell and slice the eggs. Grate the cheese coarsely.

2 dessert apples   1 Tbs lemon juice

Peel, core and slice the apples. Sprinkle the lemon juice over them and turn the slices to coat them.

4 ripe bananas   4 tomatoes

Slice the tomatoes and bananas just before you are going to serve the salad.

mayonnaise or salad dressing

Arrange the salads on individual plates, first a layer of apple, then sliced banana, then tomato and egg slices alternating, and finally the cheese. Serve as it is, or put some mayonnaise on top, and serve some more mayonnaise or salad dressing separately.

Cauliflower and cottage cheese salad

Cooking time 5–10 mins. *Quantities* for 4.

1 medium-sized cauliflower

Wash, break into sprigs and put in a little boiling salted water. Boil until barely tender, as this salad is not so good if the cauliflower is soft. Drain and cool. Arrange in a shallow dish.

4 oz sieved cottage cheese (125 g)   2 egg yolks

Beat together thoroughly using a whisk or wooden spoon.

3–4 Tbs oil

Beat in gradually, adding as much as needed to produce a consistency like mayonnaise.

2 tsp lemon juice or 1 tsp vinegar $\frac{1}{4}$ tsp French mustard
salt and pepper   a pinch of sugar
chopped fresh chervil

Beat into the cottage cheese and refrigerate the dressing until ready to serve the salad.

chopped walnuts or anchovy fillets as a garnish

Mask the cauliflower with the dressing and garnish to taste.

Chicken and almond salad

Quantities for 4.

6 oz seedless raisins (175 g)

Put in a small pan, cover with cold water, bring to the boil and leave to stand in a warm place for 5 mins to make the raisins plump up. Strain them and run cold water through to cool them quickly.

4 oz shelled almonds (100 g)

Blanch by pouring boiling water over them, leave for a couple of minutes, pour off the water and add cold water. Remove the skins by squeezing. Toast the almonds in a hot oven or under the grill until they are browned. Cool. Chop coarsely.

12 oz cooked diced chicken (350 g)	1 Tbs finely chopped onion
4 Tbs French dressing (60 ml)	1 Tbs chopped parsley
lettuce	sliced cucumber

Mix raisins, almonds, chicken, onion and parsley together and mix with the dressing. Make a nest of lettuce leaves in a serving bowl or on individual plates and put the salad on the lettuce. Garnish with the cucumber.

Curried chicken salad

Quantities for 4–6.

8 oz cold cooked chicken (250 g)	8 oz can carrots, drained and diced
½ tsp finely chopped onion	(250 g)
2 apples	3 hard-boiled eggs

Peel, core and chop the apples. Shell and chop the eggs coarsely. Dice the chicken. Mix all ingredients together.

8 Tbs mayonnaise (120 ml)	1 Tbs curry powder, or to taste
salt	

Combine these and add them to the chicken mixture, stirring gently and thoroughly. Taste for seasoning.

lettuce leaves

Line a salad bowl with washed and dried lettuce leaves, or put individual portions on plates. Add the salad and

sliced tomato or chopped herbs.

Dressed chicken salad

Quantities for 4.

4 portions of cooked chicken

DRESSING

1 oz butter (25 g)	½ pt chicken stock (300 ml)
1 oz flour (3 Tbs or 25 g)	2 egg yolks

Melt the butter in a small pan and add the flour, stirring and cooking for a few minutes. Remove from the heat and gradually stir in the stock. Return to the heat and stir until it boils. Boil for 5 mins. Remove from the heat and stir in the egg yolks. Leave to become cold, stirring occasionally as it cools.

wine vinegar	salt and pepper
mustard	½–1 Tbs sherry or brandy
sugar	

Add these to the sauce to taste, and pour the dressing over the chicken. Garnish with

cooked peas, small whole cooked potatoes, and lettuce.

Fish salad with ravigote sauce

Quantities for 4–6.

1½ lb white fish fillets (700 g)

Poach the fish, see page 138. Drain and cool. Divide in portions.

¼ pt mayonnaise (150 ml)	2 tsp chopped capers
1 slice of onion, finely chopped	2 tsp chopped parsley
2 small gherkins, finely chopped	1 tsp chopped chives
1 tsp lemon juice	2 Tbs double cream
pepper	

Mix these together to make the sauce.

lettuce leaves

Wash, drain and arrange on plates or a large platter. Put the fish on the lettuce.

4 hard-boiled eggs

8 anchovy fillets

Shell the eggs and cut them in halves lengthwise. Arrange them round the fish with an anchovy fillet on each piece of egg. Spoon the sauce over the fish and garnish to taste with

chopped parsley or chives or sliced gherkins.

Ham and broad bean salad

Quantities for 4.

12 oz diced cooked ham or boiled bacon (350 g)

10 oz can broad beans (284 g)

Remove any skin, fat or gristle from the meat. Cut the meat in strips and then across to make small dice. Drain the beans and remove the skins, easily done by pinching gently at one end. The proportions of beans and ham can be varied according to what is available.

¼ pt tomato ketchup (150 ml)
1 Tbs horseradish sauce
¼ pt double cream (150 ml), or use mayonnaise

1 tsp Worcester sauce
½ Tbs lemon juice
½ tsp dry mustard

Mix all together until well blended, and use some of this to moisten the ham and beans.

watercress or other salad greens
2 tsp finely chopped onion

4 small tomatoes, or 1 canned red pepper

Arrange beds of salad greens on individual plates. Pile the ham mixture in the centre and sprinkle with the onion. Add more of the dressing or serve the surplus separately. Garnish with tomatoes or pepper, sliced.

Herring salad

Quantities for 4.

4 fillets of salt herring

Soak in cold water overnight. Drain and remove any remaining small bones. Cut in small pieces and put in a bowl.

8 oz finely diced cooked potato (250 g)
1 dessert apple, peeled, cored and chopped

1 pickled gherkin, chopped
1 Tbs chopped onion
8 oz cooked beetroot, skinned and chopped (250 g)

Add to the herring and mix well.

1 Tbs sugar
pinch of pepper
2 Tbs water
4 Tbs wine vinegar

Mix together and combine with the salad. Press the mixture into a pudding basin or four small moulds. Unmould on to a serving dish.

1 hard-boiled egg   chopped parsley, dill or fennel

Slice or chop the egg and use it and the herbs to garnish the salad.

Horseradish and ham roll salad

4 oz cream cheese (100 g)
1 Tbs mayonnaise
1–2 Tbs horseradish sauce

Mix together.

8 slices cooked ham or boiled bacon
tomato or canned red pepper to garnish
1 lettuce, or other salad greens
salad dressing

Put the pieces of ham or bacon on a flat surface. Divide the cheese mixture between them. Roll up the ham with the cheese inside. Arrange the rolls on the salad greens and garnish to taste. Pour a little dressing over the ham or serve it separately.

Kipper salad

Quantities for 3.

2 kippers

Cook the kippers, cool and flake, removing all bones; or use kipper fillets.

2 medium-sized boiled potatoes
¾ pt chopped celery (400 ml)
2 Tbs finely chopped onion
½ tsp paprika pepper
half a chopped green or red sweet pepper

Cut the potatoes in dice and mix with the other ingredients, including the flaked kipper.

mayonnaise

Moisten the mixture with mayonnaise.

lettuce leaves   1 hard-boiled egg

Wash and drain the lettuce and arrange it in a salad bowl or on individual plates. Put the kipper salad in the lettuce leaves and decorate with the egg.

Parisian salad

Quantities for 4.

8 oz cold meat (250 g)

Trim off any skin, gristle or fat and cut the meat in strips.

4 diced cold potatoes
2 hard-boiled eggs
2 small blanched onions
4 tomatoes

Blanch the onions by covering with water, bringing to the boil and boiling for 2 mins. Drain. Chop the onions, dice or slice the eggs or tomatoes. Mix all with the meat.

French dressing
chopped parsley
lettuce

Add enough dressing to moisten the mixture. Add 4 large lettuce leaves torn in pieces and then mix in the parsley.

Pork, brussels sprouts and orange salad

Quantities for 4.

8–12 oz cold cooked pork (250–350 g)

Remove skin and surplus fat and cut the pork in small pieces. Refrigerate until ready to assemble the salad.

8 oz raw brussels sprouts (250 g)   2 large oranges

Wash and drain the sprouts and slice them as finely as possible. Peel the oranges, remove all pith and divide them in segments, reserving a few for garnishing the salad.

mayonnaise or yogurt dressing

Mix pork, sprouts and oranges with enough dressing to moisten. Garnish with oranges and serve in a salad bowl.

Tongue salad

Quantities for 4.

6 oz cooked or canned tongue (175 g)   4 hard-boiled eggs
1 medium-sized beetroot   1 apple

Skin the beetroot and peel and core the apple. Cut all the ingredients into small pieces, reserving two of the egg yolks for the dressing.

pinch of pepper
½ tsp mustard
2 Tbs single cream or evaporated milk

½ tsp salt
2 Tbs vinegar

Mash the egg yolks and seasoning and mix smoothly with first the vinegar and then the cream. Mix this into the salad.

lettuce or chicory leaves

Serve the salad in a nest of leaves.

12. Pasta and Rice

As these two cereal products have many similar uses in cooking, it is convenient to group them together. Both can be served as an accompaniment to meat, poultry and fish, instead of using potatoes; they are both used for making puddings and desserts; and they both make good main courses when combined with other ingredients such as cheese, meat, poultry, fish and vegetables. They share two other advantages, being easy to store in any dry cupboard and making good emergency foods as they are very quickly cooked.

The recipes in this chapter are for savoury ways of using pasta and rice; sweet ways will be found in Chapter 15.

PASTA

There are about 150 different shapes of pasta made, but only a few of these are commonly used in Britain, although more shops now sell a wider variety than was available a few years ago. Shops specializing in Italian foods usually have a very large selection.

The following varieties of pasta are the best known in Britain:

Canneloni is either a stuffed lasagne, rather like a stuffed pancake, or it is a large, ridged, tubular pasta (also called rigatoni). This is sometimes stuffed, a rather messy business.

Lasagne is a large, flat pasta, frequently stuffed like a pancake, but used in other ways as well. Lasagne verde is coloured green with spinach purée.

Macaroni is one of the two types of pasta most widely used in Britain, and is sold either in long sticks or cut in short pieces. Some of the macaroni sold in packets has been specially prepared for quick cooking and carries instructions on the packet.

Noodles are flat, ribbon-like pasta containing egg. They are sold loose or in packets and are used chiefly as a substitute for potatoes. For this, they are usually boiled and dressed with butter or oil. Chinese noodles are like spaghetti.

Ravioli is a very thin pasta which is not dried but is made fresh daily by firms specializing in its manufacture. It consists of a paste rolled very thinly and cut into 2 in (5 cm) squares, usually with a serrated edge. These are joined in pairs with a filling of minced meat, chopped spinach and seasonings. They are boiled in water and served with a sauce or with butter and grated cheese. They are also available canned, but these are not usually as good as the fresh ravioli.

Spaghetti is the second type of pasta most commonly used in Britain. Most people know it canned in tomato or cheese sauce or as spaghetti Bolognese.

Tagliatelle is the Italian name for noodles.

Vermicelli is like spaghetti but the sticks are very much finer and are dried either separately like spaghetti or in bundles tied in a loose knot. It is used chiefly as an ingredient in soups.

Many of the fancy shapes of pasta are made very small and are meant to be used for garnishing clear soups.

Boiling pasta

Most of the varieties sold in packets carry cooking instructions and it is advisable to follow these. Many of them have been specially prepared for quick cooking and the traditional method which follows may over-cook them. If there are no special instructions, use the following method.

Cooking time 5–15 mins depending on the variety and size; 20 mins for ravioli.
Quantities: allow 4 oz or more (100 g) per person for a main dish; 2 oz (50 g) if served with meat and vegetables.

for each lb (½ kg) pasta, allow 6–8 pt water (4 l) and 1 Tbs salt

Bring the water to the boil and add a knob of butter or margarine or a tablespoon of oil as well as the salt. This helps to prevent the water from boiling over. When the water is boiling, add the pasta gradually, keeping the water boiling all the time. If it is a long pasta, put one end in the water and as this softens the rest will curl down into the pan. Boil rapidly until a piece tested is just tender enough to bite and tastes cooked. It should still be firm. If it is cooked beyond this stage, it is pappy and uninteresting to eat and tends to clump together in a sticky mass. Drain it well in a colander or sieve. To serve plain, toss in a little butter or oil and hand grated Parmesan cheese to be sprinkled on at table.

Pasta must be kept boiling steadily and it has a tendency to boil over, especially if the pan is rather full. In this case it is better to leave the lid off the pan or else to have it just half on; the latter prevents boiling over and conserves heat.

Lasagne, stuffed

This is a good way of using up a small quantity of cooked meat.

Cooking time about 1 hr. *Quantities* for 4.

2 rashers bacon, chopped   3 oz mushrooms, chopped (75 g)

Fry the bacon for a few minutes until the fat runs, then add the mushrooms and fry for a minute or so longer. Set aside to cool.

8 oz cooked chopped meat (200 g)   1 Tbs chopped parsley
2 oz grated cheese (50 g)   1 egg, beaten
salt and pepper

Any kind of meat can be used, including cooked sausage. Mix all these ingredients with the bacon and mushrooms. Cover, and refrigerate until required.

8 lasagne or large flat egg noodles (about 6 oz or 175 g)

Add half the lasagne to a large pan of boiling water and boil for 11 mins or according to instructions on the packet. Drain them on a clean tea-towel in a single layer. Boil the second lot, making sure there is plenty of water left or they will stick together. It is a good idea to give them an occasional gentle stir with a fork while they are boiling to make sure they remain separate. Drain as before.

When ready to complete the dish, divide the stuffing between the 8 lasagne and roll them up. Put them in a single layer in a shallow baking dish, or in a double layer with a sprinkling of cheese between layers.

10½ oz can concentrated tomato soup   2–3 oz grated cheese (50–75 g)
(298 g)

Dilute the tomato soup to the consistency of a sauce and pour it over the lasagne. Sprinkle the top thickly with grated cheese and bake in a hot oven 200° C (400° F; G6) for 30 mins, or until brown on the top and bubbling. Serve hot with

mixed salad.

Macaroni and cottage cheese

Cooking time about 15 mins.
Quantities for 2–4, depending on whether it is used as a main dish or accompaniment.

8 oz macaroni (250 g)

Boil in plenty of salted water for about 10 mins or according to the directions on the packet. Drain.

1 oz butter (25 g)

Melt in the pan, return the macaroni, put over a very low heat and stir gently for a few minutes.

8 oz cottage cheese (250 g)   4 Tbs milk (60 ml)

Blend together and add to the macaroni. Simmer for 2–3 mins, or until hot.

grated Parmesan cheese

Sprinkle over the top as the macaroni is served.

Noodles with ham and soured cream

To serve as a main dish.

Cooking time about 15 mins.
Quantities for 4.

8 oz cooked ham (250 g) diced   1 lb ribbon egg noodles (500 g)

Either boil the noodles according to the directions on the packet or boil them in plenty of salted water for about 10 mins until just tender. Drain. Rinse the pan.

2 oz butter (50 g)

Melt in the pan, add the noodles and ham and mix well over a very gentle heat.

½ pt soured cream (300 ml)   salt and pepper

Add to the noodles and make sure the dish is hot.

grated Parmesan cheese

Serve the noodles on a hot dish and hand the cheese separately. Serve with mixed salad.

Spaghetti Bolognese

To many people this is simply spaghetti in a meat sauce, see page 330. The following more elaborate sauce is well worth the effort for a specially good Bolognese.

Cooking time 1½ hrs. *Quantities* for 6–8.

2 oz cooked ham (50 g)   ½ oz butter (15 g)
2 oz bacon (50 g)

Remove the rind from the bacon and chop bacon and ham into small dice.

Alternatively, mince coarsely. Heat the butter in a saucepan and fry the meat until it begins to brown.

| 1 small onion, chopped | 1 small carrot, chopped |

Add to the meat and continue cooking until the vegetables are slightly softened.

| 4 oz boneless veal (125 g) | 12 oz lean beef steak (350 g) |
| 4 oz boneless pork (125 g) | |

Chop the meat finely or mince it coarsely. Add to the ingredients in the pan and cook, stirring frequently, until the meat no longer looks red.

| ¼ pt stock (150 ml) | ¼ pt white wine (150 ml) |

Add to the meat and boil very gently until the liquid has almost evaporated.

| 2 Tbs concentrated tomato purée | salt and pepper |

Add to the meat with enough hot water almost to cover it. Cover the pan and simmer slowly, preferably in a moderate oven, until the mixture is thick, about 1 hr.

1½–2 lb spaghetti (¾–1 kg)

Boil in plenty of salted water until just tender, about 10 mins. Drain. Serve the spaghetti in a mound with the sauce on top to be mixed into the spaghetti before serving. Serve with or without grated Parmesan cheese handed separately.

Spaghetti with anchovies

Cooking time about 15 mins. *Quantities* for 4–6.

1 lb spaghetti (500 g)

Cook in plenty of boiling salted water until it is just tender, about 10 mins. Drain. While the spaghetti is cooking, prepare the anchovy mixture.

| 8 Tbs olive oil (120 ml) | 1 clove garlic |

Skin the garlic. Heat the oil in a small pan and cook the garlic in it for 3 mins. Remove the clove and discard.

12 anchovy fillets (1 small can, 2 oz or 56 g)

Drain and rinse. Cut in ½ in (1 cm) pieces and add to the oil. Keep warm, then mix with the drained spaghetti.

2 oz grated Parmesan cheese (50 g)

When the spaghetti is ready, put it in a serving dish or on individual plates and sprinkle with the cheese.

ALTERNATIVE

Make the same recipe with egg noodles.

Spaghetti with meat sauce

Cooking time 1 hr. Quantities for 4.

8 oz minced lean beef (250 g)
½ clove crushed garlic, or a pinch of dried garlic
4 Tbs olive oil
1 medium-sized onion, chopped

Heat the oil in a saucepan and fry the meat, garlic and onion in it until the meat loses its red colour.

1 oz mushrooms, chopped (25 g)

Add to the meat and fry for about 10 mins.

1 lb can of whole tomatoes (454 g)
2 Tbs concentrated tomato purée
salt and pepper

Add to the meat and simmer for about ½ hr or until the sauce is thick.

½–1 Tbs chopped fresh marjoram or basil, or 1–2 tsp dried

Add to the meat sauce, according to taste.

½–1 lb spaghetti (250–500 g)

Boil the spaghetti according to the directions on the packet, or boil it in plenty of salted water for about 10 mins. Drain and serve with the sauce on top or mixed with the spaghetti.

grated Parmesan cheese

Serve separately to be sprinkled on according to taste.

Spaghetti with tomato sauce

To serve as an accompaniment to meat, poultry or fish.

Cooking time 20–30 mins. Quantities for 2–3.

1 small onion, sliced
2 Tbs oil
½ clove garlic

Fry together in a saucepan for 5 mins, without browning. Remove the garlic.

1 lb can of whole tomatoes (454 g)

Add to the pan and cook rapidly for 5 mins to evaporate some of the liquid.

2 pieces of canned anchovy fillet, chopped

Add and cook for 10 mins or until the sauce is thick.

½–1 tsp chopped fresh marjoram, or   salt and pepper
¼–½ tsp dried

Add and keep the sauce warm.

8 oz spaghetti (250 g)

Boil according to the directions on the packet, or for 10 mins in plenty of boiling salted water. Drain and serve with the sauce on top or mixed with it, and serve separately

plenty of grated Parmesan or other dry cheese.

RICE

There are many different varieties of rice grown in different parts of the world. They vary in both size and shape of the grain, in the amount of water they absorb during cooking and in the time they take to cook. Those most commonly used in Britain include:

Brown rice which contains most of the outside branny layers of the grain and has a higher vitamin and mineral content than the more highly milled white rice. This could be an important factor to anyone living on a diet of rice and not much else. Brown rice takes longer to cook and absorbs more water than white rice; it also has more flavour, but the colour spoils the appearance of many traditional rice dishes.

Long-grain rice, of which Patna is the best-known variety, though there are others. The long thin grains stay separate provided the rice is not over-cooked, and it is the kind preferred for boiled rice and many savoury rice dishes.

Parboiled rice. This is partly cooked under steam pressure before milling. This drives some of the minerals and vitamins from the branny layers into the white interior so that, when milled, this kind of rice has a higher nutritive value than ordinary white rice; again an important factor for those whose diet has a high rice content.

Pre-cooked or quick-cooking rice. This is now sold in most stores and only requires heating before serving.

Round-grain rice. This may be quite a short, small grain, or a long one with rounded ends. Pudding rice is a round rice of short or medium length. When boiled, this kind has a tendency to clump together. Special round-grain rice is sold for making risotto, paella and pilaff, but is usually only available in some specialist shops. If you cannot get this special kind it is usually more satisfactory to use the long-grain variety for these dishes.

In the supermarket, rice is very often sold in packets with cooking instructions which it is advisable to follow.

Boiling rice

Many people boil rice by putting it in a large pan with lots of boiling water which is kept boiling hard until the rice is done. Then it is strained and kept in a warm place until it fluffs up. This method is wasteful of fuel and food value and I think either of the two following methods is better.

Quantities for 4.

METHOD 1

Cooking time 15-25 mins.

8 oz long-grain rice (250 g)   1 tsp salt
1 pt water or stock (600 ml)

Packet rice should not need to be washed, but it is as well to wash other types. Put the rice in a strainer and run cold water through it. Shake well to remove excess moisture. Put the rice in a pan with the salt and water, bring to the boil and stir once. Cover the pan and cook for 15 mins without lifting the lid. During this time keep the heat low enough for simmering. After 15 mins test a few grains by squeezing them between thumb and forefinger, when there should be no uncooked spot of rice in the middle. If all the water has not been absorbed, heat the rice gently until it evaporates, then fluff up with a fork and keep in a warm place until ready for serving.

METHOD 2

Cooking time 40 mins.

Wash the rice if necessary. Use the quantities given in Method 1, putting the rice and salt in a casserole and adding the water boiling. Cover the casserole and cook in a moderate oven 180° C (350° F; G4) until the rice is done. Fluff up with a fork and keep warm but do not allow it to go on cooking.

RE-HEATING BOILED RICE

Cold boiled rice keeps well in a covered dish in the refrigerator for up to a week, or in a cold larder for 2-3 days. To re-heat it, put the rice in a covered saucepan with a few tablespoons of water and stand the pan over a low heat. Shake the pan occasionally, or stir the rice gently, and in a few minutes the rice will be hot, fluffy and ready to serve.

Fried rice

To serve with meat, poultry or fish. Rice can be boiled in advance and kept in a cool place or in the refrigerator.

Cooking time a few mins. *Quantities* for 4.

1 lb (2 c or 500 g) dry cooked rice (8 oz or 250 g raw)	1 small onion, finely chopped
2 Tbs olive oil or 1 oz butter (25 g)	salt and pepper
	flavourings, see below

Heat the oil or butter in a pan and fry the onion gently until it softens. Add the rice and stir and heat until all the oil or butter is absorbed and the rice is beginning to brown. Season and flavour to taste and serve hot.

FLAVOURINGS

4 Tbs mixed chopped herbs
Chopped pineapple and chopped salted almonds
Raisins and chopped almonds
Fry some chopped green pepper with the onion
Fry some chopped celery and chopped button mushrooms with the onion
Add chopped raw tomato at serving time.

Kedgeree

Cooking time: the ingredients can be prepared in advance and stored in the refrigerator, then the assembly and heating will take about 5 mins; otherwise allow ½ hr.
Quantities for 4–6.

1 lb cooked flaked smoked haddock or other smoked fish (500 g); poached fish is best	4 oz rice (125 g), boiled
	2 eggs, hard-boiled

Shell the eggs and remove the yolks. Rub them through a sieve. Chop the whites. Be sure all bones are removed from the fish.

2 oz butter (50 g)

Heat the butter in a pan large enough to hold all the ingredients. Add the fish and rice and mix well.

| salt and pepper | pinch of grated nutmeg |

Season the rice and fish to taste and mix in the egg white. When the mixture is hot all through, pile it up on a serving dish. Decorate it with the egg yolk and wedges of lemon and chopped parsley.

Kedgeree with curd cheese

Cooking time 15 mins to prepare the ingredients, which can be done in advance; 5 mins final cooking.
Quantities for 4.

| 1 lb smoked fish fillets (500 g), poached in milk | 8 oz cooked fresh or frozen green peas (250 g) |
| 4 oz rice (125 g), boiled | |

Strain the fish, keeping the milk. Flake the fish and remove all skin and bone.

6 oz curd or cream cheese (175 g)

Mash this well and beat in 5 Tbs (75 ml) of the milk used for poaching the fish.

| grated rind of 1 lemon | pepper |

Add these to the cheese together with the rice, fish and peas. Cook over a low heat until the mixture is hot all through.

| chopped parsley and/or chopped green peppers or tomatoes | lemon wedges |

Garnish with these and serve.

Paella

Traditional ingredients for this are rice, saffron, vegetables, fish, shellfish, chicken or meat. Simple inexpensive ones may have just one or two ingredients and the recipe also varies in different parts of Spain. It gets its name from the two-handled iron pan in which it is cooked. A deep heavy frying pan, a sauté pan or a wok can be used instead.

Cooking time 1 hr. *Quantities* for 4.

1 dozen mussels

Scrub the mussels to remove all sand and weed. Discard any with broken shells or any which are open even a little bit. Put them in a large pan with a little water, cover and cook over a gentle heat until the shells open. Drain.

4 Tbs olive oil (60 ml)	4 pieces of frying chicken

Heat the oil and fry the chicken brown in it.

12 oz long-grain rice (350 g)	1 clove garlic

Crush the garlic and add it to the pan. Add the rice and stir over a low heat, but do not allow it to brown.

1½ pt chicken stock (850 ml)	salt
saffron	

Saffron is usually sold in shreds. Pour boiling water over a few and leave until the water is coloured. Use this during the cooking to colour the rice. Add the stock and salt to the rice, mix well and bring to the boil.

2 tomatoes	8 oz firm-fleshed white fish, e.g. rock
8 oz fresh or frozen peas (250 g)	salmon (250 g)
1 red or green sweet pepper	

Cut the tomatoes in quarters. Wash, remove seeds and cut the peppers in pieces. Remove any skin from the fish and cut it in pieces. Put all these with the rice, distributing them evenly and including the mussels in half-shells or shelled. Cook for about 7 mins and then put the pan in a moderate oven for 12 mins 190° C (375° F; G5). Then keep the paella in a warming cupboard for a further 5 mins before serving. The liquid should all be absorbed and the chicken tender. Serve from the dish.

Pilaff

This is delicious on its own for a light meal but if you want something more substantial, cooked meat such as pieces of fried liver or kidney can be added to it at the time of serving.

Cooking time about 15 mins. *Quantities* for 4.

1 pt white stock (600 ml)	salt and pepper if the stock is not
2 oz butter (50 g)	already seasoned

Put in a pan and bring to the boil.

8 oz washed and drained pilaff rice (250 g), or use long-grain rice

Add to the stock, stir and cover the pan. Reduce the heat and simmer for 15 mins without lifting the lid. Test a grain to see if it is cooked through. By this time all the stock should have been absorbed. If the rice is done and there is still some stock, heat for a minute with the lid off, but avoid over-cooking the rice. Keep in a warm place until ready to serve.

chopped fresh herbs to taste $\frac{1}{4}-\frac{1}{2}$ pt yogurt (150–250 ml)

Stir in the herbs or sprinkle them on top as the pilaff is served. Top each portion with 2–3 Tbs yogurt.

Pilau

See page 183.

Rice with egg and mint

This makes a delicious light rice dish to eat on its own with an accompanying salad or to serve with meat, for example, chicken, lamb, pork or veal.

Cooking time 20 mins. *Quantities* for 2–4.

8 oz long-grain rice (250 g)   1 pt water (600 ml)
1 tsp salt

Put in a pan and bring to the boil, stir, cover and cook over a gentle heat for 15 mins. Then test to see if it is cooked through. It should be tender and all the water absorbed. If necessary, remove the lid and allow the rice to dry.

2 eggs, beaten   1 Tbs lemon juice
1 oz grated Parmesan cheese (25 g)

Combine and stir into the hot rice.

2 tsp chopped mint or more to taste

Stir in gently and serve.

Risotto

Cooking time 25–30 mins. *Quantities* for 4–6.

4 oz fat (125 g)   6 oz onion, chopped (175 g)

Use a deep thick frying pan or a sauté pan. Heat the fat in it and fry the onion until it begins to brown.

12 oz long-grain rice (350 g)

Add to the pan and cook for a further 3 mins, stirring all the time.

2 pt hot stock ($1\frac{1}{4}$ l)

Add a quarter of the stock and stir until it boils. Continue boiling gently, adding more of the stock until all is used and the rice is tender, about 15–20 mins.

1 oz butter (25 g)
2 rashers bacon
8 oz liver, lamb's, calf's or chicken's (250 g)

Remove the rinds from the bacon and chop it. Cut the liver in small pieces. Heat the butter in a separate small pan and fry the bacon. Finally add the liver and cook it quickly until beads of blood appear on the surface. Add to the rice.

salt and pepper
4 oz grated cheese (125 g)
4 oz canned or cooked sweet red pepper (125 g)

Slice the red peppers and add to the rice. Season to taste. Serve hot with the cheese handed separately.

ALTERNATIVE

Instead of the liver use kidney or small pieces of tender beefsteak, lamb or chicken.

Saffron rice

Cooking time 20–25 mins. Quantities for 4.

8 oz long-grain rice (250 g)
1 pt white stock (600 ml)
a good pinch each of ground cloves and cinnamon
1 tsp salt
2 bay leaves
pepper
a few shreds of saffron

Put the saffron in a small bowl and cover with boiling water. Leave to infuse until cold, then strain.

Put all the ingredients in a pan, using enough saffron liquid to colour the stock yellow. More can be added later if you wish. Bring to the boil, stir, cover the pan and reduce the heat to simmering or put the pan in a moderate oven. Test the rice after 15 mins to see if it is cooked through (no hard core in the middle when a few grains are squeezed). All the water should be absorbed by this time. To dry it, fluff with a fork, cover, and stand it in a warm place for 5–10 mins. Remove the bay leaves before serving. It can be kept warm for some time, but not hot, or it will go on cooking and become a sticky mess.

13. Sandwiches and Snacks on Toast

Bread, whether used for the traditional English sandwich, the open Scandinavian sandwich or just baked beans on toast, probably forms the basis of more light meals than does any other single food. It can make a very tasty meal and one with good food value too, especially if taken with a milky drink and followed by fresh fruit. Indeed, a well-chosen sandwich meal can give better food value and be more pleasant to eat than many an indifferent meat-and-two-vegetables meal.

In this chapter I have included all types of sandwiches, plain and toasted, open and closed, with suggestions and recipes for fillings, and some recipes for snacks on toast.

ENGLISH SANDWICHES

BREAD FOR SANDWICHES

Machine-sliced bread is the quickest and simplest to use. If you prefer unsliced loaves and no machine is available for slicing, it is better to use day-old bread which is less difficult to slice by hand than new bread.

Most sliced bread is either thinly sliced or medium. Thinly sliced bread is best for all but very hearty sandwiches for the hungry.

For sandwich cakes (see below) use baps or other round loaves, and for ribbon sandwiches and sandwich loaves use tin shapes. Any kind of roll can be used.

QUANTITIES

Allow 1½–2 full rounds of sandwich per person, or according to appetite.

A small loaf usually cuts into 16 thin slices, a large loaf (1¾ lb or 794 g), into 20–30 thin slices and a quartern loaf into 50 thin slices.

Four ounces (125 g) of softened butter should be enough to spread one large loaf, and you need about 2½–3 times as much in weight for the filling.

STORING SANDWICHES

To keep sandwiches fresh, either wrap them in polythene or foil, or else pack them in a plastic box with a lid. They will keep fresh in a cold place, a cold larder or the refrigerator for 12–24 hrs; but remove them in time for the bread and filling to come to room temperature before serving.

In the freezer sandwiches will keep for several weeks but avoid any containing hard-boiled egg, salad vegetables, mayonnaise, jam or any soggy filling. It is best to use day-old bread when making sandwiches for freezing and to spread liberally with butter before adding the filling. Put the sandwiches in small packets of not more than 6 or 8 sandwiches, otherwise thawing will be slow. If they are wanted for lunch, remove them from the freezer at breakfast time and thaw at room temperature.

Whether sandwiches are stored in the refrigerator or freezer, it is better to wrap different flavours separately.

Never leave freshly made or thawed sandwiches exposed to the air in a warm room for any length of time; the bread becomes dry and the filling may become unsafe to eat.

Fancy shapes for tea-time or a buffet party

CAKES OR TORTES AND LOAVES

These look like filled and iced layer cakes but the basis is a round flat loaf like a bap, sliced horizontally into two or three layers. The layers are sandwiched with different fillings. The top is 'iced' with a soft mixture such as a spread made with cottage or cream cheese. It is decorated with salad vegetables or pickles and cut in wedges like a cake. Provide small plates and forks for eating it. These loaves can be very decorative on a buffet and suit modern tastes better than sweet iced cakes.

An alternative to the cake shape is to use a tin loaf, slice it horizontally into medium-thick layers, and sandwich these with fillings of different flavours and colours. Cut off the crusts, wrap the loaf in polythene and store it in the refrigerator with a board and a weight on top to press the slices securely together. Then it can be iced and decorated as above. For serving, it is sliced downwards as it would be for ordinary slices of bread. The fillings used should be well-flavoured and soft in texture, not dry and crumbly, or the loaf will fall apart when sliced.

These loaves can be frozen unwrapped, and then put in a polythene bag or box.

CORNUCOPIAS

Use thinly sliced, day-old white or brown bread. Trim off the crusts and spread each slice generously with butter. Cut the slices in half diagonally and roll each into a cornet shape. Pack them close together in a dish so that they keep each other in shape while the butter sets, preferably in the refrigerator.

To serve them, stand them upright in a dish and put a little of a soft filling in each, like whipped cream in a cream horn.

PINWHEELS

Use a new unsliced sandwich loaf. Remove the crusts and cut the loaf into thin slices along the length of the loaf. Place the slices on a clean damp cloth. Spread them with softened butter and a filling which has a colour to contrast with the bread. Roll each up like a Swiss roll and wrap firmly in foil. Store these in the refrigerator and slice them just before serving.

RIBBON SANDWICHES

Use fresh thinly sliced bread, both brown and white. Make the sandwiches with three slices of bread and two different coloured fillings, and either put a white slice in the middle and brown outside or vice versa. Wrap in foil and chill in the refrigerator. Cut in fingers for serving.

ROLLED SANDWICHES

Asparagus rolls made with brown bread are the best known of these, but other fillings can be used provided they are ones which will not fall apart easily.

Use thinly sliced new bread. Spread the slices with softened butter and trim off the crusts. Put a piece of freshly-cooked or drained canned asparagus on each and roll up tightly. Pack close together so that they keep each other in shape and chill them in the refrigerator.

Suggestions for sandwich fillings

Sandwich fillings should be as freshly made as possible. If made in advance, store them in covered containers in the refrigerator and when the sandwiches are made, keep them covered and cold until about 15 mins before they are to be served. For a party, when sandwiches will be required over a period of several hours, bring them out in relays instead of leaving them exposed to warm air for a long time. Stale sandwiches can be a cause of food poisoning so it is wise to take these precautions.

CHEESE-BASED FILLINGS

Cottage cheese mixed with chopped chives, very finely chopped onions or chopped pickles such as gherkins or capers. Any chopped fresh herbs can be added for extra flavour.

Grated cheese with chopped apple and celery, and mayonnaise or salad dressing to bind.

Cottage cheese and sliced or chopped radishes.

Grated cheese mixed with chopped olives, French mustard and mayonnaise.

Grated cheese mixed with chopped pineapple and mayonnaise.

Cream cheese mixed with chopped walnuts and chopped celery.

EGG-BASED FILLINGS

Mashed hard-boiled eggs mixed with salad dressing and chopped gherkins or capers.

Cold scrambled eggs mixed with chopped cooked bacon and mayonnaise.

Scrambled eggs mixed with chopped ham, and fresh chopped herbs.

Scrambled eggs flavoured with a little chopped fried onion and curry powder to taste.

Mashed hard-boiled eggs with chopped chives or onion and tomato ketchup to bind.

Mashed hard-boiled eggs moistened with mayonnaise and flavoured with French mustard and Worcester sauce.

FISH-BASED FILLINGS

Thin slices of smoked salmon with lemon juice and pepper; use brown bread.

Canned crab meat mixed with chopped cucumber and bound with mayonnaise.

Flaked cooked smoked fish moistened with mayonnaise and flavoured with chopped parsley, dill or fennel, or with a generous amount of paprika pepper.

Flaked canned salmon mixed with chopped gherkins or cucumber and chopped parsley, dill or fennel, with mayonnaise to bind.

MEAT-BASED FILLINGS

Thin slices of any cooked meat or sausage flavoured with mustard, bottled sauce or chutney.

Any minced cooked or canned meat mixed with chutney to moisten.

Chopped corned beef mixed with finely chopped onion and horseradish sauce.

Chopped ham or boiled bacon mixed with grated apple and mayonnaise.

Minced chicken mixed with chopped walnuts and cucumber, moistened with salad dressing or a sauce.

Chopped or minced chicken with chopped canned red peppers and mayonnaise.

VEGETABLE-BASED FILLINGS

Raw grated carrot mixed with chopped salted peanuts, pickle and mayonnaise.
 Chopped chives and watercress mixed with mayonnaise.
 Chopped canned asparagus with mayonnaise.
 Equal quantities of finely chopped celery and apple mixed with some chopped nuts and mayonnaise.

RECIPES FOR SANDWICH FILLINGS

Blue cheese and walnut

4 oz grated or mashed blue-vein cheese (100 g)	a few grains of cayenne pepper
2 oz melted butter (50 g)	3 Tbs mayonnaise
chopped parsley	1 oz chopped walnuts (25 g)

Mix all together thoroughly and put in a covered dish in the refrigerator to become firm.

Cheese and sherry

4 oz strong Cheddar or Cheshire cheese, grated (100 g)	1 oz soft butter (25 g)
2 Tbs sherry	pinch of paprika pepper

Mix all together thoroughly and store in a covered container in the refrigerator.

Chicken liver

See chicken liver pâté, page 72.

Curry and cheese

8 oz cottage or other soft cheese (250 g)	1 tsp very finely chopped onion
2 tsp chutney, chopped if necessary	$\frac{1}{4}$ tsp salt
1-2 tsp curry powder, according to taste	grated rind of $\frac{1}{2}$ lemon
	pinch of sugar
	milk or cream

Put the cheese in a bowl and mash it smooth. Add the other ingredients with milk or cream if necessary to make it a spreading consistency.

Egg and onion

2 oz finely chopped onion (50 g) 2 Tbs oil
pinch of pepper 4 hard-boiled eggs

Shell and mash the eggs and mix with the other ingredients.

Kipper

See kipper pâté, page 76.

Liver sausage

2 rashers bacon, grilled or fried and chopped 4 oz soft liver sausage (100 g)
4 Tbs mayonnaise 1 tsp French mustard
2 small gherkins, chopped 1 oz melted bacon fat or lard (25 g)

A soft continental sausage is the best to use for this filling. Mash it well with the other ingredients and store in a covered container in the refrigerator.

Sardine and cheese

3–4 oz can of sardines (100 g)

Mash sardines and oil thoroughly or process them in the electric blender, adding a little more oil if necessary to help the blending.

4 oz melted butter or margarine (100 g) 2 Tbs lemon juice
1 slice of onion, very finely chopped 2 oz grated cheese (50 g)
salt and pepper $\frac{1}{4}$ tsp paprika pepper

Mix with the sardine, or blend with it in the machine. Put in a covered container in the refrigerator until it has set to a spreading consistency.

Smoked cod's roe

See page 78.

SCANDINAVIAN OPEN SANDWICHES

Many different kinds of bread can be used as a base for these sandwiches, the choice depending on the ingredients used to make the sandwich and personal preferences. Among the breads are white breads of all kinds, wholemeal, brown, dark and light rye, hard breads and rusks. All are buttered generously, as this helps to keep the bread from becoming soggy when a moist topping is used.

The choice of toppings is only limited by cost and availability of ingredients; practically any meat, poultry, game, fish, eggs, cheese and cooked or raw vegetables are used and sometimes fruit as well and also pickles. The arrangement of the ingredients should look fresh, not formal and over-decorated.

The sandwiches can be very large so that one or two are enough for a light meal, or smaller ones if you want more variety of choice.

If you want to prepare them in advance it is best to prepare the ingredients, refrigerating any perishable ones, and leave the assembling of the sandwich until you are ready for serving. Because only one piece of bread is used for each sandwich, with the filling arranged on top and not covered, more filling or topping is used than for the English type of sandwich; and they are meant to be eaten with a knife and fork.

Topping for open sandwiches

CHEESE SANDWICHES

A slice of any kind of cheese, about the same size as the bread. Garnish with lettuce, radishes, pickles, fruit, watercress or other salad material available.

Any soft cheese, suitably flavoured with chopped fresh herbs, chopped pickles, or finely chopped onion or sweet pepper. Either spread the cheese over the bread or put it in a mound in the centre and surround with a garnish of various salad vegetables.

Use any of the cheese fillings given above for English sandwich fillings, spreading them on the bread and garnishing with salad vegetables.

EGG SANDWICHES

Wedges of hard-boiled egg masked with a mayonnaise flavoured with curry powder and garnished with salad vegetables.

Fried bread with a slice of cooked ham on top and then a fried egg. Garnish with lettuce and tomato wedges.

Cold scrambled egg flavoured with chopped fried bacon, fried onion and curry, chopped ham or chopped herbs. Arrange the scrambled egg on a lettuce leaf or a thin slice of ham and garnish with salad materials.

Slices of hard-boiled egg arranged in rows with other ingredients such as chopped salad ingredients bound with mayonnaise; shellfish, such as shrimps; sliced pickles; chopped beetroot mixed with horseradish sauce.

FISH AND SHELLFISH SANDWICHES

Smoked salmon paste with a garnish of chopped chives and chopped hard-boiled egg.

Sliced smoked eel garnished with hard-boiled egg and chopped chives or onion.

Pickled herring fillets with potato salad and pickled beetroot.

Cooked mussels arranged on lettuce and garnished with tartare sauce.

Fresh or canned lobster meat arranged on a nest of lettuce leaves and served with a garnish of mayonnaise and lemon.

Cold fried fillet of fish on lettuce with a rémoulade sauce.

Anchovy fillets used to garnish cold scrambled egg arranged on lettuce and garnished with chopped chives or other herbs.

MEAT SANDWICHES

Liver pâté or slices of liver sausage garnished with chopped fried bacon and fried button mushrooms.

A slice of ham garnished with spears of canned or fresh cooked asparagus and a slice of tomato.

Sliced salami sausage garnished with chopped onion and radishes.

Slice of roast lamb garnished with cucumber salad and chopped mint, dill or fennel.

Slice of roast beef garnished with potato salad and horseradish.

Slice of roast pork with pickled cucumber, tomato or apple and celery salad.

Slices of cold cooked poultry masked with mayonnaise or other cold sauce and garnished with salad vegetables.

In addition to the above suggestions, any of the fillings given for English sandwiches can be used for spreading on open sandwiches and then suitably garnished.

TOASTED SANDWICHES

There are several ways of making these hot sandwiches. Bread can be toasted, spread with butter, and made into sandwiches in the usual way. Or toast a very thick slice of bread on both sides, then split it, butter the inside and add the filling. The third method, described below, is the one I prefer.

Ingredients for the sandwiches can be prepared in advance and the family can toast their own sandwiches freshly as required. A grill or horizontal toaster is needed, and if you have a portable one the sandwiches can be made at table.

Ordinary machine-sliced white bread is usually the most satisfactory, fairly thinly sliced, though this is a matter of taste. It can be fresh or stale, but not dry.

The chosen filling is put between unbuttered slices and it is the outsides which are buttered. For this you can brush on melted butter or margarine, or use a thin spreading of softened butter or one of the soft margarines. The covering of butter or margarine should be thin but even, otherwise results will be disappointing. Crusts can be removed or left on according to taste.

The easiest way of assembling one of these sandwiches is to butter one slice, put it buttered side down on the grill rack or in a heavy frying pan, add the filling and then the top slice of buttered bread, butter uppermost. This avoids having to handle the greasy surfaces.

Toast or fry fairly slowly so that the bread browns evenly and the filling heats through. Turn with tongs or a fish slice.

Use plenty of filling of any kind you particularly like.

Filling suggestions for toasted sandwiches

CHEESE

For each slice have a thick slice of strong cheese, and spread it with mustard as you make the sandwich. Toast slowly so that the cheese begins to melt by the time the bread is browned.

CHEESE AND ANCHOVY

As above, but spread the cheese with anchovy paste or essence instead of mustard.

CHEESE AND CHUTNEY

Spread the slice of cheese with chutney instead of mustard.

CHEESE AND ONION

Use grated cheese mixed with finely chopped onion and sufficient boiling water to make a spreadable paste.

CROQUE MONSIEUR

Do this one on a griddle or in a heavy frying pan. A slice of Emmental cheese a little smaller than the bread with a slice of ham on top, the same size as the cheese.

MEAT

Use minced meat or poultry moistened with plenty of chutney or a bottled sauce.

OTHER FILLINGS

Use any of those on pages 340-42.

SNACKS ON TOAST

Baked beans and cheese

Cooking time a few mins. *Quantities* for 4.

1 lb can baked beans in tomato sauce (454 g)	2 canned red pimientos or sweet peppers, drained and chopped
4 oz grated cheese (125 g)	1 tsp Worcester sauce

Put all in a saucepan and cook over a gentle heat until the cheese is melted and the whole mixture hot.

4 slices hot toast or 4 fresh rolls

Either pour the mixture over the toast or serve it in small hot dishes with the rolls handed separately.

Cheese on toast with herbs

Cooking time a few mins. *Quantities* for 4.

4 slices toast	4 thick slices cheese the same size as the toast
2 tsp chopped fresh herbs, or to taste	

For the herbs use thyme, sage, savory or tarragon. Put the cheese on the toast and grill fairly slowly until the cheese melts and bubbles. Serve sprinkled generously with herbs.

Cheese, tomato and bacon on toast

Use the above recipe but this time add

4 small rashers bacon, diced or cut in strips	2 sliced tomatoes

Put the tomatoes on top of the uncooked cheese and herbs, the bacon on top of the tomatoes and grill until the bacon is cooked.

Crab and cheese

Cooking time about 5 mins. *Quantities* for 4.

4 oz cooked or canned crab meat (125 g)	4 slices of bread toasted on one side
mayonnaise or salad dressing to moisten	chopped fresh sage, chervil, thyme or tarragon, or use dried

Mix the crab meat with mayonnaise or salad dressing and plenty of herbs. Spread it on the untoasted side of the bread.

4 thin slices of cheese

Put on top of the crab and grill slowly until the cheese is melted.

Egg and haddock

Cooking time about 10 mins. *Quantities* for 4.

4 eggs, beaten	1 Tbs lemon juice
2 Tbs milk	pepper
8 oz cooked flaked smoked haddock (250 g)	2 Tbs grated horseradish or horseradish sauce

Combine all the ingredients.

½ oz butter or margarine (15 g)

Melt in a small pan and scramble the egg mixture.

4 slices bread   4 thin slices cheese

Toast the bread on one side and put the filling on the untoasted side. Cover with the cheese. Grill slowly until the cheese has melted and begun to brown.

Egg, cheese and bacon

Quantities for 4.

2 eggs, beaten	1 tsp paprika pepper
8 oz grated cheese (200 g)	½ tsp dry mustard
1 tsp Worcester sauce	a little garlic salt or dried garlic

Combine the ingredients thoroughly.

4 thin slices bread from a large loaf toasted on one side

Spread the mixture in a thick layer on the untoasted side.

2 rashers bacon, diced

Cover the filling with the bacon and grill until it is crisp.

Onions and cheese on toast

Cooking time 20 mins. *Quantities* for 4.

| 4 medium-sized onions, sliced | 1 oz fat (25 g) |

Heat the fat and fry the onions in it until they are tender.

| 4 slices hot buttered toast | salt and pepper |

Spread the onion on the toast and sprinkle with salt and pepper.

| 4 slices of cheese | French mustard |

Spread the cheese with mustard and place it on top of the onions. Grill, or bake in a hot oven until the cheese melts.

Rarebit, Welsh

Cooking time about 5–10 mins. *Quantities* for 4.

| 8 oz grated Cheshire or Cheddar cheese (250 g) | 2 tsp made mustard or Worcester sauce |
| 4 Tbs milk, ale or stout | 1 Tbs cornflour |

This can be prepared in advance and will keep for a week in a covered container in the refrigerator.

Mix the ingredients to a smooth paste.

4 slices of toast

Spread the cheese mixture on the hot toast and brown under the grill. Serve hot.

RAREBIT, ANCHOVY

When the rarebit has browned put some rinsed anchovy fillets on each portion and return to the grill to make them hot.

RAREBIT, BUCK

Serve a poached egg on top of each portion of Welsh rarebit.

RAREBIT, SARDINE

When the Welsh rarebit is browned put a couple of sardines on each portion and return to the grill to make them hot.

RAREBIT WITH HERBS

To the cheese mixture for Welsh rarebit add 1 Tbs chopped fresh herbs or 1 tsp dried. Chervil, chives, parsley and thyme are a good mixture of fresh herbs.

RAREBIT, YORKSHIRE

Put a thin slice of ham on the toast before spreading on the Welsh rarebit mixture. Grill slowly until the cheese is brown.

Ham rarebit

Cooking time a few mins. *Quantities* for 4–6.

2 oz butter or margarine (50 g)   2 Tbs flour
1 tsp dry mustard

Melt the fat in a small saucepan and add the dry ingredients, mix until smooth.

½ pt single cream (250 ml)   2 tsp Worcester sauce
2 oz grated Cheddar cheese   2 Tbs sherry

Add the cream gradually to the pan, stirring all the time. Add the other ingredients and cook gently until the cheese is melted.

6 oz diced cooked ham (175 g)

Add and heat for a few minutes.

4–6 slices of toast, buttered and sprinkled with paprika pepper

Pour the ham and cheese mixture on the toast and serve.

14. Fruits and Fruit Desserts

With some fruits appearance is a good guide to quality, while with others it is difficult to tell from the outside what the inside will be like. It is wise to buy from a reliable shop and pay an average price for the fruit. Fruit which is being sold at very much below the current price is often, though not always, of poor quality.

Exceptions to this generalization are soft fruits sold at the height of their season. When these are offered cheaply it usually means they are fully ripe and must be used at once, then they are a good buy for immediate use or for cooking. In the case of apples and oranges it may be that the fruit is unusually small, or not graded, which means a mixture of small and large, but perfectly sound fruit. Small fruits are often excellent value, ideal for small children. Small, thin-skinned oranges are usually very juicy and good for making drinks.

When any fruit is scarce it is usually expensive, and thus prices fluctuate from season to season, according to climatic and other conditions. This holds good for both home-grown and imported fruit. Some imported fruits are purchased for their novelty value, but can be disappointing and not worth the high prices charged for them.

It is true, of course, that fruit generally tastes best when it is grown and ripened locally. Air-freighting of fresh fruit has to a large extent overcome this difficulty for those who are prepared to pay the price.

Frozen fruits are usually more expensive than the fresh in season, but when home-grown fruit is out of season, the frozen can be cheaper than imported fresh.

When fresh fruit is out of season, canned may be a cheaper alternative than frozen but is often inferior in quality. Cheaper brands of canned fruits sometimes contain rather a lot of syrup in relation to fruit and are not as good a buy as a more expensive, well-filled can. Occasionally a fruit is canned when not fully ripe and this means lack of flavour.

Home freezing of fruit

Fruit may be frozen with or without sugar or syrup. When sugar is added to small packs, sprinkle it on as the fruit is put in. With large packs spread the fruit out on a tray, sprinkle with sugar, wait for the juice to begin to run and then pack.

To keep berries from clumping together, freeze them on trays, without sugar, and then pack in polythene bags or boxes.

When using a syrup add enough to cover the fruit varying its sweetness according to taste. Boil the sugar and water together for a few minutes and then allow it to become quite cold before use. Fruit salads, stewed fruit and similar recipes are all suitable for freezing and raw or cooked fruit purées are particularly useful.

THAWING

For serving raw it is best to thaw the fruit slowly in the refrigerator but for quicker thawing it can be emptied into a bowl and thawed at room temperature. For even faster thawing stand the bowl in cold water for $\frac{1}{2}$–1 hr. Serve raw fruit while it is still frosty. 1 lb ($\frac{1}{2}$ kg) of fruit will take about 3–4 hrs at room temperature; 8–10 hrs in the refrigerator.

Fruit for cooking can be used while still frozen, or thawed, whichever suits the recipe better. For fruit tarts, partially thaw the fruit. Thaw fruit purées at room temperature or over a gentle heat.

NOTES ON FREEZING DIFFERENT FRUITS

Apples. To freeze raw, peel, core and slice thickly, putting the slices straight into salted water to prevent discoloration. Then drain and pack. Use in the same way as fresh apples.

Apricots. Only really ripe ones are worth freezing. Cut in halves and remove stones. Slice if desired. Blanch for 2 mins in boiling water, put in ice-cold water, then drain and pack. Use as fresh apricots.

Bananas. Only satisfactory if frozen in made up dishes such as ice-cream and mousses or in a cooked sweet.

Berries. (Bilberries, blackberries, boysenberries, cranberries, loganberries, raspberries). Prepare as for serving, then freeze plain or sprinkled with sugar.

Black, red or white currants. Wash on the stalks and drain well, then strip from the stalks. Freeze plain or mix with caster sugar to coat well and then freeze.

Cherries. Freeze sour cooking cherries dry or in a syrup. Sweet red cherries in syrup are also very good, much better than most canned cherries.

Citrus fruit. Blanch the whole fruit for 2 minutes in plenty of boiling water. Plunge in cold water, peel, divide in segments removing all pith and pips. Remove coarse membranes. Pack segments in layers with sugar sprinkled between layers.

Figs. These should be fully ripe and with a tender skin. Leave whole, halve or slice and freeze without sugar.

Gooseberries. Both ripe and green gooseberries are suitable. Wash, drain, top and tail and pack plain or with sugar.

Grapes. Freeze seedless ones whole, cut others to remove seeds. Freeze plain or in a syrup.

Melon. Yellow or orange kinds are the best. Prepare portions as for serving, wrap in cellophane and put portions together in a bag or box. Alternatively, peel and dice and freeze in a syrup. Water melon makes a good ice or sorbet.

Peaches. Skin and cut in halves or slices, putting immediately into cold syrup.

Pears. Use only those of good flavour. Freeze raw sliced in a syrup, or stewed.

Pineapple. Best frozen as part of a fruit salad.

Plums, greengages and damsons. Wash, grade for size and remove any damaged ones. Freeze whole or stoned, plain or with sugar or syrup.

Rhubarb. It is best to use young, tender stalks. Wash, trim, cut in convenient lengths and freeze plain.

Strawberries. They may be frozen whole, uncovered on a tray, then packed in bags. For best flavour, halve or slice and sprinkle with sugar, then freeze.

ALPHABETICAL LIST OF FRUITS WITH NOTES ON SEASONS, BUYING AND USING

Apples

Imported all the year. Home-grown start in July and continue from store until April. Many dessert varieties are also suitable for cooking and sometimes much cheaper than the better known cooking varieties. Good apples are firm; soft or wrinkled ones are not worth buying. Apples which are sold very cheaply are often bad inside, though at the height of the season very small sound apples may also be cheap. For ways of using, see the index.

Apricots

Mostly imported. Fresh apricots are not worth buying unless fully ripe (deep orange colour); canned or dried apricots are often the better choice.

Use as dessert fruit, stewed fresh or dried; flans and pies; canned or fresh in fruit salads; to make purées for cold sweets and ices.

Bananas

Imported all the year; care needed when buying in very cold weather, khaki-coloured skins show they have been exposed to cold and will be useless. For immediate use buy fully ripe, with small black-brown flecks on the skin. For later use buy them all yellow or with the ends still green and keep them in a cool place but not the refrigerator.

Uses: for dessert, fruit salads, baked, fried, as a purée for cold sweets and ices.

Bilberries (blueberries or whortleberries)

In season from June to November, also available frozen. Fresh ones will keep 2–3 days in a covered container in the refrigerator. They have a sharp flavour, needing much sugar to sweeten them.

Uses: as for any other berry, stewed, tarts and flans, purée for cold sweets and ices.

Blackberries

In season from July to October, also available frozen (very good) or canned. Wash fresh ones if necessary, pick over and remove damaged or mouldy ones and remove any stems. Will keep 2–3 days in a covered container in the refrigerator (if unwashed).

Uses: fresh ripe in fruit salads, stewed alone or with apple, flans, with apple for pies, purée for cold sweets and ices.

Cherries

In season from June to August. Morello best kind for cooking. Both sweet and morello available canned, imported usually the best quality. For dessert, wash and leave stalks on, pick over, removing any bad ones.

Uses for dessert cherries: fruit salads and flans.

Uses for cooking cherries: flans, pies, stewed and as a purée for making cold sweets and ices.

Fruits and Fruit Desserts 355

Chinese Gooseberries (kiwiberries or fruit)

Imported from September to February. To prepare, peel off the rough brown skin.
   Use as a dessert fruit, in fruit salads, for fruit flans.

Clementines

Imported from November to mid-January. Prepare and use in the same way as oranges.

Cranberries

In season from September to February, also frozen or canned as cranberry sauce. Wash and discard any bad ones, remove stalks. Will keep 2–3 days in a covered container in the refrigerator (if unwashed).
   Use, for cranberry sauce, and as other berries in cooking. Very tart and much sugar required. See also cranberry upside-down pudding, page 409.

Currants (black, red and white)

In season from June to August, also available frozen and canned or as syrup. To prepare, strip them from the stalks, using a fork, and discarding any mouldy or shrivelled fruit. If they need washing do this before stripping from the stalks. They will keep 2–3 days, on the stalks, spread out in a shallow dish in a cool place; cover if in the refrigerator.
   Use black ones cooked, stewed, in tarts, for crumbles, purée to make cold sweets and ices; red or white as black but also raw as dessert or in fruit salads.

Damsons

In season from August to October, also canned and may be frozen.
   Use as plums, but they need more sugar.

Figs

Fresh ones imported from June to December, also canned and dried. Keep fresh ones in a cool place once they have become fully ripe.
   Use fresh figs for dessert, in fruit salads, for flans; canned as stewed fruit or in fruit salads, purée for cold sweets; dried, use stewed or as dried fruit in cakes and puddings.

Gooseberries

In season from May to July, also frozen and canned. To keep fresh gooseberries, wash, top and tail and store in polythene bag or box in the refrigerator.

Use ripe gooseberries for dessert or fruit salad; green or ripe for stewed fruit, flans, tarts and pies, purée for cold sweets and ices. Frozen, use as fresh; canned, best drained and use for a purée, though they can be used in pies and tarts.

Granadillas (passion fruit)

Imported throughout the year but mainly in the winter; the pulp is available canned or bottled. To use, cut in half and scoop out the pulp. Do not discard the seeds as these contribute to the flavour.

Use for dessert, in fruit salads, to make fruit fools and whips, as a sauce for ices and cold sweets, to flavour whipped cream.

Grapefruit

Imported all the year; best choice in winter and very early spring. Use as oranges.

Grapes

Imported all the year; English hothouse available in June and July. Wash thoroughly and discard any damaged fruit. Unless very ripe will keep 2–3 days at room temperature, longer, covered in the refrigerator. Also available canned but rather tasteless.

Use as dessert, in fruit salads, for flans alone or with other fruit, to garnish cold sweets.

Greengages

In season in August. Best eaten fully ripe for dessert but can be stewed and used in the same way as plums.

Kumquats

Occasionally imported. Usually eaten raw as dessert or in fruit salad.

Lemons

Imported all the year; at their best in the summer. To keep fresh for more than a few days, put them in a polythene bag in the refrigerator. Grated rind and juice used for flavouring many puddings and sweets. Scrub the skins before grating and grate only the yellow part. Lemons with smooth thin skins are more juicy than those with rough, thick skins.

Lichees

Fresh ones imported from January to September, canned also available.
 To prepare, remove the outer brown skin and the stones.
 Use for dessert or fruit salad, cooked or canned for a purée to make creams and whips.

Limes

Imported from March to July, usually scarce and expensive. The juice is used in the same way as lemon juice.

Loganberries

In season from June to August; available canned and also frozen. Unless very ripe the fruit can be stored for 2–3 days in a covered box in the refrigerator. Best flavour when fully ripe and usually too tart for use raw. To prepare, wash if necessary, remove the hulls and watch for grubs.
 Use fully ripe in fruit salads, stewed, for flans and tarts, in place of other berries in any recipe, purée for cold sweets and ices.

Mandarins

Some available most of the year; plentiful from December to February, also as canned. Use in the same way as oranges.

Mangoes

Imported from January to July and in September; also canned. Fresh fruit peeled and served as dessert or in fruit salad, good served sliced and dressed with lemon juice; cooked or canned purée for cold sweets and ices.

Medlars

In season from October to December. Eaten when so ripe they are almost rotten, otherwise are tasteless. Usually served as dessert.

Melons

One kind or another imported all the year; least good in the winter. Store at room temperature. If cut, cover closely and store in the refrigerator, but not for more than 2–3 days.

Use only when fully ripe otherwise they lack flavour. To test for ripeness press at the ends and they should give to gentle pressure.

Use for dessert, in fruit salads, purée to make ices. Also available canned, suitable for fruit salads. For dessert, cut in pieces and remove the seeds and pulp but leave the skin on; for fruit salad remove the skin as well and dice or slice the flesh.

Mulberries

In season in August and September, but rather scarce. Used fully ripe. Remove hulls and watch for grubs. Wash if necessary.

Use for dessert (best way) or in fruit salads. Cooked, they can be used as other berries.

Nectarines

Imported most of the year, except October and November. Always expensive and seldom worth buying as this fruit needs to ripen on the tree.

Use in the same way as peaches, except that it is usually unnecessary to remove the skins.

Oranges

Imported all the year, though late summer is usually not a very good time for top quality oranges. At room temperature they will keep several days though in a dry atmosphere the skins may become hard and dry. They can be stored for two weeks in a polythene bag in the refrigerator.

Good quality fruit should have skins which look taut and firm. Smooth skins usually mean more juicy fruit; rough skins are usually thick though the fruit may be very juicy, but you pay for the greater amount of skin.

When using oranges in fruit salads remove as much of the white pith as possible. Then with a small sharp knife cut along the segments to remove the pulp from the membrane; or divide into segments and peel off the membrane from each one. Uses are many, see the index.

Peaches

Some are imported most of the year except in October and November. Ripe peaches can be kept for 3–7 days in a polythene bag or box in the refrigerator. Fully ripe peaches need to be eaten at once. Really under-ripe ones will never ripen off the tree and are a bad buy. Canned peaches are available as peach halves or sliced peaches and are generally of good quality. Whole white peaches are also sold in cans or preserved in a syrup with brandy; also sold dried.

To skin a peach put in a bowl and pour boiling water over to cover, leave a couple of minutes, then plunge in cold water and the skins should come off easily. To stone a peach, cut the flesh right round in half and twist the halves in opposite directions. Raw peaches discolour when sliced or skinned so dress them with a little lemon juice which helps to prevent this.

Use fresh peaches for dessert, as a fruit salad on their own or with other fresh fruit, for peach Melba, pies and flans.

Pears

Home-grown are in season from August to February, imported throughout the year, canned and dried also plentiful. Avoid buying fully ripe pears as they are inclined to be over-ripe in the centre and anyway need to be used at once. It is much better to buy firm ones and keep them at room temperature for a few days until they are ready to eat. Hard, green pears will never ripen off the tree so avoid them. To prevent pears from discolouring when peeled, put them in lightly salted water to cover.

Use, as dessert, in fruit salad, stewed, for flans; canned pears, use as fresh cooked pears; dried pears, stewed alone or mixed with other dried fruits.

Pineapples

Imported throughout the year; large ones October to December. The very small ones are not a good buy as there is so much wastage in relation to the flesh. Moderate-sized ones are often a reasonable price and a better choice. The skin of a ripe pineapple is brown; avoid those with a large amount of green skin or with soft dark patches of over-ripe areas. Store whole pineapple in a cool place; cut pineapple in a polythene bag or box will keep in the refrigerator for 3–6 days. The usual method of preparing is to cut the pineapple in rings and then cut off the skin and remove the central core if it is woody. Canned pineapple is available as slices or rings, in chunks and as pulp; also crystallized.

Use fresh pineapple as dessert cut in slices with sugar and kirsch, in fruit salads, as a purée for cold sweets and ices; also see the index.

Plums

Home-grown available from June to September, imported ones most of the year. Fully ripe ones need to be used at once, otherwise they will keep in a cool place, 1–3 days in a larder, 3–7 days in a box or polythene bag in the refrigerator.

Use ripe plums for dessert or fruit salad; under-ripe stewed, in flans and pies, as purée for cold sweets. Canned plums, use as stewed fresh.

Pomegranates

Imported in April and again from September to December. To use, cut in half and scoop out the pulp. Usually served as a dessert fruit.

Quinces

In season in late autumn but rather scarce. They are always used cooked, stewed alone or with apples, also with apples in pies. When stewed to a thick jam-like pulp the mixture will set firmly when spread in a shallow dish; cut in pieces and serve with cream or milk or as a sweetmeat.

Raspberries

In season from July to October; frozen are very good to use like the fresh. Canned are suitable for many cold sweets, especially for a purée. Pick over fresh fruit carefully, removing stalks and hulls and watching for grubs. Wash only if necessary. Unwashed fruit will keep for a day in a cold larder, 2–3 days in a covered container in the refrigerator, but keeping time depends very much on the condition. Tip them out of the container in which they were sold and spread them out on a shallow dish or in a polythene box. Raspberries picked while still pink will ripen in the refrigerator. Very ripe fruit should be used at once or made into a purée and refrigerated or frozen.

Use fresh raw fruit or thawed frozen by itself with sugar and cream or in a fruit salad, for flans and purées for cold sweets and ices.

Rhubarb

In season from December to July; canned also available. Good for home freezing in pieces or sticks. Leaves must be removed and the root ends trimmed, then wash and drain. Rhubarb will keep for several days in a covered container or bag in the refrigerator.

Use stewed, for flans and pies, or a purée for cold sweets; also see the index.

Satsumas

In season from October to November. Use in the same way as oranges.

Strawberries

Home-grown from June to August, imported from January to July. Firm, ripe fruit is the best to buy; squashy over-ripe fruit will go mouldy if not used up straight away, either for mashing with whipped cream or for making a fresh purée. Good quality strawberries will keep for 1-2 days in a covered container in the refrigerator. Frozen strawberries can be used as fresh; canned strawberries are suitable for making a purée.

Use, as dessert fruit, with sugar and cream, in fruit salad, for flans, purée for cold sweets and ices.

To prepare strawberries, wash, drain and remove the hulls.

Tangerines

Some are available most of the year, plentiful from December to February. Use in the same way as oranges.

RECIPES USING FRUIT AS THE MAIN INGREDIENT

Fruit casserole or oven-stewed fruit

Temperature 160–180° C (325–350° F; G3–4).

Prepare the fruit according to the variety, cutting large fruit in slices or pieces and leaving small ones whole. Put it in a casserole or any oven dish with a lid. Add 2–4 oz (50–100 g) of sugar or honey for each pound (500 g) of fruit, and just enough water to moisten the bottom of the dish. For juicy fruits like berries and rhubarb no water will be needed, hard fruits will need ½ pt (300 ml) per pound (½ kg) of fruit. Cover the dish with a lid and cook until the fruit is tender, anything from ½ hr upwards depending on the variety, size and age of the fruit.

Fruit compote or stewed fruit

Cooking time: berries and other soft fruit 15–20 mins; quartered apples and plums 20–30 mins; cooking pears ½–1 hr or 2–3 hr for very hard fruit; quinces 1½–2 hrs.
Quantities for 4.

1 lb fruit (500 g)	4 oz sugar (100 g) more or less, as desired
½ pt water (300 ml)	

Prepare the fruit according to the variety, cutting large fruit in pieces or slicing it. Heat the sugar and water in a pan, stirring until the sugar dissolves. Bring to the boil and add the fruit. Reduce the heat to keep the liquid just below boiling. Cook until the fruit is tender. Do not allow the liquid to boil or the fruit will become a mush instead of keeping its shape. With stone fruits allow the skins to break so that the syrup will have a chance to penetrate. When the fruit is just tender, lift it from the syrup and put it in a serving dish. Boil the syrup hard until it begins to thicken a little, pour over the fruit and leave until cold.

For variety, add a little liqueur to the cold fruit or use some cider or red wine for the cooking liquid. Alternatively, add a little grated orange or lemon rind to the fruit during cooking, or a little ground spice (cinnamon, cloves, nutmeg or ginger).

custard sauce or cream   crisp biscuits

Serve with the fruit; the biscuits give a contrast of texture.

Dried fruit

Use one kind or a mixture to make a dried fruit salad. Some nuts may be added too. The quickest way to cook dried fruit is in a pressure cooker.

Cooking time: without pressure, ½–1 hr; with pressure, apples, apricots, peaches and pears 5–6 mins, prunes 6–8 mins, figs 10–15 mins.
Quantities: allow about 2 oz (50 g) dried weight per portion. It doubles in weight during cooking.

Soaking the fruit in the cooking water is not essential but it does shorten the cooking time. Soak in cold or boiling water to cover for 1–2 hrs or overnight.

For pressure cooking use 1 pt (600 ml) boiling water per ½ lb (250 g) and soak for 10 mins.

Cook the fruit in the soaking water. Lemon or orange rind or some cider or spices may be added for extra flavour. When the fruit is tender, add sugar to taste. Serve hot or cold or use in any recipe requiring cooked fruit.

Fruit kebabs

Cooking time 15–20 mins. *Quantities* for 4.

Almost any fresh, dried or canned fruit is suitable provided it is firm enough to stay on the kebab skewers during cooking. The following are two good kebabs:

NO. 1

2 firm bananas	2 or more dessert apples
2 medium-sized oranges	

NO. 2

4 oz dried apricots (100 g)	1 or 2 oranges
4 oz plump prunes (100 g)	4 oz canned pineapple chunks (100 g)

The fruit is peeled, cored and prepared as for eating raw, then cut into pieces of approximately equal size so that they will cook evenly. Cut bananas in 1 in (2½ cm) pieces, oranges in pieces about ½ in (1 cm) thick, apples in quarters or less if large. Soak dried apricots for an hour and also prunes if they are not the plump and juicy kind.

Thread the fruit on the kebab skewers alternating the different kinds.

2 Tbs honey   4 Tbs orange or lemon juice

Mix together until the honey dissolves and use the mixture to brush the fruit before cooking and during grilling. Serve the fruit on the skewers on a hot serving dish. Avoid over-cooking, or the fruit will look a mess; it really only needs to be heated all through and should still be a bit firm. Serve plain with single or whipped cream.

VARIATION

For a special occasion, flambé the kebabs at table. They can be cooked in advance and kept hot in a warming cupboard while the other courses are being served.

4 Tbs or more warm rum or liqueur (60 ml)

The kebabs must be on a hot fireproof dish such as stainless steel. Ignite the spirit and pour it over the kebabs, baste with the flaming liquid. As they are served, use a fork to slide the fruit gently off the skewers on to hot plates, pouring over them any juice left in the serving dish.

Fruit purée

Purées can be made from raw, fresh or frozen fruit; cooked fresh, frozen or dried fruit, and canned fruit. For good flavour the purée should always be a thick one so discard any liquid not needed for purposes of moistening the fruit during sieving or blending. Berry fruits with small seeds are generally more satisfactory sieved, though they can be blended and then strained. When using an electric blender to make the purée, process for the minimum time needed as long processing introduces a lot of air. If this happens let the purée stand for a while for the frothiness to subside.

When home-grown fruits are in season it is useful to make purées to store in the freezer, or to be bottled. This is a better way to freeze than making the fruit into ice-creams or other cold sweets straight away, as their freezer life is generally shorter than that of the fruit purée alone.

Best fruits for purées are the well-flavoured ones like berries of all kinds, currants (black and red), apricots (if really ripe, otherwise use canned or dried), gooseberries, rhubarb, and well-flavoured plums, or damsons. Other fruits which make good purées are bananas, melon, pineapple and papaw.

Fruit salad

Prepare 3–4 hrs in advance to allow flavours to mingle.

Quantities for 4.

½ pt water, or half cider and half water (250 ml)   2–4 oz sugar or honey (50–100 g)

Bring to the boil, stirring to dissolve the sugar. Honey will dissolve without heating. Cool the syrup before using it.

1 lb fresh fruit (500 g)

Prepare the fruit and slice or cut in small pieces. Leave small fruit whole but stone cherries and remove the hulls from berries. Add to the syrup. It is a good idea to drop the fruit straight into the syrup as it is prepared. This will help to preserve the colour of fruits like apples, peaches, pears and bananas.

kirsch or other liqueur (optional)   flaked almonds (optional)

Add 1–2 Tbs liqueur for additional flavour and the almonds for texture contrast.

CANNED FRUIT

Some mixed with fresh fruit makes a good salad. Use the syrup in the can instead of making the syrup.

FROZEN FRUIT

It is best to use just some, for example a few berries. Add these frozen to the rest of the salad and they will be thawed by the time you are ready to serve it.

DRIED FRUIT

Cooked dried fruit can be used with fresh fruit for variety; dates and figs can be chopped and mixed with fresh fruit.

TRY THESE MIXTURES

Apples with chopped dates and nuts. Use a honey syrup and add some lemon juice.
Bananas, canned grapefruit and orange juice with syrup to cover the fruit.
Grapes and tangerines, fresh or canned.
Grapefruit, chopped dates and nuts with a honey syrup.
Fresh grapefruit, cooked stoned prunes, orange juice and syrup to cover.
Greengages just by themselves in a syrup; use really ripe raw fruit.
Melon and ripe plums with honey syrup and orange juice.
Oranges and apples with a honey syrup.
Oranges, bananas, canned or stewed gooseberries and chopped dates.
Sliced peaches in a sugar syrup with liqueur.
Pears in a honey syrup with chopped preserved ginger.
Pineapple, grapefruit and chopped ginger with maraschino cherries.
Summer fruit salad of cherries, raspberries and red currants in a sugar syrup.

Apple and orange with caramel

If this is made some time in advance of serving, the caramel will melt and form a sauce so if you want the caramel to remain in crunchy pieces, add it just before serving.

Quantities for 4.

1 lb apples (500 g)

Peel, core and quarter and place in cold water to keep them a good colour.

¼ pt water (150 ml)   2 oz sugar (4 Tbs or 50 g)

Bring to the boil, stirring to dissolve the sugar. Add the apple, turning the pieces over in the syrup. Cover the pan and poach very gently until just tender, turning the apple over occasionally. Remove from the heat; leave to cool in the covered pan.

2 oz caster sugar (4 Tbs or 50 g)

Put in a small thick pan and heat, without stirring, to melt the sugar. Continue cooking until it forms a brown caramel. Pour this into a small oiled tin, about 6 in (15 cm) diameter. Leave to set and become cold, then break it up into small pieces.

1 large or 2 small oranges

Peel the rind from a small orange or half a large one and cut the rind into fine shreds. Boil these in water for 3 mins. Cut the flesh of the oranges in small pieces. Add the rind and the flesh to the apples and sprinkle with the pieces of caramel.

Apples, baked

Cooking time 40–45 mins.
Temperature 200° C (400° F; G6).
Quantities 1 large apple per portion.

water or cider to come ¼ in (6 mm) up the sides of the apples	large and perfect cooking apples
dates, raisins, nuts, chopped peel, mincemeat, and spices as optional flavourings for the stuffing	1 Tbs sugar, honey, syrup or black treacle per apple
	butter or margarine

Wash the apples and remove the cores with an apple corer. Though they may be peeled they are best cooked with the skins on, but slit the skin in a circle about half-way down the sides of the apples. This prevents the skins from bursting during cooking. Place the apples in a shallow baking dish or individual dishes and fill the centres with sweetening and fruit or spices as desired. Put a knob of butter or margarine on top of each. Pour in the liquid and bake until they feel tender when pierced with a cooking fork or skewer. Baste occasionally during cooking.

Serve hot or cold with

cream or custard.

Baked apples with rum (Jamaican apples)

Stuff the apples with apricot jam and sprinkle chopped almonds on top. Use brown sugar for the sweetening and for the liquid half rum and half water. Baste with the liquid during cooking and serve hot with cream.

Apples flambé

Cooking time about 30 mins. *Quantities* for 4.

4 oz sugar (½ c or 100 g)   ½ pt water (250 ml)

Heat in a saucepan large enough to take four apples in one layer, stir until the sugar dissolves and bring the syrup to the boil.

4 medium-sized apples   vanilla essence

Peel and core the apples, using an apple corer. Add vanilla to the syrup to taste and poach the apples in this, turning them frequently until they are tender but not broken. Lift them on to a hot metal serving dish or individual dishes of heat resistant material. Keep them hot. Boil the syrup rapidly to reduce and thicken it. Pour over the apples to give them a glaze, but there must not be a lot of syrup or it will douse the flame when the rum is ignited. Put the apples to keep hot until ready to serve them.

4 Tbs warm rum (60 ml)

Ignite, pour over the apples and serve while they are still flaming; specially attractive when served in individual dishes.

whipped, Chantilly or single cream

Hand the cream separately.

Apricot purée with almonds

Quantities for 4–6.

8 oz dried apricots (250 g)

Apricots can be cooked without prior soaking if you have not allowed time for this. Cover them with cold water, bring to the boil and boil gently, with the lid off the pan, until they are very tender, about 30 mins. Add more water if needed to prevent the fruit from boiling dry, but you do not want a lot of excess liquid.

4 oz sugar (100 g)

Add to the apricots, stir to dissolve it and continue cooking for 5 mins. Either rub the fruit through a sieve or cool it a little and then pulp it in the electric blender, in one or more lots according to the capacity of the machine.

2 Tbs blanched almonds

Chop coarsely or blend with the apricot to chop them. When the purée is cold, cover and store in the refrigerator until it is well chilled. Serve in small glasses with

whipped cream (with an optional flavouring of liqueur).

Baked bananas

Cooking time 20 mins.
Temperature 190° C (375° F; G5).
Quantities Allow 1 banana per portion.

Skin the bananas and put them in a shallow baking dish. Sprinkle with sugar and lemon juice and dot with butter. Bake, basting with the liquid occasionally, until the bananas are speckled with brown. Serve hot or cold with cream.

ALTERNATIVE

1. Use orange juice or other fruit juice in place of the lemon and a little grated orange rind as well.
2. Sprinkle the cooked bananas with coconut.

Baked bananas with prunes

Cooking time 20 mins.
Temperature 190° C (375° F; G5).
Quantities for 4–6.

4 bananas	4 Tbs lemon juice
2 tsp grated lemon rind	

Skin the bananas and cut them in four lengthwise. Put them in a shallow fireproof dish and sprinkle with the lemon rind and juice.

1 lb canned or cooked red plums or prunes (500 g)

Drain and stone the plums or prunes and put them on top of the bananas. Pour in enough of the juice barely to cover the fruit. Bake. Serve warm or chilled, with or without cream.

Fried bananas flambé

Cooking time a few mins. *Quantities* for 4.

2 oz butter (50 g)	4 large or 8 small bananas
4 Tbs rum, brandy or other spirit (60 ml)	granulated sugar

Peel the bananas just before you are ready to start cooking. Leave small ones whole, cut large ones in half lengthwise. Heat the butter in a frying pan and cook the bananas for a few minutes, turning them once. Pour the spirit over them, ignite it and sprinkle them with sugar. Baste with the liquid and serve with

lemon wedges for those who like sharpness; cream for the others.

Berries

All really ripe berries are served in the same way, the best being blackberries, red currants, raspberries and cultivated or wild strawberries. Loganberries and similar modern hybrids are good if really ripe but their full flavour emerges better after light cooking. If frozen berries are used, serve them still well chilled and firm.

Serve the prepared berries in a bowl, with a bowl or shaker of caster or icing sugar and cream (whipped or pouring), or yogurt, handed separately.

My favourite method is to give the berries a good sprinkling of caster sugar, cover and refrigerate for an hour or more before serving, or overnight if that is more convenient. The sugar dissolves and helps to bring out the flavour. Serve them with cream, ice-cream or yogurt and more sugar for those who like them sweet.

Variations on this method are to add a little kirsch as well as the sugar (2–4 Tbs to 1 lb or 500 g of berries); or use orange juice or red wine.

A very good accompaniment for strawberries or other berries is to use a mixture of half sieved curd cheese and half cream. Whip the cream and then beat in the cheese, adding a pinch of salt.

Melon en surprise

Quantities for 4.

Prepare at least 2 hrs in advance and refrigerate.

1 medium-sized ripe melon

If the melon is a round one, cut a slice off the stem end, if oval, cut a slice off one side. Scoop out the seeds and discard. Scoop out the flesh in large pieces, being careful not to pierce the skin and leaving enough flesh to keep the melon in shape. If necessary, cut a small piece of skin off the underside to make the melon sit flat on a serving dish. Cut the melon flesh in small pieces and put in a bowl.

¼ pt sweetened strawberry purée (150 ml)

Use fresh or thawed strawberries for preference, though canned ones will do. Mix the purée with the melon.

raw fresh fruit in season

Use any fruits available, preparing them as for a fruit salad and cutting them in small pieces. Add to the melon and strawberry mixture until you have enough to fill the melon shell. Fill, put back the lid, wrap the melon in foil and refrigerate it for not less than 2 hrs. Serve from the shell while the fruit is still well chilled.

Orange compote

Quantities for 4.

3 large or 4 medium-sized oranges

Scrub the oranges and grate the rind finely. Put it in a small saucepan. Remove all the white pith from the oranges. Slice them thinly, removing pips. Arrange in overlapping rows in a heat-resistant serving dish.

4 oz sugar (½ c or 100 g)   ¼ pt water (150 ml)

Add to the grated rind, heat to dissolve the sugar and boil rapidly for a few minutes. Pour over the oranges.

1 Tbs orange-flavoured liqueur

Sprinkle over the oranges, cover and leave to become cold, then refrigerate until just before serving, or serve at room temperature if preferred.

Orange and rhubarb compote

Cooking time ¾–1 hr.
Temperature 180° C (350° F; G4).
Quantities for 4–6.

1 lb rhubarb (500 g)   3 oz sugar (6 Tbs or 75 g), or to
2 oranges   taste

Trim and wash the rhubarb and cut it in 1 in (2½ cm) pieces. Peel the oranges, cut them in slices and remove the pips. Put the fruit and sugar in layers in a casserole. Cover and cook until the rhubarb is tender. Allow to become cold.

Caramel oranges

Quantities for 4.
Prepare 6–8 hrs in advance and refrigerate.

4 large oranges   caster sugar
brandy or liqueur (optional)

Peel the oranges, removing all pith. Cut the flesh in slices and remove the pips. Put the slices in overlapping rows in a shallow heat-resistant dish. Sprinkle with a little sugar and the alcohol.

4 oz granulated sugar (½ c or 100 g)   4 Tbs water (60 ml)

Heat these in a small pan, stirring until the sugar dissolves, then boil rapidly, without stirring, until it turns a deep amber colour. Pour it over the oranges and leave them in a cold place for several hours or overnight. The caramel will melt and make a sauce for the oranges.

whipped cream   chopped nuts

Use these to decorate the oranges.

Peaches with white wine or cider

Cooking time 10 mins. *Quantities* for 6.

2 oz sugar (4 Tbs or 50 g)   ½ pt Sauternes or cider (250 ml)
¼ pt water (150 ml)

Combine these in a large shallow pan, stirring until the sugar dissolves.

6 medium-ripe yellow peaches

Skin the peaches carefully. If this is difficult, immerse them in boiling water for a minute to loosen the skins. Cut them in half and remove the stones. Place them in the hot syrup as they are prepared. Cover the pan and cook over a low heat until the fruit is just tender. Leave to become cold and then chill in the refrigerator before serving. Be sure they are covered by the syrup or they may discolour.

3 Tbs rum or maraschino

Pour over the peaches just before serving them.

Stuffed peaches with almonds

Cooking time 15-20 mins.
Temperature 190° C (375° F; G5).
Quantities for 4.

1 oz toasted almonds (25 g) finely chopped or minced	½ Tbs chopped peel 1 oz caster sugar (2 Tbs or 25 g)

Mix these together.

4 large raw yellow peaches

Remove the skins. If this is difficult, immerse them first in hot water for a minute. Cut them in half and remove the stones. Put them in a shallow baking dish, hollow side up, and put the almond mixture on the top.

¼ pt white wine (150 ml)

Sprinkle the wine over the peaches and bake until they are just tender. Serve warm.

Pears amandine

Quantities for 4.

4 oz sugar (½ c or 100 g)   ½ pt water (250 ml)

Boil together for 3-4 mins.

4 pears   vanilla essence

Peel, halve and core the pears, putting them into the syrup which has been flavoured with vanilla to taste. Cook gently for about 30 mins or until just tender, turning them over frequently. Put the pears in a heat-resistant serving dish, round side up.

toasted almonds

Cut in slivers and stick all over the pears. Boil the syrup to reduce it by half.

8 oz frozen or fresh strawberries (250 g)

Add to the syrup (no need to thaw frozen ones), and cook the fruit to a pulp. Rub through a sieve. Spoon this over the pears and leave them to become cold. Then cover and chill in the refrigerator. Serve with

whipped cream.

Fruits and Fruit Desserts 373

Caramel pears

Cooking time about ½ hr. *Quantities* for 4.

2 oz sugar (4 Tbs or 50 g)   ½ pt boiling water (250 ml)

Heat the sugar gently in a small thick pan until it turns brown. Remove from the heat, let the pan cool a little, and add the boiling water. Stir until the sugar dissolves. Transfer the mixture to a pan large enough to hold the pears.

4 pears

Peel, halve and core them and poach them in the caramel syrup. When they are tender lift them out into a serving dish.

2 tsp cornflour   1 Tbs milk

Blend these to a smooth paste and add to the syrup, stirring until it thickens. Cook for a minute or two.

2–3 Tbs cream

Add to the sauce, pour it over the pears and serve them either warm or cold.

Pear cream

Cooking time about 15 mins. *Quantities* for 4.

4 firm, but not hard, pears

Peel, core and cut in large dice.

2 oz brown sugar (4 Tbs or 50 g)   4 Tbs unsweetened orange or
2 Tbs granulated sugar   pineapple juice

Put in a frying or sauté pan with the diced pears and heat, slowly, stirring to dissolve the sugar. Cover the pan and boil gently until the pears are tender. Then turn up the heat and boil more rapidly until the mixture is syrupy, stirring occasionally until the pears look glazed and almost all the liquid has gone. Remove from the pan, cool and then chill in the refrigerator.

¼ pt whipping cream (150 ml)

Whip the cream and combine it with the pear mixture just before serving. Serve in small glasses.

Honey pear compote

Cooking time $\frac{1}{2}$–$\frac{3}{4}$ hr, depending on the ripeness of the pears.
Quantities for 4.

4 oz honey (4 Tbs or 100 g) $\frac{1}{4}$ pt water (150 ml)
1 piece of preserved ginger, chopped

Put in a pan and begin to heat while the pears are being prepared.

4 firm dessert pears

Peel, halve and core and put immediately in the syrup. When they are all in, turn up the heat until the syrup boils, boil gently with the lid on the pan until the pears are just tender. If the syrup does not cover them turn them frequently during cooking to prevent discolouring. Lift them out into a serving dish and cover with the syrup. Allow to become cold, cover and chill in the refrigerator.

single cream (optional)

Hand the cream separately.

Pineapple flambé

Cooking time about 10 mins. Quantities for 4–6.

8–12 small slices of fresh or canned pineapple   about 2 Tbs kirsch

Drain the canned pineapple thoroughly, or peel fresh pineapple. Put the fruit on a large flat dish and pour a little kirsch over each slice.

1 oz butter (25 g)   2 oz caster sugar (4 Tbs or 50 g)

Heat the butter in a frying pan, add the sugar and cook gently without stirring until it turns a pale caramel colour. Add the pineapple and cook to heat it, turning or basting with the sauce.

2 Tbs orange juice (or lemon juice for a sharper flavour)   about 3 Tbs rum, brandy or liqueur

Add the spirit to the pan and set it alight. When it has burned out, add the orange juice and serve the fruit with a little of the sauce poured over it.

Prunes with walnuts

Quantities for 4.

8 oz large prunes (250 g)   hot tea, about $\frac{1}{2}$ pt (300 ml)

Put the prunes in a basin and cover them with hot, strained tea. Soak for several hours or until they are soft enough for the stones to be removed. Avoid overnight soaking as this tends to make them too soft; ½ hr is sufficient for juicy prunes. Drain them and remove the stones.

quarters of shelled walnuts

Put a piece of nut in place of each stone and close the prune round it. Put the prunes in a large pan, in a single layer.

1 Tbs sugar 2 Tbs lemon juice
¼ pt of the soaking liquid (150 ml)

Sprinkle sugar and lemon over the prunes, add the liquid, bring to the boil, cover and simmer very gently for 30 mins, adding more liquid if needed; but there should not be a lot of juice. Lift the prunes carefully into a serving dish, cool, and then chill them in the refrigerator.

¼ pt whipping cream (150 ml)

Whip until stiff and then keep refrigerated until required. Serve the prunes in individual dishes with cream on top.

Baked spiced rhubarb

Cooking time 30–45 mins.
Temperature 200° C (400° F; G6).
Quantities for 4–6.

2 lb rhubarb (1 kg)

Prepare the rhubarb by cutting off the leaves and trimming the root end. Wash well and cut it in 1 in (2½ cm) pieces. Put in a casserole.

6–8 oz sugar (¾–1 c or 175–250 g) 1 stick of cinnamon, or some ground
4 cloves cinnamon

Sprinkle the sugar and flavourings over the rhubarb. Cover and bake until it is tender but not mushy. Cool with the lid on. Serve cold, removing the stick of cinnamon before serving.

Baked rhubarb with herbs

Use the recipe above but instead of the cloves and cinnamon use 12 small sprigs of lemon balm which are cooked with the rhubarb and then removed before serving.

Alternatively, flavour the rhubarb with a handful of sweet cicely leaves, scissor-chopped and cooked with the fruit.

Angelica also goes well with rhubarb; add ½ oz (15 g or 4 Tbs) of chopped stalks, before cooking.

These herb-flavoured mixtures are very good for making a purée for rhubarb fools and other cold sweets.

Strawberries Romanoff

Quantities for 4. Prepare ½–1 hr in advance.

¾–1 lb strawberries (350–500 g), fresh or frozen	½ pt orange juice (250 ml)
1 Tbs or more of caster sugar	1 Tbs orange-flavoured liqueur or kirsch

Prepare the berries, put them in a dish and sprinkle with sugar. Add the orange juice and liqueur and leave to marinate for not less than ½ hr or until barely thawed if frozen.

To serve, pipe on top, rosettes of

Chantilly cream.

15. Puddings and Sweets

COLD SWEETS AND DESSERTS

Most of these can be made a day in advance, or weeks in advance if you have a freezer. There are only a few types of cold sweets which are not as good when frozen. Custards and milk puddings tend to separate and jellies to weep and become cloudy, but sweets with only a small amount of gelatine, such as mousses, are satisfactory. A lot depends on how long you want to keep them in the freezer. If it is only for a week or so most are satisfactory, and many more keep well for a month.

In the refrigerator, cold sweets can be kept for 24–36 hrs. It is not wise to store any containing eggs, milk, cream or gelatine for longer than this.

Be careful to remove frozen sweets from the freezer in good time to thaw them to a pleasant consistency for eating. To thaw them slowly overnight in the refrigerator is best; or do it faster at room temperature and then put them in the refrigerator until they are to be served.

Useful ingredients for cold sweets can be stored in the freezer, particularly fruit, fruit purées and egg whites and yolks left from some other recipe.

Polythene tubs or boxes are the most convenient containers for freezing sweets, though foil cups and bowls with a lid are useful, and individual metal pudding moulds or larger metal jelly moulds with double foil for a lid are very useful and versatile.

Banana mould with strawberry sauce

Quantities for 4.

- 1 Tbs gelatine dissolved in 4 Tbs hot water
- ½ pt single cream (250 ml)
- 8 oz ripe bananas (250 g)
- 1 oz sugar (2 Tbs or 25 g)
- 1 Tbs lemon juice

Either rub the bananas through a sieve and mix them with the other ingredients or put the bananas, cut in pieces, with all the other ingredients in an electric blender and blend smooth. Pour into four small moulds or a single 1 pt (600 ml) mould. Leave to set, cover and store in the refrigerator.

| 8 oz fresh or partially thawed strawberries (250 g) | sugar to taste |

Either rub the berries through a sieve or blend them to a pulp. Sweeten to taste. Unmould the banana mixture and pour the sauce over it.

Bavarois

Quantities for 6–8.

Use a 1½ pt (850 ml) mould, or individual moulds.

| 4 egg yolks | ½ pt milk (250 ml) |
| 2 oz sugar (4 Tbs or 50 g) | 2 tsp gelatine |

Mix the yolks and sugar together, add the milk and sprinkle in the gelatine. Cook very gently, preferably in the top of a double boiler, until the mixture thickens enough to coat the back of the wooden stirrer. Remove from the heat and leave to cool, stirring occasionally, until it begins to thicken and is cold.

| ¼ pt whipping cream (250 ml) | 1 oz caster sugar (2 Tbs or 25 g) |
| vanilla or other flavouring (see below) | |

Whip the cream and add the sugar to it. Whisk lightly into the cold egg mixture. Flavour and pour into the mould, the traditional one for this sweet being a ring mould with a fairly small hole. Cover and refrigerate. Unmould and serve plain or with a fruit garnish, according to the flavouring used.

FLAVOURINGS

Vanilla bavarois. Use vanilla essence or vanilla sugar.

Coffee bavarois. Use soluble coffee dissolved in the hot egg mixture, strength according to taste.

Chocolate bavarois. Melt 3 oz (75 g) semi-sweet chocolate in the hot egg mixture.

Orange or lemon bavarois. Flavour with finely grated orange or lemon rind.

Liqueur bavarois. Flavour with any liqueur, or use rum for bavarois au rhum.

Berry cream

Quantities for 4.

Use a ¾ pt (400 ml) mould, or individual moulds. Suitable for strawberries, raspberries, loganberries, blackberries, black currants and any other berries of good flavour.

8 oz fresh or frozen berries (250 g)

Put in a pan and heat very gently until the juice begins to flow, and the berries are soft. Rub them through a sieve or pulp them in the electric blender and then strain to remove pips.

2 oz caster sugar (4 Tbs or 50 g)   1 Tbs lemon juice

Add to the purée and stir until the sugar dissolves. Taste, and add more sugar if the purée is not sweet enough.

2 tsp gelatine dissolved in 2 Tbs hot water

Mix into the purée and leave until it is cold and beginning to thicken, but not set.

¼ pt whipping cream (150 ml)

Soft-whip the cream and fold it into the berry mixture. Pour into the mould, cover and refrigerate until set. Unmould and serve with

berries and/or cream.

Berry mousse

Quantities for 4–6.

Suitable for blackberries, loganberries, black currants, raspberries, strawberries and any other berries of good flavour.

4–8 oz sugar (½–1 c or 100–200 g), depending on the acidity of the berries   1 lb fresh or frozen berries (500 g)
2 Tbs lemon juice

Put the berries in a pan with the lemon and sugar and heat gently until the juice begins to run, then more rapidly until the berries are soft.

½ oz gelatine (1½ Tbs or 15 g)   3 Tbs cold water (45 ml)

Soak the gelatine in the water. Remove the cooked berries from the heat, add the gelatine and stir for a minute to dissolve it. Rub the berries through a sieve to remove the pips. Cool the purée until it begins to thicken.

2 egg whites · ¼ pt whipping cream (150 ml)

First whip the egg white until stiff and then soft-whip the cream. Fold first the cream and then the egg white into the cold berry mixture. Pour into individual dishes, cover and refrigerate until set. Serve plain or garnished with

whipped cream and a few whole berries; or run a little single cream over the top of each portion.

Blanc mange (French)

Quantities for 4–6.

Use a 1½ pt (850 ml) mould.

1 pt milk (500 ml)	4 oz sugar (½ c or 100 g)
2 in (5 cm) piece of vanilla pod, or use vanilla essence	2 in (5 cm) piece of cinnamon stick

Put in a pan and heat slowly until the sugar dissolves, bring to the boil and set aside to infuse for 5 mins or until the milk is delicately flavoured.

½ oz gelatine (1½ Tbs or 15 g) soaked in 4 Tbs cold water (60 ml)

Add to the milk and stir for a minute to dissolve the gelatine. Strain into a bowl.

¼ pt double cream (150 ml) · essence of almond
1 Tbs brandy (optional)

Stir into the milk, adding almond to taste. Pour into a mould, stand this in a pan of cold water to cool it quickly and then cover and refrigerate until set. Unmould and serve plain or with

fresh stewed or canned apricots.

ALTERNATIVE

Pour the mixture into individual glasses and leave to set. Garnish the tops with fruit or a fruit purée.

Caramel rice cream

Quantities for 4.

3 oz pudding rice (6 Tbs or 75 g) · 1 pt milk (500 ml)
2 strips of lemon rind

Put in a pan and simmer, stirring often, until practically all the milk is absorbed and the rice cooked. Over a gentle direct heat this will take 15–20 mins. It is safer to cook the rice in the top of a double boiler, when it will take 40–45 mins.

Do not cover the pan during cooking. When the rice is cooked remove the lemon rind.

4 Tbs sugar   2 Tbs water

Boil together in a small thick pan, without stirring, until it turns a deep amber colour. Pour it into the rice and stir until the caramel melts. Leave to cool.

¼ pt whipping cream or chilled evaporated milk (150 ml)

Whip until thick and light and stir into the rice. Pour into a glass serving dish or individual dishes. Garnish with

glacé cherries or drained canned fruit.

Chocolate soufflé (cold)

This is one for those who like a strong bitter-sweet chocolate flavour.

Quantities for 5–6.

Either use a 6 in (15 cm) soufflé dish with a collar of paper; or use a 1½ pt (850 ml) serving dish or individual dishes.

2 oz cocoa powder (6 Tbs or 50 g)   2 tsp instant coffee (optional)
¾ pt milk (400 ml)

Mix the cocoa and coffee to a paste with some of the milk. Add the rest of the milk and bring to the boil, whisking all the time to make sure the cocoa blends in smoothly. Remove from the heat.

3 egg yolks   3 oz sugar (6 Tbs or 75 g)

Beat together in a large basin and pour the hot milk into the basin. Mix well, return to the pan, stirring until the mixture thickens, but do not allow it to boil. Remove from the heat.

½ oz gelatine (1½ Tbs or 15 g) soaked in 4 Tbs cold water (60 ml)

Add this to the hot mixture and stir for a few minutes to dissolve the gelatine. Strain the mixture into a large basin and stand this in cold water. Whisk the mixture frequently as it cools, but do not allow to set.

5 Tbs whipping cream (75 ml)   3 egg whites

Whip the cream and beat the egg whites until they stand up in peaks but are not dry. Fold first the cream and then the egg whites into the chocolate mixture. Pour into the soufflé dish or other serving dish and leave to set. Decorate the top with

chopped nuts and piped whipped cream.

Coffee custard mould (crème au café)

Cooking time ¾–1 hr.
Temperature 180° C (350° F; G4).
Quantities for 4–6

4–5 eggs, or use some yolks (2 yolks replace 1 egg)	1 Tbs sugar pinch of salt

Beat these together just enough to mix the yolks and whites of the eggs.

1 pt hot milk (500 ml)	instant coffee

Add coffee to the milk according to taste. Pour the hot milk on to the eggs.

vanilla essence to taste

Add the vanilla and pour the custard into one large or 4–6 small greased moulds. Stand these in a baking dish with hot water coming half-way up the sides of the moulds. Bake until the custard is set (a knife inserted near the centre comes out clean). Remove from the water and leave the custard to become cold, then refrigerate to chill it well. Unmould and decorate with

whipped cream and chopped nuts.

Crème au caramel

Cooking time ¾–1 hr.
Temperature 180° C (350° F; G4).
Quantities for 4–6 small moulds, warmed.

2 oz sugar (4 Tbs or 50 g)	2 Tbs water

Heat together in a small pan, stirring to dissolve the sugar, then boil rapidly, without stirring, until the mixture is a deep amber colour. Remove from the heat at once and pour it into the moulds.

4 large eggs 1 Tbs sugar	1 pt milk (500 ml) vanilla essence

Beat the eggs and sugar to mix them. Heat the milk to boiling point, pour it over the eggs, mix, and flavour to taste. Pour into the moulds. Stand them in a shallow baking tin with hot water to come half-way up the sides of the moulds. Cook until the blade of a small knife inserted near the centre comes out clean. Remove from the water. Leave in the moulds until cold, then cover and store in the refrigerator. Loosen the top edges and turn out of the moulds. Any caramel left in the moulds can be dissolved by adding a little hot water and leaving the moulds to stand until the caramel dissolves, or by heating them gently.

Crème brulée

Quantities for 4–6.

Make the day before serving.

½ pt double cream (250 ml)   ¼ pt milk (150 ml)

Put in the top of a double boiler and heat.

4 egg yolks   1 Tbs caster sugar

Put in a basin and stir vigorously with a wooden spoon to mix well. Pour in the hot cream, stir, return to the pan and continue cooking over simmering water, stirring all the time until the custard thickens and coats the back of the spoon. Remove from the heat at once.

¼ tsp vanilla essence

Add to the custard and strain it into a shallow 1 pt (½ l) fireproof dish or individual soufflé dishes. Leave it to become cold and then refrigerate for 4–5 hours or until well chilled, when it will have thickened quite a lot.

3 oz granulated sugar (6 Tbs or 75 g), or use brown if you prefer

Sprinkle the sugar evenly over the top of the crème and place it under a heated grill until the sugar melts and caramelizes. If you have made individual ones it may be as well to stand the dishes in crushed ice to prevent the crème from becoming over-heated during grilling. With a large one, well-chilled, this is not necessary. Make sure that any of the mixture which has splashed on the sides of the dish as it was filled, has been wiped off, or it will burn and spoil the look of the finished dish. Also, see that the dishes are well filled, otherwise the caramel will cook unevenly during grilling.

Cool the crème once again and refrigerate before serving. It should be well chilled.

Custard cream

Quantities for 6.

Use a 1½ pt mould (850 ml).

1 egg   1 Tbs custard powder
2 Tbs sugar   ½ pt milk (250 ml)

Whisk the egg, custard powder and sugar to a smooth cream, adding a little of the milk. Heat the remaining milk, pour it into the egg mixture, stirring vigorously, return to the pan and stir until it just comes to the boil. Remove from the heat.

2 tsp gelatine dissolved in 2 Tbs hot water

Pour this into the custard in a steady stream, stirring vigorously to mix it in evenly. Stand the pan in a bowl of cold water to cool the custard quickly, stirring once or twice at the beginning to prevent a skin from forming. Leave the custard until quite cold but not set. Should it set you will have to whisk to break it up smoothly before adding the cream.

Flavourings. 1 tsp vanilla essence; or 2-3 tsp soluble coffee; or 3 oz plain chocolate (75 g); or 2-4 oz chopped preserved ginger (50-100 g); or liqueur, rum or brandy to taste.

Flavour the custard to taste. The coffee or chocolate should be added to the hot custard, the other flavourings when it is cool. Stir the chocolate until it melts and blends in well.

½ pt whipping cream (250 ml)

Soft-whip the cream and fold it into the cold custard. Turn the mixture into a mould and refrigerate until set. Unmould and serve plain or garnished with fruit or chopped nuts.

Fruit fool

Suitable for any berries (including gooseberries), rhubarb, dried apricots, apples and prunes.

Quantities for 4.

½ pt thick raw or cold cooked fruit purée (250 ml)	grated lemon or orange rind, or spices to taste
sugar to taste	

Sweeten and flavour the purée to taste.

½ pt whipping cream (250 ml), or use half thick custard sauce and half cream; or use all custard

Whip the cream and fold it into the purée. When custard is used, beat it into the purée before adding the cream. Put in individual dishes or glasses and serve very cold.

Golden jelly

Quantities for 4.

Use a 1¼ pt mould (700 ml).

½ oz gelatine (1½ Tbs or 15 g)   ¾ pt hot water (400 ml)

Sprinkle the gelatine into the water and stir to dissolve it.

6 oz golden syrup (6 Tbs or 150 g)   finely grated rind of 1–2 lemons
4 Tbs lemon juice

Add to the water and stir until the syrup dissolves. Pour into a mould to set. Unmould and serve with

egg custard sauce or cream.

Hamburg mousse

Quantities for 4–6.

4 egg yolks   grated rind and juice of 2 small
6 oz sugar (¾ c or 150 g)   lemons (4 Tbs juice)

Grate only the yellow part of the lemon rind and do this on the finest part of the grater. Put all the ingredients in the top of a double boiler or in a basin over a pan of boiling water. Stir and cook for about 5 mins until the sugar dissolves and the mixture thickens slightly. Remove from the heat.

4 egg whites

Whisk until the whites stand up in peaks, then whisk in the egg yolk mixture. Cool enough to pour safely into glasses, then chill in the refrigerator. Serve while still very cold.

Lemon soufflé (cold)

Quantities for 4.

Use a 1¼ pt (700 ml) serving dish, or 4 glasses.

2 tsp gelatine soaked in 5 Tbs cold   2 egg yolks
   water (75 ml)   1 oz sugar (2 Tbs or 25 g)
½ tsp grated lemon rind   5 Tbs water (75 ml)

Put the eggs, sugar, lemon and water in a basin over boiling water or in the top of a double boiler. Stir frequently until the mixture begins to thicken a little. Remove from the heat and leave for a minute. Add the soaked gelatine and stir to dissolve it.

2 Tbs lemon juice

Mix in.

| 2 egg whites | 1 oz sugar (2 Tbs or 25 g) |

Whisk the egg whites until stiff and then whisk in the sugar until the mixture is very thick. Fold the lemon mixture into the egg whites and pour it into 1 large or 4 small dishes. When it is quite cold, cover and refrigerate until set.

| sieved raspberry jam | whipped cream |

Cover the soufflé with a layer of raspberry jam and decorate with the whipped cream.

Meringue case or flan

This can be made several days in advance and stored in a covered container.

Cooking time 2 hrs.
Temperature 120° C (250° F; G$\frac{1}{2}$).
Quantities for an 8 in (20 cm) case.

| 3 egg whites | 6 oz granulated sugar ($\frac{3}{4}$ c or 175 g) |

Using a plate or flan ring as a guide, draw an 8 in (20 cm) circle on a piece of non-stick lining paper and put this on a damp baking tray.

Beat the egg whites until they are stiff enough to stand up in peaks but are not dry or grainy looking. Add half the sugar and beat until the mixture is very thick. Fold in the remaining sugar.

Spread some of the mixture in a circle on the paper to make a base for the flan. Either mould a rim with the rest of the meringue, using a spoon, or use a $\frac{3}{4}$ in (2 cm) plain piping tube to pipe a rim in several layers about 1$\frac{1}{2}$ in (4 cm) high. Bake the case until it is lightly coloured and thoroughly dried. Cool and store in an airtight container.

| fresh fruit, sweetened to taste | whipped cream |

Fill the case with fruit and decorate with cream; or mix cream and fruit together before filling the flan.

VARIATION

For a coffee meringue flan add 1–2 tsp powdered soluble coffee to the egg whites with the second lot of sugar. If granular coffee is used you will need to mix it to a paste before adding it.

To make a lemon meringue flan, add the finely grated rind of 1 lemon with the second lot of sugar.

Meringue layer cake

Use the above recipe but spread the meringue on three circles of paper. Bake until dry, about 1 hr. To serve, sandwich the layers with whipped cream and chopped fruit, preferably flavoured with a little liqueur.

Mocha dessert

Cooking time 5–8 mins. *Quantities* for 4.

3 Tbs cornflour or custard powder	2 Tbs cocoa powder
4 Tbs sugar	2 tsp soluble coffee
1 pt milk (600 ml)	pinch of salt

Blend the dry ingredients to a smooth cream with a little of the milk. Heat the remainder, pour some into the blended mixture, return to the pan and stir until it boils. Simmer for 5 mins for cornflour, 1 min for custard powder.

vanilla essence   2 Tbs soured or fresh cream

Add and mix in. Cool, stirring occasionally, until it is cool enough to pour into glasses or individual serving dishes. Allow to become cold, cover and store in the refrigerator.

soured or fresh cream

Pour a spoonful on top of each portion before serving.

Mont Blanc

Cooking time 40 mins plus time for shelling the nuts. *Quantities* for 4–6.

1 lb chestnuts (500 g)   1 pt milk (600 ml)
4 oz sugar ($\frac{1}{2}$ c or 100 g)

Shell the chestnuts, see page 16. Heat the milk and sugar until the latter is dissolved. Add the chestnuts and cook them very gently until they are quite tender and nearly all the milk has been absorbed, then rub them through a sieve.

1 tsp vanilla essence

Mix into the chestnuts. Allow the mixture to cool. To serve, heap the chestnut purée on a serving dish in a cone-shape. Smooth the sides with a knife dipped in water.

$\frac{1}{4}$ pt whipping cream (150 ml)

Whip the cream and decorate the top of the cone to look like a snow cap. Serve slightly warm or quite cold.

Orange and lemon mould

Quantities for 6–8.

6 Tbs lemon juice (90 ml)	4 Tbs orange juice (60 ml)
2–4 Tbs sugar	2 egg yolks
1 oz butter (25 g)	

Put these in a small pan or in the top of a double boiler and stir over a low heat or over boiling water until the mixture begins to thicken.

1 Tbs gelatine soaked in 2 Tbs cold water

Mix into the fruit juice and egg mixture, stir to dissolve and set aside to cool.

8 oz sieved cottage or curd cheese (250 g)	2 Tbs cream

Whisk these into the cooled mixture.

2 egg whites	2–4 Tbs sugar, to taste

Beat the whites until stiff and then beat in the sugar. Fold the egg white mixture into the cheese mixture and pour into a mould or individual serving dishes. Cover and refrigerate until set.

fresh or other fruit to garnish   cream to hand separately

Orange and lemon syllabub

Quantities for 4–6.

Make this the day before it is to be served.

1 orange   1 lemon

Squeeze the juice and strain it into a measure.

sherry or white wine   3 oz caster sugar (6 Tbs or 75 g)

Make the juice up to ¼ pt (150 ml) with the sherry or wine, add the sugar and stir to dissolve it. Put in a basin, about 1½ pt size (1 l).

½ pt double cream (250 ml)

Add to the wine and juice and whisk together until thick enough to stand up in peaks. Put in wine glasses, cover and refrigerate until required. It is normal for some liquid to collect in the bottom of the glass; this is eaten with the cream.

Orange and raisin charlotte

Quantities for 4.

Use a 1 pt charlotte mould (600 ml) or a 1 lb loaf tin (½ kg).

2 oz seedless raisins (⅓ c or 50 g)

Put in a small pan, just cover with water, put on the lid, bring to the boil and simmer for 5 mins or until the water is absorbed.

¼ pt orange juice (150 ml) ½ tsp grated orange rind
½ oz butter (15 g) pinch of salt
2 oz sugar (4 Tbs or 50 g)

Add to the raisins, bring to the boil, stirring to dissolve the sugar. Remove from the heat and cool for a minute.

2 tsp gelatine soaked in 1 Tbs cold water

Add to the pan and stir until the gelatine is dissolved. Cool and then chill until it is just beginning to set.

3–4 oz dry sponge cake (75–100 g)

Cut the sponge in thin fingers or triangles and line the mould, reserving some sponge for the top.

¼ pt whipping cream (150 ml)

Whip lightly and fold into the setting raisin mixture. Pour into the lined mould and cover the top with a thin layer of sponge. Cover and refrigerate to set and become well chilled. When ready to serve, turn it out of the mould.

cold chocolate sauce, page 66.

Cover the top of the charlotte with sauce and let some trickle down the sides, but not enough to cover it completely. Hand more sauce separately.

Pavlova

This is the recipe for a true Pavlova which should not be crisp like a meringue, but soft in the centre like marshmallow.

Cooking time 1–1½ hrs.
Temperature 120° C (250° F; G½).
Quantities for an 8–9 in tin (20–24 cm).

Line the tin with non-stick paper. If a sandwich tin is used let the paper project above the top of the tin for several inches.

3 egg whites

Beat until they are stiff enough to stand up in peaks but are not dry looking.

6 oz caster sugar (¾ c or 175 g)

Add half this to the egg whites and beat until the mixture is very thick.

1 tsp cornflour	1 tsp wine vinegar
½ tsp vanilla essence	

Mix the cornflour with the rest of the sugar and fold this gently into the egg mixture. Fold in the vanilla and vinegar, put into the tin and spread evenly. Bake until risen and lightly browned on top. Turn upside-down on a serving dish and leave to become cold before removing the paper. The cake will shrink somewhat as it cools, making a hollow to take the fruit.

½–1 lb fruit (250–500 g)   cream

Fresh fruit is the best for this, or use almost thawed fruit. The best kinds to use are raspberries or strawberries but any other can be used, though canned fruit is too sweet for a good Pavlova. Pile the fruit on top and either decorate with whipped cream or hand single cream separately. Alternatively, mix whipped cream and fruit together and pile on top of the Pavlova.

Peaches in cider jelly

Quantities for 4.

1 lb can of peach halves (454 g)

Drain the fruit, keeping the syrup. Arrange the peaches in a single layer in a shallow dish or individual dishes.

½ oz gelatine (1½ Tbs or 15 g)

Add to the peach syrup and warm over a gentle heat, stirring occasionally, until the gelatine is dissolved. Remove from the heat.

2 Tbs lemon juice   ½ pt cider (250 ml)

Add to the syrup and pour it gently over the fruit. Leave to set.

cream

Hand this separately or decorate the jelly with piped whipped cream.

Pineapple cheese

Quantities for 4–6.

14 oz can of pineapple pieces or slices (400 g)

Drain the pineapple and make the liquid up to ½ pt (250 ml) with water. Chop the pineapple.

1½ Tbs gelatine

Warm with the pineapple juice until the gelatine has dissolved.

1 egg yolk	2 oz caster sugar (4 Tbs or 50 g)
grated rind of 1 lemon	1 Tbs lemon juice

Mix together, add the gelatine mixture and cook over a low heat, stirring until the sugar has dissolved and the mixture is almost boiling. Remove from the heat.

8 oz sieved cottage cheese (250 g)

Whisk into the warmed mixture and stand the pan in cold water to cool until it starts to set.

5 Tbs whipping cream (75 ml)   1 egg white

Whip the cream and beat the egg white until stiff. Fold these into the setting mixture together with the chopped pineapple. Pour into a mould and leave to set. Unmould and garnish with fruit or serve plain.

Praline charlotte

Quantities for 4.

Use a 1 pt (600 ml) charlotte mould or a 1 lb (½ kg) bread tin.

½–¾ pt lemon jelly (250–400 ml)

Prepare the jelly and leave it to cool. Pour ¼ in (6 mm) into the mould or tin and put it into the refrigerator to set. Keep the remaining jelly warm enough to prevent setting.

blanched almonds and glacé cherries

Dip these in liquid jelly and arrange them in a pattern on the jelly in the bottom of the mould. When they are firmly set in position, spoon in more jelly to a depth of ½ in (1 cm). Put to set.

1–2 packets of sponge fingers

Cut these across in half or trim the ends, according to the depth of the mould.

Brush each with jelly and fit them close together round the sides of the mould. Put to set.

½ Tbs gelatine dissolved in 2 Tbs hot water

Keep this lukewarm.

¼ pt double cream (150 ml)   5 Tbs milk (75 ml)

Whip the cream until stiff but not buttery and gradually whip in the milk and then the gelatine.

1 oz caster sugar (2 Tbs or 25 g)   3 oz praline (75 g), see page 16

Mix these into the cream and pour it carefully into the centre of the mould. Refrigerate to set. Unmould and decorate with the rest of the jelly broken up with a fork or chopped coarsely.

Refrigerated sherry and almond cake

Quantities for 6–8.

4 oz caster sugar (½ c or 125 g)   4 oz butter (125 g)

Cream together until very soft and light.

4 oz ground almonds (1 c or 125 g)   about ¼ pt milk (150 ml)

Beat the almonds and milk alternately into the creamed mixture, using enough milk to make a soft spreadable consistency.

3 fl oz milk (6 Tbs or 90 ml)   6–8 oz sponge fingers (2 pkts or
3 fl oz sherry (6 Tbs or 90 ml)   175–250 g)

Mix the milk and sherry in a flat dish and dip the sponge fingers in for long enough to soak up some of the liquid but not long enough to become soft. Take a flat serving dish and put five of the fingers side by side. Spread them with a thin layer of the creamed mixture and put another layer of sponge fingers on top, lying in the opposite direction. Build up a cake in this way with four or five layers, keeping some of the creamed mixture back for icing the outside.

crystallized fruits or chopped nuts

Garnish the iced cake, cover with an inverted basin or cake tin and refrigerate for several hours or overnight. Cut in slices for serving.

Rice mould

I find this a most useful recipe to cook when the oven is on for a casserole. It is much nicer to eat cold than an ordinary rice pudding.

Cooking time 2–4 hrs. *Quantities* for 4.
Temperature 120–160° C (250–325° F; G$\frac{1}{2}$–3).

2 oz pudding rice (4 Tbs or 50 g)	2–3 strips lemon rind
1$\frac{1}{2}$ oz sugar (3 Tbs or 40 g)	pinch of salt
$\frac{1}{2}$ oz butter (15 g)	1 pt milk (500 ml)

Put all these in a covered casserole, large enough to be only half filled. Cook until the rice is tender. Stir occasionally.

1 egg, beaten

Remove the pudding from the oven. Discard the lemon rind. Stir in the egg and mix well. Pour the pudding into a basin and leave to become cold. Turn out and garnish in one of the ways given below.

GINGER RICE MOULD

Before putting the rice into its basin, mix in chopped ginger preserved in syrup and a little of the syrup as well. Alternatively, put the pudding in individual dishes. Garnish with sliced ginger and pour a little syrup over or round it.

APRICOT RICE MOULD

Drain a 1 lb ($\frac{1}{2}$ kg) can of apricot halves and boil the juice in a small pan until it is thick and syrupy. Cool a little and add a few drops of almond essence or a little kirsch. Unmould the rice, surround with apricot halves and brush these with the syrup. Decorate with split almonds or toasted almonds.

CHOCOLATE RICE MOULD

Omit the lemon from the recipe.

1 oz cocoa powder (3 Tbs or 25 g)

Mix this with the sugar in the recipe, and a little milk, and add to the other ingredients at the beginning of cooking. Finish as before. Unmould and serve with cooked or canned pears or with fresh sliced oranges or canned mandarin oranges.

Rice and fruit mould using canned rice

Quantities for 6.

15½ oz can of creamed rice (440 g)
1 oz chopped walnuts (¼ c or 25 g)
1 oz glacé cherries, chopped (25 g)
1 Tbs lemon juice
2 oz chopped dates (50 g)
2 oz chopped peel (¼ c or 50 g)
1 Tbs orange-flavoured liqueur, kirsch or rum

Put all these in a basin and mix thoroughly. Other mixtures of fruit, including some fresh fruit, can be used.

1 Tbs gelatine dissolved in 3 Tbs hot water

Mix into the rice.

¼ pt whipping cream (150 ml)

Beat until stiff and fold into the rice mixture. Put into a 2 pt (1 l) mould and refrigerate until set. Unmould and garnish with

chopped fruit or nuts, or serve with a fruit sauce.

Sherry mould

Quantities for 4.

1½ oz cornflour (4¼ Tbs or 40 g)   1 pt milk (600 ml)
1 oz butter (25 g)

Mix the cornflour to a smooth paste with a little of the cold milk. Heat the remaining milk with the butter. When it is almost boiling pour it into the blended cornflour, stir, return to the pan and stir until it boils. Simmer for about 5 mins, stirring frequently. Remove from the heat.

2 oz sugar (4 Tbs or 50 g)   4 Tbs sherry (60 ml)

Add to the pan and stir until the sugar dissolves. Pour into a 1 pt (600 ml) mould or individual moulds. Leave until quite cold, then cover and store in the refrigerator until required.

fruit purée or sieved jam   sherry or water

Add sherry or water to the purée or jam to make it a suitable consistency to pour over the mould.

Tortoni

Quantities for 6.

Make this a day in advance.

2 oz macaroon crumbs ($\frac{1}{2}$ c or 50 g)

To make macaroon crumbs simply crush well-baked macaroons with rolling pin or crumb them in a blender or grinder.

1 egg white   3 Tbs sifted icing sugar

Beat the egg white until stiff and gradually beat in the sugar. Set aside.

$\frac{1}{2}$ pt whipping cream (250 ml)   3 Tbs sifted icing sugar

Whip together until the cream is thick. Mix in the macaroon crumbs.

2 tsp rum

Add to the mixture and then fold in the egg whites. Divide the mixture between six small dishes or large paper or foil cups.

chopped toasted almonds

Sprinkle thickly over the tops and refrigerate for several hours until quite firm. Serve very cold.

Vacherin

This is a sweet for special occasions. There are many versions of it but the recipe I make is not too complicated, looks attractive and is not sickly sweet in spite of the meringue. The sponge and meringue can both be made several days in advance and stored separately in an airtight container. Assemble the vacherin not more than an hour before it will be required.

Quantities for 6.

1 round of sponge 7–8 in (18–20 cm)

This can be bought or made from the Genoese recipe, page 435, using only half for the vacherin.

meringue, recipe page 386

Take two rounds of non-stick lining paper the same size as the sponge. Damp the surfaces of two baking trays or use inverted sandwich tins the size of the paper circles. Stick the paper to the wet tin. Put the meringue mixture in a piping bag with a $\frac{1}{2}$ in (1 cm) plain nozzle and pipe a ring round the edge of each circle of paper. Then pipe a lattice of meringue, three bars each way. Bake until a pale fawn and thoroughly dried (time, 2-3 hrs at 120° C (250° F; G$\frac{1}{2}$)).

12 oz fresh or just thawed strawberries, or other berries (350 g)	1 pt whipping cream (500 ml)

Do not sweeten either cream or fruit and use fresh or frozen fruit rather than canned fruit which would spoil this sweet. Whip the cream and cut 8 oz (250 g) of the fruit in small pieces.

Assemble the vacherin by putting the sponge on a serving dish and spreading it with a layer of cream. Press one of the circles of meringue on top so that the cream oozes through the lattice. Spread with more cream and the fruit. Invert the other circle of meringue to have the flat bottom uppermost and put this on top of the cream and fruit. Use the remaining cream to coat the sides of the vacherin and to decorate the top. Garnish with the remaining fruit. Refrigerate until required.

Vanilla creams

Quantities for 4.

$\frac{1}{4}$ pt whipping cream (150 ml) vanilla essence	2 oz caster sugar (4 Tbs or 50 g)

Whip the cream and whip in the sugar and flavouring. Less sugar can be used if you do not have such a sweet tooth.

$\frac{1}{2}$ Tbs gelatine dissolved in 1 Tbs hot water	$\frac{1}{4}$ pt soured cream (150 ml)

Whisk the soured cream until light, fold it into the other cream and continue while you trickle in the gelatine. Pour it into four small glasses or serving dishes and leave to set, then cover and store in the refrigerator.

drained canned or stewed fruit or fresh fruit, either one kind or a fruit salad

Put a thick layer on top of the cream and serve.

ALTERNATIVE

Set the cream in 4 tiny moulds, unmould and surround with the fruit.

ICES AND FROZEN SWEETS

Ices and other frozen sweets are among the easiest desserts to make, always provided you have a suitable method of freezing. This may be the ice compartment of an old-style refrigerator, the freezing compartment of a modern refrigerator, a freezer, or an ice-cream churn used in the freezing compartment of a refrigerator. The freezing process usually takes from 3-4 hrs and then the mixture should be left to mature for 1-2 hrs before serving, but most people make these sweets days or weeks in advance depending on the sort of storage available. For long storage a freezer is essential. Freezing takes longest in the old type of refrigerator and is fastest in a freezer, but the time varies a great deal with the recipe, the kind of container used to hold the mixture (metal freezes fastest), the quantity of ice-cream in the container, and the freezing temperature.

The recipes I give here can all be frozen in either a refrigerator or a freezer and those which are stirred or beaten during the freezing process are also suitable for an ice-cream churn.

If you want to make ice-cream well in advance, a procedure I strongly recommend, it can be stored in the freezer for up to a month. After that, flavour changes may take place but the ice-cream will still be safe to eat. Be sure to take ices and frozen sweets out of the freezer in time for them to soften enough for pleasant eating. None of these sweets are at their best when still frozen hard. How long they need to thaw depends on the kind and shape of container, as well as on the quantity of ice-cream. Naturally, several small containers take less time to thaw than one large one. Shallow trays like the ice trays from a refrigerator or freezer will thaw quite fast because they are shallow and have a large area in relation to their depth. In general, the plainer ice-creams take longer to soften than those containing a lot of cream and egg. Sorbets and water ices soften fairly quickly. Chocolate ice-cream softens faster than other flavours.

There is really no substitute for personal experience in this matter of thawing times. As a rough guide, for thawing small quantities in the refrigerator allow 1-2 hrs for 2 portions; 2-4 hrs for larger amounts. In an emergency ice-cream can be softened at room temperature but I don't recommend this as the outside tends to become too soft, even runny, before the centre is softened.

When ice-cream has been frozen in a mould and you want to turn it out for serving as a whole sweet, loosen the edges with a knife and dip the mould in tepid water, or in hot water if the mould is made of a thick material. Dry the outside and put the serving dish over the top, invert it, and the ice should come out. If the surface looks rather ragged because of uneven melting, it can be smoothed with a knife. It is usually better to unmould as soon as the ice-cream comes out of the freezer and then allow it to thaw in the refrigerator. If it shows signs of becoming too soft you can always pop it back in the freezer for a short while, to check further melting.

One further word of advice: avoid over-whipping cream as this tends to produce a grainy texture in the finished product. Do what is called a soft-whip, i.e. whip until thick and light but not stiff.

Blackberry ice-cream with hot spiced sauce

Quantities for 6.

8 oz fresh or frozen blackberries (250 g)

Put in a pan and heat gently until the juice begins to flow and the fruit becomes quite soft.

1 tsp gelatine soaked in 1 Tbs cold water

Add to the fruit and stir for a minute to dissolve the gelatine. Rub the fruit through a sieve to remove the seeds. There should be about ¼ pt (150 ml) of thick purée.

2 oz icing sugar (½ c or 50 g)

Add to the blackberries and stir to dissolve. Set aside to become cold and begin to thicken.

¼ pt whipping cream (150 ml)

Soft-whip and whisk in the blackberry mixture. Freeze without stirring. Serve with

hot spiced blackberry sauce, page 70.

Brown bread ice-cream

This is an old recipe which appears in many versions in old cookery books, and some modern ones. It is essential to have real 100% wholemeal bread for the crumbs.

Quantities for 6–8.

½ pt whipping cream (250 ml)   ½ tsp vanilla essence
1 oz sifted icing sugar (¼ c or 25 g)

Whisk the cream until thick and light but not stiff. Add the icing sugar and vanilla and put the mixture in a freezing tray or box. Freeze until it begins to harden round the edges. This happens quite quickly with a mixture of this sort.

3 oz wholemeal breadcrumbs (1 c or 75 g)   3 oz caster sugar (6 Tbs or 75 g)

Mix these and put in a grill pan. Cook fairly slowly, stirring frequently until the crumbs are crisp and well toasted. Be careful to avoid burning. Allow to become cold and then break up with a fork if necessary. Tip the half-frozen ice-cream into a bowl, beat with a wooden spoon to make it smooth and then stir in the crumbs. Finish freezing.

brandy, liqueur or a sauce

Serve one of these with the ice-cream, one spoonful of brandy or liqueur per portion being enough.

Chocolate ice-cream

Quantities for 6–8.

¼ pt full cream sweetened condensed milk (150 ml)   4 oz plain chocolate (100 g), broken in pieces

Put in a double boiler or in a basin over a pan of boiling water. Heat, stirring occasionally, until the chocolate has melted and blended with the milk, about 10 mins. Remove from the heat.

½ tsp vanilla essence, or other flavouring, such as rum or instant coffee   4 Tbs water (60 ml)
pinch of ground cinnamon

Stir in gradually and then leave the mixture to become cold. Chill it in the refrigerator.

½ pt double cream (250 ml)

Soft-whip the cream and fold it into the chocolate mixture. Freeze until it begins to get very thick, then remove and beat hard to make the mixture smooth and light. Finish freezing.

Coffee ice-cream

Quantities for 4–6.

1 Tbs instant coffee
1 Tbs rum (optional)

1 oz caster sugar (2 Tbs or 25 g)
½ pt whipping cream (250 ml)

Dissolve the coffee and sugar in 2 Tbs of the cream. Add the rum. Soft-whip the cream and then whip in the coffee mixture. Half-freeze the ice-cream, then tip into a basin and beat well, before finishing freezing.

Honey ice-cream

Quantities for 8.

2 egg yolks ½ pt milk (250 ml)

Combine the yolks and milk and cook slowly, stirring all the time, until the mixture just coats the back of the wooden stirrer.

4 oz honey (4 Tbs or 100 g) 1 tsp vanilla essence

Add to the custard and mix to dissolve the honey. Cool. Freeze until it begins to set.

2 egg whites ½ pt whipping cream (250 ml)

Beat the whites until stiff. Lightly whip the cream. Tip the half-frozen custard into a bowl and beat it smooth. Fold in first the cream, then the egg white, and finish freezing without stirring.

Liqueur mousse, iced

This can be made from any liqueur, the mousse taking its name from the flavouring used, for example, 'Iced Grand Marnier'.

Quantities for 6–8.

It can be frozen in individual moulds or in a soufflé dish or cake tin about 6 in (15 cm) diameter. Line the mould with non-stick lining paper.

3 oz sugar (6 Tbs or 75 g) 5 Tbs water (75 ml)

Put in a small pan, heat to dissolve the sugar and boil for 5 mins. Remove from the heat.

4 egg yolks

Whisk these in a basin over a pan of boiling water and gradually pour in the syrup in a steady stream, whisking all the time. Continue to heat and beat until the mixture is very thick and light like whipped cream. Remove from the heat and stand the basin in a pan of cold water. Whisk frequently as it cools.

4 Tbs liqueur (60 ml) ¼ tsp vanilla

When the egg mixture is cold beat in the flavourings.

½ pt whipping cream (250 ml)

Soft-whip and fold into the egg mixture. Pour into the prepared mould, cover

Puddings and Sweets 401

and freeze. To serve, unmould, remove the paper and put the mousse in the refrigerator to soften, which it does fairly quickly. Garnish with

fruit dressed with liqueur, or serve with a fruit sauce.

Macaroon ice-cream

½ pt double cream (250 ml)

Beat until thick but not stiff.

2 oz sieved icing sugar (½ c or 50 g)   3 macaroons, crushed (about 2 oz or
½ tsp vanilla   50 g)
6 maraschino cherries, chopped

Add to the cream and mix. Put into a large mould or individual moulds and freeze.

maraschino cherries and liqueur

Unmould the ice-cream and thaw in the refrigerator, garnish with cherries and pour a little maraschino liqueuer over the ice-cream.

Strawberry ice-cream

Quantities for 6 or more.

½ pt thick strawberry purée (250 ml)

To make the purée use 1 lb (500 g) of either fresh ripe strawberries or thawed frozen ones; or use thawed frozen purée.

2 oz icing sugar (½ c or 50 g)

Add to the purée and stir until the sugar is dissolved. If you are using an electric blender for the purée, blend fruit and sugar together.

½ pt whipping cream (250 ml)

Whip until light but not stiff. Fold in the purée, combining gently but thoroughly. This mixture should not need to be beaten during freezing but for extra lightness, remove from the container when it is half frozen and beat until light. Finish freezing. Serve with

whole or sliced berries and whipped cream; or with Melba sauce.

Vanilla cream ice

Quantities for 4–6.

½ pt whipping cream (250 ml)
1 oz sifted icing sugar (¼ c or 25 g)
½ tsp vanilla essence

Whip the cream until light and thick but not stiff. Add the sugar and vanilla.

1 egg white

Beat until stiff and fold into the cream. Pour into freezing trays or a polythene box and freeze without stirring. Serve plain or as a basis for coupes and other frozen desserts.

Vanilla cream ice with yogurt

Use the recipe above but, after adding the egg white, fold in ¼ pt (150 ml) of thick yogurt which has been beaten smooth.

Lemon sorbet with mint

Quantities for 6–8.

3 strips lemon rind
¼ pt water (150 ml)

Put in a small pan and bring to the boil. Strain.

3 oz sugar (6 Tbs or 75 g)

Return the strained liquid to the pan and add the sugar. Stir until dissolved and boil for 5 mins. Cool a minute.

1 tsp gelatine soaked in 1 Tbs cold water
4 Tbs honey

Add to the hot syrup and stir until dissolved.

½ pt mint leaves (250 ml), lightly packed
¼ pt water (150 ml)

Wash the leaves and put them in the electric blender with the water. Process to chop the leaves finely. Strain into the other liquid. If no blender is available, boil the water and infuse the leaves in it until cold, then strain.

¼ pt lemon juice (150 ml)

Add and leave the mixture to become cold, then chill in the refrigerator and finally freeze until amost firm. Remove to a basin and beat to break up.

1 egg white, beaten stiff

Stir into the frozen mixture and finish freezing. Before serving, thaw until fairly soft, then stir.

Orange sorbet

Quantities for 6.

4 oz sugar (½ c or 125 g)   ½ pt water (250 ml)

Put in a small pan and heat to dissolve the sugar, then boil for 5 mins. Remove from the heat.

1 can of frozen concentrated orange juice, about 6 oz (175 ml)

Add to the syrup, stir to mix well and leave to become quite cold, then chill in the refrigerator.

1 egg white

Add to the orange mixture and whisk just enough to mix it in. Freeze until it is almost frozen, turn out into a basin and whisk by hand until it is very thick and smooth. Continue freezing until firm.

Raspberry sorbet

Quantities for 4–6.

4 oz sugar (½ c or 100 g)   ½ pt water (250 ml)

Boil together for 5 mins. Remove from the heat and cool for a minute.

½ tsp gelatine soaked in 1 Tbs cold water

Add to the hot syrup, stirring until the gelatine is dissolved. Cool.

1 Tbs lemon juice   2 Tbs orange juice
¼ pt thick raspberry purée (150 ml)

Use fresh or frozen raspberries to make the purée. For this you will need ½ lb (250 g) of fruit. Add the purée and juices to the syrup.

1 egg white

Add to the other mixture and whisk just to combine the two. Freeze. When almost frozen, tip into a bowl and beat until thick and smooth. Finish freezing.

WAYS OF SERVING ICE-CREAM

These can all be prepared either with home-made ice-cream or with commercial ice-cream.

Bombes

These are moulded ice-creams usually made with two different kinds, but sometimes with more. They can be moulded in any pudding basin covered with a foil lid, or in a plastic basin with its own lid. A 1 pt (600 ml) mould will be enough for 4–6 portions. For this you need 4–6 good portions of ice-cream made up of two or more different kinds. There can be more of one than another, according to taste.

Chill the mould in the refrigerator before starting work. Have the ice-cream frozen, but only just, and still soft enough to mould easily. Spoon in the one you are going to use for the outside layer of the bombe and use the back of the spoon to mould it evenly round the sides and base. Put the mould in the freezer to harden this layer before adding the next layer or filling the centre if you are just using two kinds. When the mould is full, level off the top, cover and return to the freezer. When you want to serve it, unmould on to a serving dish and put it in the refrigerator to soften.

The bombe is cut in slices like a steamed pudding and it helps if the knife is first warmed by dipping the blade in hot water. Should the bombe show signs of becoming rather too soft before you are ready to serve it, pop it back into the freezer to stop further thawing.

Good mixtures to try to begin with are:
Vanilla and strawberry
Coffee and liqueur or rum ice-cream
Chocolate and coffee, serve with hot chocolate sauce
Chocolate and honey, serve with hot or cold chocolate sauce.

Gâteau, frozen

This is usually made of layers of ice-cream sandwiched between layers of sponge cake. It can be one kind of ice-cream or two or more different kinds. The sponge can be home-made or bought.

Quantities for 8.

1 sponge sandwich, about 6 in (15 cm)

Take a 6 in (15 cm) cake tin or mould of a similar shape. Use a saucer or small plate a little smaller than the mould to make a guide for cutting the sponge. It needs this trimming to make it fit easily into the mould. Split each piece of the sponge sandwich into two to make four layers. Line the tin or mould with non-stick lining paper.

Rum, liqueur or fruit juice

Put the sponge layers on a flat surface and moisten (not wet) them with one of these liquids, or use rum or liqueur with a little fruit juice.

4–6 portions of ice-cream, any flavour, or use 2–3 different colours and flavours

The ice-cream should be soft but not completely thawed. Put one layer of sponge in the tin or mould, spread it with a thick, even layer of ice-cream, then put in another layer of sponge and repeat the layers until the tin or mould is full, finishing with sponge on top. Cover and freeze.

chopped nuts or fresh or preserved fruit

$\frac{1}{4}-\frac{1}{2}$ pt whipping cream (150–250 ml)

About 2 hrs before you want to serve the gâteau, turn it out on to a serving dish and strip off the lining paper. By the time you are ready to serve it the sponge should be thawed and the ice-cream beginning to soften. It is better to thaw rather too long than to have the centre frozen hard.

Whip the cream, using the larger amount if you want to decorate the gâteau with piped cream. Ice the cake all over with whipped cream. You can do this as soon as it is unmoulded or later on as convenient. Decorate with piped cream or nuts or fruit.

To serve, cut in wedges like a cake.

Banana and black currant coupe or sundae

Quantities for 4.

2 bananas

2 Tbs lemon juice

Skin and slice the bananas and toss them in the lemon juice. Do this as near to serving time as possible since the bananas will gradually discolour in spite of the lemon juice.

2 portions strawberry ice-cream
black currant syrup

2 portions vanilla ice-cream
chopped nuts

Put half a portion of each ice-cream in serving dishes. Arrange sliced bananas round it and pour the black currant syrup over and round it. Sprinkle with chopped nuts.

Cherry coupe or sundae

Quantities for 4.

¼ pt whipping cream (150 ml)   about 1 Tbs sieved raspberry jam

Whip the cream until thick and mix in enough jam to colour the cream pink. Cover, and refrigerate until ready to assemble the ice-cream.

4–8 oz (125–250 g) canned or stewed   4 portions of vanilla ice-cream
black or morello cherries

Put a portion of the ice-cream in each dish, cover with a layer of cherries and decorate with the cream.

Coffee chocolate coupe or sundae

Quantities for 4.

2 oz salted almonds, chopped (50 g)   4 portions of coffee ice-cream
hot chocolate sauce

Put portions of ice-cream in serving dishes. Pour over it the chocolate sauce and sprinkle the top with almonds.

Coupe Jacques

Quantities for 4.

8 oz fresh fruit salad (250 g)   1 Tbs kirsch

Combine and refrigerate until ready to assemble the coupe.

4 small portions of strawberry   4 small portions of lemon sorbet
ice-cream

In each serving dish put a mixture of the two ices side by side. Add a portion of the fruit salad.

Melon and ginger coupe or sundae

Quantities for 4.

4–8 oz diced fresh or canned melon   4 pieces of crystallized ginger,
(125–250 g)   chopped

Combine these and refrigerate until ready to serve.

4 portions of vanilla ice-cream   4 Tbs grated chocolate

Put some of the melon and ginger in each dish, add the ice-cream and sprinkle with chocolate.

Pears Helène

Quantities for 4.

4 small or 2 large firm, ripe pears   ½ pt water (250 ml)
4 oz sugar (125 g)   vanilla

Peel, halve and core the pears. Heat water, sugar and vanilla to make a syrup. Poach the pears in this and leave them to become cold.

4 portions of vanilla ice-cream   hot chocolate sauce

Put a portion of ice-cream in each dish and arrange one or two pear halves on top. Pour over the hot chocolate sauce or hand it separately.

Profiteroles filled with ice-cream

Make small cream puffs or profiteroles, see page 442. Fill these with ice-cream of any flavour and serve with hot chocolate sauce.

Strawberry Melba

Quantities for 4.

4 portions of vanilla ice-cream   8 oz strawberries, fresh or just
Melba sauce, page 69   thawed (250 g)

Put the ice-cream in the bottom of serving dishes. Cover it with a layer of strawberries, slicing very large ones. Cover these with the sauce.

Stuffed oranges

medium-sized oranges   orange sorbet

Cut a slice off the stem end of each orange and keep it for a lid. Use a small, sharp knife to cut out a cone-shaped piece of orange flesh and then a small spoon to extract the rest of the flesh and juice. Put the orange shells and tops in the refrigerator to chill them. Fill each one with partially frozen sorbet, replace the lids, wrap each in foil and freeze. Remove them from the freezer in time to allow the sorbet to soften very slightly. Serve garnished with

small orange, bay or laurel leaves.

HOT BAKED PUDDINGS

Apple cheese crumble

Cooking time 40–50 mins.
Temperature 190° C (375° F; G5).
Quantities for 4.

2 oz grated Cheddar cheese (½ c or 50 g)   1 lb cooking apples (500 g)

Peel and slice the apples. Put apples and cheese in layers in a 1½ pt (1 l) baking dish or pie dish.

3 oz plain flour (½ c or 75 g)   ½ tsp ground cinnamon
3 oz brown sugar (6 Tbs or 75 g)   pinch of grated nutmeg

Mix in a bowl.

2 oz butter or margarine (50 g)

Rub into the dry ingredients or mix in by machine. Sprinkle over the fruit and cheese and bake until the apples are tender. Serve hot or warm.

Baked banana mousse
(for the blender)

Cooking time 30–40 mins.
Temperature 190° C (375° F; G5).
Quantities for 4–6.

1½ oz softened butter (40 g)   2 Tbs sugar
2 egg yolks   ¼ pt sherry (150 ml)
1 lb bananas (500 g)   ¼ pt milk (150 ml)

Skin the bananas and cut them in pieces. Put all the ingredients in the goblet and blend until smooth.

2 egg whites

Beat until stiff. Tip the blended mixture into a bowl and fold in the egg whites. Pour into a well-greased baking or soufflé dish, 2 pt size (1¼ l). The dish should be not more than three-quarters full. Bake until the mixture is set. Serve plain or with single cream.

Cranberry upside-down pudding

Cooking time 30-35 mins.
Temperature 190° C (375° F; G5).
Quantities for 4.

1 oz butter (25 g)

Melt this in an 8 in (20 cm) sandwich tin.

4 oz soft brown sugar (½ c or 125 g)

Sprinkle over the bottom of the tin.

6 oz prepared cranberries (2 c or 175 g)

To prepare the cranberries pick over, removing stalks and over-ripe or withered berries. Wash and drain. Spread them on top of the sugar. There is no need to thaw frozen ones.

2 oz butter (50 g)	½ tsp vanilla essence
2 oz caster sugar (¼ c or 50 g)	1 egg

Cream the butter and sugar, add essence, and then beat in the egg.

2 oz self-raising flour (6 Tbs or 50 g)   pinch of salt

Sift these into the creamed mixture and stir until blended. Spread over the cranberries and bake until the cake feels springy when pressed lightly in the centre. Turn out on a serving dish and serve upside-down and still warm, with cream.

ALTERNATIVE

Instead of cranberries use 8 oz (250 g) raw, stoned morello cherries or red currants, stripped from the stalks.

Fruit crisp or crumble

Cooking time 1 hr.
Temperature 180° C (350° F; G4).
Quantities for 4.

1 lb apples, rhubarb or plums (500 g),   spice or grated lemon rind
  or ½ lb berries (250 g)

Peel, core and slice apples. Wash and cut rhubarb into short pieces. Remove stones, slice large plums. Prepare berries in the usual way.

Put the fruit in an ovenproof dish. Add 4 Tbs water (none for berries). Add spice or lemon to taste.

2 oz plain flour (6 Tbs or 50 g)	4 oz light brown sugar (½ c or 100 g)
1 oz rolled oats (¼ c or 25 g)	2 oz butter or margarine (50 g)

Mix the dry ingredients in a basin. Melt the fat and stir it into the flour mixture until it makes a crumbly consistency. Use a fork for mixing and avoid having the fat too hot. Sprinkle the crumble on top of the fruit and bake until the fruit is tender and the top golden brown. Do not over-cook or the juice will bubble through and spoil the crisp top. Serve hot or cold with

cream or custard sauce.

Hazel nut soufflé
(for the blender)

Cooking time 20–30 mins.
Temperature 190° C (375° F; G5).
Quantities for a 1½ pt (1 l) soufflé dish or other baking dish, well greased.

3 oz toasted hazel nuts (75 g)	2 oz caster sugar (50 g)
1 oz butter or margarine (25 g)	¼ pt hot milk (150 ml)
3 egg yolks	

To toast the nuts, cook them in a moderate oven until they begin to brown. There is no need to rub off the skins. Put all ingredients in the goblet and blend until the nuts are finely chopped. Tip into the milk pan and heat, stirring vigorously until the mixture thickens. Remove from the heat.

3 egg whites, beaten stiff

Fold carefully into the nut mixture and put in the prepared dish. Bake until well risen and lightly browned. It should still be soft in the centre. Serve at once, plain or with

single cream or a thin chocolate sauce.

Queen's pudding

Cooking time 1 hr.
Temperature 180° C (350° F; G4).
Quantities for 4–6.

4 oz fresh breadcrumbs (1½ c or 100 g)   ½ oz butter (15 g)
1 oz sugar (2 Tbs or 25 g)

Put these in a bowl.

1 pt hot milk (500 ml)

Pour on to the crumbs and leave to stand for a few minutes for the crumbs to become soaked and the butter to melt.

2 egg yolks, beaten
pinch of salt
½ tsp vanilla essence or a little grated lemon rind

Add to the crumb mixture, mix and pour into a pie dish or other baking dish. Bake for about 45 mins or until it is set in the middle. Remove from the oven and leave to stand for a few mins.

2–3 oz jam (2–3 Tbs or 50–75 g)

If the jam is stiff, soften it with a little hot water. Spread a thin layer over the top of the pudding.

2 egg whites   2 oz sugar (4 Tbs or 50 g)

Beat the egg whites until they stand up in peaks. Fold in the sugar and pile the meringue on top of the pudding. Return to the oven and cook until the meringue just begins to colour, about 10–15 mins. Serve hot or warm.

Rhubarb meringue

Cooking time 50–60 mins.
Temperature 180° C (350° F; G4).
Quantities for 4.

1 lb rhubarb (500 g)

Wash, trim and cut in 1 in (2½ cm) pieces.

4 oz sugar (½ c or 125 g)   grated rind of 1 orange
¼ tsp salt

Mix these with the rhubarb.

1 pkt sponge cakes (4 small trifle sponges)

Grease a baking dish and cover the bottom with thin slices of sponge cake. Cover this with about a quarter of the rhubarb and continue the layers until the rhubarb is all used. Cover the dish and bake for ½ hr or until the rhubarb is tender.

2–4 oz granulated sugar (4–8 Tbs or 50–125 g)   2 egg whites

Beat the egg whites until stiff and fold in the sugar. Pile this on top of the pudding and bake uncovered for 15-20 mins until pale brown and set. Serve hot or cold.

ALTERNATIVE

Use canned or stewed rhubarb instead of the raw fruit and sugar. Layer it with the sponge and put the meringue on top. Bake.

Rice pudding with bay leaves and raisins

Cooking time 2 hrs.
Temperature 150° C (300° F; G2).
Quantities for 3-4.

1 pt milk (500 ml)	1 large bay leaf, or 2 small
½ tsp coriander seeds	

Put in a pan and bring to the boil. Set aside to infuse and become almost cold. Strain the milk.

1½ oz pudding rice (3 Tbs or 40 g)	pinch of salt
1 Tbs sugar	3 oz seedless raisins (½ c or 75 g)

Put in a baking dish with the milk and cook slowly, stirring once or twice during the first hour. Serve hot.

ALTERNATIVE

Let the pudding get cold and then mix in some cream to make it soft. Serve cold with fruit.

Swedish apple soufflé

Cooking time 1 hr.
Temperature 180° C (350° F; G4).
Quantities for 4.

2 oz soft brown sugar (4 Tbs or 50 g)   4 Tbs water

Heat the sugar and water together in a pan until the sugar dissolves.

1½ lb apples (700 g)

Peel, core and quarter and cook in the syrup until they are soft. Place them in a fireproof dish and leave to cool.

2 egg whites	2 Tbs ground almonds
2 oz sugar (4 Tbs or 50 g)	almond essence
2 tsp ground rice or semolina	

Beat the egg whites until stiff. Fold in the other ingredients, adding almond essence to taste. Spread this over the apples and bake until lightly brown and set, about ½–¾ hr. Serve hot or cold with

custard sauce or whipped cream.

STEAMED PUDDINGS

The essential with cooking steamed puddings, whether you put the pudding in a steamer or cook it in a saucepan, is to keep the water boiling steadily and to use boiling water if it is necessary to top up. In a saucepan the water should come about half-way up the sides of the pudding basin.

The top of the pudding needs to be securely covered to prevent water from getting in. Some pudding basins have their own metal lids but a piece of foil pressed over the top and firmly down the sides for a couple of inches is perfectly adequate.

Steamed puddings can be made in advance and re-heated, as with a Christmas pudding, and they may also be frozen. Freezing is not necessary with a Christmas pudding as it will keep for a year or more in a cool dry store. But it is very convenient to have a supply of other frozen puddings, especially if they have been frozen in individual portions.

Cool puddings thoroughly before wrapping and freezing. Turn them out of the pudding basins and wrap in foil or polythene. They can then be put back in the basins for re-heating or left in the foil and re-heated in a steamer or in the oven.

Thaw the puddings before re-heating. This will take 6 hrs for a large one, less for individual portions. Then steam for ½–1 hr depending on the size, or heat in the oven at 180° C (350° F; G4) for 15–20 mins for small ones. Large ones are really better heated by steaming.

In the recipes the cooking time has been given for the whole mixture; individual puddings take about three-quarters of that time.

Chocolate pudding

Cooking time 1½–2 hrs, or 1 hr in individual moulds. *Quantities* for 4.
Grease the pudding basin or moulds.

2 oz butter or margarine (50 g)   2 oz sugar (4 Tbs or 50 g)

Cream together until light and fluffy.

1 egg ½ tsp vanilla essence

Beat the egg into the creamed mixture and add the vanilla.

4 oz self-raising flour (¾ c or 100 g) 2 Tbs cocoa
pinch of salt milk to mix

Sift these together and stir them lightly into the creamed mixture, adding enough milk to make a soft dropping consistency. Fill the basin or moulds not more than ¾ full, cover with foil and steam. Turn out and serve with

chocolate sauce or custard sauce.

Christmas pudding

Recipes for these are legion and many families have one handed down from mother to daughter. They are very easy things to make so do not be put off by the fuss some people make about the preparation of the pudding. It does not even have to be made months in advance, just make it when convenient; a week beforehand is enough.

Cooking time 4 hrs when preparing and 2–3 hrs on the day it is served.
Pressure cooking 1½ hrs when preparing and 25–30 mins on the day it is served.
Quantities for a 2 pt (1¼ l) basin, enough for 8 or even more.

2 oz plain flour (6 Tbs or 50 g) 1 tsp mixed spice
½ tsp grated nutmeg ¼ tsp salt
¼ tsp ground cinnamon

Sift these into a large mixing bowl.

4 oz prepared suet (¾ c or 125 g) 2 oz fresh breadcrumbs (⅔ c or 50 g)
4 oz sugar (½ c or 125 g) 2 eggs, beaten
1 lb mixed dried fruit (3 c or 500 g), 2–4 Tbs brandy or other spirit
  including some mixed peel

Mix all the ingredients together very thoroughly, adding enough liquid to make a fairly soft consistency. Steam for the first time, covered with a foil lid. Allow to become cold, cover with fresh foil and store in a dry cool place.

PRESSURE COOKING

When the pudding is first made use 2½ pt (1¼ l) of boiling water and steam without pressure for 30 mins to allow the pudding to begin to rise, then bring to pressure and continue cooking. On the day of use, steam for 25–30 mins at pressure all the time with 1 pt (½ l) of boiling water. Either allow the pressure to reduce at room temperature or hold the cooker under the cold tap.

TO SERVE THE PUDDING

Have the serving dish very hot and the brandy or rum (4 Tbs or more) to hand, together with holly for the top and a heated spoon for serving. Pour the brandy or rum round the pudding on the hot dish, not over the pudding. Set the spirit alight and baste the pudding with the burning liquid.

SAUCE FOR THE PUDDING

Hard sauce or Cumberland rum butter, page 68; or egg custard sauce flavoured with sherry or brandy; or pouring cream.

Coconut pudding

Cooking time 1 hr. *Quantities* for 4.

4 oz desiccated coconut (1 c or 100 g)   ½ pt milk (250 ml)

Heat together in a small pan over a very gentle heat, for about 10 mins or until the milk is absorbed. Stir it frequently. Remove from the heat and allow to cool a little.

2 oz butter (50 g)   2 oz caster sugar (4 Tbs or 50 g)

Cream together thoroughly.

2 oz breadcrumbs (½ c or 50 g)   2 egg yolks
2 oz sponge cake crumbs (½ c or 50 g)   ½ tsp vanilla essence

Add these to the creamed mixture together with the coconut.

2 egg whites

Beat until stiff and fold into the cake mixture. Put in a greased basin, about three-quarters full, and steam for 1 hr. Turn out and serve with a sauce such as jam sauce, custard sauce or cream.

Jam layer pudding

Cooking time 2 hrs. *Quantities* for 4.

8 oz self-raising flour (1½ c or 200 g)   ¼ tsp salt
4 oz grated suet (100 g)   ¼ pt water (150 ml)

Put the dry ingredients in a bowl and mix to a soft dough with cold water.

Divide into four pieces. Roll one piece to fit the bottom of a greased 1½ pt (1 l) basin.

8 oz well-flavoured jam or marmalade (200 g)

Spread a layer of jam or marmalade on the pastry in the basin. Roll each of the other pieces a little bigger than the last and layer them with jam or marmalade, finishing with pastry. Cover the top of the basin with foil and steam the pudding for 2 hrs.

Remove the pudding from the pan and leave it to stand for not less than 5 mins before turning it out. It can be left in a warming cupboard while the first course is served. Run a knife round the sides of the pudding to loosen it and turn it out on to a hot serving dish. Serve plain or with

custard sauce, or a jam sauce using more of the same jam.

Treacle pudding

Cooking time 2 hrs. *Quantities* for 4–6.

4 oz caster sugar (½ c or 100 g)   2 eggs
4 oz butter or margarine (100 g)

Cream the fat and sugar until light and fluffy and then beat in the eggs one at a time.

8 oz black treacle (8 Tbs or 200 g)   4 Tbs milk

Should the treacle be cold enough to be stiff, warm it slightly before using it. Add treacle and milk to the creamed mixture.

8 oz self-raising flour (1½ c or 200 g)

Add to the mixture and stir in gently. Put in a greased 2 pt (1¼ l) basin, cover with foil and steam for 2 hrs. Allow to stand for a while before turning it out on to a hot dish. Serve with

custard sauce or single cream.

SWEET PANCAKES

Basic recipe

Quantities for 8 pancakes.

For how to freeze, see page 38.

4 oz plain flour (¾ c or 125 g)	1 oz caster sugar (2 Tbs or 25 g)
2 eggs	½ pt milk (250 ml)

Put the flour and sugar in a basin and make a well in the centre. Add the eggs and start mixing from the centre, gradually working in the flour and adding milk until half the quantity has been used. Beat well and then add the remaining milk. Pour into a jug.

lard

Heat a little in an 8 in (20 cm) frying pan, pour out any surplus and pour in a thin film of the batter. Cook until brown underneath, turn or toss and cook the other side. Serve with lemon juice and caster sugar or in one of the ways below.

ALTERNATIVE METHOD OF MIXING

Put all the ingredients in the goblet of the electric blender and process at high speed for 1 minute.

Banana pancakes

Quantities for 8 pancakes.

2 large ripe bananas	1 Tbs lemon juice
caster sugar	

Skin the bananas and mash them with the lemon and sugar to taste. As each pancake is cooked, spread it with some of the banana mixture. Roll up and keep hot. Serve sprinkled with caster sugar.

Banana pancakes flambé

4 Tbs rum	caster sugar

Use the recipe above and when all the pancakes are ready, warm the rum, ignite it and pour over the pancakes. Sprinkle with caster sugar and serve with lemon wedges.

Orange marmalade pancakes

Add some grated orange rind to the pancake mixture before cooking it and spread them with orange marmalade before rolling or folding and serving.

Stuffed pancakes

8 oz sieved cottage cheese or mashed curd cheese (250 g)

cream

Mix in enough cream to make the cheese a soft spreading consistency.

jam

As each pancake is made, spread with jam and then with the cheese. Roll up.

pouring cream or sweetened whipped cream

An optional extra to serve with the pancakes.

ALTERNATIVE

Add chopped dried or crystallized fruit to the cheese mixture and a little spirit or liqueur to taste. Finely grated orange or lemon rind are other good flavourings.

Flans, pies and tarts

Recipes for making pastry, shaping flans and covering pies will be found in Chapter 1, Basic Dumpling, Pancake and Pastry Recipes. Here, too, is information on freezing pastry, flans, pies and tarts.

Any of these sweets which contain cream, milk, eggs or gelatine in the filling should be given refrigerated storage if not used up on the day of preparation. Unless they are meant to be served very cold, remove them from the refrigerator in time to allow them to reach room temperature before serving.

Apple dumplings

Cooking time 30 mins or more.
Temperature 200° C (400° F; G6).
Quantities for 4.

short-crust pastry using 8 oz flour (1½ c or 200 g), or use 12 oz ready-made pastry (350 g)
4 medium-sized cooking apples
brown sugar
margarine or butter
pinch of grated nutmeg or ground cloves

Peel and core the apples. Roll the pastry into a rectangle about ¼ in (6 mm) thick. Cut it into four squares. Put an apple on each piece and fill the centre with sugar. Add a knob of fat and a pinch of either of the spices. Moisten the edges of the pastry with water and then mould it up over the apple, making a good seal at the top. Turn the dumpling upside-down on a baking tray and cook until the pastry is crisp and the apple feels soft when you pierce it with a fine skewer. Serve hot or cold with

custard sauce or cream.

Apple flan

Cooking time ½–¾ hr, plus time to stew some apples.
Temperature 200° C (400° F; G6).
Quantities for a 7–8 in flan (18–20 cm).

1 lb cooking apples (500 g)	½ oz butter (15 g)
¼ tsp grated lemon rind	1 Tbs water; omit this if the apples are juicy
2 Tbs sugar	

Use half the apples first. Peel, core and slice them and mix with the other ingredients. Stew to a thick pulp. Cool.

short-crust pastry using 4 oz flour (100 g), or use 6 oz ready-made (175 g)

Roll thinly to line a flan ring or tin. Spread the cold apple pulp in the bottom.

granulated sugar

Peel, core and slice the rest of the apples very thinly. Arrange them on the apple pulp in a spiral design. Sprinkle with sugar and bake until the pastry is firm, ½–¾ hr.

2 oz apricot jam (2 Tbs or 50 g)   1 Tbs water

Heat together until runny, sieving if necessary to make a smooth glaze. As soon as the flan comes out of the oven brush this glaze all over the apples. Cool the flan and then lift it on to a serving dish. Serve cold.

Apple tart or double-crust pie

Cooking time 30–45 mins.
Temperature 220° C (425° F; G7).
Quantities for an 8 in (20 cm) tart.

6 oz flour made into short-crust pastry (175 g), or use 10–12 oz (300–350 g) ready-made

Use a flan ring or pie plate. Divide the pastry into two pieces, one a little bigger than the other. Use the larger piece for the bottom and the smaller for the top.

1 lb apples, cooking or dessert (500 g)
1 tsp grated lemon rind
¼ tsp grated nutmeg or ground cinnamon

2 tsp lemon juice
pinch of salt
4–6 oz sugar (½–¾ c or 100–150 g)

Peel and core the apples and slice fairly thinly. Put apples, flavourings and sugar in the pastry. Cover with pastry, sealing the edges carefully. Cut small slits all over the top.

Place the tart on a baking tin in case juice boils over and bake until the pastry is lightly browned and the fruit cooked, shown by juice appearing in the slits in the top.

cream or custard sauce   caster sugar

Serve the tart hot or cold, sprinkled with sugar, and hand the cream or sauce separately.

Apple tart with fennel seeds

Use the recipe above but omit lemon and spices and substitute 2 tsp fennel seeds.

Apricot flan or apricots à la bourdaloue

Cooking time 40 mins. *Quantities* for an 8 in (20 cm) flan.

4 oz flour (100 g) made into short-crust pastry with egg, page 41

Line the flan ring and bake blind for 15–20 mins.

2 oz macaroons (50 g)

Crush with a rolling pin, grate, or crumb in the electric blender. Tip into a basin.

2 eggs, beaten
1 oz flour (3 Tbs or 25 g)
4 oz caster sugar (½ c or 100 g)

pinch of salt
½ pt milk (250 ml)

Mix the eggs into the sugar and flour to make a smooth cream, gradually adding the milk. Put in a pan and stir until the mixture thickens and comes to the boil. Cook gently for 2–3 mins.

1½ oz butter (40 g)

Add to the pan and stir until the butter melts. Add half the macaroon crumbs. Cool the mixture, stirring occasionally to prevent a skin from forming.

not less than 1 lb (500 g) canned apricot halves, or 1 lb fresh apricots poached in syrup

Drain the fruit. Spread half the macaroon sauce on the bottom of the flan case.

Arrange a layer of fruit on top of this, keeping back a few pieces for decoration. Cover the fruit with the rest of the mixture. Sprinkle the remaining macaroon crumbs over the top and decorate with fruit.

ALTERNATIVE

Make the same recipe with other fruit such as bananas poached in vanilla-flavoured syrup; canned or fresh cooked peaches; or use poached pears or apples.

Berry tart or pie

Make and bake in the same way as apple tart, page 419. For an 8 in (20 cm) tart use:

1½ lb berries (700 g)   4 oz sugar (½ c or 100 g)
2 Tbs flour sprinkled over the fruit

The flour is for thickening the juice slightly as the fruit cooks. For sharp fruit like black currants and gooseberries you may want to use some more sugar.

Coconut flan

Quantities for a 7 in (18 cm) refrigerated flan case, page 42, or sponge flan case, page 42.

Prepare 8–12 hrs in advance and refrigerate.

1½ oz sugar (3 Tbs or 40 g)   ¼ tsp salt
2½ Tbs cornflour   ½ pt milk (250 ml)

Mix the dry ingredients with a little of the milk. Heat the rest of the milk and pour it into the blended mixture, stirring well. Return to the pan and stir until it boils. Simmer for 5 mins, stirring frequently. Remove from the heat.

1 egg yolk, beaten

Stir into the cornflour mixture,

½ oz butter (15 g)   ½ tsp vanilla essence
2 oz desiccated coconut (⅓ c or 50 g)

Mix in and pour the filling into the prepared flan case. Cool, and then refrigerate until required. Serve garnished with

whipped cream or fresh or canned fruit.

Fruit flan

Quantities for an 8 in (20 cm) flan.

Make the flan and bake blind, see page 42. Leave to cool. Put on a serving dish.

1 lb fruit (500 g) fresh, frozen, canned or bottled

Drain stewed or canned fruit, remove any stones and arrange the fruit in the flan case.

1 Tbs potato flour or arrowroot   ½ pt syrup (250 ml)

Mix the flour to a smooth paste with the syrup from canned, stewed or bottled fruit. For fresh or frozen fruit use a sugar and water syrup or fruit juice. Put the blended flour in a small pan and stir until it comes to the boil. Pour over the fruit and leave to cool.

ALTERNATIVE

Instead of using flour for thickening dissolve 1½ Tbs gelatine in the hot syrup, leave until cold and beginning to thicken and spoon over the fruit.

For fresh ripe or frozen fruit use ½ pt (250 ml) of any appropriately flavoured packet jelly. Allow it to become cold and begin to thicken, then spoon over the fruit. Leave to set. Garnish any flan with

whipped cream.

Fruit pies

Cooking time 30–45 mins.
Temperature 220° C (425° F; G7).
Quantities for 4–6.

For the fruit use any of these:

- 2 lb apples (1 kg), 2 cloves or a little grated nutmeg
- 1 lb apples (500 g) and 1 lb blackberries (500 g)
- 2 lb (1 kg) apricots, peaches, plums, remove stones
- 2 lb rhubarb (1 kg) cut in 1 in (2½ cm) pieces, add some grated lemon rind
- 2 lb gooseberries (1 kg), topped and tailed

In addition

¼ pt or less of water (150 ml)
4 oz or more of sugar (½ c or 100 g)

6 oz flour made into short-crust pastry (175 g)

Put the fruit in a pie dish piling it well up in the middle. Roll the pastry and cover the pie, see page 43. Place the pie dish on a baking tray and cook until the pastry is lightly browned and the fruit cooked.

Sprinkle the top with sugar and serve with

cream or custard sauce.

Honey and cinnamon cheese flan

Cooking time 35–40 mins.
Temperature 190° C (375° F; G5).
Quantities for an 8 in (20 cm) flan.

4 oz flour made into short-crust pastry (100 g), or use 6 oz ready-made (175 g)

Roll the pastry to line a flan ring, prick the bottom and refrigerate while the filling is prepared.

8 oz sieved cottage cheese (250 g)	2 oz liquid or melted honey (2 Tbs or 50 g)
2 oz caster sugar (4 Tbs or 50 g)	

Combine these thoroughly.

2 eggs, beaten	1 tsp ground cinnamon

Gradually beat into the cheese mixture. Pour into the pastry shell and bake until the filling is set and the pastry lightly browned. Serve warm or cold.

Lemon chiffon pie

Quantities for an 8 in (20 cm) refrigerated flan, page 42.

½ Tbs gelatine	2 Tbs cold water

Put the water in a small pan and sprinkle in the gelatine.

5 Tbs lemon juice (75 ml)	2 oz sugar (4 Tbs or 50 g)
½ tsp grated lemon rind	2 egg yolks

Add to the pan, stir and cook over a gentle heat without boiling until it thickens slightly (it thins when the sugar melts and then thickens). Remove from the heat.

2 egg whites	2 oz sugar (4 Tbs or 50 g)

Beat the whites until stiff and then beat in the sugar. Fold in the lemon mixture and pour into the flan case. Leave to set and store in the refrigerator.

whipped cream to garnish or hand separately.

Lemon meringue pie

Cooking time 15–20 mins for the pastry; 15–20 mins for the meringue; 7–8 mins for the filling.
Temperature: pastry 200° C (400° F; G6); meringue 160° C (325° F; G3).
Quantities for a 7–8 in pie (18–20 cm).

4 oz flour made into short-crust pastry (100 g), or use 6 oz
ready-made pastry (175 g)

Roll the pastry thinly to line a flan ring or pie plate. Bake blind.

3 Tbs cornflour $\frac{1}{2}$ pt water (250 ml)

Mix the cornflour to a smooth cream with a little of the water.

grated rind of 1 lemon

Add to the rest of the water and bring to the boil. Pour into the cornflour, mix well, return to the pan and stir until it boils. Boil gently for 5 mins.

2 egg yolks

Add to the pan and heat and stir until the eggs thicken the mixture. Avoid further boiling.

3–4 oz sugar (6–8 Tbs or 75–100 g)   juice of 1 lemon
1$\frac{1}{2}$ oz margarine (40 g)

Add to the pan and mix until the margarine melts. Pour into the cooked pastry case.

2 egg whites   3 oz sugar (6 Tbs or 75 g)

Beat the egg whites until stiff and then beat in half the sugar; fold in the rest. Pile the meringue on top of the filling and bake until it is lightly coloured and set. Allow to cool and serve warm or cold.

Pineapple and orange flan

Quantities for a 7–8 in (18–20 cm) refrigerated flan, page 42.

Prepare 6–8 hrs in advance and refrigerate.

about 15$\frac{1}{2}$ oz can of pineapple slices   2 Tbs potato flour or arrowroot
(375 g)

Keep back one slice of pineapple for garnishing. Mix the potato flour or arrowroot to a smooth paste with a little of the juice. Make a purée of the rest of the pineapple and the juice, either in the electric blender or by rubbing through a sieve. Add the blended starch to this and stir in a pan until it comes to the boil. Remove from the heat.

½ oz butter (15 g)   1 Tbs lemon juice
caster sugar

Add to the pineapple mixture and pour into the flan. Sprinkle with caster sugar and leave to become cold.

1 can of mandarin oranges

Drain and use these and the remaining piece of pineapple to cover the top of the flan with fruit.

2–3 Tbs sieved apricot jam   a little warm water
a little kirsch

Combine and spoon over the fruit to glaze it. Leave to become cold and then cover and refrigerate.

Pumpkin pie

Cooking time 45 mins.
Temperature 220° C (425° F; G7).
Quantities for a 7 in (18 cm) flan or pie plate.

short-crust pastry using 4 oz flour (100 g), or use 6 oz (175 g) ready-made

Roll the pastry thinly and line the flan ring or pie plate. Refrigerate while the filling is prepared.

8 oz fresh or canned pumpkin purée   1 tsp ground ginger
   (250 g)   pinch of salt
1 Tbs golden syrup   1 egg yolk
pinch of grated nutmeg   4 Tbs milk (60 ml)
1 Tbs brown sugar

Mix all together thoroughly.

1 egg white

Beat stiffly and fold into the pumpkin mixture. Pour into the pastry case and bake until the pastry is lightly browned and the filling set. Serve hot or cold.

Treacle tart

Cooking time 20 mins.
Temperature 220° C (425° F; G7).
Quantities for a 7 in (18 cm) tart.

short-crust pastry using 4 oz flour (100 g), or use 6 oz (175 g) ready-made pastry

Roll the pastry thinly and line a flan ring or pie plate. Refrigerate for about 20 mins before adding the filling.

6 oz syrup or treacle, or half and half (150 g)

3 oz fresh breadcrumbs (1 c or 75 g)
grated rind of 1 lemon (optional)

If the syrup is very stiff warm it slightly. Spread it over the bottom of the tart and sprinkle the lemon rind on top. Add the breadcrumbs and leave the tart to stand for $\frac{1}{2}$ hr so that the crumbs begin to sink into the syrup. Bake until the pastry is lightly browned. Serve hot or cold.

16. Cakes, Biscuits, Scones and Bread

Those who like to do their own baking have probably been brought up on the home-made variety and prefer it to the commercial product. Those brought up on the shop variety are usually quite happy with it and often really prefer it, especially the bread and biscuits.

I think a modern home cook should do her own baking only if she enjoys it as a creative hobby and is prepared to become skilled at it. Some feel they should do it because they have been told that it saves money. This may or may not be true depending on the quality, quantity and type of baked goods the family enjoys. Apart from bread all these are luxuries, not necessities, in a healthy low-cost diet. If economy is important it is better to eat fewer cakes and biscuits and spend the money instead on the more essential foods such as bread, milk, cheese, meat, vegetables and fruit.

The recipes I have included in this chapter are not meant for everyday food to fill the hungry but for an occasional special treat for tea or a party.

Those who like to bake, but only eat a little cake occasionally, can make use of the freezer for prolonging its useful life and the same goes for home-made bread and other baked goods.

For short-term storage of up to a week (more for fruit cakes and biscuits), it is best to keep all baked goods in either airtight tins, polythene boxes or polythene bags. Cakes with a cream filling should either be filled just before serving them, or covered and stored in the refrigerator. It is a waste of space to store other baked goods in the refrigerator and this includes bread, which does not in fact keep any fresher than it would in an airtight box or bag in a kitchen cupboard.

To freeze bread and buns

Provided they are properly wrapped to prevent evaporation, they will keep in good condition for up to a month. Always cool all baked products thoroughly before freezing them otherwise they will go soggy when thawed.

Polythene bags are usually the most satisfactory containers, particularly for sliced bread when you may only want to remove a few slices at a time and then re-seal the bag.

Unless bread or buns are meant to be served hot or toasted, thaw them at room temperature in the unopened wrapper. If removed from the wrapper, bread especially tends to become soggy with condensation. Thawing a 1 lb (½ kg) loaf will take 7 hrs while a 2 lb (1 kg) loaf can take up to 12 hrs.

To thaw by heating, foil-wrap the loaf and put it in a fairly hot oven – 190° C (375° F; G5) – for up to 30 mins. It should then taste like freshly baked bread, but you will find that any not eaten up straight away will go stale very rapidly.

Sliced bread will thaw quickly when the pieces are spread out on a rack and it can be toasted while still frozen.

Yeast rolls and scones are better if heated to thaw them, especially if you want to keep a crisp crust. Foil-wrap and heat at 180° C (350° F; G4) for 10–15 mins. For soft rolls and buns, thaw at room temperature in the unopened bags and leave in the bags until you want to use them.

To freeze cakes

Those which are well worth freezing are the light sponge cakes which tend to stale fairly quickly, and cakes with cream fillings or other moist, easily perishable fillings.

Once it is thawed, a frozen cake goes stale more quickly than a fresh one, so if you only want to use a little of it at a time it is better to cut it in portions for freezing. Delicate cakes, like iced cakes, are better frozen unwrapped on a tray, then wrap or put in boxes. The same applies to small cakes which might easily be damaged by close packing.

Thaw cakes at room temperature, large ones up to 12 hrs, small cakes and portions will take 2 hrs, less in a warm room. Unwrap iced cakes, leave others wrapped for thawing.

To freeze biscuits

Freeze cooked biscuits in polythene bags or boxes and thaw 2–3 hrs in the unopened package. They can be thawed more quickly by putting them on trays in the oven at the lowest setting for 5–10 mins.

Raw doughs for making freshly cooked biscuits can be frozen in a block or sausage shape. Thaw enough to be able to slice off the number of biscuits you want, then re-seal the packet. Bake the biscuits on well-greased trays or on non-stick paper as you would for unfrozen dough.

Cake tin sizes

In each recipe I have given the size of tin I have used for making the cake. If your tins are not approximately the same size as these, use one a trifle bigger and reduce the cooking time a little.

The same applies to small cakes and biscuits. If you can make more than the number I give in the recipe, reduce the cooking time, if you make less and therefore larger ones, increase the cooking time.

LARGE CAKES

Almond fruit cake

Cooking time 2–3 hrs.
Temperature 150° C (300° F; G2).
Quantities for an 8 in cake tin (20 cm).
Use a non-stick tin or line it with paper.

8 oz butter (250 g)
4 eggs

8 oz caster sugar (1 c or 250 g)
8 oz ground almonds (2 c or 250 g)

The butter and eggs should be at room temperature. If necessary, warm the mixing bowl before starting to cream the butter and sugar together. When the mixture is light and fluffy beat in the eggs one at a time, alternating these with some of the ground almonds. Add the rest of the almonds.

1 oz chopped preserved ginger ($\frac{1}{4}$ c or 25 g)
12 oz sultanas (2 c or 350 g)
grated rind of 1 orange

4 oz plain flour ($\frac{3}{4}$ c or 125 g)
3 oz chopped mixed peel ($\frac{1}{2}$ c or 75 g)
pinch of salt

Stir the flour and salt into the creamed mixture, then the fruit and lastly the orange rind. Put in the prepared tin, smoothing the top of the mixture. Bake until a fine skewer inserted in the centre comes out clean. Leave the cake in the tin to cool. When it is quite cold store it in an airtight tin or box where it will keep fresh for several weeks.

Austrian hazel-nut gâteau

Cooking time 40 mins.
Temperature 190° C (375° F; G5).
Quantities for a 7 in (18 cm) cake tin.
Use a non-stick tin or line the bottom with a circle of non-stick paper.

8 oz shelled hazel nuts (250 g)

Toast the nuts by baking them in a moderate oven until the skins will rub off easily, though this is merely used as a test for the toasting and the skins are left on for this cake. Cool the nuts. Either mince them or chop coarsely in the electric blender. In the blender do them in several small lots switching on/off until they are chopped. Tip them into a bowl.

3 egg yolks   6 oz caster sugar (¾ c or 175 g)
1 Tbs rum

If the eggs are cold, warm the bowl. Add egg yolks and the other ingredients and whisk until thick and light.

3 egg whites

Whisk until stiff enough to stand up in peaks. Fold in the nuts and the egg yolk mixture and turn it into the prepared tin. Bake until the cake is lightly browned. Invert the cake tin over a rack and leave it to fall out as it cools. Leave until cold.

butter cream, page 448, or whipped cream

Slice the cake through the centre and fill it with whipped cream or butter cream flavoured with rum, vanilla or finely ground toasted hazel nuts. It can be iced with more butter cream and decorated with hazel nuts.

A coffee-flavoured butter cream also goes well with this cake.

Bienenstich

This is a delicious cake to serve at tea-time or with coffee, or serve warm as a dessert.

Cooking time 30 mins.
Temperature 190° C (375° F; G5).
Quantities for 16–20 good-sized pieces.

2 oz butter or margarine (50 g)   4 oz granulated sugar (½ c or 100 g)
1 Tbs milk   ½ tsp vanilla essence

Heat together in a small pan until the fat melts. Remove from the heat.

4 oz roughly chopped hazel nuts or blanched almonds (100 g)

Add to the pan and set aside to cool.

4 oz sieved cottage cheese (100 g)   4 Tbs milk
4 Tbs salad oil   2 oz sugar (4 Tbs or 50 g)
pinch of salt

Put in a bowl and mix well.

8 oz self-raising flour (1½ c or 250 g)

Add the flour a tablespoon at a time, mixing each in before adding the next, until about half has been added. Then work in the rest, finishing by kneading very lightly to make a smooth ball. Roll out into a rectangle about ¼ in (6 mm) thick. Put on an oiled baking sheet or tin, lifting it up with the aid of the rolling pin, wind it round and then unwind on to the tin. Spread with the nut mixture and bake until well-browned. Cut in pieces while it is still hot and cool it on a wire rack. Serve warm or cold.

Cheese cake, baked

Cooking time 1 hr.
Temperature 150° C (300° F; G2).
Quantities for an 8 in (20 cm) tin.
A loose bottom tin is the best to use for this, otherwise use a deep flan ring or a deep sandwich tin lined with foil and having the ends projecting above the edges of the tin for easy removal after baking.

3 oz butter or margarine (75 g)   1 Tbs golden syrup

Heat together in a small pan until melted.

6 oz digestive biscuit crumbs (175 g)   1½ oz caster sugar (3 Tbs or 40 g)

Add to the melted mixture, blend well and press down into the bottom of the tin and up the sides to make a case. Put it in the refrigerator while the filling is being made.

1 lb sieved cottage cheese (500 g)   2 oz caster sugar (4 Tbs or 50 g)
2 eggs, beaten

Beat these together thoroughly.

¼ pt evaporated milk (150 ml)   1 tsp vanilla essence

Gradually beat these into the other mixture. Pour it into the prepared tin and bake until the filling is set. Allow to become cold, cover and refrigerate until chilled. Lift it carefully on to a serving dish.

jam

Spread a layer over the top of the cheese mixture and serve as a cake or cold sweet.

Cheese cake, refrigerated

Quantities for an 8 in (20 cm) tin. A tin with a loose bottom is best and it should be deeper than a sandwich tin. Alternatively, use an ordinary cake tin with a piece of foil as a lining, having the edges projecting above the top of the tin so that the cake can be lifted out on the foil.

3 oz cornflake or biscuit crumbs (75 g)	2 oz very soft butter or margarine (50 g)
1 oz sifted icing sugar ($\frac{1}{4}$ c or 25 g)	

Mix these together thoroughly until very well blended. Tip into the tin and press flat.

1 Tbs gelatine soaked in 4 Tbs cold water	4 oz granulated sugar ($\frac{1}{2}$ c or 125 g)
3 egg yolks	4 Tbs milk

Put the egg yolks in a small pan or a double boiler and beat to mix them. Add the sugar and milk and stir over a gentle heat until the sugar has dissolved and the mixture begins to thicken. Remove from the heat, add the soaked gelatine and stir until it dissolves. Set the mixture aside to cool, but not long enough to set. Meanwhile prepare the remaining ingredients.

1 lb sieved cottage cheese or low-fat curd cheese (500 g)	pinch of salt
grated rind of $\frac{1}{2}$ lemon	1 tsp vanilla essence

Combine in a mixing bowl.

3 egg whites   2 oz granulated sugar (4 Tbs or 50 g)

Beat the egg whites until they stand up in peaks. Beat in the sugar until the mixture is very thick. Set aside.

5 Tbs whipping cream (75 ml)

Put in a small basin and whisk lightly, not until stiff. Add the egg yolk mixture to the cheese mixture and beat until it is quite smooth. Fold in the cream and lastly the egg whites. Pour into the tin and spread evenly. Cover with a lid of foil and refrigerate for at least 8 hrs. Remove from the tin and then lift it off the base on to a serving dish, using a fish slice or similar utensil.

cornflake or biscuit crumbs or finely chopped nuts

whipped cream
fresh or drained canned fruit

The cheese cake may be served plain or decorated by coating the sides with crumbs or nuts and the top with piped cream and fruit. Refrigerate again until required.

Chocolate Swiss roll

Cooking time 7–10 mins.
Temperature 200 °C (400° F; G6).
Quantities for 1 Swiss roll tin.
Use a non-stick tin or grease and line with non-stick paper.

3 eggs

Put in a warmed bowl and whisk until very light and fluffy.

2 oz fine brown sugar ($\frac{1}{4}$ c or 50 g)

Add to the eggs and continue whisking until the mixture is so thick that when the beater is removed the impression remains for a few seconds.

1 oz cornflour (3 Tbs or 25 g)
pinch of salt

1 oz cocoa (3 Tbs or 25 g)
$\frac{1}{4}$ tsp vanilla essence

Sift cornflour, cocoa and salt together and fold them gently into the egg mixture, together with the vanilla. Spread evenly in the tin and bake until it feels springy when pressed lightly with the finger tips. Loosen the edges with a knife and turn the cake on to a piece of greaseproof paper which has been dusted with caster sugar. Remove non-stick paper if used. Trim the edges of the cake with a knife and roll it up with the greaseproof paper inside. Leave until cold.

$\frac{1}{4}$ pt double cream (150 ml), or use butter cream, page 448

rum (optional)

Either whip the cream until it is stiff but not buttery, flavouring if desired, or make the butter cream. Unroll the sponge, remove the paper and spread on the cream. Roll up again.

icing sugar

Sprinkle the top thickly with sifted icing sugar.

Chocolate Venetians

chocolate Swiss roll, recipe above
granulated sugar

vanilla-flavoured butter cream, pages 448–9

Instead of rolling the cake, cool it flat on a rack. When it is cold cut it into three even strips lengthwise. Sandwich these together with the butter cream and ice the top thinly with the same butter cream. Sprinkle the top with granulated sugar and cut the cake into about 10 portions.

Rich fruit cake

Cooking time 3½–4 hrs.
Temperature 140° C (275° F; G1).
Quantities for an 8–9 in tin (20–23 cm).

Line the tin with non-stick paper coming a few inches above the top of the tin. A mixture as rich as this rises very little so the tin can be filled to within ½ in (1 cm) of the top. If you prefer a wider, thinner cake use a larger tin and reduce the cooking time.

2 lb currants (1 kg)
3 oz ground almonds (75 g)
8 oz sultanas (200 g)
¼ tsp grated nutmeg

8 oz mixed chopped peel (200 g)
½ tsp each of ground cinnamon and mace

Mix these together in a bowl, adding a little of the flour (see below) as this helps to separate the pieces of fruit.

8 oz butter (200 g)
1 oz black treacle (1 Tbs or 25 g)

8 oz sugar (200 g), half fine brown and half caster

Cream these together in a large mixing bowl or by machine.

8 oz plain flour (1½ c or 200 g)
¼ tsp baking powder

4 eggs
pinch of salt

Mix the dry ingredients together. Beat the eggs into the creamed mixture one at a time with a little of the flour. Add remaining flour and stir in thoroughly.

2 Tbs brandy or rum

Add this with the fruit and mix very thoroughly. Put in the prepared tin and spread the top evenly, making a slight depression in the centre. Bake until a fine skewer inserted near the centre comes out clean. When the top is sufficiently browned, protect it by placing a piece of foil or greaseproof paper on top. Leave the cake to cool in the tin.

Before covering the cake with almond paste, page 448, turn it upside down, make a few skewer holes in the bottom and sprinkle it with rum or brandy, allowing this to soak in (about 3 Tbs).

Genoese sponge

Cooking time 20–30 mins.
Temperature 190° C (375° F; G5).
Quantities for a 10 × 8 in tin (25 × 20 cm), or two 8 in (20 cm) sandwich tins. Use non-stick tins or line the bottoms with a piece of non-stick paper.

3 eggs	4 oz caster sugar (½ c or 100 g)

Either have the eggs at room temperature or warm the mixing bowl. Whisk the eggs until light, add sugar and whisk until the mixture is very thick so that when the whisk is withdrawn the mixture takes a few seconds to level out.

3 oz plain flour (⅔ c or 75 g)	3 oz melted butter (75 g), not hot
1 Tbs cornflour	

Sift the flour and cornflour together and use a metal spoon (not electric beater) to fold it in gently. Finally fold in the warm butter, gently and thoroughly. Spread evenly in the prepared tin. Bake until it feels springy in the centre when lightly pressed with the finger tips. It should also be showing signs of shrinking from the sides of the tin. Leave in the tin for a few minutes and then turn it out on to a wire rack to cool. This is the classic sponge used as a base for making small iced cakes and petits fours. It is also often split into layers, filled and iced and called a gâteau; or it can be filled with jam or lemon curd and the top dusted with icing sugar; or fill with whipped cream and jam. See also lemon gâteau, rum punch gâteau and praline gâteau, pages 437–8.

Gingerbread

Cooking time 45 mins.
Temperature 180° C (350° F; G4).
Quantities for a tin about 9 in (24 cm) square. Use a non-stick tin or line with non-stick paper.

4 oz plain flour (¾ c or 100 g)	1 tsp mixed spice
1 Tbs ground ginger	pinch of salt

Sift these into a mixing bowl.

2 oz sultanas (⅓ c or 50 g)	4 oz wholemeal flour (¾ c or 100 g)
1 oz chopped peel or crystallized ginger (2 Tbs or 25 g)	1½ oz fine brown sugar (3 Tbs or 40 g)

Add to the mixing bowl and combine well.

8 oz golden syrup or black treacle   4 oz butter or margarine (100 g)
(8 Tbs or 200 g)

Melt together but do not allow to become very hot.

1 tsp bicarbonate of soda   ¼ pt milk (150 ml)

Warm these together, stirring to dissolve the soda.

1 egg, beaten

Use the syrup or treacle, milk and egg to mix the dry ingredients to a smooth batter. Pour into the prepared tin. Bake until it feels springy to the touch when lightly pressed with the finger tips. It should also be showing signs of shrinking from the sides of the tin. Turn out of the tin. When cold, cut in squares or store whole and cut as required. This will keep several weeks in an airtight box and improves with keeping.

Greek yogurt cake

This is similar to a Madeira cake in appearance and texture, though it is a little more moist, and keeps moist too. Although the proportion of sugar used is higher than in a traditional British cake, the result is not sickly sweet.

Cooking time 1¼ hrs.
Temperature 180° C (350° F; G4).
Quantities for a 6 in (15 cm) cake tin. Use a non-stick tin or line it with non-stick paper.

4 oz softened butter or margarine   8 oz caster sugar (1 c or 250 g)
(125 g)

Warm the mixing bowl and the butter or margarine if it is not already soft. Mix together with a wooden spoon or by machine, going slowly until the two ingredients are blended, then beat a little in the usual way for a creamed mixture.

¼ pt thick yogurt (150 ml)

Add and beat again very thoroughly.

3 eggs   grated rind of ½ lemon

Beat in gradually, beating very thoroughly and not worrying if it appears to curdle.

8 oz self-raising flour (1½ c or 250 g)

Add the flour in three or four lots, beating well between each addition, until the mixture is a smooth thick batter. Spread evenly in the tin and bake until a fine skewer inserted in the centre comes out clean. Leave in the tin to cool for about 15 mins, then turn out on a cake rack to finish cooling. Serve as it is or sprinkled with

vanilla-flavoured icing sugar.

Honey cake (Swiss)

Cooking time 30 mins.
Temperature 180° C (350° F; G4).
Quantities for a Swiss roll tin about 13 × 9 in (33 × 23 cm).
Line the tin with non-stick paper or foil having the sides projecting about an inch (2½ cm) above the edges of the tin.

4 oz blanched almonds (100 g)

Grind half the almonds to a fine meal and chop the rest coarsely. This can be done in the electric blender or in a mincer. Tip the nuts into a mixing bowl.

8 oz self-raising flour (1½ c or 200 g)   8 oz caster sugar (1 c or 200 g)
1 oz chopped mixed peel (25 g)

Add to the almonds.

6 oz honey (6 Tbs or 150 g)   ½ tsp mixed spice
1 tsp ground cinnamon   1 egg, beaten

If the honey is not already liquid, warm to soften it or put egg, spices and honey in the electric blender to liquidize them. Mix these into the dry ingredients, kneading to make a stiff dough. Roll or pat out on a floured board to fit the tin, smoothing the top with a knife. Bake until the centre feels set when lightly pressed. Turn out on a rack and leave to become cold.

lemon glacé icing, pages 449–50, using 8 oz icing sugar (200 g)

Ice the top of the cake thinly, leave to set and then store it for three days, either wrapped in foil or in a polythene bag. During this time it softens and is then cut in fingers for serving. It is very sweet and small pieces are enough. It keeps very well in an airtight box or polythene bag.

Lemon gâteau

a Genoese sponge baked in sandwich   lemon-flavoured butter cream,
  tins, page 435   pages 448–9
lemon curd   chopped toasted nuts or coconut

Split the cold sponge into four layers and sandwich with lemon curd. Ice the top and sides with lemon butter cream an coat the sides with the nuts or coconut. Pipe more butter cream on top for decoration.

Praline gâteau

a Genoese sponge baked in sandwich tins, page 435
praline butter cream, pages 448–9
finely crushed praline or chopped toasted almonds

Split the cold sponge to give four layers. Sandwich these with praline butter cream. The top can be iced with the same cream or simply sprinkle the top with crushed praline. If it is iced, sprinkle the top with chopped toasted almonds.

Rum punch gâteau

1 Genoese sponge baked in sandwich tins, page 435
rum
sieved apricot jam
chocolate butter cream, pages 448–9, or butter icing, pages 448–9
blanched almonds
crystallized violets

Split the cold sponge to give four layers and sprinkle each layer with a few drops of rum.

If necessary, soften the jam with a little hot water. Flavour it with rum and sandwich the layers of cake with the jam.

Cover the top and sides with a layer of butter cream or icing and decorate with almonds and violets.

Victoria sandwich

Cooking time 20 mins.
Temperature 190° C (375° F; G5).
Quantities for two 7 in (18 cm) sandwich tins.
Use non-stick tins or grease and line the bottom with a circle of non-stick paper.

4 oz butter or margarine (125 g)   4 oz caster sugar (125 g)

Cream together until very light.

2 eggs

Add one at a time, beating each in thoroughly.

4 oz self-raising flour (125 g)   pinch of salt
few drops vanilla essence   1 Tbs warm water

Sift flour and salt together and stir into the creamed mixture with the essence and water. Spread evenly in the tins and bake until the cakes feel springy when pressed lightly in the centre. Leave in the tins to cool for 15 mins and then turn them out on to a cake rack to finish cooling. When cold, join together with jam or other filling.

Upside-down cake

Cooking time 30–40 mins.
Temperature 190° C (375° F; G5).
Quantities for a tin 6 × 8 in (15 × 20 cm) or a round tin of a similar capacity. Do not use a smaller one than this or the cake will be too thick and rather dull.

1 oz butter (25 g)	canned, fresh, or crystallized fruit
soft brown sugar	(see below)

Melt the butter in the cake tin and sprinkle in a thick layer of brown sugar. Drain canned fruit. Suitable fruits are pineapple, peaches, apricots, crystallized or glacé fruits of any kind, and some nuts as well. Arrange fruit to cover the sugar.

3 oz butter (75 g)	1 egg
3 oz caster sugar (6 Tbs or 75 g)	vanilla or other flavouring

Cream the butter and sugar together until light and then beat the egg in thoroughly.

6 oz self-raising flour (1¼ c or 175 g)	milk if needed to make a soft
pinch of salt	consistency

Stir into the creamed mixture. Spread the mixture thinly and evenly over the fruit. Bake until a skewer inserted in the middle comes out clean. Turn the cake out on to a serving dish. Serve warm or cold as a cake or cold sweet with cream handed separately.

Walnut gâteau

Cooking time 40 mins.
Temperature 190° C (375° F; G5).
Quantities for a 7 in (18 cm) tin.
Use a non-stick tin or line it with non-stick paper.

1 oz fresh breadcrumbs (25 g)	3 oz shelled walnuts, chopped (75 g)

Put in a bowl and set aside.

3 egg yolks
1 Tbs rum or 1 tsp vanilla essence
3 oz caster sugar (6 Tbs or 75 g)

Put in a warmed bowl and whisk together until very thick and light.

3 egg whites

Beat until stiff enough to stand up in peaks. Fold the egg yolk mixture and the crumb and nut mixture into the egg white, alternately. Put in the prepared tin, smooth the top and bake until the cake is firm in the centre. Turn it out on a rack to cool.

butter cream, page 448, or whipped cream   icing, optional

When the cake is cold, split it in half and fill with butter cream flavoured with chocolate or coffee, or with whipped cream. It is very good just like this but can be iced and decorated if you wish.

SMALL CAKES AND BISCUITS

Almond fingers

Cooking time 15–20 mins.
Temperature 180° C (350° F; G4).
Quantities for 3 dozen fingers.

4 oz butter (100 g)
1 egg yolk
2 oz caster sugar (4 Tbs or 50 g)

Cream the butter and sugar together thoroughly and beat in the egg yolk.

8 oz plain flour (1½ c or 200 g)
pinch of salt
1 tsp baking **powder**
milk

Sift the dry ingredients together and add to the creamed mixture, mixing and kneading to make a smooth dough. Add milk only if necessary to make a pliable dough. Roll out on a floured board to make a thin rectangle, keeping the sides as straight as possible (approximately ⅛ in (3 mm) thick).

1 egg white, beaten stiff
2–3 oz chopped blanched almonds (¼–½ c or 50–75 g)
about 4 oz icing sugar (¾ c or 100 g) sifted

Mix the icing sugar into the egg white, using enough to make a spreadable mixture. Spread it evenly over the biscuit and sprinkle the almonds on top. Use a sharp knife to cut the biscuit into finger shapes. Lift these on to baking trays, leaving a little space between each. Bake until the biscuits are a very pale gold colour. Leave on the baking tray to cool and then lift them off carefully with a palette knife. When they are quite cold, store them in an airtight box.

Brazil nut cookies

Cooking time 15–20 mins.
Temperature 180° C (350° F; G4).
Quantities for 4 dozen cookies.

4 oz butter or margarine (100 g)   4 oz caster sugar ($\frac{1}{2}$ c or 100 g)

Cream these together very thoroughly.

1 egg

Add to the creamed mixture and beat again.

4 oz shelled Brazil nuts, finely minced ($\frac{1}{2}$ c or 100 g)   6 oz plain flour (1 c plus 3 Tbs or 150 g)
1 tsp vanilla essence $\frac{1}{4}$ tsp salt

Add the vanilla and then mix in the other ingredients. Use either a plain piping tube and bag or a biscuit forcer to shape the cookies, or drop them on the baking tray in small spoonfuls. There is no need to grease the tray or leave room for spreading. Bake until they are firm to the touch and are just beginning to colour. Cool on a rack and store in an airtight box. They keep very well.

Caraway biscuits

Cooking time 15 mins.
Temperature 180° C (350° F; G4).
Quantities for 3 dozen 2$\frac{1}{2}$ in (5 cm) biscuits.

8 oz plain flour (1$\frac{1}{2}$ c or 250 g)   4 oz butter or margarine (125 g)

Put the flour in a bowl and rub in the fat.

4 oz caster sugar ($\frac{1}{2}$ c or 125 g)   pinch of grated nutmeg
1 Tbs caraway seeds

Mix into the flour thoroughly.

1 egg, beaten   1 Tbs sherry

Add the sherry and as much egg as is needed to mix the dry ingredients to a softish dough. Roll it out on a floured board to about ⅛ in (3 mm) thick and cut in rounds using a plain or fluted cutter. Put fairly close together on a non-stick or greased baking tray and cook until the biscuits are lightly coloured and crisp. Cool on a rack and, when quite cold, store them in an airtight container.

Cheese biscuits with herbs

Cooking time 15–20 mins.
Temperature 200° C (400° F; G6).
Quantities for 2 dozen 2¼ in (5½ cm) biscuits.

4 oz plain flour (¾ c or 125 g) few grains cayenne pepper
pinch of salt pinch of dry mustard

Put in a bowl.

1½ oz butter or margarine (40 g)

Rub into the flour until the mixture looks like fine breadcrumbs.

4 oz grated strong cheese (1 c or 1 Tbs chopped fresh herbs, or 1 tsp
125 g) dried herbs or fennel seeds

Suitable herbs are sage; sage and chives mixed; mint or marjoram alone or mixed; lemon or common thyme; dill; fennel; cumin; crushed coriander seeds.
Rub the herbs and cheese into the flour to distribute them evenly.

1 egg, beaten

Use to mix the ingredients to a stiff dough, adding only as much egg as is needed for this purpose. Roll out not more than ⅛ in (3 mm) thick and cut in shapes. Use any remaining egg, mixed with a little cold water, to brush the tops. Bake until they are crisp and lightly browned.

Choux pastry for éclairs, cream puffs or buns and profiteroles

Cooking time 20–40 mins.
Temperature 220° C (425° F; G7).
Quantities for 12 éclairs or cream puffs, or 24 small cream puffs or profiteroles.

1 oz butter (25 g) ¼ pt water (150 ml)
pinch of salt

Put these in a small pan and bring to the boil. Remove from the heat.

2 oz plain flour (6 Tbs or 50 g)

Add all at once and mix in. Return to a moderate heat and beat and cook until the mixture forms a ball in the centre of the pan, leaving the sides clean. Remove from the heat and cool for a few minutes, but do not allow the mixture to become cold.

2 eggs

Beat in one at a time, making sure the first one is well mixed in before adding the second. Beat until the mixture is smooth and shiny and then stop.

For shaping cream puffs or profiteroles the mixture may be put on greased trays in small heaps; but for shaping éclairs it is more satisfactory to use a piping bag and plain nozzle ($\frac{1}{2}$ in or 1 cm). Pipe the mixture in 2-3 in (5-8 cm) lengths, leaving plenty of room for rising.

Do not open the oven door for the first 20 mins for profiteroles, or 30 mins for large cream buns or éclairs. When they seem brown and firm, open one to make sure it is cooked in the middle. It is quite a good idea to slit all of them at this stage and dry them with the oven turned off. Use them while they are fresh as they become flabby with keeping too long.

They may be filled with whipped cream and frozen, then thawed at room temperature. A better way is to freeze them unfilled and thaw on trays in the oven at 120° C (250° F; G$\frac{1}{2}$) for 10-15 mins or until they are crisp; then cool and fill.

For serving, cream puffs or buns are usually filled with whipped cream or ice-cream and the tops dusted with sifted icing sugar. Profiteroles are filled in the same way and served as a dessert with chocolate sauce. Éclairs are filled with whipped cream and the tops iced with a chocolate glacé icing.

Lemon biscuits

Cooking time 15-20 mins.
Temperature 180° C (350° F; G4).
Quantities for 4 dozen biscuits.

4 oz butter or margarine (125 g)   4 oz caster sugar ($\frac{1}{2}$ c or 125 g)

Cream together until light.

1 egg   finely grated rind of 1 lemon

Beat the egg into the creamed mixture and add the lemon rind.

8 oz plain flour (1$\frac{1}{2}$ c or 250 g)   1 tsp baking powder
pinch of salt

Sift these into the creamed mixture. The dough should be a soft one suitable for putting in a biscuit forcer or cookie press. The metric version is a trifle stiffer than the original. If you prefer to roll the mixture and cut it into biscuits, put the dough in the refrigerator until it becomes firm enough for this. Roll it on a floured board. With a forcer, make finger shapes, using a fluted nozzle.

Bake the biscuits on greased trays until they are just beginning to colour; over-cooking spoils the fresh lemon flavour. Allow to cool on racks. These biscuits will keep fresh for several weeks in an airtight box or tin.

Little Cupids

Cooking time 15–20 mins for the pastry shells.
Quantities for 12 or more tarts made in bun tins.

short-crust pastry using 4 oz flour (100 g), or 6–8 oz ready-made (175–250 g)

Roll to line the bun tins and bake blind at 220° C (425° F; G7). Allow them to become cold before filling.

4 oz macaroon or ratafia crumbs (125 g)	3 Tbs sherry or brandy

Mix in a basin and leave for a few minutes for the liquid to soak into the crumbs.

¼ pt whipping cream (150 ml)	glacé cherries and angelica

Whip the cream until stiff but not buttery. Stir in the crumb mixture. Put the cream in the tart shells and garnish with cherry and angelica, or other garnish. Keep cold until required.

Macaroons

Cooking time 30–40 mins.
Temperature 160° C (325° F; G3).
Quantities for 18 medium-sized macaroons.
Either use non-stick baking trays or line the trays with a sheet of non-stick paper or foil.

6 oz ground almonds (1½ c or 175 g)	1 Tbs ground rice or fine semolina
8 oz caster sugar (1 c or 250 g)	

Put these into a mixing bowl.

2–3 egg whites

Beat until stiff but not dry. Gradually work them into the dry ingredients, using enough egg white to make a fairly stiff mixture suitable for rolling into balls in the hands; or add a little more egg to make it soft enough for piping with a forcing bag and plain nozzle. Leave room for the macaroons to spread.

18 blanched almonds

Press one on top of each macaroon and bake until they are lightly coloured and firm on the outside. If you are making them for macaroon crumbs they should be crisp all through so continue cooking at a lower temperature or with the heat turned off. Cool them on a rack and when they are quite cold, store in an airtight box.

Meringues

Cooking time 1 hr or more.
Temperature 120° C (250° F; G$\frac{1}{2}$).
Quantities for 18 meringues.

2 egg whites
4 oz sugar ($\frac{1}{2}$ c or 125 g)

vanilla essence or other flavouring

If a very fine textured meringue is preferred, use caster or icing sugar, or a mixture of both. Granulated sugar gives a very good meringue with a crunchy texture which is more interesting than the usual commercial meringue. Some cooks use half granulated sugar and half caster.

Beat the egg whites until they are stiff enough to stand up in peaks but are not dry or granular. Add up to half the sugar and beat again until the mixture is very thick. Fold in the remaining sugar and flavouring. Shape straight away. This can be done with two spoons, or use a forcing bag and a plain or star nozzle; put on non-stick paper on a damp tray.

Bake until they are almost done but still feel soft inside when one is tested by pressing the underside gently with the thumb. Press them all to make a hollow for the cream and then continue baking until they are crisp. The oven can usually be turned off for the final drying. Allow to become quite cold and store in airtight boxes, where they should keep crisp for at least a week.

whipped cream

Flavour to taste and use to join the meringues in pairs.

Note. If you prefer the meringues to remain white, use a lower baking temperature. I prefer mine to have a slight colour; they look better and taste better.

FLAVOURINGS

Instead of vanilla use:
1–1$\frac{1}{2}$ tsp powdered soluble coffee mixed with the sugar and folded in (granular soluble coffee will give a speckled effect); the finely grated rind of 1 lemon,

added with the last of the sugar and folded in; almond essence for flavouring; shape the meringues in fingers and sprinkle the tops with shredded blanched almonds.

Nut biscuits

Cooking time 15–20 mins.
Temperature 180° C (350° F; G4).
Quantities for 2 dozen 2½ in (5 cm) biscuits.

4 oz hazel nuts (100 g)   1 oz unblanched almonds (25 g)

Mince these finely or chop them in the electric blender in two lots, using the on/off technique. Put in a mixing bowl.

6 oz caster sugar (¾ c or 150 g)

Add to the nuts.

2 egg whites, beaten stiffly

Stir into the sugar and nuts.

about 3 oz plain flour (6 Tbs or 75 g)

Stir into the other mixture, using sufficient flour to make a stiff consistency suitable for rolling. Roll on a floured board to about ¼ in (½ cm) thick and cut in rounds with a fluted cutter. Either use non-stick baking trays or line them with a sheet of non-stick paper. Bake until the biscuits are lightly browned and firm.

chocolate icing and chopped hazel nuts

Either serve the biscuits plain or ice and decorate. They are fairly hard when first baked, rather like a gingernut, but soften with keeping, especially if they are iced. The flavour is very good.

Potato biscuits

These are excellent for serving with cheese.

Cooking time 25 mins.
Temperature 180° C (350° F; G4).
Quantities for 3 dozen 2½ in (6 cm) biscuits.

4 oz plain flour (¾ c or 100 g)   4 oz rolled oats (1 c or 100 g)
1 tsp salt

Mix these in a basin.

3 oz butter or margarine (75 g)

Rub into the flour mixture.

4 oz cold mashed potatoes ($\frac{1}{2}$ c or 100 g)

Knead the potatoes into the mixture until a stiff dough is formed. Do not add liquid. Roll out very thinly on a floured board and cut in rounds, using a plain cutter. Place on trays and cook until the biscuits are crisp but only slightly coloured. Cool on a rack and store in an airtight tin.

Shortbread biscuits

Cooking time 15 mins.
Temperature 180° C (350° F; G4).
Quantities for 3 dozen biscuits.

4 oz butter or margarine (125 g)	4 oz caster sugar ($\frac{1}{2}$ c or 125 g)
1 egg yolk	1 Tbs marsala or sherry

Cream the fat and sugar until light, beat in the egg and wine.

6 oz plain flour (1 c plus 3 Tbs., or 175 g)	pinch of salt
	1 oz cornflour (3 Tbs or 25 g)

Add these to the creamed mixture, stir and then work with the hands to make a pliable mixture. Shape it into a block like a butter pat, 1 in (2$\frac{1}{2}$ cm) thick. Wrap it in foil and put it in the refrigerator until it is firm enough to slice easily. Slice the block in $\frac{1}{4}$ in (6 mm) slices and bake on non-stick trays or line them with a sheet of non-stick paper. Leave a little room for spreading. Bake until pale brown and crisp. Cool on a rack and store in an airtight box.

Small marzipan cakes

Genoese sponge made in one flat cake, page 435

Stamp out rounds of cake with a 1$\frac{1}{2}$–2 in (4–5 cm) plain cutter.

8 oz (250 g) ready-made marzipan, or use the recipe on page 448

Roll the marzipan thinly and cut strips the same width as the thickness of the cake and long enough to wrap round the sides. Cut rounds to fit the tops.

sieved apricot jam

Thin the jam with a little hot water and brush the sides of the sponge with it. Wrap a strip of marzipan round each, brush the tops and press a round of marzipan on top of each cake.

glacé cherries

Put half a cherry in the centre of each, sticking it in position with a little jam.

ALTERNATIVE

Before wrapping the marzipan round the cakes, sprinkle them with a very little brandy, rum, sherry or kirsch.

ICINGS AND CAKE FILLINGS

Almond paste or marzipan

8 oz icing sugar (1½ c or 250 g) or 4 oz icing sugar plus 4 oz caster sugar	8 oz ground almonds (2 c or 250 g)

Mix these together in a basin.

2 egg yolks	few drops of almond essence
few drops of vanilla essence	¼ tsp rose water
2 Tbs lemon juice	

Beat the egg yolks and add the flavourings. Use this to mix the almonds and sugar to a stiff paste. Knead very thoroughly. If the paste is made in advance, wrap it in polythene and store it in a cool place. When rolling the paste to cover a cake, roll it between two pieces of polythene. To cover a cake, cut a circle the size of the top of the cake and a long strip to go round the sides. Brush the cake with melted jelly to make the paste stick. Store it for up to a week before covering the paste with royal icing. This allows the paste to dry out and give a firm basis for the icing.

The paste can be coloured with food colourings worked in a very little at a time. When models of fruit are made from marzipan the colouring is painted on afterwards with a brush.

This amount of almond paste is enough to cover a fruit cake weighing about 2 lb (1 kg), but this depends on the area of the cake and how thick you want the paste to be.

Butter cream
(to use as icing or filling)

6 oz butter (175 g)	12 oz icing sugar (2½ c or 350 g)

Warm the mixing bowl to soften the butter. Sift the sugar and cream it with the butter.

2 egg yolks

Beat into the creamed mixture and beat until smooth and light.

flavouring to taste

Add one of the following:
vanilla or other essence
rum or a liqueur
finely grated orange or lemon rind
1–2 Tbs soluble coffee
4 oz melted chocolate (125 g)
2 oz crushed praline (50 g)

ALTERNATIVE

Omit the egg yolks and use equal weights of butter and icing sugar.

Butter icing

This is sweeter than butter cream and sets more firmly.

Quantities for the inside and top of an 8 in (20 cm) sandwich cake.

4 oz butter (125 g)   8 oz icing sugar (1½ c or 250 g)

Warm the mixing bowl to soften the butter and cream it with the sifted icing sugar.

milk, water or fruit juice

Beat in enough liquid to give the right consistency for spreading and piping. For piping it should be thick enough to hold its shape well and a little thinner for easy spreading. This icing does not set hard.

CHOCOLATE BUTTER ICING

Add 2 oz (50 g) of melted chocolate or 2 oz (6 Tbs or 50 g) of cocoa powder mixed to a paste with a little boiling water. Flavour with vanilla or rum.

CHOCOLATE ORANGE ICING

As above but add the grated rind of ½ orange.

COFFEE BUTTER ICING

Use 2 Tbs instant coffee, or to taste, and flavour with vanilla or rum.

MOCHA ICING

Flavour with a mixture of chocolate and coffee.

ORANGE OR LEMON BUTTER ICING

Use the grated rind of 1 orange or lemon and some juice for mixing.

LIQUEUR ICING

Flavour with liqueur, rum, brandy or sherry.

SPICY ICING

Add ¼ tsp each of ground nutmeg, cloves and cinnamon.

Glacé icing

8 oz icing sugar (1½ c or 200 g)   flavouring and colouring
about 2 Tbs water or fruit juice

Sieve the icing sugar and beat in enough liquid to make the icing thin enough to coat the back of a spoon without running off too freely. Beat well until it is glossy and add colouring and flavouring.

CHOCOLATE GLACÉ ICING

Add 2 oz (50 g) melted chocolate or 4–6 Tbs cocoa mixed to a paste with a little boiling water. Add a tiny knob of butter to help give a shine.

COFFEE GLACÉ ICING

Add 2 Tbs instant coffee, or to taste.

LEMON OR ORANGE GLACÉ ICING

Use lemon or orange juice for mixing the icing.
A glacé icing is not spread, but poured over a cake and allowed to flow. Spreading destroys the shine.

Royal icing

Quantities 3 lb (1½ kg) icing sugar for a 12 in (30 cm) round cake; 2 lb (1 kg) icing sugar for an 8 in (20 cm) cake; 1 lb (½ kg) icing sugar for a 4 in (10 cm) cake.
The cake will need two coats of icing, allowing a few days between each.

1 lb icing sugar (3 c or 500 g)   2 egg whites
juice of ½ lemon   water if necessary

Sieve the icing sugar. Beat the egg whites until stiff and beat in the sugar and lemon juice, beating hard until the mixture is thick and light. Use a palette knife to spread it first over the top of the cake and then the sides. Dip the knife in hot water to give a final smoothing. An icing turntable is a help with doing the sides and when decorating but one can be improvised by putting the cake board on an inverted basin. To get smooth sides, hold the palette knife upright against the side of the cake and rotate it slowly.

Left-over icing can be kept for use later if it is left in the basin with a clean damp cloth pressed over the surface to prevent it from drying out.

BREAD AND SCONES

This section includes both yeast and baking powder breads. Some people are nervous of using yeast but it is not difficult to handle provided you remember a few points. The most important is that yeast mixtures must be fully risen before they are baked, whereas baking powder mixtures do their rising in the oven. So you have to have patience with yeast and give it time. The time it needs varies with the amount of yeast used and the temperature at which it is kept during rising. It works best in a really warm room or a warm airing cupboard; though if you want to do long, slow rising it will be satisfactory overnight in the refrigerator.

Yeast can be dried or fresh. Fresh yeast works a little faster initially than dried but there is very little difference. You will find that most of my recipes recommend mixing the yeast with liquid and a little sugar and leaving it to begin working and become frothy before mixing the dough. I think this is very important, especially with dried yeast, as you may have been sold old, tired stock; also, if you happen accidentally to add water or other liquid which is too hot, it will kill the yeast. So always do this preliminary work to see that the yeast is really active before you proceed.

If you have a strong mixing machine with a dough hook, this takes the hard work out of kneading and mixing the dough. Follow the maker's instructions for the amount to mix in one go and for the timing.

Kneading, by hand or machine, is done to make a bread dough elastic. This helps it to rise and give a good loaf, and also produces a fine, even texture. Insufficient kneading produces a coarse open texture. Each time a dough is kneaded some of the gas (carbon dioxide) produced by the yeast is lost, and a further rising period is required to make it light again. Hand kneading is a stretching and folding process done with the palms of the hands and is continued until tiny bubbles are seen beneath the surface, and the dough is springy and elastic when pressed with a finger.

YEAST, BREAD AND ROLLS

Baba au rhum

Today one seldom gets a really good baba in either a restaurant or cake shop so if you enjoy this kind of light, rich yeast mixture it is worthwhile making it yourself. It is, in fact, much easier than making a good loaf of bread. Individual portions can be baked in deep bun tins but the traditional tin is a savarin or ring mould, or small moulds.

Cooking time about 20 mins for small ones, 30 mins for a large one.
Temperature 200° C (400° F; G6).
Quantities for 4–6 small moulds or one 7 in (18 cm) mould. Grease the moulds thoroughly with unsalted butter.

4 oz plain flour (¾ c or 125 g)	¼ oz fresh yeast (10 g), or 1 tsp dried
4 Tbs milk (60 ml)	1 Tbs sugar

Put the flour into a basin and make a well in the centre. Heat the milk to lukewarm, blend the yeast with it and pour into the well. Sprinkle the sugar on top of the liquid and leave the bowl in a warm place until the yeast is frothy.

2 eggs, beaten	1 oz raisins (2 Tbs or 25 g)
2 oz butter (50 g), almost melted	

Add these to the yeast mixture and then mix all together. Beat hard for about 5 mins. Pour the mixture into the moulds, half-filling them. Stand small moulds on a baking tray. Put in a polythene bag and close the opening. Put in a warm place until the mixture rises almost to the tops of the moulds. This will take an hour or more. Towards the end of this time heat the oven.

Remove the baba from the bag and bake until the top feels springy in the middle when lightly pressed and the sides are beginning to shrink from the mould.

4 oz sugar (½ c or 125 g)	5 Tbs water (75 ml)
4 Tbs rum	

Boil sugar and water together for a minute, then add the rum. Turn the hot baba on to a serving dish and pour the rum syrup all over the top. Serve hot or cold, as a dessert or cake. Cold ones are often served with whipped cream and a fruit garnish.

Soft dinner rolls

Cooking time 15 mins.
Temperature 220° C (425° F; G7).
Quantities for 18 rolls.

1 tsp sugar	1 tsp plain flour
½ oz fresh yeast (15 g), or 2 tsp dried	¼ pt warm milk (150 ml)

Mix milk, sugar and flour in a small bowl and sprinkle the yeast on top. Put in a warm place to become frothy.

12 oz plain bread flour (2½ c or 350 g)	½ tsp salt
	1 oz butter or margarine (25 g)

Mix the flour and salt in a bowl and rub in the fat.

1 egg, beaten

Use this and the frothy yeast mixture to mix the flour to a sticky dough. Beat well until it leaves the sides of the bowl clean. Put the bowl in a large polythene bag and close the opening or tuck the end under. Put in a warm place to rise until double in size, about 1 hr. Do not worry if it rises too much at this stage, better to over-rise than under.

Turn the dough on to a very lightly floured board or table top and knead it lightly with the knuckles, which will reduce the bulk somewhat, but it should still feel soft and light. Shape into rolls, see below. Put on greased or non-stick baking trays, put the trays in polythene bags and put in a warm place for them to rise to double in bulk, ½ hr or more. Heat the oven.

Brush the rolls lightly with a little beaten egg and water or milk and bake until brown and firm to the touch.

SHAPING ROLLS

The simplest way is to roll the dough into a ball and flatten slightly. Put them on the trays so that when they increase to double in size they will be almost touching each other.

Clover Leaf Rolls. Shape a piece of dough into a long, thin sausage and cut off pieces weighing about ¼ oz (10 g) each. Roll each piece into a ball and put them in greased patty tins in sets of three balls in each. Rise to double in bulk and bake.

Figure Eights. Roll 1 oz (25 g) pieces of dough into an 8 in (20 cm) rope about ½ in (1 cm) thick. Pinch the ends together to make a loop and then twist the loop to make a figure eight. Put to rise until double in bulk and bake.

Crescents. Roll a 6 oz (175 g) piece of dough into an 8 in (20 cm) round about

⅜ in (9 mm) thick. Cut into 6 wedges. Starting at the wide end roll each piece towards the point. Place on a tray with the point tucked under and the ends curved round to make a crescent shape. Put to rise until double in bulk and bake.

Braids. Roll strips of dough about 18 in (20 cm) long and ⅜ in (9 mm) thick. Plait three of these strips together and cut them into 3–4 in (8–10 cm) lengths. Pull each slightly to lengthen it and put to rise to double in bulk, then bake.

Poppy Seed Rolls. After brushing any of the rolls with milk or egg prior to baking, sprinkle with poppy seeds.

Soft dinner rolls with herbs

Use the above recipe, adding ½–1 tsp mixed crushed dried herbs with the egg used for mixing the dough. Instead of crushed herbs, herb seeds can be used. Suitable herbs are: marjoram, thyme, mixed herbs, fennel or dill seeds, crushed coriander seeds.

Vienna bread

This is a soft white plait of bread, easy to make and keeps very well.

Cooking time about 20 mins.
Temperature 220° C (425° F; G7).
Quantities for 2 loaves.

1 tsp sugar	¼ pt lukewarm milk (150 ml)
1 tsp flour	½ oz fresh yeast (15 g), or 2 tsp dried

Mix the sugar, flour and milk in a small basin, sprinkle in the yeast and whisk well. Put in a warm place until frothy.

1 lb plain bread flour (3 c or 500 g)	1 tsp salt

Sift into a mixing bowl.

2 oz butter (50 g), melted	about ¼ pt warm milk (150 ml)
1 egg	

Beat the egg and cool the butter a little. Use these, the yeast mixture, and more milk to make a sticky dough. Beat thoroughly until it leaves the sides of the basin clean, and is no longer sticky. Put the bowl in a polythene bag and close the opening or tuck the ends under the bowl. Put in a warm place to rise to double in bulk.

Turn the dough out on to a lightly floured board and divide in two, then each piece in three. Roll each of these into a long sausage about 1 in (2½ cm) thick and make two thick plaits with the six pieces, pressing the ends firmly together. Place on greased or non-stick trays, put in polythene bags in a warm place to double in bulk. Bake until firm. Tap the bottom of one and if it sounds hollow it is done. Cool on a rack.

Vienna plaits with fennel seeds

Make as above but mix 1 Tbs fennel seeds with the flour and salt.

Wholemeal bread

Cooking time ½–¾ hr.
Temperature 220° C (425° F; G7).
Quantities for two 1 lb (½ kg) loaves or three slightly smaller loaves.

1 tsp flour	¼ pt lukewarm water (150 ml)
½ oz fresh yeast (15 g), or 1 Tbs dried	1 tsp sugar

Put in a small bowl and whisk together. Put the bowl in a warm place until the mixture becomes frothy.

1½ lb plain 100% wholemeal flour (4 c or 700 g)	½ oz lard (15 g)
	1 Tbs salt

Put flour and salt in a mixing bowl and rub in the lard.

about ½ pt lukewarm water (300 ml)

Use this water and the yeast mixture to mix the flour to a soft dough, using more or less water as required. Knead the dough thoroughly by hand or machine, until it is smooth and elastic to the touch. Put the bowl in a large polythene bag and close the opening or tuck the ends under the bowl. Put in a warm place until the dough doubles in bulk, 1 hr or more. Do not worry if it over-rises at this stage. This is better than under-rising.

Turn the dough on to a lightly floured table top or board and knead lightly, or knead by machine. Divide the dough into two or three equal pieces, roll each into a sausage shape and put in the oiled tin. Put back in the polythene bag and leave in a warm place until the dough almost reaches the tops of the tins. Avoid over-rising at this stage or the loaf will be coarse in texture and inclined to be dry. Bake until brown. Turn one out and tap the bottom, a hollow sound shows it is cooked. Cool on a rack and when quite cold store in polythene bags.

Wholemeal bread with herbs

Make as the recipe above but add 1½ Tbs caraway, dill or fennel seeds after the lard has been rubbed in. Alternatively, for just one herb loaf in a batch knead the seeds in after the dough has had its first rising.

BAKING POWDER OR QUICK BREADS AND SCONES

Banana loaf

Cooking time 1 hr.
Temperature 180° C (350° F; G4).
Quantities for a 1 lb (½ kg) loaf.
Use a non-stick or well-oiled tin.

4 oz self-raising flour (¾ c or 125 g)	1 oz margarine (25 g)
½ tsp salt	

Put flour and salt in a basin and rub in the margarine.

2 oz shelled nuts, chopped (50 g)	1 egg, beaten
3 Tbs golden syrup	8 oz ripe bananas, mashed (250 g)

Add the nuts to the flour. Soften the syrup if necessary, by warming it, and use the egg, bananas and syrup to mix the flour. Turn into the prepared tin and bake until firm in the centre. Turn out on a rack to cool. When it is quite cold store it in a covered box or polythene bag for 24 hrs before cutting.

ALTERNATIVE METHOD

Use the electric blender to blend bananas, soft margarine, syrup and egg until smooth and use this for mixing the flour and nuts.

Cheese loaf

Replacing some of the milk used for mixing an ordinary cheese loaf by yogurt gives it a pleasant sharp flavour. This goes well with the cheese flavour and seems to make the loaf more moist, especially on the second day of cutting.

Cooking time 1 hr.
Temperature 180° C (350° F; G4).
Quantities for a 1 lb loaf tin (½ kg)
Use a non-stick tin or oil it well.

8 oz self-raising flour (1½ c or 200 g)   3 oz strong grated cheese (75 g)
½ tsp salt

Mix these in a bowl.

1 egg, beaten   milk to mix
5 Tbs yogurt (75 ml)

Beat the yogurt into the egg and add about 5 Tbs (75 ml) of milk. Use this to mix the dry ingredients to a stiff cake consistency, adding more milk as necessary. Turn the mixture into the prepared tin, smooth the top and bake. Turn out on a rack to cool. Serve spread with butter, and also marmalade if you like this combination of flavours.

ALTERNATIVE METHOD

Instead of grating the cheese, cut in pieces and put in the electric blender with the egg, yogurt and some milk. Blend to a smooth mixture and then add to the flour.

Cheese loaf with herbs

Use the recipe above, either with yogurt or using all milk for mixing. To the flour add ½ Tbs chopped fresh herbs or herb seeds or ½ tsp dried powdered herbs. Suitable herbs are: sage, marjoram, thyme, dill, fennel, basil or savory; use just one or a mixture.

Cheese scones with herbs

These are delicious to serve at tea-time or instead of bread with a salad meal. Use any of the herbs which go well with cheese, sage, marjoram, thyme, dill, fennel, basil or savory. Use just one herb or a mixture. Dried herbs are generally more satisfactory than fresh ones.

Cooking time 10–15 mins.
Temperature 250° C (475° F G9).
Quantities for 12 scones.

8 oz self-raising flour (1½ c or 200 g)   ½ tsp salt

Put in a mixing bowl.

2 oz butter or margarine (50 g)

Rub into the flour.

2 oz finely grated strong cheese ($\frac{1}{2}$ c or 50 g) $\frac{1}{2}$–1 tsp dried crushed herbs, depending on strength of flavour

Mix into the flour using your fingers to distribute them evenly.

about $\frac{1}{4}$ pt milk (150 ml)

Use a knife for mixing and add milk to make a very soft, almost sticky dough. Roll out on a floured board to about $\frac{1}{2}$ in (1 cm) thick and cut in rounds about $2\frac{1}{4}$ in (6 cm), or cut in squares. Put on a baking tray, brush the tops with milk and bake until golden brown. Serve hot or warm.

Girdle scones

Useful to make for eating in place of bread in an emergency, or to have fresh and hot for tea-time. They can be cooked on a girdle or griddle, in an electric frying pan, or in a heavy iron frying pan over a direct heat.

Cooking time 20–25 mins. *Quantities* for 8 large scones.

8 oz self-raising flour ($1\frac{1}{2}$ c or 200 g)   2 oz margarine (50 g)
pinch of salt

Mix the flour and salt in a bowl and rub in the margarine.

1 egg, beaten   milk to mix, about $\frac{1}{4}$ pt (150 ml)

Use this to mix the flour to a very soft dough. Form the dough into a ball and roll it out on a floured board to make a circle about $\frac{1}{2}$ in (1 cm) thick. Pat the edges into a neat shape. Cut it into 8 triangles.

Heat an electric pan to about 180° C (350° F) or use a girdle or pan over a moderate heat. Grease the cooking surface lightly with lard. Cook the scones, turning when they are brown on one side and have risen. Use a palette knife or fish slice for turning them. Cook until the second side is browned and the scones cooked through. They are best served while still warm, with butter and jam, or clotted cream and jam, or just with butter.

Cheese girdle scones

Add to the above recipe, after the margarine has been rubbed in,

2–3 oz grated strong cheese (50–75 g).

Sweet girdle scones

Add to the recipe for girdle scones, above, after the margarine has been rubbed in,

2 Tbs sugar.

Cakes, Biscuits, Scones and Bread 459

Whole wheatmeal girdle scones

Make the recipe above for girdle scones, substituting 100% whole wheatmeal self-raising flour for the white flour. These are very good eaten warm or cold, especially with honey for a sweet spread, or plain with cheese.

Soured cream scones

These are very light with a pleasant flavour and keep fresh longer than ordinary scones. They are also very good toasted.

Cooking time 10–12 mins.
Temperature 250° C (475° F; G9).
Quantities for 10 2½ in (5 cm) scones.

8 oz self-raising flour (1½ c or 200 g)	½ tsp salt

Put into a mixing bowl.

1½–2 oz butter or margarine (40–50 g)

Rub into the flour.

4 Tbs soured cream (60 ml)	4–6 Tbs milk (60–90 ml)

Combine the cream and 4 Tbs of the milk. Use this to mix the flour to a soft dough, adding the remaining milk as needed. Roll out on a lightly floured surface to about ½ in (1 cm) thick and cut in rounds or other shapes. Put on a baking tray, brush the tops with milk and cook near the top of the oven until they are lightly browned. Cool on a rack. Use warm or cold. When they are quite cold store them in a polythene bag.

Treacle loaf

Cooking time 1 hr.
Temperature 180° C (350° F; G4).
Quantities for a 1 lb (½ kg) loaf.
Use a non-stick tin or line the bottom with non-stick paper and grease the sides.

8 oz self-raising flour (1½ c or 200 g)	½ tsp mixed spice
½ tsp salt	½ tsp ground ginger

Sift into a mixing bowl.

2 oz margarine (50 g)	8 Tbs milk (120 ml)

Warm these together just to melt the margarine, cool a little.

2 Tbs black treacle   1 egg, beaten
2 oz fine brown sugar (4 Tbs or 50 g)

Add these to the margarine and milk, stir to dissolve the sugar and use to mix the dry ingredients to a soft consistency. Put in the prepared tin and bake until firm in the centre. Turn out on a rack to cool. When quite cold store in a polythene bag for 24 hrs before cutting.

17. Drinks

ALCOHOLIC DRINKS

Today wines at fair prices are available in Britain from all over the world. The wines that most people drink at home are those they know and like, or those which have been recommended to them. When drinking out, the choice is limited to the wine list presented, and the 'best' is not necessarily the most expensive. A lot depends on the policy of the management and the clientele. Most wine waiters in this country tend to treat you fairly, and there is no disgrace in asking for advice. No one can know the content of all the cellars available.

A wine gives pleasure via three senses, taste, smell and sight. Assuming the wine is good, the first two qualities are governed by the state of your palate. Smoking and eating highly-seasoned foods will radically alter your sense of taste and appreciation of delicate flavours. It is necessary to find from experience something that suits your own palate.

The shape of the glass used is important for getting the best flavour from a wine. It is not easy in Britain to buy retail the standard clear wine glass found on every good European table. The shape should be such as to enhance the aroma when drinking, or, in the case of sparkling wines, to show and preserve the play of bubbles. Many modern glass designers are spoiling wine drinking by exaggerating their own fantasy for colour and form. It is noteworthy that many of these come from non-wine countries.

The 'best'? Certainly not necessarily that with the highest alcoholic content (which rarely exceeds 10%). Some wines, notably champagnes, are more expensive to produce than others. Within any one type, commercial competition largely takes care of price levels against quality.

Broadly, the very best white wines come from Germany and reds from France. The best vintages, that is wines from grapes of a specific year's harvest, can be checked from a number of reliable sources and when the product is really noble it has to be paid for. Non-vintage wines, which are quite pleasant, are a matter of experiment and advice.

Certain traditions of wine drinking exist but if you like it a different way, drink what you like when you like it. Red wine is generally best with meat or poultry. Champagne, hock or Moselle go with any course in the meal. A sweet white wine is best kept for the sweet course or dessert, though many women like it throughout the meal. Dry wines are best with fish and hors d'œuvre. Any wine can be served with cheese, though many people prefer a red wine, or madeira.

Red wine is best served at room temperature, uncorked about an hour before drinking. Young red wines and rosés should be slightly chilled. White wines are served chilled.

WINE CUPS

These are cold drinks with a basis of wine and often flavoured with fruit, spices and herbs.

RECOMMENDED HERBS

Angelica leaves for a muscatel flavour
Balm, use generously as the flavour is mild
Basil, the tender young tips
Bergamot leaves or flowers
Borage leaves and flowers
Burnet, young leaves for a cucumber flavour
Costmary, tiny piece for a bitter minty flavour
Mint leaves of any kind
Rosemary leaves and flowers
Verbena, lemon, for a perfumed lemon flavour.

Leaves are infused with the other ingredients, flowers are used as a garnish.

Hock cup

Quantities for $2\frac{1}{4}$ pt ($1\frac{1}{4}$ l).

1 oz sugar (2 Tbs or 25 g)
$\frac{1}{2}$ pt boiling water (250 ml)

$\frac{1}{2}$ lemon, peeled and sliced thinly, and/or herb leaves

Put sugar, lemon and herbs in a heat-resistant jug and pour in the boiling water. Cover the jug and leave to infuse for 15 mins.

1 small glass sherry   1 bottle of hock or Chablis

Add to the jug and leave the mixture to infuse for an hour. Strain and then chill in the refrigerator.

about ½ pt (250 ml) of chilled soda water

Add just before serving.

Claret cup

Quantities for 1¼ pt (700 ml)

2 tsp mixed spice   1 bottle claret
1 oz caster sugar (2 Tbs or 25 g)   ½ pt cold water (250 ml)

Mix these in a jug, stirring until the sugar has dissolved.

½ small lemon

Peel the rind very thinly and add this to the drink. Chill before serving.

Mulled wine
(to serve hot)

Quantities for just under 1 pt (½ l).

1 dessert apple

Wash the apple and bake it in a moderate oven for about 10 mins to heat it through, 190° C (375° F; G5).

a pinch of mixed spice   2 Tbs sweet sherry
2 Tbs honey   1 bottle red wine

Put in a pan and heat almost to boiling. Serve in a bowl with the apple floating on top. Use a ladle for filling the glasses, which should be warmed.

Grog
(to serve hot)

Quantities for 1.

1 slice lemon   1 tsp brown sugar

Put these in a heat-resistant tumbler.

boiling water   2 Tbs rum

Fill the tumbler three-quarters full with boiling water. Stir well and add the rum. Serve at once.

Vermouth with soda water and herbs

About a quarter fill tumblers with French or Italian vermouth. Fill up with chilled soda water. Add a slice of lemon, a lump of ice and sprigs of either mint, borage, lemon balm or lemon verbena.

Egg nog
(to serve hot or chilled)

Quantities for 1 large or 2 small glasses.

1 egg	pinch of salt
1–2 tsp sugar	2 Tbs sherry, marsala or madeira
8 fl oz milk (200 ml)	grated nutmeg

The milk may be hot or chilled. Whisk the egg with the sugar, salt, and wine, and pour in the hot or cold milk. Stir well and serve with a little nutmeg on top.

NON-ALCOHOLIC DRINKS

Banana egg flip
(for the blender)

Quantities for 1 large or 2 small glasses.

1 egg	2 Tbs milk
1 small ripe banana	1 Tbs caster sugar
¼ pt single cream (150 ml)	vanilla essence

Peel and cut up the banana. Put all the ingredients in the goblet of the blender and process until smooth. If you want the drink to be really cold, use egg, cream and milk straight from the refrigerator.

Fruit punch

Quantities for 25 glasses.

2 lb sugar (4 c or 1 kg) 2 qt water (2¼ l)

Put in a pan and boil for 10 mins. Cool.

6 oranges

Peel, remove as much white pith as possible and cut the oranges into slices. Add to the syrup.

6 more oranges   6 lemons

Extract the juice and add it to the first mixture.

4 sliced bananas   8 oz small green grapes, stoned
8 oz cherries, stoned (250 g)   (250 g)

Add, and chill the punch thoroughly in the refrigerator.

1 qt chilled ginger ale (1 l)   1 pt chilled strained tea (600 ml)
2 qt chilled soda water (2¼ l)   ice cubes

Add these to the chilled punch just before serving it.

VARIATION

Infuse herb leaves with the syrup, adding them when it is hot and straining them out before adding the fruit. Suitable herbs are angelica, balm, borage, mint, rosemary or lemon verbena.

Grapefruit and mint drink
(for the blender)

Quantities for a little over 1 pt (600 ml).

1 medium-sized grapefruit

Peel off the yellow rind thinly and put it in the blender goblet. Remove as much of the white pith as possible and discard it. Cut the fruit in pieces, removing pips, and put the fruit in the goblet.

2 oz caster sugar (4 Tbs or 50 g), or   ¼ c mint leaves (75 ml)
  to taste   1 pt cold water (600 ml)

Add to the grapefruit and blend until the grapefruit is pulped and the mint finely chopped. The mixture will then be a delicate green colour. Strain into a jug, cover and refrigerate until well chilled. Garnish each glass with

a small sprig of mint.

Grapefruit and orange drink
(for the blender)

Quantities for 1½–2 pt (1 l).

1 medium-sized grapefruit

If the grapefruit is a thin-skinned one simply wash it and cut it in pieces. If the skin is thick, peel off the outside yellow and put it in the blender goblet. Remove the white pith and discard it. Cut the rest of the fruit in pieces and put it in the goblet.

1 pt water (600 ml)   4 oz sugar (½ c or 125 g)

Add to the goblet and blend for a few seconds. Strain.

1 orange   ½ pt water (300 ml)

Wash and cut up the orange and blend it with the water for a few seconds. Strain and add to the grapefruit juice. Chill before serving.

Herb teas

The majority of herb teas are better made with dried herbs but some, such as lemon balm, mint, sage, sweet cicely and bergamot are equally good made with fresh leaves.

1 Tbs scissor-snipped fresh leaves per cup, or 1 tsp dried crushed herbs (not powdered finely), or herb seeds

These quantities can be varied according to taste, perhaps using less of the stronger herbs.

METHOD

Heat the tea-pot in the usual way, add the herb and pour in boiling water. Stir and leave to brew for 5 mins. Stir again and strain into the cups. Serve without milk.

Optional additions are lemon or orange juice (1-2 tsp per cup), or a small slice of orange or lemon, and sugar. Some like to make mint tea very sweet; other herbs suitable for making a sweetened tea are lemon balm, lemon verbena, bergamot, sweet cicely, sage and rosemary. The rest are usually too spicy for sugar, but this is a matter of taste.

HERBS SPECIALLY RECOMMENDED

Bergamot, fresh or dried
Dill seed
Lemon balm, fresh or dried
Lemon verbena, fresh or dried
Lemon verbena with eau de cologne mint in equal quantities
Lovage
Mint, fresh or dried
Rosemary
Sage, especially with lemon or orange juice
Savory, strong but good

Sweet cicely, very good for an anise flavour
Thyme for a strong flavour

Iced coffee

This is very good made with soluble or instant coffee or coffee concentrate.

METHOD 1 FOR 1 GLASS

The simplest way is to put 1 tsp or more of soluble coffee in the goblet of the electric blender, add 6–8 fl oz (175–200 ml) chilled milk and blend for a few seconds. For a sweetened drink add caster sugar to taste before blending.

METHOD 2 MAKES 1½ pt (1 l)

Make ½ pt (250 ml) of your usual coffee, but double strength. Mix with ½ pt (250 ml) of chilled milk and pour into a jug with ice cubes to make a total of 1½ pt (1 l). Serve.

METHOD 3

Make your usual brew of coffee, cool, chill in the refrigerator. Serve with chilled milk or cream and sugar to taste.

Lemonade

Quantities for just over 2 pt (1¼ l).

4 lemons   4 oz sugar (½ c or 125 g)

Scrub the lemons and peel off the yellow rind thinly. Put this in a jug with the sugar.

2 pt boiling water (1¼ l)

Pour on to the lemon and sugar and stir until the sugar dissolves. Leave to become cold. Strain and add the lemon juice. Serve iced or with cubes of ice in it.

Lemonade
(for the electric blender)

Quantities for 1¾ pt (1 l).

2 medium-sized thin-skinned lemons   2 oz sugar (4 Tbs or 50 g), or 2 Tbs
1¾ pt cold water (1 l)   honey

Scrub the lemons and cut them in large pieces, or leave whole according to the type of blender. Very large powerful ones will deal with whole lemons. Put the fruit in the goblet with the sugar and some or all of the water. Blend to chop the lemons coarsely. Strain. Taste for sweetening and then chill the lemonade in the refrigerator or serve it straight away with ice cubes.

VARIATION

Blend a few fresh mint leaves with the lemons.

Mint julep

Quantities for 8.

6 oz sugar (¾ c or 175 g)   ½ pt water (300 ml)

Heat to dissolve the sugar and bring to the boil. Boil for a minute or two.

3 Tbs chopped fresh mint

Add to the hot syrup and leave to cool. Then cover, and store in the refrigerator to chill it well.

¼ pt lemon juice (150 ml)   ¾ pt orange juice (400 ml)
1 qt dry ginger ale (1¼ l)

Put these in the refrigerator to chill. When ready to serve the julep, strain the mint syrup into a jug and add the chilled juices and ginger ale. Serve well chilled and garnished with

sprigs of mint, eau de cologne or other variety.

Orangeade in the blender

METHOD 1

Quantities for 1 large glass or two small.

Peel 1 small orange, slice it and remove the pips. Put it in the goblet, cover with cold water and blend for a few seconds. It can be served as it is or strained. For a sweet drink add sugar to taste.

METHOD 2

Quantities for 4–6 glasses.

2 medium-sized thin-skinned oranges,   1–2 oz sugar (2–4 Tbs or 25–50 g)
  or 1 orange and 1 lemon   1 pt cold water (600 ml)

Wash the fruit thoroughly. Cut it in pieces and put it in the goblet with the water and sugar. Blend for a few seconds, just to break up the skins coarsely. Strain at once.

This method produces a very good flavour and colour without bitterness. Over-blending or using very thick-skinned fruit will make it bitter.

Orange egg flip

Quantities for 1 large or 2 small glasses.

1 egg	1 Tbs sugar
6 oz chilled orange juice (175 ml)	

Put it in the goblet, blend until frothy and serve.

Spiced mocha drink
(for the blender, hot or cold)

Quantities for 4–6.

4 Tbs drinking chocolate	1 Tbs instant coffee
½ tsp vanilla essence or 1 tsp rum	pinch of ground nutmeg
¼ tsp ground cinnamon	¼ pt hot water (150 ml)

Put in the goblet and blend for 30 seconds. Tip into a pan.

¾ pt milk (400 ml)	whipped cream

Add the milk to the pan and bring to the boil. Serve with a spoonful of cream on each portion.

TO SERVE COLD

Process as before in the goblet and then add ice-cold milk or some ice and cold milk. Serve with cream as before.

Yogurt for drinking

This makes the ordinary thick yogurt into a drink like the filmjolk or surmelk of Sweden and Norway.

Quantities for 2 good-sized glasses.

½ pt plain yogurt (300 ml)	¼ pt milk (150 ml)

Remove these from the refrigerator just before mixing them. Either whisk them together or put in the electric blender and blend until smooth and frothy. If liked still thinner, add more cold milk.

Yogurt and fruit juice drink

Quantities for 2 small glasses.

¼ pt yogurt (150 ml) ¼ pt fruit juice (150 ml)
sugar to taste

Chill yogurt and juice either before or after mixing. Either whisk to a smooth drink or put in the electric blender for a few seconds. Serve very cold.

Yogurt and mint drink

Quantities for 4 glasses.

½ pt thick yogurt (300 ml) ½ pt cold water (300 ml)
pinch of salt

Put the yogurt in a bowl and whisk it until smooth, then beat in the water and salt to taste. Alternatively, mix the ingredients for a few seconds in the electric blender.

8–10 leaves of fresh mint, or a pinch of dried powdered mint

Either chop the fresh leaves finely and add, or blend the leaves with the yogurt for a few seconds to chop the mint finely. Put the drink in a jug, cover and chill in the refrigerator.

Yogurt and soda water drink

This may be a bit sharp for some people but it is a very refreshing drink, especially on a hot day.

Quantities for 2 glasses.

1 bottle soda water (8½ fl oz or ¼ pt yogurt (150 ml)
240 ml)

Have the yogurt and soda water well chilled. Put in the electric blender or beat together to mix well and make frothy. If desired, add an ice cube before serving.

18. Planning and Preparing Meals

PLANNING MEALS

To make a good job of family catering, forethought and planning are needed. The hand-to-mouth existence of the meal-at-a-time plan is not likely to provide interesting and varied meals, and is still less likely to provide healthy ones. The weekly plan is the best unit for most people, and a week starting on Thursday or Friday the most easily worked. This allows for one big shopping day to cover the basic needs of the week, the amount of possible advance shopping obviously depending on circumstances such as storage facilities and transport of goods.

It is unlikely that the week's plan will be followed in all details, as unforeseen events such as visitors, meals out, food unavailable or too dear, all necessitate last-minute changes. But a plan helps to reduce the time and worry of daily planning. The busier a woman is, the more useful such a plan can be.

Not only can food be bought in advance, but it may also be prepared in advance. While one meal is cooking, food can be partly prepared for the next meal and, if adequate refrigerator or freezer space is available, for further ahead than this.

How does one make a start with what, to the beginner, may seem a daunting task? The best thing to do is get a piece of paper large enough to hold an outline of meals for the week and rule it thus:

Meals	Fri.	Sat.	Sun.	Mon.	Tues.	Wed.	Thurs.
Breakfast							
Midday							
Evening							

The number of meals depends on convenience and family customs. Three meals are right for most people except those with very small appetites, and those with specially large needs such as children who are growing fast. Between-meal snacks for these should be nourishing ones like a milky drink and a sandwich rather than sweet drinks, sweets, biscuits and cakes.

If yours is a household where week-end cooking is the most important, start with planning the meals for Saturday and Sunday. Many people with freezers follow the main shopping day with a session in the kitchen, cooking food in advance for the rest of the week. This suits some but is not practical for others and can lead to monotony.

When the scheme for the week has been made out, check it for the following points:

1. Have you planned meals which you can easily cook in the time available, for example if there is a complicated dish with lots of ingredients to be prepared, or you plan to try a new recipe (which always takes longer than a familiar one), are all the other items ones which are quick and easy or can be made in advance?

2. Is there variety of texture, flavour and colour to make the meals interesting, and is there something in each which requires chewing (especially important for children)?

3. Have you planned to include each day at least some of the following very important foods? They are the main sources of protein, vitamins and minerals needed for good health.

MILK AND/OR CHEESE

A minimum of ½ pt milk (300 ml), more for children.
The following are good alternatives to fresh milk:

1 oz hard cheese (25 g)
2 oz soft cheese (50 g), cottage, curd, etc.
4 Tbs evaporated milk (60 ml)
1 oz dried milk powder (25 g)
½ pt natural yogurt (300 ml), more if fruit yogurt.

BUTTER OR MARGARINE

These are the only solid fats which provide vitamins A and D, the latter very scarce in other foods. The alternative is a daily dose of cod liver or halibut liver oil.

MEAT, GAME, POULTRY, FISH, EGGS

Try to include one of these at two meals daily. The cheapest are as good for you as the more expensive. When you are on a tight budget, extra cheese can be an alternative to these.

VEGETABLES AND FRUIT

Try to allow for two portions daily from this list; they are nutritionally our most valuable ones. Use others as available in addition to these.

Freshly cooked cabbage, brussels sprouts, spinach or cauliflower
Freshly cooked potatoes, or vitamin-enriched potato powder
Raw green vegetables such as watercress, cabbage, brussels sprouts
An orange
A grapefruit
A dose of blackcurrant syrup or rosehip syrup
2 tomatoes
5 tablespoons (a small glass or 75 ml) fresh, canned or frozen orange or grapefruit juice
¼ pt fresh or canned tomato juice (150 ml)

BREAD AND CEREALS

Allow 2–3 oz daily (50–75 g or 2–3 medium-thick slices) for people leading sedentary lives. Children, teenagers and very active adults need more. When on a tight budget use larger amounts of bread in place of cakes and biscuits, it is cheaper and better for you. If possible, include some whole-grain breakfast cereal, hard breads, or wholemeal bread for the roughage they contain.

Planning the shopping

Make up a shopping list from the menus you have planned, dividing the food into appropriate groups likely to be found in the same shop or part of the supermarket, for example, meats, fish, dairy foods, fruit and vegetables, bread and cereals, groceries.

Most newspapers and many radio programmes give really up-to-date information about foods in season and which are cheap of their kind. These are invaluable both for helping you to plan menus at different seasons and to plan economically. Generally speaking, fresh foods are cheapest at the height of their season and throughout the book I have given fresh food seasons where appropriate.

Storing food

If you are going to buy foods in advance, proper storing is obviously important to avoid wastage. In the introduction to each chapter I have given hints on the correct storage for the different foods, but the following list is a useful summary of the foods which are highly perishable and should not be purchased far in advance unless you have adequate refrigerated storage.

DAIRY FOODS

Fresh milk and cream
Yogurt, soured or cultured cream and butter milk
Opened canned, sterilized or UHT milk and cream
Eggs in the shell or separated
Cottage, curd and cream cheese
Butter and other fats

FISH

All raw, cooked and thawed fish and shellfish
Open cans of fish and shellfish
Made-up fish dishes such as fish pies, fish cakes and so on

FRUIT AND VEGETABLES

Soft fruits
Salad vegetables
Green vegetables and fresh herbs
Cooked vegetables and opened cans

MEAT

All raw, cooked, thawed meat, game and poultry and offal. Made-up dishes containing any of these, pies, casseroles, sandwiches and so on
Opened cans of meat

PUDDINGS

Any made with milk or cream
Any made with gelatine, especially if eggs, cream or milk are also included
Custard and other cold egg puddings

SAUCES AND SOUPS

All except unopened canned and packet ones or bottled sauces

Preparing the meal: how to make your own step-by-step working plan

The beginner usually finds the most difficult thing about preparing a meal is to have everything ready at the right time. This is a question of planning, organization and experience. Provided that you are prepared to do a little planning on paper it is really very simple.

Take the menu you have planned, write down the names of the dishes with the approximate cooking times. Make a list of which ingredients will need some preparation before cooking can be started. These you can often do the day before and store them, see Advance Preparation and Cooking, below. Some recipes give you a preparation time as well as a cooking time, but preparation times vary a lot with individual skills and often assume you will have no interruptions. It is always wise to do as much preparation as possible well ahead for this is often the part of a meal which takes more of the cook's time than the cooking itself.

Write down when you should start cooking each dish to have it ready by the meal time, and this is all the working plan you really need provided the preparation of ingredients has been done in advance. This is a much simpler way of working than the complicated interlocking of preparation and cooking. You will also be able to see from this sort of plan whether there are too many things to be started at the same time; you may then want to alter the menu slightly. Remember, too, to allow time for things to heat up, for example, for the pan to come to the boil, the casserole to heat through. Add a bit extra on to the time to allow for this.

It is always a good idea to include something in the menu which can be made completely the day before, or earlier in the day for an evening meal; or even far in advance for the freezer.

ADVANCE PREPARATION AND COOKING

Batters

Completely mixed pancake and other batters can be made well in advance, put in a covered container and stored in the refrigerator. Cooked pancakes can be made in advance, put in a pile on a plate, covered with a polythene bag and kept for two or three days in the refrigerator. To re-heat, spread them out on a baking tray and heat in a slow oven. Or, if they are stuffed pancakes, add the stuffing and heat the two together in a moderate oven for $\frac{1}{2}-\frac{3}{4}$ hr. If the stuffing is made in advance, store it separately. Pancakes can also be frozen and then re-heated to thaw them, see page 38.

Breadcrumbs

These are often needed in quite small quantities and when the recipe specifies fresh breadcrumbs it means these, not the dried packet ones. Breadcrumbs will keep several days in a polythene bag in the refrigerator, almost indefinitely in the freezer, and they thaw very quickly when tipped out of the storage bag or box.

Casseroles

Most of these can be cooked completely the **day** before, cooled and stored in the refrigerator. Before serving, bring them back to boiling point and boil for 10–15 mins. This is the best kind of recipe for cooking meat or poultry in advance. Most other ways are spoilt if the dish is re-heated; they always tend to taste like re-heated leftovers. Leftovers should be used up but I think it is a pity to treat food like this unless it is absolutely necessary; go for simple fresh cooking rather than for re-heating complicated dishes. For freezing cooked meat dishes, see page 156.

Cheese

Grated cheese is used in many recipes and it is a good plan to keep some in a polythene bag in the refrigerator, or for longer storage in the freezer. A little removed from the bag will thaw very quickly.

Cold sweets

All kinds can be kept either in individual dishes, covered with a lid of foil, or in a serving bowl with a cover. Some should have refrigerated storage, see Storing Food, page 473. For freezing, see page 377.

Cream

Whipped cream will stay whipped for several hours, but cover it closely and store in the refrigerator.

Eggs

Hard-boiled ones can be kept for several days in the refrigerator.

Fish

Many recipes use cooked fish as an ingredient. This can be cooked in advance, covered and stored in the refrigerator. Then combine it with sauce or dressing just before serving. For freezing fish, see page 123.

Fruit

All kinds can be prepared in advance, especially fruit salad, grapefruit and other citrus fruits and fruit juices; also fruit for dessert which is nicest when chilled, for example, fresh peaches or fresh strawberries. Avoid advance peeling of fruits which discolour, for example, apples, pears, peaches and bananas, unless they will be covered by syrup as in fruit salad. If breakfast grapefruit is prepared the night before, cover it closely and store in the refrigerator to preserve the vitamins. For freezing fruit, see page 352.

Garnishes

Parsley and other herbs can be washed, drained and stored in a covered dish or polythene bag in the refrigerator. Chopped herbs, herb butters for grills, tomatoes, cucumber and other garnishes can be prepared and stored.

Hors d'œuvre

Most ingredients for these can be prepared in advance and stored in the refrigerator in polythene bags or boxes.

Meat and poultry

This can be prepared for cooking and stored in the refrigerator or freezer. Casseroles can be cooked in advance for re-heating. For freezing meat, see pages 155-6, and poultry, page 220.

Pastry

This benefits from being made in advance and refrigerated before baking. For flans, add the filling just before cooking. For freezing pastry, see page 39.

Pies

Pies and tarts with raw fruit can be prepared in advance, refrigerated and cooked when required. Savoury pies can be cooked in advance to serve cold, otherwise store pastry and ingredients separately and combine just before cooking. For freezing pies, see page 39.

Salad foods

Salad greens should be washed, drained and stored in covered boxes in the refrigerator. Cucumber can be sliced, sprinkled with salt and left for several hours in a cool place (not refrigerated). Drain off any liquid before serving. Sliced beetroot sprinkled with lemon juice or vinegar doesn't need refrigerating either. Make potato salad and store it in a covered container in the refrigerator. Other dressed salads (not lettuce) can be stored for 2-4 hrs with safety, if covered and in the refrigerator.

Sauces

Most can be made in advance and re-heated, or kept warm in a bain-marie for a short period. If the recipe contains egg or cream add these after the sauce has been re-heated, just before serving. For freezing sauces, see page 46.

Soups and stocks

When these have been made in advance they should be kept in covered containers in the refrigerator. Those with egg and cream in the recipe can be cooked up to the stage before this, then refrigerated, and the remaining ingredients added just before serving. Make sure the soups have been brought to the boil before you add the finishing touches. This ensures that they will be hot. For freezing soups, see page 80.

Vegetables

Apart from washing, peeling, draining and storing in polythene bags in the refrigerator, avoid advance preparation. Don't cook in advance and re-heat because flavour and vitamin content deteriorate too much. Rather than do this, serve a salad or use frozen vegetables.

GARNISHING

Garnishing has always been an important part of the art of cooking and serving food. Garnishes are used to add colour to foods which are basically colourless, for example, white soups and fish dishes, or they are used to enhance a dish by serving it with contrasting or harmonizing colours, for example, a selection of different coloured vegetables served with meat. Garnishes are also used to add flavour to a dish, and a great deal of French cookery owes its diversity to the type of garnish used, the dish then being labelled with the name of the basic ingredient 'à la' whatever the garnish may be. These garnishes are traditional; they form a large part of any French cookery book.

Foods with uninteresting shapes are also helped considerably by garnishes with plenty of form and character of their own, for example, sprigs of fresh herbs or herb flowers, the shape of slices of lemon or tomato, rings of sweet peppers, shaped pieces of toast, fried bread or pastry. These last items also provide contrast in texture which is very welcome with soft foods, as is the crisp biscuit served with sweet dishes which are soft in texture.

Whether one's taste is for elaborate or simple garnishes, one basic principle is the same, namely that the food being decorated should live up to the promise of its appearance. Far too many of the cooks and chefs who have a liking for elaborate garnishing regard the flavour and quality of the dish of secondary importance. Garnishing is easy, good cooking more difficult, and to be able to say of a cook that the food produced both looks good and tastes good is high praise indeed.

Some useful garnishes

ANCHOVY FILLETS

Sold in tins or jars as straight fillets or rolled and stuffed. Use on hot or cold meats, fish, vegetables, eggs and salads.

CARROT STICKS AND SHREDDED CARROTS

Make good garnishes for grills, salads, hot or cold meat or fish. To make sticks, peel carrots and cut in matchsticks; keep in iced water. Sprinkle grated carrot with lemon juice and keep it in a covered dish.

CELERY

Small celery leaves, whole or shredded, make attractive garnishes for any savoury dish. For special decorations make curled celery. With a sharp, thin vegetable knife, cut very thin slices of washed celery down the length of the stick. Then hold one end, and with the knife in the other hand, pull it firmly along the strip curling it as you go. Put in iced water where the curling process will continue. Drain well before using.

CHERRIES

Use maraschino cherries for garnishing sweet or savoury foods; use glacé cherries for sweet foods; canned cherries for sweet or savoury dishes, especially duck, chicken, grills and salads.

CHOCOLATE

Buy this as vermicelli, chips or polka dots; or grate block chocolate coarsely and use to garnish cold sweets. Cocoa powder mixed with sugar, or drinking chocolate (both used dry), are also useful.

COCONUT

Desiccated or shredded, useful on dark-coloured sweets or ices. It can also be coloured by putting a spoonful or two of the coconut in a jar, adding a drop of colouring and shaking well. Then spread out on a piece of kitchen paper to dry. Alternatively, toast it under a grill or in a hot oven to make it brown; shake frequently and avoid scorching.

COFFEE

Instant coffee to sprinkle on ices and cold sweets just before serving; use plain or mixed with sugar.

CROÛTONS

Small squares or cubes of toasted or fried bread. Use for garnishing soups and savoury dishes. With soups, serve them separately so that they are still crisp when added.

CUCUMBER

Peeled or unpeeled, cut in circles or at an angle to make ovals. Chunks of cucumber can be hollowed to make cups which are then filled with mayonnaise or a savoury filling and used to garnish cold and hot fish or meat.

EGGS

Hard-boiled and stuffed, sliced or chopped. Rub the yolks through a sieve to give a garnish for soups, salads and savoury dishes. Use chopped whites for garnishing dark foods.

GLACÉ FRUITS

Rinse in warm water and drain before use, whole or cut up.

HERBS

Use any fresh ones as a green garnish, scissor-snipped, chopped, as leaves or small sprigs. The best ones to use as leaves or small sprays are balm, bay, caraway, chervil, coriander, curry plant, dill, fennel, mint, nasturtium, burnet, parsley, rosemary, sage, sweet cicely and tarragon.

Edible herb flowers make most attractive garnishes, fresh or dried. Best (all edible) are anchusa, bergamot, borage, caraway, chives, hyssop, lavender, marigold petals, marjoram, nasturtium, rosemary, sage and thyme. Mixed flowers, chopped if large, make a pretty garnish to sprinkle over salads.

LEMONS

Use lemon wedges as the garnish when the juice is to be squeezed on the food by the diner; when the lemon is for decoration only, it can be cut into a variety of shapes. Very thin slices are cut across the lemon, pips removed and a little chopped parsley put on each slice. Or cut thin slices through almost to the middle on two opposite sides, then twist the pieces in opposite directions to make wings. If the lemon is peeled in strips before cutting slices they will have a serrated edge.

Cups made from squeezed lemons are used to hold cold sauces or mayonnaise and also for serving lemon sorbets.

MUSHROOMS

Use grilled, or boil for 5-8 mins in a little stock or water, drain and keep hot.

NUTS

Use any kind, whole, halved or chopped. Toasted almonds are useful for chicken, fish à la meunière, in rice dishes and for garnishing sweets and ices. Toasted hazel nuts and roast peanuts make good alternative garnishes. For toasting nuts, see page 16.

OLIVES

Use plain black, red or green ones or stuffed ones, whole or sliced (pimento stuffed best for this).

ORANGES

Use sections or slices for grilled meat or fish, on salads and other savoury dishes. Use drained canned mandarin oranges for sweet garnishes.

PAPRIKA PEPPER

For adding a dash of bright red to white and other pale foods, including soup. Use a pinch, a sprinkling from a perforated tub or make patterns with it.

PICKLES

For cold dishes, especially, cocktail onions, gherkins or pickled cucumbers, pickled walnuts and any others with a good shape.

RADISHES

Used whole, cut in fine slices or as 'roses'. To make the roses use a sharp, pointed knife and carve the petals from the root end to within $\frac{1}{4}$ in (6 mm) of the stem end. Lever up the red part from the white to free the petals. Put in iced water until required.

SWEET PEPPERS

Use fine slices of raw green or red peppers, or chopped. Canned red ones are very useful, best cut in strips.

TOMATOES

Use firm ripe ones of small or medium size. To skin, plunge in boiling water for a minute, then in cold, and the skins will peel off easily. Small unskinned tomatoes make a good garnish when the centres are scooped out and the cup filled with mayonnaise or a savoury filling. Baked stuffed tomatoes make a good garnish for hot meats and fish, see page 301.

EMERGENCY MEALS

The occasion may be unexpected guests, but probably more often it is because something has delayed you and kept you from preparing the meal you had planned. To be ready for these occasions you want to have some popular menus in reserve, ones that you know how to prepare in the minimum time. I think it is worth while writing these down somewhere for quick reference, perhaps including a selection of menus, plain and posh. Then be sure you keep the necessary ingredients in stock, replacing as they are used. Include in the menu some luxury canned or frozen foods which will help to disguise the fact that it is a scratch meal.

Whether or not you have a freezer will, of course, have a lot to do with the kind of emergency meals you can plan. The following are just some ideas to start you off if you haven't already got yourself organized to cope with emergency situations.

STARTERS

Canned artichoke hearts to be drained and dressed with French dressing.

Canned smoked cod's roe to serve with thin slices of hot toast and plenty of lemon.

Pâté in small cans. Choose from liver, smoked trout, grouse, smoked goose, prawn and others.

Canned prawns to make a quick fish cocktail or open sandwich.

SOUPS

Obviously canned or packet or your own make from the freezer, some of the family favourites as well as some luxury ones, for example, turtle, bisque d'homard, bouillabaisse, cock-a-leekie, pheasant or wild duck.

MAIN DISH

This is a bit tricky if you don't want the meal to be too obviously out of a can. If you have a freezer, steaks, chops or fish which can be cooked without thawing are a good choice. A reserve of casseroles and other made up dishes are useful, depending on how long you can spare for the heating up. Useful canned foods are frankfurters with sauerkraut; curried eggs using a canned sauce or one from the freezer and freshly cooked rice; canned chicken or duck to be heated up in your favourite sauce. If you have a freezer make your favourite recipes and freeze them in single portions, which heat up much faster than a larger quantity and will be much better than similar commercial articles.

For vegetables, the best in my opinion are salads, assuming you keep a supply of washed and drained salad vegetables in the refrigerator; or use frozen.

If you have a freezer always keep some sauces in stock as these can be quickly heated. There are also plenty of good canned sauces you might choose from as a reserve for serving with quickly-cooked frozen fish or meat, for example, Béarnaise, lobster, madeira wine, Newburg, Robert or Sanafyana (tomato and sweet pepper).

SWEET COURSE

This is easy if you keep a well-filled fruit bowl or have cheese and biscuits always in stock. Most people like canned fruit, so keep some exotic ones such as guavas, lichees, green figs, mangoes, melon cubes, ginger in syrup or papaw. Most useful for the freezer owner are ready-to-bake fruit tarts, or ice-cream, while those who like something more substantial can have canned steamed puddings, which heat up quite quickly.

Index

advance preparation and cooking, 475–82
alcoholic flavourings, 19–20
allspice, 21, 23
almond(s)
  and sherry cake, refrigerated, 392
  fingers, 440
  fruit cake, 429
  in stuffed peaches, 372
  paste, 448
  praline, 16
  salad with, 319
  with apricot purée, 367
anchovy
  and cheese toasted sandwiches, 346
  butter, 57
  canned fillets as flavouring, 125
  fillets as garnish, 479
  methods of cooking, 125
  rarebit, 349
  sauce, 46
  with spaghetti, 329
anise, 21
apple(s), 353
  freezing of, 352
  with cheese, 97
  Recipes
  and horseradish sauce, 55
  and lamb pie, 181
  and orange with caramel, 365
  and pork pie, 192
  and prune stuffing, 28
  baked, 366
    with rum, 366
  cheese crumble, 408
  dumplings, 418
  flambé, 367
  flan, 419
  salads with, 306, 307, 308, 309, 312, 314
  sauce, 46
  Swedish, soufflé, 412
  tart or double crust pie, 419
  tart with fennel seeds, 420
  with roast loin of pork and prunes, 187
apricot(s), 354
  à la bourdaloue, 420
  flan, 420
  freezing of, 352
  purée with almonds, 367
  rice mould, 393
artichokes, globe, 352
  boiled, 252
  bottoms for soup, 81, 85
  vinaigrette, 72
artichokes, Jerusalem, 253–4
  boiled, 253
  with cheese, 253
asparagus, 254–6
  boiled, 254
  cream soups, 81, 85
  freezing of, 251
  use of in soups, 81

aspic jelly, 19
aubergine, 256-7
aurore mayonnaise, 63
avocado pear, 71

baba au rhum, 452
bacon, 194-8
  accompaniments to, 196
  sauces for, 48, 52
  storing sliced, 156
  rashers, cooking of, 196-7
  Recipes
  and broad bean stew, 258
  and curd cheese flan, 97
  and liver with red wine, 212
  and nut stuffing, 27
  baked, rashers with cider, 197
  boiled, 194-5
  grilled, with kidneys, 210-11
  with leek purée, 278
  in madeira sauce, 196
  omelet, 111
  rolls, 197
  with cheese and egg, 348-9
  with cheese and tomato on toast, 347
  with (poached) eggs and green pea purée, 288-9
  with fried eggs, 109
  with fried eggs and green pea purée, 109-10
  with scrambled eggs, 117
bain-marie, *see* double boiler
baking blind, 42
balm, 21
banana(s), 354
  freezing of, 352
  with cheese, 97
  Recipes
  and black currant coupe or sundae, 405
  baked, 368
  baked, mousse, 408
  baked, with prunes, 368
  egg flip, 464
  fried, flambé, 368-9
  loaf, 456
  mould with strawberry sauce, 377-8
  pancakes, 417
  flambé, 417
barbecue basting sauce, 25
basil, 21, 23, 24
  butter, 57
bass, 125
basting sauces, 24-6
batters, advance preparation and cooking of, 475-6
bavarois, 378
bay leaves, 21, 23
  with rice pudding and raisins, 412
bean, white, salad, 317
beans, 257-62
  and mushrooms, 260-61
  baked, 259
  boiled green, 261
  butter, 260-61
  dried, 260
  freezing of, 251
  salads with, 312, 321
beans, baked, and cheese, 347
beans, broad, 257-8
  and bacon stew, 258
  boiled, 258
  for soup, 81
  freezing of, 251
  in fennel sauce, 259
  salad with, 321
beans, butter, 259
beans, French, 261
  freezing of, 251
  in cream sauce, 261
beans, haricot, 259
beans, runner, 261
  Béarnaise, 262
  freezing of, 251
Béarnaise sauce, 56
beating, 34
béchamel sauce, 46-7
beef, 154, 158-74
  accompaniments to, 158, 160, 169
  boiled, 169

beef—*cont.*
  casseroles, 163–7
  fried, 160–61
  grilled, 160, 162
  leftovers, 172
  minced, 169–70
  pies, 163–8
  pressed, 169
  roasting temperatures, 158
  stews, 163–6
  Recipes
  boiled salt, 169
  Bourguignon, 164
  braised steak with soured cream, 164
  burgers, 170
  cakes, 173
  casserole with olives, 165
  casserole with seven herbs, 165–6
  curry, 166
  fondue Bourguignonne, 161–2
  fricadelles, 173
  goulash, 167
  grilled marinated, steak, 162
  hash, 173–4
  kebabs, 162
  layered pancakes, 174
  sausage to serve cold, 171
  steak and kidney pie, 167–8
  steak and kidney pudding, 168–9
  steak Diane, 162–3
  steak Mirabeau, 163
  Strogonoff, 161
  zucchini moussaka, 171–2
beer, as flavouring, 19
beetroot
  freezing of, 251
  pickled, with cheese, 97
  salads with, 307, 309, 310, 312
  soup, 90
berries, 369
  cream, 379
  freezing of, 352
  mousse, 379–80
  preparation of, 369
  serving of, 369
  tart or pie, 421
bienenstich, 430–31
bilberries, 354
  freezing of, 352
  serving of, 369
biscuits, 427–47
  almond fingers, 440–41
  caraway, 441–2
  cheese, with herbs, 442
  freezing of, 428
  lemon, 443–4
  macaroons, 444–5
  nut, 446
  potato, 446–7
  shortbread, 447
  with cheese, 96
black currant(s), 355
  and banana coupe or sundae, 405
  cream, *see* Berry cream
  freezing of, 352
black grouse, *see* Blackcock
black treacle, as flavouring, 24
blackberries, 354
  cream, *see* Berry cream
  freezing of, 352
  ice-cream with hot spice sauce, 398
  sauce, spiced, 70
  serving of, 369
blackcock, 241–2
blanc mange (French), 380
blanching, 13, 251
blender, use of for sauces, 49
blender cream soups, 81
blending, 34
bloaters, 125
  smoked, 141
blueberries, *see* Bilberries
boiling, 29–30
bombes, 404
bone stock, 18
boning, 13
  fish, 124–5
bortsch, 82, 90
bouquet garni, 23

boysenberries, freezing of, 352
brandy, as flavouring, 20
Brazil nut cookies, 441
bread, 427, 428, 451–60
  banana loaf, 456
  cheese loaf, 456–7
  freezing of, 427–8
  rolls, 452–4
  sauce, 47
  treacle loaf, 459–60
  Vienna, 454–5
  Vienna plaits with fennel seeds, 455
  wholemeal, 455
  with herbs, 456
  with cheese, 96
breadcrumbs, 14
  advance preparation of, 475–6
  for stuffings, 26
bream, 125
Breton sauce, 56
brill, 125
broccoli, sprouting, freezing of, 251
broccoli, white, 271
brochettes, 32–3
brown bread ice-cream, 398–9
brussels sprouts, 262–3
  boiled, 263
  freezing of, 251
  Lyonnaise, 263
  salads with, 307–8, 323
  storing, 262
buck rarebit, 115, 349
buckling, smoked, 78
buns
  freezing of, 427–8
  pastry for, 442–3
butter cream, 448–9
butter icings, 449–50
butters, savoury or compound, 57–8
  anchovy, 57
  basil, 57
  curry, 57
  garlic, 57
  maître d'hôtel, 57
  mint, 57
  mustard, 57
  paprika, 58
  parsley, 57
  rosemary, 58
  tarragon, 58

cabbage, 263–7
  boiled, 264
  fried, 264
  leaves, stuffed, 265–6
  red, 266–7
  salads with, 308, 310
  sauerkraut, 267
  storing, 263–4
  white, with herb seeds, 266
  with caraway or capers, 267
  with cream sauce, 265
cakes, 427–48
  freezing of, 428
  hard sauce, filling for, 68
  icing for, 448–51
  large, 429–40
  rubbing in ingredients, 36
  small, 440–48
  Recipes
  almond fruit, 429
  Austrian hazel-nut gâteau, 430
  bienenstich, 430–31
  Brazil nut cookies, 441
  cheese, baked, 431–2
  cheese, refrigerated, 432–3
  chocolate Swiss roll, 433
  chocolate Venetians, 434
  cream buns, 442–3
  cream puffs, 442–3
  éclairs, 442–3
  Genoese sponge, 435
  gingerbread, 435–6
  Greek yogurt, 436–7
  honey (Swiss), 437
  lemon gâteau, 437–8
  little Cupids, 444
  praline gâteau, 438
  profiteroles, 442–3
  rich fruit, 434–5

cakes—*cont.*
  rum punch gâteau, 438
  sherry and almond, refrigerated, 392
  small marzipan, 447–8
  upside-down, 439
  Victoria sandwich, 438–9
  walnut gâteau, 439–40
canned fish, storing of, 123
canned soups with yogurt, 80–81
cannelloni, 325
caper(s), 21
  sauce, 48
  with sauerkraut, 267, 315
capsicums, *see* Sweet peppers
caramel
  crème au, 382
  oranges, 371
  pears, 373
  rice cream, 380–81
  with apple and orange, 365–6
caraway biscuits, 441–2
caraway seeds
  with sauerkraut, 267
  with turkey paprika, 240
cardamon, 21
carrots, 268–71
  and celery, 269
  and cheese quiche, 270
  boiled, 268
  casserole of, 269
  freezing of, 251
  mould with green peas, 270–71
  salad with, 306
  sticks and shredded as garnish, 479
  sticks, with cheese, 97
  storing, 268
  use of in soups, 81
  Vichy, 269
  with parsnips, 287
casserole(s), 163–7, 178–84, 191–4, 227–31
  advance preparation and cooking, 476
  cooking, 30
  storing, 156, 157

Recipes
  beef, with olives, 165
  belly of pork, 191–2
  chicken, with curd cheese and spicy sauce, 228
  fruit (for dessert), 361–2
  of carrots, 269
  of lamb cutlets, 180
  of ox liver, 211–12
  of spare ribs (pork), 192
  spiced lamb, 184
  (veal) with rosemary or thyme, 205
  (beef) with seven herbs, 165–6
cauliflower, 271
  boiled, 271
  freezing of, 251
  Milanaise, 272
  salad, 308
  soup, 82
  storing, 271
  with walnuts, 272
Cayenne pepper, 20
celeriac, 22
celery, 22, 273
  and carrots, 269
  and mustard sauce, 274
  and tomato soup, 83
  as garnish, 479
  braised, using whole head, 273–4
  cream soups, 81, 83, 85
  freezing of, 251
  salads with, 307, 308, 309, 314
  turnip-rooted, 272–3
  with cheese, 97
  with yogurt, 274
Chantilly cream, 65
charlotte
  orange and raisin, 389
  praline, 391–2
Cheddar fondue with beer, 100
cheese, 94–102
  accompaniments to, 96–7
  advance preparation, 476
  buying for cooking, 95
  fillings for sandwiches, 340–42, 346

flans, 97–9
flavours and texture, 94–5
fondues, 99–100
salads with, 318–19
serving of, 96
snacks with, 346–50
storing, 95–6
topping for open sandwiches, 344
Recipes
and baked beans, 347
and carrot quiche, 270
and crab, 348
and honey cinnamon flan, 423
and onion quiche, 286
and rosemary stuffing, 27
and watercress soup, 89
apple crumble, 408
bacon and curd, flan, 97–8
biscuits, with herbs, 442
cake, baked, 431–2
cake, refrigerated, 432–3
cottage, and leek quiche, 278–9
cottage, and macaroni, 327–8
creams (for starter), 71–2
flan, 98
with herb pastry, 98–9
fondue, 99–100
fondue, Cheddar, with beer, 100
girdle scones, 458
kedgeree with curd, 334
loaf, 456–7
with herbs, 457
omelet, 111
on toast with herbs, 347
pineapple, 391
pudding, 100–101
sauce with poached fish, 138–9
scones with herbs, 457–8
soft, with herbs, 101–2
soufflé, 101
with chicory and ham, 275–6
with courgettes and cream, 280
with egg and bacon, 348–9
with leeks and cream, 277
with onions on toast, 349

with scrambled eggs, 117, 118, 119
with tomato and bacon on toast, 347
cherries, 354
as garnish, 479
coupe or sundae, 406
freezing of, 352
sauce, 65–6
chervil, 22, 23
with stuffed eggs, 108
chestnut(s)
purée, 16
shelling and skinning of, 16
stuffing, 27–8
chicken, 219–34
accompaniments to, 222
carving, 220
casseroles, 227–9
freezing of, 220
leftovers, 231–4
preparation of, 220
salads, 319–20
sauce for, 49–51
stuffing for, 28
young, 223
Recipes
à la King, 231–2
à la Marengo, 229–30
and ham turnovers, 232–3
and rice soup with yogurt, 84
barbecue, 225
braised, 222
casserole with curd cheese and spicy sauce, 228
casserole with green peppers, 228
casserole with herbs and lemon, 229
cream soup, 81, 84–5
crème de volaille princesse, 84–5
curried, 231
curried, salad, 319
curried, soup, 91,
fondue, 224–5
fricassée, 233–4
fried, flambé with cream, 224
fried, joints, 223

Index 489

chicken—*cont.*
  goulash, 230
  in a pot, 222–3
  liver omelet, 111
  liver pâté, 72
  mousse, 72–3
  pie, 233
  roast, 219
  sauté of, with herbs and olives, 226
  Spanish, 227
  spatchcock, 225
  stuffed, pancakes, 234
  with tarragon sauce, 226–7
chicory, 274–6
  boiled, 275
  Polonaise, 275
  preparation of, 275
  salads with, 306, 309, 310
  storing, 275
  with cheese, 97
  with cheese and ham, 275–6
chillies, 20
Chinese gooseberries, 355
chives, 22, 23, 24
  salad with, 310
chocolate
  as flavouring, 24
  as garnish, 480
  coffee coupe or sundae, 406
  ice-cream, 399
  icings: butter, 449
    glacé, 450
    orange butter, 449
  mocha sauce, 66
  pudding, 413–14
  rice mould, 393
  sauce, 66
  soufflé (cold), 381
  Swiss roll, 433
  Venetians, 434
chopping up food, 14–15
chops, storing of, 156
Christmas pudding, 414–15
chutney and cheese toasted sandwich, 346

cider
  as flavouring, 19
  baked bacon rashers with, 197
  sauce, with marinated pork chops, 189
cinnamon, 22
  and honey cheese flan, 423
  with fried lamb and soured cream, 178
citrus fruit, freezing of, 353
claret cup, 463
clarified butter, 15
clementines, 355
cloves, 22, 23
cocoa, as flavouring, 24
coconut
  as garnish, 480
  flan, 421
  pudding, 415
cod, 125
  smoked, 141
cod's roe, smoked, 78
coffee
  as garnish, 480
  chocolate coupe or sundae, 406
  custard mould, 382
  ice-cream, 399
  iced, 467
  icings: butter, 449
    glacé, 450
cole slaw with walnuts, 310
coley, 125
compotes
  fruit, 362
  honey pear, 374
  orange, 370
  orange and rhubarb, 370
condiments, 20
conger eel, 125
consistencies in mixing, 35
consommé
  cold, with mushrooms, 90
  hot, with mushrooms and herbs, 84
cooking processes and techniques, 29–36
  beating, 34

blending, 34
boiling, 29
brochettes, cooking of, 32
casseroles, 30
creaming fat and sugar, 35
double boiler, use of, 30
flamber, to, 35
folding in, 36
frying, 31
grilling, 32
kebabs, cooking of, 32
liquidizing, 34
mixing, consistencies in, 35
poaching, 33
pressure cooking, 33
purées, making of, 34
rubbing in, 36
sauté, 33
whisking, 34
coriander, 22
corn, sweet, *see* Sweet corn
coupes, 405-6
  banana and black currant, 405
  cherry, 406
  coffee chocolate, 406
  Jacques, 406
  melon and ginger, 406
courgettes, 276, 279-82
  cooked in butter, 279
  in paprika sauce, 281
  salad with, 310
  stewed with tomatoes, 281
  storing, 279
  with cheese and cream, 280
crab, 125, 146-8
  boiling of, 146
  dressed, 147
  fondue, 147
  hot buttered, 147
  preparation of, 146
  scallops, 73
cranberries, 355
  freezing of, 352
  sauce, 49
  upside-down pudding, 409

crawfish, 125
cream
  buns, 442
  puffs, 442
  sauce, 139
  whipped in advance, 476
  with cabbage, 265
  with courgettes and cheese, 280
  with French beans, 261
  with fried chicken flambé, 224
  with leeks and cheese, 277
  with new potatoes, 294
  with poached fish and mushrooms, 139
  with prawns, 151
  with scampi flambé, 151
cream cheese and horseradish sauce, 58
cream dressing, 61
cream of asparagus soup, canned, 81
cream of celery soup, canned, 81
cream of chicken soup, canned, 81
cream of chicken soup, 84
cream of tomato soup, canned, 81
creaming fat and sugar, 35
crème au café, 382
crème au caramel, 382
crème brûlée, 383
crème d'artichauts, 85
crème d'asperges vertes, 85
crème de céleri, 85
crème de volaille princesse, 84
croque monsieur, toasted sandwich, 346
croûtons, as garnish, 480
cucumber
  and green pepper cocktail, 73
  as garnish, 480
  salad with salmon, 134, 136
  salads with, 311, 317
  sauce, 49
  with cheese, 97
Cumberland sauce, 58
cumin, 22
curd cheese,
  and bacon flan, 97

curd cheese—*cont.*
  in chicken casserole with spicy sauce, 228
currants, black, red, white, 355
  see also under individual colours
curried chicken, 231
  soup, 91
curried eggs, 106
curry
  and cheese sandwich, 342
  and yogurt dressing, 64
  beef, 166
  butter, 57
  chicken salad, 319
  lemon, dressing, 62
  mayonnaise, 62
  powder and pastes, 22
  sauce, 50
custard
  coffee, mould, 382
  cream, 383
  sauce, 66

dab, 126
damsons, 355
  freezing of, 353
desserts, 351–426
  bombes, 404
  cold, 377–96
  cold, made in advance, 377
  flans, 418, 419–24
  fruit, 351–76
  hot baked puddings, 408–12
  ices and frozen sweets, 397–407
  pies, 418, 419–25
  steamed puddings, 413–16
  tarts, 418, 419–21, 426
digestive biscuits, with cheese, 96
dill, 22
dog fish, 126
double boiler, 45
  use of, 30
drinks, 461–70
  alcoholic, 461–4
  non-alcoholic, 464–70

duck and duckling, 235–6
  accompaniments to, 235–6
  roast, 235
  sauces for, 52
  stuffing for, 26, 28–9
  wild, 245
  with mint, 236
dumplings, 37

éclairs, 442
eel(s), 78, 126
  fresh water, 126
  methods of cooking, 126
  skinning of, 134
  smoked, 78
  stewed, 134
eggs, 103–21
  as garnish, 480
  baked, 104–5, 107–8
  boiled, 106
  fillings for sandwiches, 341
  fried, 109
  hard-boiled, 106–7, 476
  omelets, 110–15
  poached, 115–16
  sauces for, 46, 47
  scrambled, 117–19
  size of, 103
  storing, 103
  stuffed, 108
  topping for open sandwiches, 344
  Recipes
  and haddock, 348
  and haddock toasted sandwiches, 146
  and ham pie, 198
  and herb quiche, 120
  baked, with herbs, 104
  banana, flip, 464
  Crécy, 115
  curried, 106
  en cocotte, 104
  fried, with bacon, 109
  with bacon and green pea purée, 109
  Mornay, 116
  nog, 464

orange, flip, 469
patties, 120
poached, in green sauce, 116
Raymond, 105
scrambled, 117–19
  with bacon, 117
  with cheese, 117
  with cheese and parsley, 118
  with cream cheese, 118
  Lyonnaise, 117
  with sweet peppers and tomatoes, 118
  with vegetables and cheese, 119
stuffed, au gratin, 108
  with chervil, 108
Swiss, 115
with bacon and green pea purée, 288
with cheese and bacon, 348
with mushrooms, 107
with rice and mint, 336
with yogurt and paprika, 105
emergency meals, 482–3
escallops, 126
Espagnole sauce, 50
essences, 21

faggot, *see* Bouquet garni
fennel, 22
  mayonnaise, 63
  salads with, 307, 309
  sauce, 51
  seeds with Vienna plaits, 455
  with apple tart, 420
  with broad beans, 259
fenugreek, 22
figs, 355
  freezing of, 353
fines herbes, 23
  omelet with, 112
fish, 122–53
  (*see also* under individual fish and shellfish)
  à la meunière, 129
  baked, 130–31, 134–5, 139
  boiled, 132–3

boning, 124–5
buying, 122
cakes, freezing of, 124
cleaning, 124
cooked in advance, 476
cooking fillets, 134–41
cooking large whole fish, 132–4
cooking small whole fish, 128–30
cooking smoked fish, 141–5
en papillote, 128, 134, 136
filleting, 124
fillings for sandwiches, 341
freezing of, 123
fried in butter, 129
fried in deep fat, 137–8
grilled, 129, 135
leftovers, 146
marinaded, 130
poached, 132–3
quantities guide, 122–3
rissoles, freezing of, 124
sauces for, 46, 47, 48, 49, 51, 55, 57, 58, 60
scaling, 124
seasons for, 125–7
shellfish, 146–53
skinning, 124, 134, 136
smoked, as starter, 78–9
stock, 18
storing, 123
stuffing flat fish, 130–31
stuffing for, 26, 27, 28
topping for open sandwiches, 345
yields for shelled fish, 123
Recipes
à la Bretonne, 127
cocktail, 74
  leftovers for, 146
flambé with tarragon sauce, 132
fricassée, 137
mousse, 74
  leftovers for, 146
poached with cheese sauce, 138
poached with mushrooms and cream sauce, 139

fish—cont.
  salad with ravigote sauce, 320
  stuffed fillets, 140
flaky pastry, quick, 40
flamber, to, 35–6
flaming, see Flamber
flan(s), 39, 41–2, 418–26
  baking blind, 42
  freezing of, 39
  refrigerated, 42
  Recipes
  apple, 419
  apricot, 420
  bacon and curd cheese, 97
  cheese, 98–9
  coconut, 421
  honey and cinnamon cheese, 423
  meringue, 386
  mushroom, 284
  pineapple and orange, 424
  shellfish, 153
  smoked haddock, 142, 146
  sponge, 42
  tomato, 302
flavourings for savoury and sweet cooking, 21–4
  for mayonnaise, 63
flounder, 126
flour, seasoned, 20
folding in, 36
fondues, 99–100
  Bourguignonne, 161
  Cheddar, with beer, 100
  cheese, 99
  chicken, 224
frankfurters with paprika potatoes, 218
freezing, 39
  buying meat for, 154–5
  cheese, 95–6
  cooked meat dishes, 156–7
  eggs, 104
  game, 220, 241
  pastry, 39
  poultry, 220
  soups, 80
  vegetables, 251–2
French beans see Beans, French
French dressing, 61
French mustard, 20
French omelet, 110
frozen fish
buying, 122
  methods of cooking, 125
fruit, 351–79
  (*see also* under individual fruits)
  and rice mould, 394
  as flavouring, 24
  as main ingredient in recipes, 361–76
  buying, 353–61
  casserole or oven-stewed, 361
  compote or stewed, 362
  crisp or crumble, 409
  desserts, 351–79
  dried, 362–3, 365
  flan, 422
  fool, 384
  freezing, 352–3
  juice and yogurt drink, 470
  kebabs, 363
  pies, 422
    freezing of, 39
    prepared in advance, 477
  punch, 464–5
  purée, 364
  rich, cake, 434–5
  salads, 364–5
  sauce, nos. 1 and 2, 67
  sauces for, 65
  seasons for, 353–61
  synthetic, flavouring, 21
  use of, 353–61
  with cheese, 97
frying, 31–2

game, 240–49
  (*see also* under individual birds, hare and venison)
  casseroles, 241
  chips, see Potato crisps

freezing of, 220, 240–41
hanging, 240
methods of cooking, 241–9
roasting, 241
sauce for, 50–51
seasons for, 241–8
storing, 240–41
stuffings for, 26–9
gammon, 195–8
accompaniments to, 196
boiled, 195–6
fried, in sweet mustard sauce, 198
with leek purée, 278
garlic, 22
butter, 57
garnishes, 479–82
advance preparation, 477
gaspacho, 91
gâteau
Austrian hazel-nut, 430
frozen, 404–5
lemon, 437–8
praline, 438
rum punch, 438
walnut, 439–40
gelatine, 15
Genoese sponge (cake), 435
gherkins, pickled, with cheese, 97
giblet stock, 18
ginger, 22, 23
and lemon marinade or basting sauce, 25
and melon coupe or sundae, 406–7
rice mould, 393
sauce, 67
with roast spare rib of pork and sage, 188
gingerbread, 435–6
glacé fruits, as garnish, 480
glacé icing, 450
golden jelly, 385
golden syrup, as flavouring, 24
goose, 237
accompaniments to, 237
roast, 237
sauce for, 52
stuffing for, 28, 29
gooseberries, 356
Chinese, 355
freezing of, 353
goulash, 167
chicken, 230
pork, 193
granadillas, 356
grapefruit, 356
and beetroot salad, 312
and mint drink, 465
and orange drink, 465–6
grapes, 356
freezing of, 353
with cheese, 97
grating, 16
gravy, 51
Greek yogurt cake, 436
green peas, *see* Peas
green pepper and cucumber cocktail, 73
green sauce, 60
greengages, 356
freezing of, 353
girdle scones, 458–9
grilling, 32
grog, 463
grouse, 241–2
accompaniments to, 242
roast, 242
guinea-fowl, 242–3

haddock, 126
and egg, 348
with poached egg, 115
haddock, smoked, 141
baked, 141
flan, 142
grilled, 141
omelet, 113
pancakes, 142–3
pie, 143–4
poached, 142
hake, 126
halibut, 126

496 Index

ham, 194–8
  accompaniments, 196
  boiled, 195–6
  leftovers, 198
  salads with, 321, 322
  sauce for, 52
  Recipes
  and chicken turnovers, 232–3
  and egg pie, 198–9
  and veal plate pie, 208–9
  and madeira sauce, 196
  mousse, 199
  omelet, 111
  rarebit, 350
  with chicory and cheese, 275–6
  with noodles and soured cream, 328
Hamburg mousse, 385
hard sauce, 68
hare, 246–8
  accompaniments to, 247, 248
  casseroles, 241
  frozen, 241
  jugged, 246, 247–8
  roast, 247
hazel nut(s)
  Austrian, gâteau, 430
  soufflé, 410
  toasted, 16
herb teas, 466–7
herb(s), 21–4, 26
  and egg quiche, 120
  and sherry basting sauce or marinade, 25
  and yogurt dressing, 64
  as garnish, 480–81
  casserole with seven, 165–6
  in consommé with mushrooms, 84
  marinade, with roast shoulder of lamb, 175
  pancakes, 38
  pastry, cheese flan with, 98–9
  salads with, 305–6
  seasoning, 23–4
  seeds with cabbage, 266
  vinegar, 24
  with baked eggs, 104
  with baked rhubarb, 375–6
  with cheese biscuits, 442
  with cheese loaf, 457
  with cheese on toast, 347
  with cheese scones, 457–8
  with chicken and lemon casserole, 229
  with grilled lamb chops, 176
  with rarebit, 350
  with sauté of chicken and olives, 226
  with soft cheese, 101–2
  with soft dinner rolls, 454
  with vermouth and soda water, 464
  with wholemeal bread, 456
herring(s), 126
  boiled, 128
  kippered, 144
  pickled, 21
  salad, 321–2
  with cheese and cream, 75
  with dill and tomato, 75
hock cup, 462–3
hollandaise sauce, 52
  with asparagus, 254
  with halibut, 126
  with salmon, 133–4
  with sole, 136
honey
  and cinnamon cheese flan, 423
  as flavouring, 24
  cake (Swiss), 437
  fudge sauce, 68
  pear compote, 374
  sauce, 68
hors d'oeuvre, 71–9
  prepared in advance, 477
horseradish, 22
  and apple sauce, 55–6
  and cream cheese sauce, 58
  salads with, 307, 322
  sauce, 59
  with herrings, 126
huss, *see* Dog fish

ice-cream, sauces for, 65, 66, 67, 68, 69, 70
ice-creams, 397–407
    blackberry, with hot spiced sauce, 398
    brown bread, 398–9
    chocolate, 399
    coffee, 399
    honey, 400
    liqueur mousse, 400–401
    macaroon, 401
    profiteroles filled with, 407
    strawberry, 401
    vanilla cream, 402
    vanilla cream with yogurt, 402
    ways of serving, 404–7
icings, 448–51
    butter, 449–50
    glacé, 450
    royal, 450–51
ingredients, preparation of, 13–17

jam
    layer pudding, 415–16
    sauce, 68–9
Jamaican apples, 366
jelly
    cider, with peaches, 390
    golden, 385

kebabs
    (beef), 162
    cooking of, 32–3
    fruit, 363–4
    (lamb) with yogurt marinade, 177
    (pork) with pineapple, 191
kedgeree, 333–4
kidney(s), 209–11
    and steak pie, 167–8
    devilled, 209–10
    grilled, and bacon, 210
    omelet, 112
    pancakes, 210–11
kipper(s), 144
    paté, 76
    salad, 322

kiwiberries, see Chinese gooseberries
kumquats, 356

lamb, 154, 174–86
    accompaniments to, 175, 176, 184–5
    carving of, 157
    casseroles, 178–84
    frying, 177–8
    grilling, 176–7
    leftovers, 184–6
    pies, 181, 185–6
    roast, 174–5
    sauces for, 49, 51
    soup, 85
    stews, 178–84
    stuffing for, 27
    Recipes
    and apple pie, 181
    braised, shank, 179
    burgers, 185
    chops, baked au gratin, 178–9
        grilled, with herbs, 176
    cutlets, fried minute, 177–8
        casserole of, 180
    devilled neck, 180–81
    fried, with cinnamon and soured cream, 178
    kebabs with yogurt marinade, 177
    navarin of, 182
    pie, 185–6
    pilau, 183
    ragout of, 183–4
    shepherd's pie, 186
    shoulder, roast, with herb marinade, 175
    soup, 85
    spiced, casserole, 184
    with tarragon, 181–2
lasagne, 325
    stuffed, 327
leeks, 276–9
    and cottage cheese quiche, 278–9
    boiled, 277
    preparation of, 276–7

leeks—*cont.*
  purée with grilled bacon or gammon, 278
  storing, 276
  vinaigrette, 313
  with cheese and cream, 277
leftovers
  beef, 172–4
  chicken, 231–4
  fish, 146
  lamb, 184–6
  pork, 198
  storing, 156
  veal, 209
lemon sole, 126
lemon(s), 357
  and ginger marinade or basting sauce, 25
  and orange mould, 388
  and orange syllabub, 388
  and sage sauce, 52
  as garnish, 481
  biscuits, 443–4
  butter icing, 449–50
  chiffon pie, 423
  curry dressing, 62
  gâteau, 437
  glacé icing, 450
  meringue pie, 424
  sauce, 69
  soufflé, 385
  stuffing, 28
  with chicken and herb casserole, 229
  with mint sauce, 59
lemonade, 467
lentil soup, 86
lettuce and sorrel salad, 316
lichees, 357
limes, 357
ling, 126
liqueur icing, 450
liqueur mousse, iced, 400
liquidizing, 34
little Cupids, 444

liver, 211–13
  sausage sandwich, 343
lobster, 126, 148–50
loganberries, 357
  cream, *see* Berry cream
  freezing of, 352
  serving of, 369

macaroni, 326, 327
  and cottage cheese, 327
macaroon ice-cream, 401
macaroons, 444
mace, 22, 23
mackerel, 126
  pâté, 77
  smoked, 78
madeira
  as flavouring, 20
  sauce, bacon in, 196
  sauce, ham in, 196
maître d'hôtel butter, 57
  with bass, 125
mandarins, 357
mangoes, 357
marinades, 24–5
  ginger and lemon, 25
  herb, with roast shoulder of lamb, 175
  sherry and herb, 25
  wine, 26
  yogurt, with lamb kebabs, 177
marinated chops with cider sauce, 189
marjoram, 22, 23
marrow, 279–82
  baked, 282
  cooked in butter, 279
  in paprika sauce, 281
  Lyonnaise, 280
  roast, 282
  stewed with tomatoes, 281
  storing, 279
marsala, as flavouring, 20
marzipan, 448
  small, cakes, 447
mayonnaise, 45, 62
  made in electric blender, 63

storing, 45
variations of, 63
with salmon, 134
measures, 9–11
meat, 154–218
(*see also* under individual meats)
buying frozen, 154–5
carving, 157
fillings for sandwiches, 341, 347
fondue, sauces for, 58, 60
for freezer, 154–5
freezing, cooked, dishes, 156–7
pies, freezing of, 39
prepared in advance, 477
salads, 323–4
sauce, with spaghetti, 330
storing, 155–6
thawing frozen, 155
topping for open sandwiches, 345
medlars, 358
Melba sauce, 69
melon, 358
and ginger coupe or sundae, 406
as starter, 77
en surprise, 369
freezing, 353
salad with, 311
meringue(s), 445
case or flan, 386
layer cake, 387
rhubarb, 411
mint, 22, 24
and grapefruit drink, 465
and yogurt drink, 470
butter, 57
julep, 468
salad with, 310
sauce, 59
with lemon, 59
with lemon sorbet, 402
with rice and egg, 336
mixed herb vinegar, 24
mixing, consistencies in, 35
mocha dessert, 387
mocha drink, spiced, 469

mocha icing, 449
Mont Blanc, 387
moulds
apricot rice, 393
chocolate rice, 393
ginger rice, 393
orange and lemon, 388
rice, 393
and fruit, 394
sherry, 394
moussaka, zucchini, 171–2
mousses
baked banana, 408
berry, 379
chicken, 72
fish, 74, 146
ham, 199
Hamburg, 385
liqueur, iced, 400
mulberries, 358
mullet, grey and red, 126
mushroom(s), 22, 282–4
as garnish, 481
baked, 283
dried, 282
freezing of, 251
fried, 283
grilled, 283
preparation of, 282
salads with, 313
storing, 282
Recipes
and beans, 260
creamed, 283
flan, 284
in cold consommé, 90
in (hot) consommé, 86
omelet, 112
sauce, 53
soup, 86
stock, 18
with eggs, 107
with poached fish and cream sauce, 139
with spinach, au gratin, 298
with (veal) chops or cutlets, 203

mussels, 126, 150
  à la marinière, 150
mustard, 20
  butter, 57
  dressing, 63
  French, 20
  sauce
    cold, 60
    hot, 53
    with herring, 126
    sweet, with fried gammon, 198
    with celery, 274
mutton
  (*see also* Lamb)
  carving of, 157
  sauces for, 48, 51
  soup, 85

nasturtium, 22
  and cucumber salad, 311
  seeds, use of, 48
nectarines, 358
noodles, 325–6, 327
  with ham and soured cream, 328
nutmeg, 22, 23
nut(s), 16
  and bacon stuffing, 27
  as garnish, 481
  biscuits, 446
  toasted, 16
  with cheese, 97

offal, storing, 156
olives
  and chicory salad, 309
  as garnish, 481
  casserole with, 165
  with cheese, 97
  with sauté of chicken with herbs, 226
omelets, 110–15
  frying pan for, 110
  Recipes
  aux fines herbes, 112
  bacon, 111
  cheese, 111
  chicken liver, 111
  French, 110
  ham, 111
  kidney, 112
  made with egg whites, 114
  mushroom, 112
  onion, 112
  smoked haddock, 113, 146
  soufflé, 110, 113
  soured cream, 113
  Spanish, 114
  Swiss eggs, 115
omelette aux fines herbes, 112
onion(s), 22, 285–6
  chopped, 285
  freezing of, 251
  storing, 285
  Recipes
  and cheese quiche, 286
  and cheese toasted sandwich, 346
  and egg sandwich, 343
  and potato soup, 88
  and sage stuffing, 29
  baked, 285
  stuffed, 285
  omelet, 112
  pickled, with cheese, 97
  sauce, 53
  with boiled sheep's tongue, 215
  soup, 92
  with cheese on toast, 349
orange(s), 358
  and apple with caramel, 365
  and chocolate butter icing, 449
  and grapefruit drink, 465
  and lemon mould, 388
  and lemon syllabub, 388
  and pineapple flan, 424
  and raisin charlotte, 389
  and rhubarb compote, 370
  as garnish, 481
  butter icing, 450
  caramel, 371
  compote, 370
  egg flip, 469

glacé icing, 450
marmalade pancakes, 418
salads with, 306, 308, 309, 314, 323
sauce, 70
sorbet, 403
stuffed, 407
orangeade in the blender, 468
osso buco, 206
oysters, 126

paella, 334-5
pancakes, 37-8, 417-18
banana, 417
banana, flambé, 417
basic recipe for, 417
herb, 38
kidney, 210
layered (with beef), 174
prawn, 151
smoked haddock, 142, 146
storing, 38
stuffed (dessert), 418
stuffed chicken, 234
paprika pepper, 20
as garnish, 481
butter, 58
mayonnaise, 63
potatoes with frankfurters, 218
sauce, with marrow or courgettes, 281
soup, 87
turkey, with caraway seeds, 240
with eggs and yogurt, 105
parsley, 22, 23
butter, 57
with bass, 125
sauce, 54
with hot salmon, 134
soup, 87
with scrambled eggs with cheese, 118
parsnips, 286-7
baked, 287
cooked in butter, 287
freezing of, 251
preparation of, 286-7
roast, 287
storing, 286
with carrots, 287
partridge, 243
passion fruit, *see* Granadillas
pasta, 325-31
(*see also* under individual names)
boiling, 326
sauce for, 54
pasties, 39
freezing of, 39
kipper, 144
pastry, 37-44
advance preparation, 477
baking blind, 42
choux, 442
covering for pies, 43
flan cases, 41-2
freezing of, 39
puff, 43-4
quiche cases, 41
quick flaky, 40
rubbing in ingredients, 36
short crust, 40
vol-au-vents, 43
pâté
chicken liver, 72
kipper, 76
mackerel, 77
storing, 156
Pavlova, 389
peaches, 359
freezing of, 353
in cider jelly, 390
stuffed with almonds, 372
with white wine or cider, 371
pears, 359
armandine, 372
caramel, 373
cream, 373
freezing of, 353
Hélène, 407
honey, compote, 374
with cheese, 97

peas, green, 288–90
  and peppers, 289
  freezing of, 251
  French method of cooking, 288
  in carrot mould, 270
  purée, 109
  with fried eggs and bacon, 109
  with (poached) eggs and bacon, 288
  soup, 92
  storing, 288
  use of in soups, 81
pease pudding, 289
peppercorns, black and white, 20
peppers, see Sweet peppers
pheasant, 243
  accompaniments to, 243
  stuffing for, 29
piccalilli with cheese, 97
pickled fish, storing, 123
pickles
  as garnish, 481
  with cheese, 97
pie(s), 39, 41, 43, 418–26
  advance preparation and cooking, 477
  covering of, 43
  freezing of, 39
  storing, 156
  Recipes
  apple double crust, 419
  berry, 421
  chicken, 233
  fruit, 422
  ham and egg, 198
  lamb, 185
  lamb and apple, 181
  lemon chiffon, 423
  lemon meringue, 424
  pork and apple, 192
  pumpkin, 425
  shepherd's, 186
  smoked haddock, 143
  spinach, 299
  steak and kidney, 167
  veal and ham plate, 208

pigeons, 244
pilaf, 335
pilau, 183
pimientos, see Sweet peppers
pineapple, 359
  and orange flan, 424
  cheese, 391
  flambé, 374
  freezing of, 353
  with kebabs (pork), 191
piquant dressing, 64
plaice, 126
  fillets, stuffed, 140
planning
  meals, 471–4
  shopping, 474
plover, 244
plums, 360
  freezing of, 353
poaching, see Boiling
pomegranates, 360
poppy seeds, 22
pork, 187–99
  accompaniments to, 187, 188
  boiled, 194–5
  casseroles, 191–2
  fried, 188, 190
  grilled, 188–9
  leftovers, 198–9
  pies, 192, 198
  roast, 187–8
  sauce for, 52
  stews, 191–4
  stuffing for, 28–9
  Recipes
  and apple pie, 192
  belly of, casserole, 191
  boiled salt or pickled, 194
  casserole of spare ribs, 192
  chops, fried, 188
    grilled, 188
    marinated with cider sauce, 189
    with sauerkraut, 189
  cutlets or chops with sweet corn, 193
  fried, and green peppers, 190

goulash, 193
kebabs with pineapple, 191
roast loin, with apple and prunes, 187
roast spare ribs with sage and ginger, 188
salad, with brussels sprouts and orange, 323
sauté of, fillet, 190
Portuguese baked fish, 139
potatoes, 292–6
and onion soup, 88
baked jacket, 293
baked stuffed, 294
biscuits, 446
chips, 295
freezing of, 251
creamed, 293
crisps, 295
game chips, 295
mashed, 293
new, 292
with cream, 294
ofentori, 294
preparation of, 292–3
salads with, 307, 314–15
scalloped, 296
storing, 292–3
poultry, 219–40
(see also under individual birds)
carving, 220
freezing of, 220
preparation of, 220
in advance, 220, 477
salads, 319–20
sauces for, 49, 50, 51, 52, 55, 60
storing, 221–2
stuffings for, 26–9
praline, 16
charlotte, 391
gâteau, 438
prawns, 126, 150–52
pancakes, 151
with cream sauce, 151
preparing meals, 474–83
pressure cooking, 33

profiteroles
choux pastry for, 442–3
filled with ice-cream, 407
prune(s)
and apple stuffing, 28
with baked bananas, 368
with roast loin of pork and apples, 187
with walnuts, 374
puddings, 408–16
hot baked, 408–13
sauces for, 62–7, 68–70
steamed, 413–16
puff pastry, 43–4
pumpkin, 297
methods of cooking, 297
pie, 425
punch, fruit, 464
purée(s)
apricot, with almonds, 367
fruit, 364
green pea, 109, 288
making of, 34–5

quail, 244
Queen's pudding, 410
quiche(s), 39, 41–2
asparagus, 255
carrot and cheese, 270
cases for freezing, 39
egg and herb quiche, 120
kipper, 145
leek and cottage cheese, 278
making cases, 41–2
onion and cheese, 286
quick flaky pastry, 40
quinces, 360

rabbit, 248
casseroles, 241
frozen, 241
sauce for, 51
wild, 248
radishes,
as garnish, 482
with cheese, 97

ragout
  lamb, 183
  turnip, 303
raisin(s)
  and orange charlotte, 389
  sauce, 70
  with rice pudding and bay leaves, 412
raspberries, 360
  cream, *see* Berry cream
  freezing of, 352
  sauce for, 69
  serving of, 369
  sorbet, 403
ratatouille with yogurt, 77
ravigote sauce, 320
ravioli, 326
red currants, 355
  freezing of, 352
  serving of, 369
red fish, 126
refrigerated flan, 42
refrigerated sherry and almond cake, 392
rémoulade sauce, 60
  with salmon, 136
  with sole, 127
rhubarb, 361
  baked spiced, 375
  baked, with herbs, 375
  freezing of, 353
  meringue, 411
rice,
  boiling, 332
  fried, 333
  savoury dishes, 331–7
  sweet dishes, 380, 393–4, 412
  varieties of, 331–2
  Recipes
  and chicken soup with yogurt, 84
  and fruit mould using canned rice, 394
  apricot, mould, 393
  caramel, cream, 380
  chocolate, mould, 393

ginger, mould, 393
kedgeree, 333
  with curd cheese, 334
mould, 393
paella, 334
pilaf, 335
pudding with bay leaves and raisins, 412
risotto, 336
saffron, 337
  with egg and mint, 336
risotto, 336
rissoles, fish, freezing of, 124
rock salmon, *see* Dog fish
rolls, bread, 452–4
  shaping of, 453–4
  soft dinner, 453
    with herbs, 454
  with cheese, 96
rosemary, 22
  and cheese stuffing, 27
  butter, 58
  in veal casserole, 205
royal icing, 450–51
rubbing in ingredients, 36
rum
  as flavouring, 20
  punch gâteau, 438
  with baked apples, 366
rusks, with cheese, 96
rye bread, with cheese, 96

saffron rice, 337
sage, 22
  and lemon sauce, 52
  and onion stuffing, 29
  with roast spare ribs of pork and ginger, 188
saithe, *see* Coley
salad(s), 304–24
  advance preparation of foods for, 478
  cold halibut for, 126
  for accompaniments, 306–17
  herbs and other flavourings for, 305–6

ingredients for, 304–5
main dishes, 318–24
storing vegetables for, 304
Recipes
apple and chicory, 306
apple, carrot and orange, 306
banana and cheese, 318
beetroot, apple and potato, 307
beetroot, with horseradish and fennel, 307
brussels sprouts and celery, 307
brussels sprouts and orange, 308
cabbage, celery and apple, 308
cauliflower, 308
celery, apple and beetroot, with fennel, 309
chicken and almond, 319
chicory and beetroot, 310
chicory and olive, 309
chicory and orange, 309
cole slaw with walnuts, 310
courgette, with mint and chives, 310
cucumber and melon, 311
cucumber and nasturtium, 311
cucumber, Swedish style, 311
curried chicken, 319
dressed chicken, 320
fish, with ravigote sauce, 320
fruit, 364
grapefruit and beetroot, 312
green bean and apple, 312
green leaf, 312
ham and broad bean, 321
herring, 321
horseradish and ham roll, 322
kipper, 322
leeks vinaigrette, 313
mixed, 313
mushroom, cooked, 313
mushroom, raw, 313
orange, 314
orange, apple and celery, 314
Parisian, 323
pork, brussels sprouts and orange, 323
potato, 314

potato, with yogurt dressing, 315
sauerkraut, with capers, 315
sorrel and lettuce, 316
sweet pepper, 316
sweet pepper and tomato, 316
tomato, 316
tomato and cucumber, 317
tongue, 323
Turkish cucumber, 317
white bean, 317
salad dressings, 61–4
cream, 61
French, 61
lemon curry, 62
mayonnaise, 62–3
mustard, 63
Turkish, 64
yogurt, 64
salmon, 126, 133
smoked, 79
steaks en papillote, 136
steaks or cutlets, grilled, 136
salsa verde, 60
salt, 20
spices, 21–2
salted fish, storing, 123
sandwiches, 338–47
bread for, 338
fancy shapes for, 339–40
fillings, 146, 340–43, 346–7
leftovers for, 146
open, 344–5
storing, 339
toasted, 345–7
topping for open, 344–5
Recipes
blue cheese and walnut, 342
cheese and sherry, 342
curry and cheese, 342
egg and onion, 343
liver sausage, 343
sardine and cheese, 343
sardine
and cheese sandwich, 343
rarebit, 349

satsumas, 361
sauce Mornay, 48
sauce(s), 24-6, 45-61, 65-70
  blender, 47
  butters, 57-8
  for basting, 24-6
  making in advance, 45, 478
  savoury, cold, 55-61
    hot, 46-55
  sweet, 65-70
  Recipes
  anchovy, 46
  apple, 46
  apple and horseradish, 55
  Béarnaise, 56
  béchamel, 46
  bread, 47
  Breton, 56
  brown butter, 47
  caper, 48
  cheese, 48
  cranberry, 49
  cream cheese and horseradish, 58
  cucumber, 49
  Cumberland, 58
  curry, 50
  Espagnole, 50
  fennel, 51
  green, 60
  hollandaise, 52
  horseradish, 59
  lemon and sage, 52
  meat, 330
  mint, 59
    with lemon, 59
  Mornay, 48
  mushroom, 53
  mustard, 53, 60
  onion, 53
  parsley, 54
  ravigote, 320
  rémoulade, 60
  salsa verde, 60
  soured cream, 60
  spicy, 228
  tartare, 61
  tomato, 54
  velouté, 55
  white, 46
  with beef, 158
sauerkraut, 267
  salad, 315
  with caraway or capers, 267
  with pork chops, 189
sausages, 216-18
  accompaniments to, 216
  baked, 217
  continental, 78, 216
  fried, 216
  grilled, 217
  storing, 156
  recipes
  English beef and pork, 216-17
  frankfurters with paprika potatoes, 218
  Norfolk pork, 217
  smothered, 218
  to serve cold, 171
sauté, 33
savory, 22
scallops, 127
  (*see also* Escallops)
  baked, 152
scampi, 127, 152
  flambé with cream sauce, 151
scones, 427-8, 451, 456-9
  cheese, with herbs, 457
  girdle, 458
  soured cream, 459
seasoned flour, 20
sesame seeds, 22
shallots, 22
shellfish, 146-53
  (*see also* under individual fish)
  buying, 123
  flan, 153
  storing, 123
  topping for open sandwiches, 344-5
  yields for shelled fish, 123

sherry
    and almond cake, refrigerated, 392
    and cheese sandwich, 342
    and herb basting sauce or marinade, 25
    as flavouring, 20
    mould, 394
short crust pastry, 40, 41, 43–4
    pie covering, 43
    with egg, 41
shortbread biscuits, 447
shredding, 17
shrimps, 127, 152
sieving and sifting, 17
silverside, 169
skate, 127
smelt, 127
smoked fish
    buying, 122
    for starters, 75–6
    storing, 123
snacks on toast, 347–50
    baked beans and cheese, 347
    cheese, tomato and bacon, 347
    cheese, with herbs, 347
    crab and cheese, 348
    egg, cheese and bacon, 348
    egg and haddock, 348
    ham rarebit, 350
    onions and cheese, 349
    rarebit, Welsh, 349
        variations of, 349–50
snipe, 244
soft cheese with herbs, 101
sole, 127
    fillets, stuffed, 140
    Véronique, 140
sorbets, 402–3
    lemon, with mint, 402
    orange, 403
    raspberry, 403
sorrel and lettuce salad, 316
soufflé omelet, 113
soufflé(s)
    cheese, 101

chocolate (cold), 381
hazel nut, 410
lemon, 385
Swedish apple, 412
soupe Flamande, 88
soups, 80–93
    canned, with yogurt, 80–81
    cold, 90–93
    consommés, 84, 90
    hot, 81–9
    made in advance, 80, 478
    Recipes
    beetroot, 90
    blender cream soup, 81
    bortsch, 82, 90
    cauliflower, 82
    celery, 83
    celery and tomato, 83
    chicken and rice, with yogurt, 84
    consommé with mushrooms and herbs, 84
    cream of chicken, 84
    crème de volaille princesse, 84
    curried chicken, 91
    Flamande, 88
    gaspacho, 91
    lamb or mutton, 85
    lentil, 86
    mushroom, 86
    onion, 92
    paprika, 87
    parsley, 87
    pea, 92
    potato and onion, 88
    straciatella, 89
    watercress and cheese, 89
soured cream
    omelet, 113
    sauce, 60
    scones, 459
    with braised steak, 164
    with fried lamb and cinnamon, 178
    with noodles with ham, 328
spaghetti, 326, 328–31
    Bolognese, 328

spaghetti—*cont.*
  with anchovies, 329
  with meat sauce, 330
  with tomato sauce, 330
spiced blackberry sauce, 70
spiced lamb casserole, 184
spiced mocha drink, 469
spiced salt, 20
spices, 21–2
spicy icing, 450
spicy sauce, in chicken casserole with curd cheese, 228
spinach, 297–9
  au gratin with mushrooms, 298
  boiled leaf, 298
  for soup, 81
  freezing of, 251
  pie, 299
  preparation of, 298
  storing, 298
sponge flan, 42
sprats, 127
  grilled, 129
  smoked, 79
spreads, storing, 156
spring onions, 97
sprouts, brussels, *see* Brussels sprouts
starters, 71–93, 104
  hors d'oeuvre, 71–9
strawberries, 361
  cream, *see* Berry cream
  freezing of, 353
  ice-cream, 401
  Melba, 407
  Romanoff, 376
  sauce for, 69
  sauce with banana mould, 377
  serving of, 369
steak, 159–68
  and kidney pie, 167
  and kidney pudding, 168
  braised, with soured cream, 164
  Diane, 162
  grilled marinated beef, 162
  Mirabeau, 163
  storing, 156
stock(s), 17–19
  bone, 18
  fish, 18
  giblet, 18
  made in advance, 478
  mushroom, 18
  vegetable, 19
storing food, 473–4
  See also under individual foods
stout, 19
straciatella, 89
stuffings for meat, game and poultry, 26–9
  bacon and nut, 27
  cheese and rosemary, 27
  chestnut, 27
  lemon, 28
  prune and apple, 28
  sage and onion, 29
  walnut, 29
sugar
  as flavouring, 24
  creaming fat with, 35
sundaes, *see* Coupes
swedes, 300
sweet corn
  and tomatoes, 300
  creamed, 300
  for soup, 81
  on-the-cob, 300
  with cutlets or chops (pork), 193
sweet girdle scones, 458
sweet peppers, 22, 290–92
  and peas, 289
  as garnish, 482
  freezing of, 251
  fried, 290
  green, and cucumber cocktail, 73
  green, with fried pork, 190
  grilled, 291
  Italian dish of green, 291
  preparation of, 290
  salads with, 316
  storing, 290

stuffed, 292
  with cheese, 97
  with scrambled eggs and tomatoes, 118
  with yogurt, 291
sweets (desserts), 351–426
  (see also Desserts)
  cold, made in advance, 476
Swiss eggs, 115
Swiss roll, chocolate, 433
syllabub, orange and lemon, 388

tagliatelle, 326
tangerines, 361
tarragon, 22
  butter, 58
  sauce, with fish, 132
  sauce with sauté of chicken, 226
  with lamb, 181
tartare sauce, 61
  with halibut, 126
  with salmon, 134, 136
tarts, 39–40, 418–26
  advance preparation, 477
  apple, 419–20
    with fennel seeds, 420
  berry, 421
  freezing of, 39–40
  treacle, 426
teal, 245
terrine
  liver, 76
  veal, 208
thyme, 23
  in veal casserole, 205
tomato(es), 300, 301–2
  as garnish, 482
  freezing of, 251
  methods of cooking, 301
  preparation of, 301
  salads with, 316–17
  storing, 301
  Recipes
  and celery soup, 83
  and (sweet) corn, 300

cream soup, 81
flan, 302
juice cocktail, 79
salad, 316
sauces, 54–5
  with spaghetti, 330
stuffed, 301
with cheese, 97
with cheese and bacon on toast, 347
with scrambled eggs and sweet peppers, 118
with stewed marrow or courgettes, 281
tongues, 213–15
  calf's, boiled, 214
  ox, boiled, 213
  salad, 323
  sauce for, 48
  sheep's, boiled in onion sauce, 214
tortilla, 114
tortoni, 395
treacle
  loaf, 459
  pudding, 416
  tart, 426
tripe au gratin, 215
trout, 127, 133
  smoked, 79
turbot, 127
turkey, 237–40
  accompaniments to, 239
  devilled, 239
  paprika with caraway seeds, 240
  roast, 238
  stuffing for, 27
Turkish dressing, 64
turmeric, 22
turnips, 302–3
  ragout, 303
turnovers
  chicken and ham, 232
  freezing of, 39

upside-down cake, 439

vacherin, 395
vanilla creams, 396
  ice, 402
  ice with yogurt, 402
veal, 200–209
  accompaniments to, 201
  fried, 201–4
  leftovers, 209
  roast, 200–201
  sauce for, 49
  stuffing for, 27, 28
  Recipes
  and ham plate pie, 208
  blanquette of, 204
  casserole with rosemary or thyme, 205
  chops or cutlets à l'hongroise, 202
  chops or cutlets, fried, 201
  chops or cutlets with mushrooms, 203
  escalopes flambées, 203
  escalopes, fried, 201
  escalopes Parmesan, 204
  galantine, 207
  Italian, stew, 206
  osso buco, 206
  roast stuffed, 200–201
  terrine, 208
vegetable(s), 17, 19, 250–303, 304–24
  (*see also* under individual vegetables and salads)
  advance preparation, 478
  fillings for sandwiches, 342–3, 344–5, 346–7
  for flavouring, 21–2
  freezing of, 250–52
  frozen for soups, 80
  sauces for, 47, 51, 55, 57
  stock, 17–18, 19
  storing, 250
  to use in cream soups, 81
  use of frozen, 252
  with scrambled eggs and cheese, 119
velouté sauce, 55
venison, 248–9
  casseroles, 241
  frozen, 241
  grilled, cutlets, 249
    steaks, 349
  jugged, 249
  roast, 249
vermicelli, 326
vermouth
  as flavouring, 20
  with soda water and herbs, 464
Victoria sandwich (cake), 438
Vienna bread, 454
Vienna plaits with fennel seeds, 455
vinegars, 24
vol-au-vents, 43
  lobster, 149

walnut(s)
  cauliflower with, 272
  gâteau, 439
  salad with, 310
  sandwiches with, 342
  stuffing, 29
  with prunes, 374
watercress
  and cheese soup, 89
  with cheese, 97
weights and measures, 9–11
Welsh rarebit, 349
  variations of, 349–50
wheatmeal girdle scones, 459
whisking, 34
whisky, as flavouring, 20
white currants, 355
  freezing of, 352
white sauce, *see* Béchamel sauce
whitebait, 127
whiting, 127
wholemeal bread, 455
  with herbs, 456
whortleberries, *see* Bilberries
widgeon, 245
wild duck, 245
wine, 461–2
  cups, 462–3
    claret, 463

hock, 462
  marinade and basting sauce, 26
  mulled, 21, 463
witch sole, 127
woodcock, 246

yeast, 451–2
yogurt
  and fruit juice drink, 470
  and mint drink, 470
  and soda water drink, 470
  dressing, 64
    with salads, 315
  for drinking, 469
  Greek, cake, 436
  in chicken and rice soup, 84
  marinade with lamb kebabs, 177
  with canned soups, 80–81
  with celery, 274
  with eggs and paprika, 105
  with ratatouille, 77
  with sweet peppers, 291
Yorkshire pudding, 159
Yorkshire rarebit, 350

zucchini, *see* Courgettes
zucchini moussaka, 171